RACE RELATIONS

LITIGATION

IN AN AGE OF

COMPLEXITY

CONSTITUTIONALISM AND DEMOCRACY

KERMIT HALL AND DAVID O'BRIEN, EDITORS

RACE RELATIONS LITIGATION IN AN AGE OF COMPLEXITY

STEPHEN L. WASBY

UNIVERSITY PRESS OF VIRGINIA

Charlottesville and London

THE UNIVERSITY PRESS OF VIRGINIA

Copyright © 1995 by the Rector and Visitors
of the University of Virginia

FIRST PUBLISHED 1995

ISBN: 0-8139-1572-4 (cl)
      0-8139-1573-2 (p)

Library of Congress Cataloging-in-Publication Data

Wasby, Stephen L., 1937–
    Race relations litigation in an age of complexity / Stephen L. Wasby.
        p.   cm. — (Constitutionalism and democracy)
    Includes index.
    ISBN 0–8139–1572–4 (cloth). — ISBN 0–8139–1573–2 (pbk.)
    1. Civil rights—United States—History.   2. Discrimination—Law and
legislation—United States—History.   3. Actions and defenses—United States
—History.   I. Title.   II. Series.
    KF4749.W37   1995
    342.73'0873—dc20
    [347.302873]   94-47132
                                                               CIP

PRINTED IN THE UNITED STATES OF AMERICA

To the memory of
my father

Milton Charles Wasby

a first-rate contract writer
and
a warm, gentle man
who always showed an interest in my work

CONTENTS

Preface

Can The Bumblebee Fly?

We are told that according to the laws of aerodynamics, the bumblebee is not supposed to fly. Yet fly the yellow-and-black-striped winged creature does. What, you ask, does this have to do with civil rights litigation, which involves those who are white and black and brown? If civil rights litigation has to be undertaken with limited resources in the face of increased complexity in the political environment, in relations between the proliferating groups pursuing civil rights, and in litigation itself, the bumblebee of civil rights litigation should have remained grounded. Yet it has indeed flown, at least under certain circumstances, although less in a straight line than in an erratic pattern. In short, civil rights litigation efforts are highly contingent and extremely problematic.

For many years, the common picture of civil rights litigation, particularly that pursued by organizations like the NAACP Legal Defense Fund and culminating in the landmark ruling in *Brown v. Board of Education* (1954), was one of success with relative ease after a well-planned and carefully crafted litigation campaign. (Citations to cases may be found in the Table of Cases at the end of the volume.) Emphasis was given to the planned character of the litigation campaign, the implementation of a blue print through a series of cases. In a principal recounting,[1] the *Brown* litigation was characterized as a story of "un-problematic success"[2] which minimized difficulties and unplanned events that created deviations from straight-line progress to an ultimate Supreme Court victory.

Deriving from a skepticism about earlier studies' overemphasis on the planned nature of litigation "campaigns," this study presents a rather different picture of efforts to achieve civil rights litigation starting roughly ten years after *Brown,* one that calls attention to the problematic elements, the "humps and bumps," in the situation. The underlying theme is that, although organizational litigators attempt "planned litigation for social change" in which they choose areas of law on which to focus their efforts and cases in which to invest resources, many aspects of that litigation turn out to be unplanned, and much about the litigation is not simple and linear. We must be careful not to confuse retrospective statements about planned strategy, which form part of the participants' logic of justification, with the complicated reality that actually unfolded. Instead of taking at face value statements by Charles Houston, the NAACP's first full-time attorney, that he was pursuing a legal strategy, we must recognize that at times those statements represented post hoc portrayals of a reality in which Houston was traveling around the country putting out brush-fires. We must also recognize that such portrayals can be an important organizational tactic, necessary to restrain the natural tendency of some of those involved in the litigation to slip out of harness and to persuade potential supporters and contributors that something was actually being done, as they would not be likely to aid a bumblebee that apparently could not fly. In his important work on pre-1950 civil rights litigation, Mark Tushnet has suggested quite reasonably that although this argument "presents a more complex view of the realities of litigation," it "stresses too much the novelty of the problems . . . found in . . . interviews with contemporary public interest lawyers."[3] Yet, by comparison with what others have written about the more recent period, the problems emphasized in the present study do appear novel and warrant considerable attention.

We must be careful not to take too far the argument that the bumble-bee can never become airborne, that it is difficult to carry out a litigation campaign because of external events and internal difficulties. Some recent civil rights litigation has been undertaken systematically and does contain elements of planning; examples are efforts to enforce Title VII of the Civil Rights Act of 1964 and to overturn the death penalty. Yet such campaigns account for only some civil rights litigation, and even within these campaigns one finds unplanned elements. Indeed, one can say that in such litigation, Murphy's Law prevails, with Murphy sitting on the edge of the lawyer's desk. The result is failure to maintain direction; there are so many humps and bumps that the litigation does not proceed along a straight line. That is the essential message conveyed in these pages. This emphasis on constraints and difficulties comes from the mouths of those in the trenches of civil rights litigation. Thus before saying, "What, another book on civil rights!" the reader should try to keep in mind that the focus here is not on the civil rights movement. Instead, it is on the litigation process, to which little attention has been paid, and the problems associated with it.

The period covered by this exploration of race relations litigation by interest groups begins in the late 1960s and extends through the early 1980s. It thus begins in the waning of the civil rights movement and extends into the subsequent conservative era. In this regard, it is important to recognize that the use of litigation began before the civil rights movement and continued after its conclusion. In this study principal attention will be devoted to four major areas of race relations litigation that are the traditional foci of civil rights activity: schools (desegregation of elementary and secondary schools, not desegregation of higher education); jobs (employment discrimination law under Title VII); housing; and voting rights. Two newer areas—criminal justice concerns, particularly capital punishment, and welfare—will also receive some attention. Because Title II of the Civil Rights Act of 1964, which the Supreme Court promptly upheld, resolved issues of public accommodations and public facilities, those subjects will receive little attention.[4]

The principal purpose of the study is to explore the environmental, intraorganizational, and interorganizational factors that affect the litigation strategy of major interest groups active in the area of civil rights and to describe and explain the difficulties of that litigation, with a focus on its problematic aspects and contingent nature. Another major, related purpose is to ascertain the extent to which our prior picture of earlier civil rights litigation applies in a period of increasing complexity. Should it be replaced by a more sophisticated picture that shows the complexity of interest-group litigation? Such pictures have now been provided for litigation on church-state relations and sex discrimination, on behalf of children, and by the handicapped and the mentally ill,[5] and, particularly, the revised picture of NAACP litigation in the period of developing civil rights litigation campaigns. Much earlier literature was based on the notion that civil rights groups turn to the courts because these groups carry less weight in other "political" arenas or were effectively without power in those arenas, particularly prior to the 1960s. Recently, serious questions have been raised about the "dubious predominance" of the "political disadvantage theory," yet litigation is still a crucial activity for racial minorities, and "courts may indeed have a higher proportion of politically disadvantaged groups on the plaintiff's side than one would find in other political arenas because legal resources partially (though not entirely) offset political resources."[6]

This study focuses on the principal groups litigating concerning civil rights, primarily those organizations litigating on behalf of blacks, although examples will also be drawn from litigation by conservative groups and the government, as the discussion here is relevant to litigation they and other groups conduct. The intent is not to slight efforts made on behalf of, for example, Hispanics, women, the disabled, or gays and lesbians, but to recognize that civil rights litigation as we have come to know it was initiated by organizations working on behalf of blacks and that their litigation activities served as the model for litigation activities by others seeking enforcement of their rights, including the law reform activity by the government's Legal Services Program. The groups examined in this study include the premier civil rights litigators like the NAACP Legal Defense and Educational Fund (LDF), thought foremost in carrying out litigation through planned litigation campaigns, the NAACP, and the Lawyers' Committee for Civil Rights Under Law, as well as the American Civil Liberties Union (ACLU) and less prominent participants. Organizations litigating less frequently and individual attorneys using cases primarily to obtain relief for individual clients are underrepresented in this study.

The focus is on the principal actors' views of the way in which they and the organizations with which they were affiliated dealt with civil rights cases or situations that might have become cases. This is not a study of the correlation of specified variables with litigation success, but an examination of organizations' litigation processes, *from the litigators' perspective,* using a framework that is in a sense inductive: factors that seemed worth examining further were identified from diverse literature and people knowledgeable about litigation. The traditional literature on interest groups said very little about interest groups' relation to the courts, except for the groups' role in judicial selection, which, like other lobbying, took place in the legislative arena. The most recent scholarly work and texts on interest groups contain the same relative emphasis.[7] Until relatively recently, studies of interest group litigation generally focused on test cases and amicus curiae ("friend of the court") activity, not on the variety of factors affecting litigation. As late as 1980, we were told that previous studies "have noted the importance of various factors in the success of interest group litigation, although nowhere have the effects of the set of factors been studied systematically or their potential impact on the initial decision to litigate discussed."[8]

Interest in the mobilization of law[9] stimulated this study, which is also related to current work on cause lawyering, because civil rights lawyers were certainly litigating on behalf of a cause. However, no particular social theory drives this study. Since much civil rights litigation is undertaken to help produce social change, the study undoubtedly will cast some light on the conditions under which litigation produces social change; these conditions, however, are not its focus. This study also does not speak to whether the judicial rulings obtained are effective in producing the litigators' goals.[10]

The law, the legal strategies, and the outcomes do not merely reflect their environment, yet civil rights litigators are affected, and constrained, by the environment while to an important extent they remain independent actors capable of making choices they hope will affect that environment positively. The environment to which principal attention will be given is the period from the mid-1960s through the early 1980s. Examples will also be drawn from earlier periods, including that of the civil rights movement, which concluded as the period under intensive examination began. According to someone long associated with the NAACP, in 1954 the NAACP had a "simplified view of the world," but the period starting in the 1960s was "much more complex," and "like an archeological dig: after each level, you find another one." From a one-ring circus, with the courts being the only arena of activity, now there was a three-ring circus. Instead of dealing almost exclusively with the courts over constitutional questions, after passage of the Civil Rights Act of 1964 and the Voting Rights Act of 1965, civil rights organizations also had to deal with statutes and administrative regulations in most areas of race relations law. This made more difficult their decisions as to how to divide resources among litigating, legislative lobbying, and monitoring of executive agencies.

The 1964 Act, like the Voting Rights Act of the following year a product of the civil rights movement, not only marked a watershed in civil rights law as the first major civil rights statute since Reconstruction, but also significantly changed civil rights activity and civil rights litigation. Up to that time, such litigation, except for black unionists' challenges to union action as a breach of the duty of fair representation created by the National Labor Relations Act, had previously been almost exclusively constitutional litigation. Although most school desegregation litigation remained focused on constitutional issues, the emphasis in other areas shifted largely to statutory interpretation. The change was most obvious in employment litigation. Title VII for the first time created a federal law of employment discrimination separate from labor law, and led to a regime of federal court litigation that followed federal or state administrative action, with the courts taking into account—and at times giving great weight to—Equal Employment Opportunity Commission (EEOC) regulations when interpreting the statute. (Attacks on discrimination in government employment were based on constitutional provisions until 1972 when government employees were brought under the law, making the new regime basically the same for them.)

Likewise, under Title VI, which provided that no agency receiving federal funds could discriminate on the basis of race, the HEW Desegregation Guidelines provided the basis for administrative-judicial interaction. Such interaction increased with the administrative rule that a school district under court order to desegregate would be considered in compliance with the guidelines, with the regulations also affected when courts increased desegregation requirements for school districts. Challenges to affirmative action programs in employment and education raised both statutory questions (under Titles VI and VII) and constitutional issues.

Before the passage of the Voting Rights Law of 1965, voting rights law had been based almost entirely on the Constitution. The new law added both statutory interpretation and administrative aspects, because under Section 5 of the Act, voting procedures in affected ("covered") jurisdictions had to be precleared by the Department of Justice. (Voting rights litigation increased after the 1982 amendments to the Voting Rights Act and continued unabated into the 1990s, because of decennial legislative redistricting.) Passage of the Fair Housing Act of 1968 and the Supreme Court's rediscovery that same year of the Civil Rights Act of 1866 in *Jones v. Mayer* shifted federal housing discrimination law to a statutory basis.

Apart from the complexity introduced by these changes, civil rights litigation itself became increasingly complex. Instead of statutorily imposed segregation, there was less clear-cut discrimination in education, jobs, and housing, which forced litigators to probe far beneath the surface to prove their cases and thus increased the resources required to pursue these problems through litigation. There were also more civil rights issues about which to litigate. Litigating organizations' external environment also became more complex because there were more groupings seeking their rights in court, with civil rights no longer only for blacks, but also for women, Hispanics, and the disabled.

These changes in the legal and litigating environment took place in a period of increasing disagreement as to how best to attain civil rights. Shortly after the civil rights movement's high point in the mid-1960s, when the 1964 and 1965 laws were passed, it began to recede as public opinion and elected politicians' positions on civil rights became less supportive, with Northerners resisting school desegregation and white males challenging employment discrimination remedies that threatened them. This paralleled the shift from the executive branch support of the Johnson administration, weakened at the end as the nation's attention shifted to Vietnam, to the more mixed stance of the Nixon presidency, which produced a Supreme Court that, after a short lag, was markedly less liberal on civil rights. After heightened acceptance for civil rights organizations' goals during the Carter years of the late 1970s, the much more severely conservative Reagan administration, reflecting and reinforcing decreased national commitment to remedying problems of racial inequality and racism, moved aggressively to cut back on the civil rights community's victories.

In the environment of the 1980s, far different from the heady days of 1964 and 1965—and perhaps more historically representative—civil rights litigators had to proceed against an unfriendly administration before an unfriendly Supreme Court, and were compelled more frequently not only to attack discriminatory practices undisturbed, and perhaps even condoned, by the government, but also to move against government action aimed at overturning prior victories. This illustrates that much litigation by groups is defensive rather than initiated as part of a planned campaign. We should also not forget that the 1980s led even some of those at the heart of the civil rights battle to question use of the legal system, and litigation in particular, to achieve civil rights. As one professor, who used the legal system all his life to achieve protection for civil rights, observed, "The next time I'll be out there in levi's with a gasoline can, but I'll be too old to run."

When this study was written, there was a Democratic president after a dozen years of conservative Republican presidency. President Clinton's election led to some optimism about achieving civil rights but he backed away from a controversial nominee to be Assistant Attorney General for Civil Rights, a position that remained unfilled more than one year into his term. At the turn of the decade, immediately before his election, the picture of civil rights was a decidedly mixed one. It was captured by the November 1989 *New York Times* headline, "Racial Incidents and Black Progress."[11] There were instances of progress by, and acceptance of, racial minorities, but simultaneously there were many instances of violence against members of racial minorities, not only in the South, but also in the North. These events were symbolized by the Rodney King beating in Los Angeles and by the Howard Beach and Crown Heights incidents in New York City, serving, respectively, as symbols of the conflict between white ethnics and African-Americans and between African-Americans and Jews. Even when gains have occurred or battles over discrimination seem to have been resolved, tensions remained not far below the surface, so that one can say that racism took new forms but did not disappear.

The economic picture, on balance, also has not been favorable, and deteriorated toward the end of the period on which this study focuses. Likewise, although "the social status of American blacks has *on average* improved dramatically, both in absolute terms and relative to whites" over the fifty-year period ending in 1989, it has remained at a plateau or declined since 1970. Those at the bottom of the economy were in a seriously deteriorated position, as the civil rights struggles played out in the courts in a way irrelevant to the very poor of the inner cities. This situation stemmed in part from the poor state of the nation's economy, but also from continuing employment discrimination in which outright racial barriers to employment were replaced by seemingly neutral requirements with differential racial impacts.[12]

Sources

This study is a synthesis of material from interviews and secondary sources, including not only previous studies of interest group litigation and accounts of civil rights litigation in earlier and present times, where case studies of school desegregation litigation are particularly numerous, but also materials on law and social change, public interest law, and institutional reform litigation, which provide useful conformation even when group litigation is not central to their accounts. The general literature on interest groups, with its standard focus on the legislative arena and a more recent emphasis on what incentives prompt individuals to join groups or how organizations providing public goods can avoid the "free rider" problem, is not a major source.[13] The concern of the present study is instead what organizations' lawyers do.

Interviews.   Lawyers who had an organizational association with race relations law—as either staff attorneys or cooperating attorneys with the NAACP, the NAACP Legal Defense Fund, the Lawyers' Committee for Civil Rights Under Law, or other organizations active in race relations litigation—were selected from case records and organizational publications for possible interviews. To obtain a variety of perspectives on group-related civil rights litigation, included were senior staff attorneys, subject-matter specialists, other attorneys closely involved in organizations' litigation planning, and cooperating attorneys with varying degrees of involvement in major race relations cases and litigating either in their own states and communities or in several cities across the country.

Of fifty-seven lawyers with whom contact was attempted, forty-one were interviewed, a success rate of 74.4 percent. (Eight declined interviews, three could not be reached, and five were willing to be interviewed but scheduling problems prevented an interview.) Most interviews took place in 1982, with a few taking place in 1984, 1985, and 1986. They generally lasted from forty-five minutes to an hour, but some were longer and some respondents later volunteered additional information. The structured interviews, based primarily on open-ended questions, allowed respondents to discuss matters they thought especially salient. Factors that might affect the litigation in which the respondents or their organization had been involved received particular attention, and aspects of the particular cases in which cooperating attorneys had been involved were explored. (Material in quotation marks without attribution is drawn from the interviews, as they were undertaken on the condition that quotations would not be attributed to individuals.)

Writing about civil rights litigation without talking to lawyers does not allow us to go beyond formal organizational statements or allow a look at litigators' perspectives or provide their insights into litigation dynamics and thus generally provides an inadequate picture. Yet interviews pose a risk, not only because people either don't remember their actions accurately,[14] or engage in self-justification, but also, particularly crucial for this study, because respondents "consistently overestimate the predictability of past events once they know how they turned out."[15] Because lawyers are articulate and able to reconstruct past events to fit preconceived notions, a tendency to reconstruct past events might lead them to picture litigation as highly planned—more planned than it is in fact[16]—and thus to provide an overly symmetrical picture of "planned litigation." Thus perhaps we need to discount somewhat statements suggesting that elements of civil rights litigation did involve planning and conscious choice.

Lawyers' association with groups might also lead to overemphasis on the groups' role in race relations litigation. However, group involvement has been heavy in civil rights litigation—heavier than in other areas of civil rights and civil liberties litigation.[17] This fact helps to satisfy our primary goal, which is to provide a more complete picture of factors affecting litigation by interest groups. A reverse risk is that the individual lawyer, even when associated with organizations, will be emphasized at the expense of the larger picture. Yet because individual lawyers are not interchangeable, and because organizations are seldom homogeneous or monolithic, with perspectives differing even within any single organization's full-time staff, attention must be given to individuals, and talking to more than one person affiliated with a particular organization can provide a balanced perspective on that entity, without masking intraorganizational tensions and inconsistencies.

The Book's Structure

Aspects of civil rights litigation are highly interrelated. For example, an organization's resources affect which cases it can undertake, but winning significant cases allows it to obtain more resources. Likewise, because more complex cases require greater resources, litigation complexity affects which cases a group can undertake. An organization's participation in a case as amicus curiae is related both to its resources and to interorganizational relations. These interrelations provide numerous options for this book's structure, which was altered more than once during its construction.

The book starts with a look at the environment in which civil rights litigation takes place. Next the political environment, including public opinion and congressional and executive actions concerning civil rights, is examined; particular attention is given to litigating interest groups' relationships with government. The next chapter deals with the effects of Supreme Court decisions, particularly effects on ongoing litigation, as those decisions become part of the dynamics of ongoing cases and affect the particular cases that groups initiate or appeal and even the areas of law in which they litigate. Another aspect of the environment is the growth of public interest law and the proliferation of civil rights litigators; there the reader will find discussion of characteristics of the principal civil rights litigation organizations, followed by examination of organizations' acquisition and allocation of resources, including attorneys' fee awards.

The book turns next to litigation strategy. Attention is focused on the reasons for an organization's use of litigation, the increased complexity of litigation, and litigators' choice of forum, the federal or state courts. Then the development of litigation strategy or "planning" is discussed. This discussion is followed by a look at organizations' choice of areas of law in which to litigate; their choice of cases, including the source of cases, the beginning of their involvement in cases, their control of litigation, and their decision to participate as an amicus curiae in a case.

Next the internal dynamics of litigation, especially in individual cases, is examined, followed by a look at relations between staff attorneys and "cooperating attorneys" along with the subject of attorney-client relations, which is closely tied to questions of legal ethics. The concluding chapter focuses on interorganizational relations in civil rights litigation, and includes a separate section about the at-times troubled relations between the NAACP and the NAACP Legal Defense and Educational Fund. The book ends with some conclusions based on the themes of litigation strategy and planned litigation.

A Note on Terminology

In discussing civil rights, the question arises as to the names to use for particular minorities, itself a term that has been called into question. During the period under study, standard usage shifted from "Negro" to "black," which will receive predominant usage although Justice Thurgood Marshall continued to use the former term longer than most younger members of his race and "African-American" was becoming the term of choice in the early 1990s. Because the latter was not used much during the period on which this book focuses, to use it here would be to rewrite history inappropriately.

There has been little consensus on the proper appellation for those who are part of or stem from Spanish-speaking cultures. Some have suggested that Hispanics should not be treated as a single minority, as judges have tended to do, but should be differentiated on the basis of assimilation. In the 1990s, "Hispanic" has been challenged by "Latino," which some find underinclusive and others find unsatisfactory as a designation for particular group identifications ("Chicano" was used earlier) and the Mexican-American Legal Defense Fund and the Puerto Rican Legal Defense Fund are separate organizations. "Indian" has been replaced by "Native American." Somewhat ironically in view of earlier displeasure with "hyphenated American" designations, "Asian-American" has displaced "Oriental." As the term in use at the time, "Japanese-American" will be used in discussion of the World War II exclusion of that group from the West Coast.

Acknowledgments

This book had its genesis when Hubert Locke, Director of the William O. Douglas Institute (formerly, The Institute for the Study of Contemporary Social Problems), prompted by his concerns about our nation's race relations, suggested that I look into litigation by civil rights groups, which seemed an interesting complement to my earlier work on the Supreme Court's strategies in its race relations rulings. I am grateful for his stimulus and moral support through the project's early stages. Small grants from the Johnson Fund of the American

Philosophical Society and from the Office of Research and Graduate School of Public Affairs at the University at Albany made possible travel to conduct most interviews.

Most appreciated is the willingness of many exceptional, energetic, and committed lawyers to make time available to be interviewed; by agreement, they remain anonymous when I quote them. I wish to pay particular tribute to the late Allison W. Brown, Jr., an unsung co-operating attorney who gave substantial service to the American Civil Liberties Union and the NAACP Legal Defense Fund. Some of the lawyers were generous in their continuing reactions to my work and thus have helped keep me on the right track. I particularly want to thank Harold ("Nick") Flannery, Barry Goldstein, and Herbert Hill, whose gravelly telephone voice often kept me from sin and error. I also wish to thank Professors Robert Belton of Vanderbilt University Law School, himself a civil rights litigator, Karen O'Connor of Emory University, and Mark Tushnet, preeminent chronicler of an earlier period of civil rights activity, for their assistance at early stages of the project; Lee Epstein, Washington University, who read the *whole* thing and was enthusiastically supportive; and David O'Brien, University of Virginia, in whose series this volume appears. I owe an especial debt to Susan Daly, whose always astute comments regularly led me closer to coherence, and to Matthew Holden, Jr., University of Virginia, from whose sage counsel I have benefited over the years. I am particularly grateful for his substantial assistance in developing the material, of which he should really be a coauthor, on the relationship between the NAACP and the NAACP Legal Defense Fund.

Material from this project was first presented at professional meetings and seminars and in published articles. I wish to acknowledge use of material from "How Planned Is 'Planned Litigation'?" (*American Bar Foundation Research Journal,* 1984), where the basic argument was laid out; "The Multi-Faceted Elephant: Litigator Perspectives on Planned Litigation for Social Change" (*Capital University Law Review,* 1986); "A Transformed Triangle: Court, Congress, and Presidency in Civil Rights" (*Policy Studies Journal,* 1993); and "The Supreme Court's Impact on Litigation" (*Akron Law Review,* 1993). Seminar and panel participants and readers of publications made many helpful comments and provided new perspectives. Particularly helpful were Ed Still, a preeminent civil rights lawyer who enjoys talking to social scientists, and Tony Freyer, University of Alabama, for their comments on "Some

Horizontal and Vertical Dynamics of Civil Rights Litigation: Litigator Perspectives" (at the Southern Political Science Association meetings, Birmingham, Alabama, 1983); those who attended colloquia at the U.S. Naval Academy in 1991 and at the U.S. Military Academy in 1993; Joel Grossman, University of Wisconsin at Madison; Christine Harrington, New York University; Ann Chih Len, University of Chicago; and Frances Kahn Zemans, American Judicature Society.

At a less serious level, also deserving acknowledgment—and bearing all the responsibility for errors—are the cats. Particularly helpful (?) was the late Ernie, who loved to chew on the end of my pencil when I was correcting the manuscript or to lie upside down on my papers, looking at me until I put aside less important things and paid him attention. Was he taking or giving inspiration? Addie Napolitano, one of the world's best preparers of manuscripts, deserves special commendation for taking a manuscript with more arrows and inserts than Carter had liver pills and making sense of it. (She was feeling left out when the cat got an acknowledgment, but she *really* is more important.) Without her, and without Joanne Partridge at the University of Victoria, who helped in preparation of the index, the project couldn't have been completed.

RACE RELATIONS

LITIGATION

IN AN AGE OF

COMPLEXITY

1

The Political Environment

of Civil Rights Litigation

Any civil rights action takes place in an environment of many elements, among them the nation's demographics, including the racial groupings in the population and their spatial location; the economy, which intersects with demographics to provide a distribution of racial groupings by income and occupation,[1] and the political environment, which itself has several components, only some of which we can touch on in this chapter. In this treatment of selected elements of the political environment, we begin with public opinion, the attitudinal environment, including important components of ideology such as change in the very meaning of *civil rights* itself and ideological division in the minority community. Then we turn to perhaps the most important environmental element, the policy matrix in which organizations function—the actions of president, Congress, and Supreme Court, and crucial changes in the interaction among them on civil rights. We end by discussing interest groups' relations with the government generally.

Because civil rights groups have sought action from government, not the reverse, discussion of environment properly focuses on how those contemplating litigation have contended with that environment.

What was true of an earlier period is applicable to the more recent time: "In general, social and political developments provided the framework within which the NAACP acted." That the environment has not *dictated* particular responses but "could have accommodated rather wide variations in the legal status of segregation," makes the environment a less powerful explanation for the specifics of group action than organizations' internal aspects.[2] Litigating civil rights organizations are not *apart* from the environment but instead are *a part* of it and intersect with it; they affect the environment and are affected by it. At times the environment appears neutral or benign, to be acted upon; at other times, it seems to provide pressures directing, if not driving, action. Fortunate interest groups operate in a supportive environment facilitating their success, but the environment may also provide resistance to their efforts. *Brown v. Board of Education* illustrates the former situation: elite public opinion favored the NAACP's goal, particularly because of its importance for the nation's fight against communism.[3] However, in the very different 1980s, civil rights groups faced an unsupportive public opinion and a presidential administration seeking to reverse their past victories.

Public Opinion

Some say that external demand such as public opinion is more important than internal demand in influencing civil rights actions. Opinion about civil rights issues seems to produce a picture of long-term improvement in race relations, in which people respond to surveys with socially acceptable statements supporting racial equality, so that whites' resistance to blacks is less blatant. However, there are also negative images in the picture. White liberals shifted from their mid-1960s endorsement of breaking down barriers to racial minorities' political and economic participation, an endorsement stimulated by the civil rights movement, to believing that blacks had received enough, were demanding too much, and had deprived whites of what was due them. As Kenneth Clark stated on the twentieth anniversary of passage of the 1964 Civil Rights Act, liberals felt they had gone far enough and had become "tired of the battle for democracy."[4] One's view of race relations is decidedly a function of one's own race, as an early 1989 Harris survey showed, "with a majority of whites believing that blacks are treated equally in America and a majority of blacks disagreeing."[5] This disparity in view is not simply a result of different evaluations using the same framework: whites and blacks approach the problem of racial inequality from different foci. "Even whites who think discrimination contributes to black-white inequality tend to view it as a problem created and maintained by prejudiced individuals. Blacks view discrimination as a result of both prejudiced individuals and broader social processes."[6]

Someone who had worked for many years on civil rights characterized the situation this way: "In the early 1970s, they gave us ten years to implement the law. Now they have said, 'We don't want any more. We aren't interested.' " Supporters of civil rights may have believed not only that equality had been achieved but also that programs like President Johnson's War on Poverty had resolved the economic difficulties of the disadvantaged.[7] More likely, after 1966 advances in civil rights policy were hindered by a shift in salience of issues, with the Vietnam conflict particularly increasing in salience, the political and financial support of white liberals, who had been the core of support for civil rights during the civil rights movement, now went to antiwar organizations.[8] Tightening economic circumstances in the early 1970s further deflated enthusiasm for the economic components of the 1960s civil rights program and produced greater resistance to civil rights, particularly by white males. And efforts to achieve anti-discrimination policy in housing, more than efforts to achieve school desegregation, had "mobilized the forces of racism and conservatism in a counterattack on the civil rights movement."[9]

One thus saw "substantially less support for policies intended to implement principles of racial equality" than for the principles themselves.[10] More specifically, "Principles of equality are endorsed less when they would result in close, frequent, or prolonged social contact, and whites are much less prone to endorse policies meant to implement equal participation of blacks in important social institutions. In practice, many whites refuse or are reluctant to participate in social settings (e.g., neighborhoods and schools) in which significant numbers of blacks are present."[11] However, when people were subjected to disliked policies, some came to accept them. For example, in the face of strong overall opposition to busing among both whites and blacks, there was increased acceptance of the practice where it had been used to aid desegregation for three or more years.[12]

Public attitudes may have made a difference in public policy such as legislative action. Evidence suggests "Congress responded strongly, perhaps primarily, to the public's preferences when it considered EEO [Equal Employment Opportunity] legislation." The degree of public support in a region for equal employment opportunity legislation was strongly related to the extent to which members of Congress from that region voted for such legislation. Moreover, "*passage* of legislation was related to the salience of civil rights to the public." Intense public concern led to major legislation, while demonstrations, rather than directly producing legislation, served to "sensitize Congress to public opinion." However, the civil rights movement, including interest groups, had only a "secondary" effect on Congress. Congress also seemed to take into account public opinion on the pace of integration; the defeats of both housing and employment discrimination laws came at the point of highest resistance in 1966, while reduced resistance provided the opportunity for passage of legislation such as the Open Housing Act of 1968.[13] Longitudinal evidence also seems to suggest that external events, that is, elements in the environment, explain congressional voting on civil rights more than do changes in legislators' attitudes.[14]

The Meaning of "Civil Rights"

The meaning of *civil rights* is an important aspect of public opinion, particularly elite opinion; neither white nor black conservatives gave the term the same meaning as did established civil rights organizations. The change in meaning became apparent when, instead of seeing civil rights as something to be sought for the nation's good— Lyndon Johnson's justification for the 1964 Civil Rights Act—opponents of further legal protection of civil rights called civil rights a "special interest."

For some, civil rights has meant an individual's opportunity, unfettered by government barriers, for access to the political and economic systems, or a "level playing field" with no specific results guaranteed. These meanings are close to the position argued by those who attacked de jure segregation and wished the Supreme Court to strike down the laws and other official actions that mandated and enforced separation of the races. They were seeking, to use the phrase of the first Justice Harlan's phrase from his dissent in *Plessy v. Ferguson*, a "color-blind" Constitution. Yet once the Court struck down such official barriers, the resistance that led to the failure of most efforts to bring about compliance also led those seeking to obtain the rights confirmed in *Brown* to press for bringing white and black children together—what some have called integration instead of desegregation. This shift from the rights aspect to the remedy aspect of civil rights led to requests for race-conscious judicial remedies, which came to be called "quotas" regardless of the type of plan used.[15] Thus cases starting with an identifiable individual who had suffered direct discrimination would result in a group-based remedy. These changes shifted the focus from the individual to group rights.

Some whites who had previously supported the effort that led to *Brown* and had sought enforcement of desegregation became disaffected as they saw this shift from the efforts to eliminate group classifications from the law to group-based notions of remedy. As those who had originally argued for color-blindness supported group remedies, conservative Republicans, who been in the background during the struggle to enforce *Brown* in the 1950s and early 1960s or whose resistance had led to numerical race-conscious remedies, now advocated attention to individual merit and to "race neutral" remedies. Stephen Carter observed that "the ideal of colorblindness did not become enshrined as an untouchable part of the political firmament until government began, albeit sluggishly, to make some affirmative use of color to undo some of the crimes that racism has wrought. At that point a legal barrier was needed, and the rhetoric of the colorblind Constitution suddenly supplied it."[16] In such situations, civil rights leaders saw a reversal in which laws enacted to expand blacks' rights were used to limit opportunities for special consideration in employment and education where discrimination had existed.

The changed political environment revealed other turnarounds on civil rights. Conservatives who had earlier argued that federalism concerns—more bluntly, "states' rights"—militated against national government intervention on behalf of civil rights forgot those concerns when the administration intervened against quotas that had been adopted in the hope of avoiding resegregation. In the Starrett City housing project in New York City, government officials, who had done little to enforce housing discrimination laws, intervened to try to set aside quotas used to maintain a racially diverse community. When increased black registration resulting from the Voting Rights Act led to election of black mayors, who then set about dealing with discrimination in municipal employment, the national administration ignored earlier concerns about keeping hands off and intervened on behalf of whites to upset consent decrees to which the local officials had agreed. Likewise, although conservatives had earlier argued against the use of "judicial activism," which they effectively associated with liberal causes to achieve social change, the Reagan administration did not hesitate to call for the judiciary's use to restore prior patterns.

In another ironic twist, the Voting Rights Act, once criticized for making states and counties captive provinces of the national government, was used by whites. Bringing lawsuits to gain greater representation on legislative bodies, such as city councils, where blacks had obtained majorities, whites ignored their earlier claim that the Act applied only to deprivation of an individual's right to vote, not to vote dilution. When some Republicans sought to use the law to increase the election of white Republicans by concentrating the black voting-age population in other legislative districts, that particular turnaround strayed sufficiently far from principled opposition to use of the VRA to promote complaints even within conservative ranks that those Republicans had distorted the law in the same way civil rights groups had done.[17]

Ideological Division in the
Minority Community

Because there are differences among African-Americans, Latinos, and Asian-Americans, we cannot speak of "minorities" as a single category. Nor can the African-American community be considered ideologically homogeneous although major national organizations, particularly the NAACP, have come to speak for it as a single entity. The proliferation of groups like the Congress of Racial Equality (CORE), the Student Nonviolent Coordinating Committee (SNCC), and the Southern Christian Leadership Conference (SCLC), whose members "took to the street," made obvious the disagreement about means to be used to achieve rights. There was also ideological division among those willing to use litigation. Although, in the struggle to eliminate mandated segregation, there was consensus within the black community on the goal of desegregation, questioning voices arose as attainment of the goal receded. Even desegregation produced by court orders was questioned on pragmatic grounds by some black parents whose children bore the brunt of busing; a significant portion preferred not busing but instead an enrollment policy of open access/

freedom of choice. In some large cities like Detroit and Atlanta, local black leaders opted for plans emphasizing educational quality over desegregation, which produced conflict within the NAACP. Divergence in San Francisco's black community even led at one point to local NAACP pressure to build new schools in the ghetto rather than in a location conducive to greatest integration.[18] Derrick Bell gave voice to the division, arguing for greater attention to matters of class and against pursuing racial balance remedies and "desegregation by the numbers," which he called an "ineffective means of translating educational rights into meaningful remedies," used at the expense of quality education in the immediate community, where blacks were likely to remain.[19]

Disagreement within the black community also occurred in other civil rights policy areas. Thus, although the NAACP Legal Defense Fund had vigorously attacked seniority systems for keeping employed blacks "in their place," some black unionists supported seniority as better in the long run and objected to using other considerations to protect minority workers in layoffs. Division over quotas was also evident in internal NAACP debate over the content of its *Bakke* brief and over whether a racial group is better off "packed" into a legislative district in which it can elect one of its own as its representative or distributed across several districts, in all of which it might have some influence.[20] More recently, a growing number of black intellectuals, such as Thomas Sowell, Shelby Steele, and Stephen Carter, adopted positions like those of the white neoconservatives who had shifted from supporting the civil rights movement to opposing busing and affirmative action programs now advocated by the civil rights community from which they had detached themselves. They have questioned affirmative action programs or argued against them for not helping undereducated, unemployed blacks; for stigmatizing those who benefited from the programs; and for increasing whites' resentments.

The Presidency

The president's efforts to lead, or to block, legislative action and to implement and enforce policy are central to the achievement of civil rights. Those efforts have a substantial symbolic effect either when the president, on behalf of the government, takes action on behalf of minorities, thus serving to increase the extent to which all citizens are considered included in the polity,[21] or, on the other hand, takes action that appears to impede minorities' access to the system. There is noticeable variation from one presidency to the next in administrative and litigative actions to enforce civil rights,[22] and those actions affect how interest groups can spread their scarce resources. When an administration is supportive of efforts to achieve civil rights, there can be implicit cooperation in which the administration undertakes some efforts and civil rights organizations undertake others. At other times, when the administration is hostile to the goals of the civil rights community, civil rights groups must use resources to fend off agency actions.

The more complex civil rights environment of the mid-1960s began with the Civil Rights Act of 1964 and the Voting Rights Act of 1965, which marked a watershed and functioned "as congressional and presidential legitimations of the Supreme Court decisions on race— legitimations backed up by the use and threat of greater use of federal force."[23] Lyndon Johnson's civil rights activity and clear and unequivocal public stance made him "the least ambiguous, and demonstrably most vigorous [president], in his pursuit of civil rights policies."[24] His administration was obviously the high point in presidential attention and commitment to civil rights and activity to achieve them, although implementation of school desegregation was slowed by internal bureaucratic politics and resistance by strong local party leaders,[25] and both civil rights commitment and efforts began to wane because of the Vietnam war. Johnson's activity was so striking because it followed the minimal action of Eisenhower and Kennedy, who, despite mythology, did relatively little to advance civil rights. Their inactivity made them unlike Harry Truman, who, immediately after World War II, moved strongly toward increasing equality in the nation.[26]

Eisenhower's best-remembered civil rights action was his sending the 82nd Airborne into Little Rock, Arkansas, when mobs, stirred up by Governor Orval Faubus, prevented the integration of Central High School,[27] but this action was not representative. Despite the revisionist view of Eisenhower as a strong president with a "hidden hand," his hand "hardly touched the civil rights issues at all" while he concealed his "intense racial conservatism."[28] His conservatism was perhaps most evident in his never making a public statement in support of *Brown v. Board of Education*, but it also was clear from his administration's disinclination to protect blacks even when they were faced with violence in their attempt to bring about civil rights in the South. For Eisenhower, dealing with violence was for the states, not for the national government.[29]

However, with the Republican president and the Democratic Senate majority leader (Lyndon Johnson) working together pragmatically, the first civil rights legislation since Reconstruction was enacted during Eisenhower's presidency. The Voting Rights Act of 1957 allowed the attorney general to obtain injunctions against interference with voting rights, elevated the civil rights unit in the Department of Justice to division status, and created the U.S. Commission on Civil Rights. The Voting Rights Act of 1960 allowed states to be made defendants in the injunction suits, gave the attorney general access to voting records, and allowed federal courts to appoint voting referees empowered to register voters.

John Kennedy's civil rights stance, like Eisenhower's, has also been mythologized.[30] Kennedy, like Eisenhower, moved quite slowly on civil rights matters. For example, he did not make good on his promise to end discrimination in housing "at the stroke of a pen" until two years after the promise, and then only in limited form. His administration's response to violence aimed at civil rights workers was also minimal. Faced with a situation comparable to that in Little Rock— Mississippi's resistance to admitting James Meredith to the University of Mississippi—Kennedy failed to act forcefully and then had to resort to calling in the troops, with bloodshed the result.

The coming of the Nixon administration illustrates the importance of changes in, and transitions between, administrations. In the Nixon's administration's first school desegregation action, after HEW Secretary Robert Finch said he was unwilling to accept HEW's Desegregation Guidelines without reexamination, Finch asked for an extension of time to desegregate Mississippi school districts despite the lack of desegregation there for more than ten years after *Brown,* with belated action taken only after threatened withdrawal of federal funds. Finch's action put the government and the NAACP Legal Defense Fund on opposite sides of a Supreme Court school desegregation case for the first time. The administration also supported a congressional moratorium on busing and a constitutional amendment that would have prohibited assignment of pupils to particular schools because of race. However, HEW Secretary Elliot Richardson quietly enforced the Supreme Court's desegregation standards, and there was "no overt effort at wholesale displacement of the executive role in enforcing civil rights." Thus one could properly call the Nixon administration's record one of "consolidation, advancement—and retreat." [31] Moreover, in an instance of innovative activity, the administration developed the Philadelphia Plan, designed to increase the number of minority employees in federally financed construction projects. A look back from the 1990s thus shows the transition between the Johnson and Nixon administrations to be very different from that between the Carter and Reagan administrations. Although the former may have looked at the time to civil rights organizations as a major retrogression, it now appears much more benign. [32]

Like Nixon, President Ford was generally moderate on civil rights. Ford adopted Nixon's stance on busing. He directed Attorney General Edward Levi to find a case for imposing limits on the practice and conveying mixed messages in the heated Boston school desegregation situation, that one should obey the law, but a judicial solution is not the best. However, he promulgated regulations and guidelines for enforcement of civil rights statutes and, " 'when forced to do things, did so with a sense of the spirit of the law instead of trying to undercut it.' " [33]

President Jimmy Carter did not have Johnson's strong pro-civil rights commitment, but differences from the Nixon-Ford period were evident. Carter supported improvements in civil rights legislation; concentrated enforcement of employment discrimination laws in the Equal Employment Opportunity Commission; and took a stronger general enforcement stance, although actual practice did not match this stance. Particularly noteworthy were a serious commitment to seeking out minorities and women for the federal judiciary and the appointment of people from the civil rights groups to policy and enforcement positions. For example, Carter appointed Drew Days III, a former NAACP Legal Defense Fund lawyer, as Assistant Attorney General for Civil Rights. (Days was President Clinton's solicitor general.)

The Reagan administration, not only reflecting but going beyond contemporary public opinion, provided a severe and abrupt disjuncture from preceding administrations, both Democratic and Republican, in presidential support for civil rights. The administration overturned existing policy, challenged statutes and judicial rulings on racial integration, and dismantled enforcement machinery. The principal change was advocacy of less federal government enforcement to eliminate discrimination, and a concomitantly greater role for state and local governments.

Reversing positions constructed by the Nixon, Ford, and Carter administrations, the Reagan administration declared that only "identifiable victims" of employment discrimination could be recompensed; affirmative action programs were to be stopped; the intent test was to be used in voting discrimination and school desegregation cases; and voluntary compliance with fair housing rules was to be emphasized. Where others acted to eliminate discrimination and its effects, the administration joined those "seeking to restrict or curtail rules that were established to remedy civil rights violations." [34] The administration intervened in school cases where busing was already in place and regularly moved to reopen consent decrees in which earlier discrimination complaints had been settled. It did so particularly when the Supreme Court provided further support in rulings based on the administration's position.

The administration's view was translated into an enforcement record that was weaker than that of all predecessors, Democrat and Republican. The Justice Department's Civil Rights Division was restructured to constrain liberal career attorneys who had resisted, even rebelled at, the change;[35] there was less government litigation in employment (particularly in major pattern-or-practice cases), voting rights, and housing.[36] Limited housing litigation was focused on places like Oak Park and Starrett City where, even though the law was technically being violated, efforts were being made to maintain desegregation. Nonetheless, enforcement was relatively strong in some areas of the law such as voting rights, and there was support for new housing legislation, enacted in 1988, which increased HUD's enforcement powers and strengthened state and local civil rights agencies' implementation of fair housing policy.

Chicago, where the Johnson administration had failed to remove the city's federal school funds, perhaps best illustrates the administration's action on school desegregation. At first delaying implementation of a 1980 decree in which the Chicago school board was to adopt an acceptable desegregation plan by March 1981, the Reagan Justice Department shifted to support of voluntary rather than mandatory busing, opposed court orders for financing to upgrade black and Hispanic schools, and failed to make available promised federal desegregation funds. After a federal judge ordered federal payments toward desegregation, Reagan vetoed a congressional appropriation for that purpose.[37]

Fragmentation delayed immediate reaction to administration-produced change, but eventually major civil rights organizations, joined by some leading black Republicans, reflected the very low poll ratings blacks gave the president and became highly negative toward the Reagan administration.[38] They were infuriated when the president said that civil rights leaders exaggerated the amount of racism to maintain the civil rights cause and their own positions and questioned whether the leaders wanted civil rights efforts to succeed. Civil rights leaders' opposition was focused by the nomination of Assistant Attorney General for Civil Rights William Bradford Reynolds to be deputy attorney general, and the Senate Judiciary Committee rejected the nomination.

Especially significant was the Reagan administration's effort, in what can be called "The Eclipse of an Outspoken Agency," to quiet the U.S. Civil Rights Commission's independent voice which was critical both of conditions limiting civil rights and of the government itself. That critical stance continued after Reagan took office. For example, the commission wrote in a letter to the president about the end of federal leadership in equal educational opportunity; reaffirmed its support for mandatory busing; and the new chairman, Clarence Pendleton, made a statement about the administration's lack of cooperation in providing information. That lack of cooperation led the commission to issue subpoenas to the Departments of Labor and Education to obtain information concerning civil rights enforcement.

An Office of Management and Budget directive that reports and legislative testimony by commission members and staff be cleared for consistency with the administration's position was followed by the president's firing of the three most critical commission members. After an angered Congress allowed the commission's authorization to expire, a compromise was reached on the process of selecting commission members (four were to be appointed by the president, four by congressional leaders). The result was that the commission's position became largely an echo of the administration's civil rights views. For example, the commission asserted that the term "civil rights" had become debased through attention to group remedies and, altering its position, said that racial preferences were unjustified discrimination.

Pendleton also criticized civil rights leaders (including Jesse Jackson, Vernon Jordan of the Urban League, and NAACP Executive Director Benjamin Hooks) for making an "industry" of racial politics. Even an administration appointee declining reappointment said the commission had lost its moral strength and purpose and was no longer an important voice The new commission's critics, including minority legislative caucuses and a number of congressional Republicans, suggested defunding, and the House Appropriations Committee so voted. Staff was reduced and most regional offices were closed; the commission was barely kept alive. President Bush's selection of a well-respected black Republican, Arthur A. Fletcher, as the commission's new chair led to congressional reauthorization of the commission and to somewhat increased funding.

President Bush's administration had important elements of continuity with the Reagan administration. The Bush administration offered an anti-"quotas" justification for vetoing a civil rights bill, phased out regulations on preferences and quotas in hiring and promotion in federal agencies and private companies, limited college and university scholarships for minorities, and appointed Clarence Thomas to the Supreme Court. However, the administration was viewed more favorably by the civil rights community because of the selection of a moderate former state legislator, John Dunne, to be Assistant Attorney General for Civil Rights, more Justice Department enforcement activity, particularly on voting rights, better communication with the civil rights community, and a less contentious civil rights posture.

The Supreme Court

Crucial for civil rights litigators in the 1960s was that the Supreme Court had been favorable to civil rights, most notably with *Brown v. Board of Education* in 1954, although that ruling had taken on almost mythic proportions, and there was a tendency to ignore the Court's lack of activity with respect to school desegregation. (There was no action concerning employment discrimination from World War II until the Civil Rights Act of 1964 was passed.) We look here first at trends from the late Warren Court (mid-1960s through 1969) through the Burger Court (1969 through 1986), and then turn to a brief summary of the Court's substantive civil rights action.

The justices' support for civil liberties and rights was at its highest in the late Warren Court, and civil rights lawyers were generally quite positive about the Court. Able to obtain far more from the Supreme Court than from the other branches of government, they overestimated what the Court did produce. Indeed, while the Court's record on civil rights was strong, it was less than 100 percent—some thought far less, although few were willing to be critical in public. The criticism by Lewis Steel, then on the NAACP staff, received the most attention. According to Steel, the "Nine Men in Black Who Think White" showed a lack of serious commitment to racial equality by delaying implementation of civil rights through "all deliberate speed," dealing timidly with sit-ins and demonstrations, and striking down "only the symbols of racism while condoning or overlooking the ingrained practices which have meant the survival of white supremacy in the United States, North and South." The result was "a cautious Supreme Court [that] has waltzed in time to the music of the white majority—one step forward, one step backward and sidestep, sidestep." [39]

Perhaps most indicative of the Warren Court's action on race relations was its handling of cases on sit-ins and civil rights demonstrations. Accepting a large number of cases, the Court wrestled with the question of a proprietor's right to refuse service to someone because of race and to reinforce that refusal by summoning the police to arrest for trespass those sitting-in. The Court used a variety of strategems to reverse convictions of those arrested for sitting-in but never decided the central issue. In an interplay of lawyers' and judges' strategies, civil rights lawyers who understood the Court's reluctance to deal with the central issue "creatively developed arguments that permitted decisions to be made on narrower grounds." [40] Once Congress enacted the public accommodations section of the 1964 Civil Rights Act, the Court strongly affirmed that action. However, the Court's rulings upholding laws prohibiting picketing at jails and courthouses indicated limits to its agreement with the civil rights movement. [41]

Although, from the beginning, many saw the early Burger Court to be quite different from the Warren Court, it produced a mixed record on individual rights, upholding busing and giving a broad reading to the new federal employment discrimination law while showing reluctance like the Warren Court's to invalidate private discriminatory action. By the mid-1970s, however, the Court had made it more difficult for those with civil rights claims to obtain access to the courts and, when they did achieve access, made it more difficult to prove civil rights claims. The most important thread running through the Burger Court's race relations cases was its requirement that violations be proved on the basis of causation and intent. The watershed case was *Washington v. Davis* (1976), which required proof of discriminatory intent in job discrimination cases brought under the Constitution. The rule that remedies be limited to the extent of the (intentional) violation reinforced the Court's stance. In taking this position, the Court gave greater weight to the interests of whites, for example, their claim that they were "innocent victims" who had unfairly lost jobs in affirmative action programs.

The Court's action, and nonaction, can be seen in school desegregation, employment discrimination, affirmative action, and voting rights cases. After the 1955 "with all deliberate speed" decision on implementation of school desegregation, the Court avoided major involvement in school desegregation questions for over a decade, becoming engaged again only after Congress and the executive branch had begun to dominate the field. During that period—until the late 1980s—private actors, including parents, civic activists, ministers, journalists, and academics, had played larger roles, and the Court of Appeals for the Fifth Circuit became the primary judicial actor pressing ahead, as it gave great weight to and reinforced the HEW Desegregation Guidelines. Most important was that court's en banc ruling in the *Jefferson* case on Louisiana and Alabama school districts,[42] in which the court ordered "affirmative action" by the school districts to reorganize into "unitary, nonracial systems in which there are no Negro schools and no white schools—just schools."

Only after this activity did the Supreme Court make a substantial contribution, by confronting "freedom-of-choice" desegregation plans, which assigned children to neighborhood schools or their earlier-assigned schools and then allowed transfers. These plans produced some desegregation of previously all-white schools but little or none at previously all-black schools. Going beyond the HEW Guidelines, the justices ruled that "freedom of choice" plans not producing results were not acceptable and that school boards had an obligation to dismantle dual school systems effectively and to bring about "meaningful and immediate progress" toward eliminating de jure segregation. Only then did the Court, in *Alexander v. Holmes County*, one of Chief Justice Burger's first cases, finally make the point that the end of "all deliberate speed" had come: school districts were to give up their dual systems "at once" and operate unitary systems "now and hereafter."

Having finally disposed of the "when" question, the Court was able to turn to standards for desegregation and to remedies. Its stance on both elements varied over time. The Court's major ruling on the extent of desegregation and on remedy came in 1971. In the *Swann* case, the Court, speaking unanimously through Chief Justice Burger, said that not every school had to reflect the community's overall racial composition and some one-race schools could exist, but school officials had to explain their continuation and could not use school construction to perpetuate or reestablish segregation. At least as important was the justices' reinforcement of district judges' authority and discretion to order remedies, including adjustment of attendance zones and cross-busing of students. In other cases, the Court continued to head off efforts to avoid desegregation,[43] even ruling in *Runyon v. McCrary* (1976) that racially discriminatory private schools could be sued under 42 U.S.C. Sec. 1981, the Reconstruction era civil rights law. (In its major open housing decision, *Jones v. Mayer* in 1968, the Court had used that law to rule that denial of purchase of property because of race could be attacked as a "badge of slavery.") Then, in the more significant *Bob Jones University* case (1983), the Court ruled that schools that discriminated on the basis of race were not entitled to receive a tax exemption for being "organized and operated exclusively for religious, charitable, . . . or educational purposes."

In the Court's first desegregation case from the North, in which it ruled that the Denver school board acted improperly by manipulating attendance zones, selecting school sites, and using a "neighborhood school" policy to achieve segregated schools, the majority considerably eased the burden of plaintiffs bringing such cases. However, the Court then limited remedies in northern metropolitan school cases. In 1974 in the Detroit case, it ruled against interdistrict remedies. An indication that the Court had reached a turning point was the dissenting justices' complaint about the ruling's retrogressive effect and its crippling of the judiciary's ability to remedy segregation. The Court then ruled in the first Dayton case that district courts must match their remedies to the "incremental segregative effect" of school board actions taken with the intent to discriminate, so that a systemwide remedy was allowed only if a violation had a systemwide impact.

However, indicating the somewhat erratic nature of its rulings, only two years later the justices upheld systemwide remedies for both Dayton and Columbus, Ohio.[44]

When voters rescinded desegregation efforts, the Court was less supportive of civil rights claims, in particular upholding California voters' adoption of a state constitutional amendment limiting state court-ordered busing, although at the same time, a narrow majority of the Court found that Washington State voters had violated the Constitution by adopting an initiative prohibiting school boards from assigning students away from neighborhood schools for desegregation.[45]

The Court's first major pronouncement on the substance of Title VII did not come until 1971. In *Griggs v. Duke Power Co.*, which paralleled *Brown* in its importance in its area of law, the Court ruled that, under the statute, an employer's discriminatory intent need not be shown and that employment practices that were facially neutral could be challenged for having "disparate impact"—a differential effect on minorities—unless the provisions were job-related. However, only a few years later the Court reversed direction in *Washington v. Davis* (1976), declaring that under the Constitution, to be invalid an employment test "must ultimately be traced to a racially discriminatory purpose"; it was not improper merely because of different racial results. This requirement that "disparate treatment"—actions taken *based* on race— be shown was particularly important because it was applied not only in employment cases but also in school, housing and voting cases.

Although rulings on questions of remedy began with victories for civil rights claimants, the Court reversed direction. The justices first ruled that once unlawful discrimination was found, back pay should generally be granted and that showing an employer's "bad faith" was not necessary; they said that lower courts could award both "benefit-type seniority" (the basis for counting vacation time and pension benefits) and "competitive-type" seniority (the basis for bidding for jobs and for layoffs).[46] Later, however, the Court said in the 1977 *Teamsters* case that although seniority systems established with a discriminatory purpose could be attacked, Title VII protected "bona fide" seniority systems that perpetuated discrimination, and that, because the law provided no relief from discrimination predating the statute, retroactive seniority could only be awarded from the date of Title VII's enactment. Even if the new, post-Act, seniority systems perpetuated earlier discrimination, they were valid unless one could show intent to discriminate.

The Court's most controversial discrimination cases of the 1970s and 1980s were those brought by whites who felt that race or gender-based remedies created improper "reverse discrimination." Their claims focused on the use of numbers ("quotas") to determine the proportion of minorities or women hired or promoted, starting with the federal government's requirement that federal contractors provide affirmative action plans including numerical goals and timetables. The Court's first substantive pronouncement on affirmative action, by a very badly divided Court, came in the famous *Bakke* case in 1978. Dealing with both statutory (Title VI) and constitutional (Fourteenth Amendment) questions, different majorities found setting aside positions for disadvantaged minority students improper but said that the goal of achieving a diverse student body was sufficiently compelling that race could be one element in an admissions decision. The Court's internal division meant that *Bakke* provided few principles for later cases, nor was the Court's direction clear or consistent. Initially the Court ruled that Title VII did not prohibit all private, voluntary, race-conscious affirmative action plans, particularly temporary plans used to eliminate manifest racial imbalance in the workforce, and then upheld Congress's creation of the 10 percent Minority Business Enterprise (MBE) "set-aside" for federal public works projects.[47] Then the Court showed that it would be less supportive of affirmative action combined with restraints on seniority, that is, when some whites with greater seniority might be laid off to protect the jobs of some blacks.[48] Yet at the same time, by upholding affirmative action plans, justices were saying that those who were not actual victims of discrimination could legitimately benefit from affirmative action provisions that reserved some promotions for minorities, and that pervasive discrimination and the agency's obstinacy about hiring blacks justified a requirement that for each promotion opening in the Alabama state police one white and one black were to be promoted.[49]

Both the late Warren Court and the Burger Court not only sustained the Voting Rights Act of 1965 and its revisions against constitutional challenge but also held a wide range of election changes subject to the Act's coverage and Section 5 preclearance, sustained Justice Department preclearance processes, and placed the burden of proof on submitting jurisdictions to show a change was *not* discriminatory. The Court did not, however, give as much support to vote dilution claims, that is, claims that the force and effect of people's votes had been weakened by devices such as municipal annexation of territory containing a high concentration of whites and use of multimember districts in state legislative elections or at-large municipal elections. The Court did recognize the Attorney General's authority under the Voting Rights Act of 1965 to demand some "affirmative action," such as insisting that the nonwhite majority in some state legislative districts be increased to 65 percent, before preclearing a change in voting procedures.

The Transformed Triangle: Congress and the Rescue of Civil Rights

In the 1950s and into the early 1960s, one could not have imagined Congress, with or without the president's assistance, providing strong support for civil rights when the Supreme Court refused to provide it. Yet now the 1970s and 1980s saw a reversal of position—a *transformed triangle*—in the relations among the Court, Congress, and the president on civil rights policymaking. After earlier congressional resistance and limited executive action, tri-branch support of civil rights from 1963 through 1966 provided a brief heady time for those seeking support for civil rights.[50] However, as efforts were made to bring about school desegregation in the North, support for civil rights soon dissolved in a backlash, leaving a liberal Supreme Court facing a less supportive administration and an increasingly conservative Congress. Then the Court itself shifted, with its new Republican-appointed conservative majority limiting rather than advancing civil rights. This shift led to another: instead of turning to the Supreme Court because Congress was resistant, civil rights advocates turned to Congress to overcome a resistant Court. Congress repeatedly responded positively to restore what the Court had taken away, at times overriding the president to do so.

This increase in congressional support, for which civil rights groups had worked hard, was aided by the Democrats' control of the House throughout the Reagan and Bush presidencies, and control of the Senate except for six years. Greater linkage between lobbying and the Court's actions also made a difference. In particular, the successful effort to overturn *City of Mobile v. Bolden* (1980), returning the law to an earlier test to be used under Section 2 of the statute, a test that was easier for plaintiffs to satisfy, included use of major voting rights litigators Frank Parker and Armand Derfner as lobbyists. The Lawyers' Committee for Civil Rights Under Law shifted Parker from its Mississippi office and set up a Voting Rights Project at its Washington, D.C., headquarters, while Derfner hung his hat at the Joint Center for Political Studies, a think-tank focusing on blacks' political activities.

Congress's first modern rescue of civil rights groups from an adverse Supreme Court ruling came after the Court had severely limited federal courts' award of attorneys' fees. Congress's response, the Civil Rights Attorneys Fees Act of 1976, provided attorneys' fees to the prevailing party in civil rights cases. In other actions, Congress protected substantive civil rights interests and came to the aid of minorities and women faced with adverse Supreme Court rulings.[51] For example, after the *Grove City College* ruling that the antidiscrimination provision of Title IX (sex discrimination in education) applied only to specific programs that received federal funds, not to the entire institution, Congress, in the aptly titled Civil Rights Restoration Act, returned to what had been understood to be the status quo ante, saying that if an institution received any federal funds, antidiscrimination law applied to the entire institution.

The most striking congressional civil rights reversal of the Supreme Court came after a set of June 1989 rulings changing the standard for proving a Title VII violation, excluding racial harassment on the job and race-based denial of promotions from coverage under civil rights laws, and facilitating reopening of employment discrimination consent decrees by those claiming reverse discrimination. The Bush administration, although conceding that some of the rulings should be reversed, argued that the proposed Civil Rights Act of 1990 would require "quotas" in employment, and President Bush vetoed it. However, he ultimately agreed to the Civil Rights Act of 1991, at the heart of which was a provision restoring the *Griggs* disparate impact standard for proving employment discrimination. The two-year lapse between the Court's rulings and the passage of the 1991 act allowed Congress to reverse two 1991 Supreme Court rulings in the same law.[52]

Relations with Government

Amicus briefs are sometimes considered the judicial equivalent of lobbying of the legislative and executive branches, but there is much more to the relations between litigating interest groups and the government. Relations between civil rights litigators and the government are characterized by division of labor, cooperation, and conflict.

When litigating interest groups and government agencies engage in division of labor, the government pursues some cases and interest groups pursue others. This takes place even without communication: there are "no Spain, Portugal discussions" between interest groups and the government. Instead an interest group, seeing where the government places its effort, invests its resources elsewhere. Likewise, the government looks to see where the NAACP, similar organizations, and private counsel have undertaken cases and avoids activity there. Comparative advantage also explains why the government concentrates on certain subjects and interest groups concentrate on others. For example, a former government litigator noted that discrimination in the provision of municipal services was one problem where "if anyone could get at it, it would have to be the government, because of problems of standing and the enormous financial resources required."

Interest groups and government also participate on the same side of some cases. In job discrimination cases, a private plaintiff, represented by an organization, and the EEOC may each file its own complaint, or, after private civil rights litigators have initiated a suit, the government may enter the case or file a nearly identical one. Such participation does not necessarily result from joint planning. There may, however, be conscious parallelism between a group and the Justice Department even though one party may keep its distance from other other, as the Justice Department did in its amicus role in a federal court prison conditions case in Ohio, where department staff interviewed prisoners without the plaintiff's attorneys' knowledge or presence, and where its attitude was described as, "We're the United States. We'll do what we want. We're invited in by the court."[53]

Even if the administration is supportive of civil rights, relations between civil rights groups and the Justice Department concerning the content of the government's amicus briefs may be only a "one-way street." An organization "would show the government its brief," a former Department of Justice official noted, "but the government wouldn't release its document—although it would tell LDF generally what DOJ would do, the approach it would take." Relations can, however, be two-way. At times the Justice Department, having heard that an LDF or ACLU case was to be appealed, would initiate contact and ask for the group's briefs. Justice's participation was more likely "if government had unique perspectives." One assistant attorney general for civil rights is reported to have "encouraged attorneys in his Division to maintain contacts with private civil rights organizations so as to better identify cases for potential amicus support or assistance."[54] Cooperation is facilitated if there is no friction over who receives credit for action taken. A housing litigator who said he wanted "results, not credit" claimed to be quite willing to let government agencies receive the credit for what his organization and the government worked on together.

Interest groups and government action in the same case may occur because one wishes to press further than it anticipates the other will. For example, a civil rights group may join a suit to assure that the government does not either drop its suit or accept a limited settlement, say, an employment consent decree that does not embody the group's goals.[55] The latter concern led the NAACP to intervene in the government's Yonkers education case of the 1980s, where communication was facilitated by the NAACP's lawyer having moved from Justice to the NAACP and the government's lawyer being a former colleague. Conservative groups engage in the same strategy. A lawyer for a conservative public interest law firm explained, "It helps the department when we come in as an amicus curiae taking a more extreme viewpoint. . . . That way *they* can't be called extremist."[56] This is an example of a more general phenomenon: the target of moderate and more extreme interest groups will not pay attention to the moderates until the more extreme activists begin to take action that makes the moderates far more attractive. The government likewise has entered privately initiated cases to protect a position more appropriate than the one that initial plaintiffs sought. For example, when the NAACP argued for an expansive set of remedies in education and employment cases, the Reagan Justice Department, saying it must protect the civil rights of all individuals, would intervene seeking less.[57]

Government entry into a case complicates the work of interest group litigators while the government's presence constrains group control of litigation. This is even more true because the federal government's top lawyers are skillful. Thus the presence of Solicitor General Robert Bork as an amicus curiae in the *Fowler* death penalty litigation made the NAACP Legal Defense Fund's task more difficult because it had to "face a skilled opponent, who approached litigation in much the same way it did—as a means to bring about broad policy change."[58] Litigating interest groups can, however, serve to constrain the government, particularly if the government has been able to litigate without such groups being part of the picture. In voting rights litigation, the Department of Justice initially controlled litigation but the development of new litigating organizations with voting rights concerns limited the government's discretion.[59]

When interest groups act first and the government then joins the game, the groups, perhaps because of government default, take the role of "private attorney general" to develop and implement precedent, which agencies use in subsequent administrative or litigative action. This pattern occurred in both employment discrimination and school desegregation. LDF, for example, "by nudging constitutional doctrine along, . . . provided the legal footing and political cover for OCR [Office of Civil Rights] to evolve administrative enforcement standards for Title VI."[60] The agencies may not object to being prodded to adopt particular stands or to invest more resources in enforcement, because interest group action may give agency factions support to resist opposition.[61] Defendant government agencies occasionally are even willing to lose cases. One lawyer who litigated against a northern city school district observed, "It helps to have a sympathetic defendant," such as a school board which "even helped with suggestions at discovery." Similarly, in prison condition cases, defendant administrators, who "know you should get what you wanted" but because of budgetary restraints cannot volunteer it, did not mind a court ordering them to provide it or entering into a consent decree to the same end.

Some interaction between litigating interest groups and the government goes beyond "parallel play" or implicit cooperation. Trying to extend resources, interest groups may bring matters to the government's attention in the hope the latter will undertake litigation or provide some support with an amicus brief, or at least not take a contrary position. For example, in the *Bakke* case, groups strenuously sought to engage government on their side, and the general counsel of both the NAACP and the LDF tried to dissuade Solicitor General Wade

McCree from including an antiquota argument in the government's brief.[62] When groups bring matters to the government's attention, the government itself may also benefit. One former Justice Department official pointed out that some cases brought to the department's attention by interest groups "provided the opportunity to get involved where the government hadn't been involved."

There can even be explicitly shared responsibility, as there was in the development of EEOC regulations and desegregation guidelines, and in litigation, when government assisted interest groups with difficult resource problems in important employment discrimination cases.[63] Such assistance, in addition to funds for Legal Services Program backup centers, may include provision of government funds to organizations for litigation. The EEOC made loans to employment discrimination litigators,[64] and the Lawyers' Committee had a contract with EEOC to train lawyers in Title VII litigation. The Reagan administration did not renew the contract, so that such services decreased.

The absence of government cooperation, which may result from its inaction in dealing with an issue, can become a general failure to enforce civil rights provisions, one that may compel litigators to sue the government to force action, as in the *Adams* litigation to obtain agency enforcement of Title VI. Lack of government cooperation can, however, be more than inaction: the government may take the initiative against groups. This was most obvious in the post-*Brown* Southern counterattack against the organizations themselves. More recent was the Reagan administration's exclusion from the federal fund drive of groups "that seek to influence . . . the determination of public policy through . . . litigation on behalf of parties other than themselves."[65] Some efforts are less visible if not particularly subtle, for example, the Kennedy administration's efforts to isolate or at least co-opt Dr. Martin Luther King, Jr.[66] To influence groups to shift their focus of attention, the administration also tried to channel activity away from sit-ins and Freedom Rides and into challenges to voting discrimination by working with private foundations to provide funding for a multiorganization Voter Education Project.

Oppositional government action is particularly important for planned litigation by civil rights groups, because it forces the organizations to engage in defensive litigation regardless of whether the government's intent was to deplete the groups' resources. The activity occupies the groups' attention and thus distracts, and detracts, from their ability to engage in litigation campaigns. Their only plan must be to devote scarce resources to defeat the administration's on-slaught, thus leaving far less with which to pursue their remaining agenda. Groups do, however, fight back against debilitating govern-ment activity; their counterattacks include opposition to administra-tion nominees (e.g., the successful opposition to the nomination of William Bradford Reynolds to be deputy attorney general[67]); attacks on governmental bodies seen as inimical to civil rights goals (e.g., a 1983 NAACP proposal to cut the budget of the Reagan administra-tion's Civil Rights Division); and attempts to reverse disliked Supreme Court rulings.

These government actions to which groups respond are evidence that in relations between groups and the government, no assumption can be made that government is passive, only being acted upon. In-deed, government is an active participant—at times cooperating in the effort to advance civil rights, at other times resisting, and at still other times actively seeking to turn back the clock, thus requiring inter-est groups to adopt a responsive mode. In this sense, interest group activity results from government activity.[68]

2

The Supreme Court's

Impact on Litigation

Because of the Supreme Court's importance for interest group litigation, before proceeding with other elements of the litigation environment and with interest groups' decisions about civil rights litigation, we examine the wide range of the Supreme Court's effects on civil rights litigation. Particular attention is given to the Court's importance for litigating organizations' survival and functioning, and especially their ability to bring cases.

Lawyers' Attention to the Court
and Its Direction

We should not be surprised that many lawyers pay attention to the Supreme Court of the United States as more than an intellectual exercise. They are particularly likely to pay it heed if they are engaged in certain types of litigation like civil rights litigation. After all, they are expected to follow precedent, and Supreme Court rulings are the ultimate precedent. And even if developing precedent is not the lawyers' goal, they will pay heed to the Supreme Court, because if they win in the lower courts, their opponents may seek to drag them there. However, their attention to the Court, or the weight they give it, is not equal at all stages of litigation. Some attorneys think the Court's rulings are "less crucial in going from the district court to the court of appeals" than from the court of appeals to the Supreme Court, and that "what the Supreme Court does really comes into play after a major lower court decision" as lawyers decide whether to seek certiorari. According to litigators, "seldom is a case keyed solely on the Supreme Court," although "tactics in trying a case" are. The Supreme Court's actions "more affected *how* a case was brought, not whether," particularly when cases, like the sit-in cases, "had to be brought" to respond to civil rights workers' actions. "Causes addressed" may not be affected, but, as part of lawyers' efforts to alter precedent, there is a desire to frame issues to satisfy the Court's majority. For example, litigators seeking to protect the rights of the mentally ill shifted their argument in *O'Connor v. Donaldson* (1975) from a "right to treatment" to due process, in part for tactical reasons "dictated by an assessment of the attitudes of the members of the Supreme Court" and of Chief Justice Burger's antagonism to his former D.C. Circuit colleague David Bazelon.[1]

Despite the importance of Supreme Court rulings, they constitute only one vector affecting attorneys' actions, because in the short run, lawyers must devote their immediate attention to the trial judge, whose rulings are crucial in forming the record that may later be used in an appeal. Thus the lower courts are often more central to attorneys in the litigation process. When the Supreme Court does decide cases, the lower court has "filtered and shaped the legal issues for the Supreme Court."[2] And, having established basic rules, the justices may rely on the lower courts to implement the Court's broad guidelines. And when the Supreme Court leaves lower court rulings undisturbed, as it does in most cases, their word is final, not only as to particular cases but also for doctrine in some important areas of the law. Thus the Court's nonparticipation in school desegregation law after its "all deliberate speed" pronouncement in *Brown II* made the Fifth Circuit the lead court for defining the pace of desegregation. And when the Supreme Court did not develop clear doctrine, for example, on "what degree of integration is necessary in specific schools to eliminate the effects of systemwide violations," that ambiguity made the

Sixth Circuit "in effect the functional court of last resort" for many important school desegregation cases resulting from the NAACP's attack on northern segregation.[3]

Lawyers engaged in planned civil rights litigation analyze the Supreme Court's rulings closely to see which issues have been settled and which left unresolved. Lawyers certainly give attention to opinions of the Court, and to the size of the Court's majority, although at times they misjudge it.[4] They also watch concurring and dissenting opinions. In the first Detroit school case, *Milliken v. Bradley* (1974), the majority refused to tie schools and housing together, thus limiting the way in which litigators can present school cases, but civil rights lawyers paid considerable attention to Justice Stewart's suggestion in his concurrence that a link between housing discrimination and school desegregation might be accepted.

Even dissents from certiorari denials receive close scrutiny. The dissent by Justices Goldberg, Brennan, and Douglas from the denial of review to two 1963 death penalty cases,[5] in which they argued that the Court should decide the constitutionality of the death penalty for rape, told interested lawyers of the justices' interest in the death penalty's constitutionality.[6] However, their not mentioning racial discrimination as a consideration was also "an omission which lawyers close to the Court took to mean that in 1963 it was still too early for many to accept that an interracial rape was not a more serious crime than an intraracial rape." However, those following the case carefully "readily concluded that, *if proven*, a claim that the Southern states reserved the death penalty for blacks who raped whites was an even more compelling constitutional argument against capital punishment for the crime of rape" than some arguments the justices mentioned.[7]

Lawyers also watch the receptivity of the Supreme Court and lower courts to particular types of cases and claims and the Court's pattern of granting review. The Supreme Court directly affects what types of cases are brought to it both through its supporting or rejecting certain claimed rights and by the frequency with which it grants or denies review to particular types of cases.[8] For example, in the 1950s and 1960s, the Court's apparent unwillingness to grant review to challenges to urban renewal and related housing issues served to depress the number of housing cases brought to the Court.[9] However, litigators may attempt to change such patterns. Concerned about earlier denials of review to challenges to racial restrictive covenants, the NAACP put more effort into getting the "right" cases to the Court and into framing petitions for review.[10]

Reaction to shifts in the Court's openness to civil liberties and civil rights claims is affected by perception of state courts and whether the latter will be more receptive. In some instances, the Supreme Court's closing the door means that litigators have little choice but to proceed in state court if they wish to pursue their claims at all. In mental health litigation, *Pennhurst* (1981) led lawyers to question whether they should have proceeded in federal court, and their changed view led them to call the Supreme Court's attention to a recent Massachusetts case; the case was remanded for reconsideration in light of that ruling.[11]

Changes in direction.   The existence and nature of changes in the Supreme Court's overall direction have regularly received lawyers' particular attention. Sometimes, this is because there is hope of better reception in the future. Albion Tourgee, the principal lawyer in the *Plessy* case, was concerned that the timing of that challenge to Jim Crow laws was inappropriate because of the Court's post-1877 conservative posture on race relations, but felt the situation might improve with time.[12] Likewise, in *Frank v. Mangum* (1915), a federal habeas corpus due process challenge to a case in which mob influence had been present, the Court had defined due process narrowly and deferred generally to state judicial processes. This did not make it likely that the convictions of blacks in connection with riots in Phillips County, Arkansas, could be overturned, but the defendants' lawyers were aware that *Frank* was not unanimous and that several members of the *Frank* majority had left the Court, while Holmes, who had dissented there, remained. In this instance, however, the personnel changes did not favor the NAACP, as the Taft Court had become more, not less, conservative.[13]

Changes in the Supreme Court's direction are important because when cases reach the Court can determine their outcome. An NAACP lawyer has observed that if the increasingly liberal Justice Blackmun of the early 1980s had been sitting in the first Detroit school case in 1974, it "would have left a whole new picture." Likewise, an NAACP Legal Defense Fund attorney has suggested that had the issue of the discriminatory effect of seniority systems reached the Supreme Court when certiorari was first sought, the "thoroughly briefed and researched" case probably would have been won. However, when the issue was finally decided in 1977 in *Teamsters,* the issue "was not as central and was not as thoroughly treated," and the Supreme Court ruled adversely and in a footnote wiped out appeals court rulings favoring LDF's position.

In a particularly striking example, the "political ambience" and the composition of the Supreme Court changed significantly from the time welfare cases were initiated to the time those cases reached the Court. In the brief span between the Supreme Court outlawing durational residence requirements for welfare benefits in *Shapiro v. Thompson* and its deciding cases concerning the level of AFDC benefits in *Dandridge v. Williams,* President Nixon had made appointments to the Court and the AFDC program had become a political liability, so that a Court earlier willing to support due process claims in *Goldberg v. Kelly* would not support redistributive ones.

In the Burger Court's early years, civil rights lawyers, expecting conservative rulings to erode earlier victories, paid particular attention to the Court's direction. Because "from an organizational point of view, the decision to go up has as a component who is sitting on the court," nominations to the Court are watched closely. Some civil rights lawyers were still sanguine about the Burger Court after the nominations of southern federal judges Clement Haynsworth and G. Harrold Carswell were unsuccessful, leading to the confirmation of Justice Harry Blackmun. However, the controversy helped create a conservative aura before the Burger Court handed down any decisions. Attention to the Court's anticipated shift affected lawyers' actions, including those of Legal Services Program lawyers,[14] and when the Court did not become as conservative as expected, there was some surprise, although it was coupled with realistic evaluation of what the Court had done.

Perceptions of shifts in the Court's approach have led lawyers to state publicly their concern about avoiding "bad" Supreme Court precedent. NAACP Legal Defense Fund Director-Counsel Jack Greenberg remarked that "Certain cases should not be brought if they are likely to be lost. Lawyers ought to try to avoid creating a new *Plessy v. Ferguson* and should apply energies where they will be most productive."[15] Thus, when an NAACP branch president argued against bringing school desegregation litigation in Omaha because it might eventually reach the newly conservative Supreme Court, which might use the case to issue retrogressive precedent, the local NAACP withdrew from active participation in the case.[16]

Typical of national organizations' reactions was statement by one of the ACLU's legal directors that the organization had made " 'a very conscious decision' and was 'doing everything we can to keep away from the Supreme Court'." [17] Ironically, the same attorney, later anticipating President Reagan's appointments, talked about increasing the number of cases taken to the Court before matters got even worse; and later in the Reagan administration, the ACLU said it would take more cases to the Court then because matters would be worse later.[18] Conversely, and further illustrating that groups' "rhetorical and behavioral reactions . . . were not necessarily consistent," the ACLU in reacting to *Miller v. California,* expressed great concern but "took the occasion to de-emphasize its obscenity litigation." [19] Thus we should be wary of accepting at face value lawyers' public statements about *not* taking cases to a more conservative Supreme Court. Out of the public eye, some litigators say that they go ahead nonetheless. For example, a former senior ACLU attorney said, "There was always talk of being more selective" in the cases taken "as Supreme Court positions changed," but "we don't stop litigating . . . That's the only Supreme Court we've got!" He added that "we don't select who is prosecuted" and thus needs defending. A former attorney for a national civil rights organization also conceded that "if they have a big case, lawyers will go up with the case, even if they might lose," perhaps, as another lawyer observes, because unless they can tell group members they are going to the Supreme Court, the members won't make contributions. Another leading civil rights litigator, although he had had "a lot less trepidation with the Warren Court than with the Burger Court," put it concisely: "Many cases have gone forward anyhow, or *Brown* wouldn't have happened."

Litigating interest groups' multiple goals lead to multiple reasons why lawyers pursue cases even with a diminished likelihood of victory. A major reason for proceeding is that there are principles to defend: "We've got to continue to defend civil liberties. There is a need to keep the flame alive inside the courts and out." Particularly with cases brought both for precedent and for "propaganda" purposes, an organization could "win even when losing." There was also strategy: "If the ACLU would trim, the [Court's] ultimate position would be further off the mark." Lawyers' "enormous egos" were offered as another reason, as is an organization's momentum. Other pending cases may also create a situation requiring continued litigation. Thus, even after the 1935 *Schechter Poultry* ("sick chicken") case, government attorneys found the Agricultural Adjustment Administration's powers had to be tested in the Supreme Court because of "a flood of cases filed by processors seeking injunctions to restrain the AAA from collecting the processing tax."[20]

The Range of Effects

What is the range of possible effects of the Court's rulings? They can be both large and small, as *Brown v. Board of Education* illustrates. The ruling's "indirect consequences," later wrote NAACP attorney Robert Carter, "have been awesome. It has completely altered the style, the spirit, and the stance of race relations." In addition, because, as Carter notes, it "has promised more than it could give," by being primarily only symbolic,[21] the ruling had negative effects, including contributing "to black alienation and bitterness, to a loss of confidence in white institutions, and to the growing racial polarization of our society."[22]

"Mobilization, exit, or continuance" are possible responses to the Court's rulings. Mobilization and exit, perhaps polar responses, have varying meanings. "Exit" may mean only departure from litigation on one subject, perhaps coupled with attention to an area of law on which the group had not previously focused or to a new approach. However, it may also mean withdrawal from all litigation, perhaps to focus on legislation or administrative proceedings. Civil rights litigators' dropping of particular litigation campaigns after negative rulings, as the ACLU did after *Miller v. California* (1973), exemplifies exit,[23] as does the reduced enthusiasm and then the ending of the Legal Defense Fund's attack on the bail system after the Supreme Court denied certiorari in a case in which review had been sought.[24] The Detroit case, which one civil rights lawyer called "a contradiction of everything the Court had held about the ability of a court to remedy constitutional violations," was said to be "the only big setback that caused people to reevaluate existing litigation," at least the metropolitan school cases. As a civil rights attorney succinctly put it, "After *Milliken*, we didn't go running around bringing interdistrict cases."

The Supreme Court's ending of some campaigns (for example, challenges to exclusionary zoning or to the property tax basis for financing education) forced people to turn elsewhere, although at times, ironically, this was to their advantage, when they were able to obtain favorable state court rulings. Supreme Court rulings on welfare law led to a significant reduction—indeed, almost elimination—of litigation efforts on that subject. There have been many other such examples over the years. For example, *Prigg v. Pennsylvania* (1842) caused a serious setback to litigation in aid of fugitive slaves that had brought together organizations of diverse antislavery persuasion. More than fifty years later, *Plessy v. Ferguson* "so disheartened advocates of racial desegregation that it took nearly a decade and a half before they organized to attempt to overturn it or to mitigate its effects."[25]

Particularly when housing litigators sought to go beyond simple housing discrimination cases to challenge suburban exclusionary zoning, Supreme Court rulings made prospects for successful judicial action unlikely. The Court did so by restricting standing in *Warth v. Seldin*, upholding laws requiring local referenda only on low-cost housing, so long as race was not the stated reason for the requirement, in *James v. Valtierra* (1971), which had negative implications for other challenges to exclusionary devices, and sustaining ordinances limiting the number of unrelated individuals who could occupy a dwelling, in *Village of Belle Terre v. Boraas* (1974).[26] The last ruling, in a case on which people had pinned their hopes because it was the first on suburban zoning reaching the Supreme Court in over forty-five years, was thought especially damaging because the Court showed little interest in non-residents' concerns and "seemed to endorse a wide range of exclusionary devices."[27]

Supreme Court rulings also have had heartening effects, leading to "continuance" of litigation efforts. For example, the 1941 ruling in *United States v. Classic* "gave an enormous lift to NAACP lawyers" because, contrary to *Grovey v. Townsend* (1935), it seemed to bring primaries within the Fourteenth Amendment's reach.[28] NAACP lawyers were likewise elated in 1948 when *Shelley v. Kraemer* struck down enforcement of racial restrictive covenants. Women's rights groups gained optimism for their efforts from the Court's equal pay ruling in *Phillips v. Martin Marietta* (1971), coupled with a contemporary California Supreme Court ruling.[29] In Title VII litigation, positive rulings on procedural issues "made matters easier." In particular, *Love v. Pullman Co.* (1972), saying technical construction of rules was inappropriate, "allowed expansion in many ways in the lower courts." And the "extraordinarily broad" ruling in *Griggs v. Duke Power Co.* (1971) "obviously encouraged a whole bunch of cases testing selection devices."

Government lawyers could be affected in the same way. National Recovery Administration (NRA) attorneys "assigned to the job of taking code violators to court began their task buoyed with optimism" by *Nebbia v. New York* (1934), upholding a state milk pricing law against a due process claim. However, as other enthusiasts have done, they overread the ruling and overlooked the fact that the case was based on the due process clause, not the commerce clause, the basis for challenges to the NRA.[30] In another instance of overreading, after the Supreme Court denied an interdistrict remedy in the Detroit school case and refused to invalidate property tax financing of local education, Delaware's lawyers in the Wilmington school case "were so confident of their chances on appeal that they took their case directly to the Supreme Court in 1975," but the Court handed down a one-line ruling against them.[31]

The Court's decisions could also produce mixed reactions, in part because interest groups respond differently depending on what they see for themselves in a ruling. After the Court invalidated the particular version of the white primary at issue in *Nixon v. Herndon* (1927), NAACP lawyers were "delighted to win," but longer-run concerns made them react more cautiously because the Court's use of the Fourteenth Amendment Equal Protection Clause rather than the Fifteenth Amendment required proof of "state action," thus leaving a basis for other devices that would limit black voting.[32] In the reverse situation, where an opinion was more favorable than the immediate outcome, ACLU-associated lawyers found that the 1943 *Hirabiyashi* curfew case, although decided adversely, made framing their strategy for the *Korematsu* relocation case easier by leaving open both the question of support for relocation in military findings and the relationship between evacuating and detaining people.[33]

Another aspect of mobilization is that the Court's rulings can serve as a catalyst for establishment of litigating interest groups. For example, the Media Coalition, with a litigation focus different from the ACLU's, came into existence soon after *Miller* to protect its members' commercial interests; and Americans for Effective Law Enforcement, an organization presenting the position of police and other law enforcement officials in criminal procedure cases, had originated earlier in response to the Warren Court's decisions. There is little question that *Roe v. Wade* served to spur the development of pro-life organizations, including some using litigation as a tool, and that *Gregg v. Georgia* (1976), upholding the constitutionality of capital punishment, prompted action by groups seeking abolition of the death penalty; most major groups whose sole task was to fight capital punishment came into existence within about a year after *Gregg* was decided.[34] The Court's decisions thus increased the proliferation of litigating groups; because, in the ACLU's absence, "numerous groups representing narrow interests began to litigate"; obscenity litigation also became more decentralized.[35]

Clearly related to "continuance" is the Court's removal of threats to an organization's very existence, at times seeming to rescuing them from extinction, and of impediments to their functioning, thus allowing them to continue to serve as litigators. Continuance can also mean an organization's continuing to litigate on subjects on which it had earlier litigated or, whether because of conscious evaluation of the Court's rulings or interia, its repeating arguments rather than reframing them.[36] Reframing arguments to fit the Court's rulings is a part of continuing pursuit of existing objectives, as is pressing for reversal of disliked decisions.

Particularly when the Court limits protection of civil rights, its rulings cause litigators to delete arguments or retreat from their principal points. An example is provided by the effect of the *Washington v. Davis* requirement that intent to discriminate be proved. That case came down from the Supreme Court one month before the trial in *City of Mobile v. Bolden*, and the lawyers pressing that case had to try to distinguish *Washington v. Davis* to avoid its application to their voting rights cases. Such effects are not only recent. Thus "the inauspicious beginnings of Supreme Court litigation involving slavery" produced a narrow legal focus in manumission societies' early-nineteenth-century litigation to assure blacks' freedom.[37] Lawyers may, however, proceed with their arguments despite such auguries, perhaps because they have invested time in developing them. During the test of Louisiana's requirement that races be separated in transportation that produced *Plessy v. Ferguson*, the Supreme Court upheld Mississippi's provision for separate cars as applied only to intrastate travel.[38] Although this cast doubt on an interstate commerce argument the Louisiana lawyers wanted to use, they continued to pursue it, perhaps because they read the ruling not to answer the key issue of mandatory assignment of passengers by race. However, when the Louisiana high court read the Supreme Court decision to exclude interstate passengers from the state's separate transportation law, the test case was "seriously undercut."[39]

At other times, rulings may prompt lawyers to proceed with an otherwise abandoned case or to add to, rather than limit, their requests. As the *Sullivan v. Little Hunting Park* challenge to a resident's exclusion from use of a community swimming pool progressed through the state courts, "manna from heaven" was provided in the "wholly unanticipated" decision in *Jones v. Mayer* (1968), leading the plaintiff's lawyer to seek certiorari instead of ending the litigation. The Supreme Court's reentry into the school desegregation fray with the 1968 *Green-Raney-Monroe* trilogy, effectively eliminating "freedom of choice" desegregation plans, led plaintiffs in the then-pending *Swann* litigation to move for further relief and to initiate the Forsyth County (Winston-Salem) school case.[40]

Perhaps the best-known instance of a shift in approach is the effect on the NAACP's attack on segregated education of the Court's attention to intangible factors when the Court ordered desegregation of state law schools in *Sweatt v. Painter* (1950). This led the NAACP to shift toward a more direct attack on "separate but equal." Marshall, on reading the *Sweatt* and *McLaurin* opinions, found them " 'replete with road markings telling us where to go next'—to begin the direct attack on segregation." Three weeks after the Court ruled, NAACP attorneys met to map out strategy and produced a resolution, adopted by the NAACP's Board of Directors, that future litigation would seek no relief other than desegregation.[41] However, because in *Sweatt* the NAACP had both argued against inequalities, including intangibles, and had attacked *Plessy*, *Sweatt* may not have started the attack on "separate but equal" but made it irrevocable. Here there was interaction between the litigators and the Court because the NAACP, knowing that use of intangibles would be a major step toward an outright attack on *Plessy*, had tried to nudge the Court toward such use, and the justices knew that adoption of intangibles as part of inequality committed them to going further.[42]

The extended nature of planned litigation for social change makes it more likely that changes in the Court's posture will affect its dynamics at some point. A Supreme Court ruling in mid-litigation can undermine the heart of a litigant's legal theory. Thus *Pennhurst v. Halderman*

(1981), which failed to take an expansive view of the rights of those in institutions for the mentally retarded, caused mental patients to view "with much trepidation" the state's taking to the Supreme Court a case in which they were involved.[43] Prison litigation was likewise affected by Supreme Court rulings. While the appeal in the *Rhodes v. Chapman* attack on "double-celling" in prisons was pending in the Sixth Circuit, the Supreme Court decision in *Bell v. Wolfish,* a case on jail conditions for pretrial detainees which many took to indicate the Court's general outlook on prison conditions, increased the likelihood that the appeals court would decide against the plaintiff, who had won in the trial court.[44] The decision in *Rhodes* itself affected Alabama prison litigation that was in process. After the trial judge's rulings, the appellate court found *Rhodes* applicable, saying it enunciated a new standard that had to be applied to the trial judge's orders.[45]

Supreme Court rulings may require immediate reconsideration of plans and affect timing. When *United States v. Butler* (1936), invalidating the Agricultural Adjustment Act, came as National Labor Relations Board (NLRB) lawyers were pressing for an acceleration of a decision in a test case, those lawyers delayed Wagner Act test in the Supreme Court.[46] If a new Supreme Court ruling is handed down after the court of appeals has completed its work on a case, lawyers may have to take initial defensive action in certiorari petitions and Supreme Court briefs. The likelihood of such effects is increased if lower court judges hold cases for a pending Supreme Court ruling, perhaps to protect themselves from reversals.

Effect on Organizations

Survival

The Supreme Court has a direct effect on interest groups as organizations, preserving organizational survival, providing footing for the organizations, and affecting their ability to pursue litigation. The Supreme Court removed a major financial risk to the NAACP in the Port Gibson, Mississippi, boycott case, *NAACP v. Claiborne Hardware Co.* (1982); that case provides the best example of nongovernment actions threatening an organization's financial basis, actions to which it must respond. White merchants whose trade was damaged by a boycott claimed boycott leaders threatened reprisals against nonsupporting blacks and obtained a $1.2 *million* judgment against boycott participants and the NAACP. The NAACP avoided bankruptcy by staving off execution of the judgment, and then the Supreme Court ruled unanimously that the NAACP could be held liable only if it were shown to have authorized or ratified improper conduct and then only for the violence, not for the boycott's economic effects. The Court thus lifted a large financial cloud from the NAACP and terminated a serious financial drain of resources expended in self-defense.

The Court's actions have also affected the personal financial well-being of organization leaders. The Court's refusal to allow the libel case that later produced *New York Times v. Sullivan* to be shifted from state to federal court led to state auction of the property of four ministers who were officials of the Southern Christian Leadership Conference (SCLC) and the attachment of other property; enforcement of later judgments in the case would have resulted in taking of family possessions of those relatively prosperous ministers, but the Court's far-reaching libel ruling protected the civil rights leaders from further financial threats.

Unfavorable Supreme Court rulings can also contribute to organizational well-being by providing an excuse for raising funds. For example, the ACLU based pleas to its contributors on negative Supreme Court rulings and the Reagan administration's civil rights posture. Likewise, the Court's ruling in *Bowers v. Hardwick* (1986), upholding the application of sodomy statutes to private consensual homosexual behavior, helps explain the growth of the Lambda Legal Defense and Education Fund, with one result of the case being a dramatic increase in contributions.

The most important set of cases affecting organizations stemmed from the South's post-*Brown v. Board of Education* counterattack against the NAACP. The most protracted litigation was *NAACP v. Alabama,* resulting from the state attorney general's efforts to enjoin the NAACP from conducting further activities in the state and to obtain organizational documents, including the names and addresses of all NAACP members there.[47] Because the Supreme Court's initial favorable rulings were insufficient to end the state's efforts, in the interim before the last of *four* rulings the organization was preoccupied with the attack and was effectively put "out of business" in Alabama, while it also had to deal simultaneously with government efforts against it in five other states. It is an interesting irony that the unavailability in Alabama of the NAACP, with its litigation orientation, was a factor facilitating the growth of direct action—what we have come to know as the civil rights movement.

The Court's consistent support of the right of association helped keep the organization intact. The Court first upheld the NAACP's standing to assert its members' associational rights—a decision on the law of standing with important long-term effects—and ruled that the NAACP did not have to produce membership lists. The Court unanimously overturned a municipal ordinance in Arkansas requiring an organization wishing an occupational license to submit membership lists; an Arkansas state requirement that school teachers list all organizations to which they had belonged in the last five years; Louisiana laws requiring annual complete membership lists and barring organizations affiliated with groups on the Attorney General's list or cited by the House Un-American Activities Committee; and Florida's efforts, through state legislative anti-Communism investigations, to obtain NAACP membership lists.[48]

Virginia's efforts were of a different sort—hindering NAACP litigation through laws that barred stirring up litigation (barratry) or raising or expending money for litigation. Winning a favorable ruling also took the NAACP more than one trip to the Supreme Court, but Justice Brennan's opinion in *NAACP v. Button* (1963) provided strong support for organizational litigation in aid of constitutional rights, particularly where an organization like the NAACP was not seeking money through litigation. The Court reaffirmed that ruling fifteen years later in the 1978 *Primus* case after South Carolina disciplined an ACLU-affiliated attorney for advising women of their legal rights and informing one woman that the ACLU would provide free legal assistance.

The Law of Procedure

Particularly significant among the Supreme Court's effects on organizations' ability to conduct litigation are rulings on basic procedural aspects of cases, particularly on access to the courts, including the law of standing and rules for bringing class actions (in which one or more named plaintiffs sue on behalf of "all others similarly situated") and obtaining attorneys' fees.

Standing and class actions. The Burger Court's tightening of the rules on standing made bringing certain types of civil rights suits far more difficult. Perhaps the clearest effect came from *Allen v. Wright* (1984); the ruling severely limited standing to challenge government action unless one could show that success in the lawsuit would eliminate the deprivation of rights claimed, and specifically blocked standing a challenge to Internal Revenue Service decisions on tax-exemption of private schools said to engage in racial discrimination. This decision complicated efforts to enforce school desegregation and, perhaps most significantly, ended the *Adams* litigation, the NAACP Legal Defense Fund's effort to force the (then) Department of Health, Education and Welfare to enforce Title VI of the 1964 Civil Rights Act, which lasted twenty years before being dismissed.[49]

While the initial *Adams* plaintiffs, whose complaint focused on the government's failure to combat segregation in higher education, had been chosen carefully and were replaced by other students as they eventually graduated, the separate *WEAL* case had been brought in the name of organizational, not individual, plaintiffs, and had not been made a class action. The latter litigation strategy was certainly reasonable under the rules on standing at the time, but was problematic nonetheless because no specific injury was claimed and the question of standing was not addressed directly.[50] When *Allen v. Wright* was decided in 1984, a serious problem was created. Although the Carter administration had not contested the *Adams'* plaintiffs' standing, the Reagan administration was certainly happy to use *Allen v. Wright* to defeat the *Adams* lawsuit. In 1984, the D.C. Circuit remanded the case for a determination of standing in light of the *Allen* ruling, and in 1987, the judge dismissed the entire case because plaintiffs had not proved that action against the officials would change public higher education.[51] On appeal, the D.C. Circuit granted standing but then came to the same conclusion: the action could not be brought against government officers with the responsibility for monitoring and enforcing compliance with Title VI because "Congress has not explicitly or implicitly authorized the grand scale action plaintiffs delineate."[52]

The Court's rulings, stemming in part from the new majority's desire to limit federal court intrusion into local affairs, especially affected challenges to police misconduct and to housing practices. The Court first, in *O'Shea v. Littleton* (1974), denied standing to plaintiffs who had claimed illegal bonding, sentencing, and jury fee practices; the justices said the plaintiffs had not identified the injury *they* had suffered or were personally likely to suffer. Then *Rizzo v. Goode* (1976) denied standing to those challenging police practices against minority citizens of Philadelphia because they were complaining only about a small, unnamed minority of officers. This led the NAACP Legal Defense Fund to "write off" police brutality cases. Then *Warth v. Seldin* (1975) required a showing that without zoning rules excluding low- and moderate-income residents, plaintiffs would have been able to buy or lease in the municipality and that a court ruling would provide appropriate relief. This ruling seriously hindered—indeed, almost precluded—civil rights litigation and was then thought insurmountable.[53]

If these rulings illustrate the Court's obstacles to civil rights litigation, *Gulf Oil Co. v. Bernard* (1981) illustrates its ability to assist litigation, if only by striking down procedural limitations on lawyers' communication with potential employment discrimination class members. Justice Lewis Powell thought it significant that the case was brought by the NAACP Legal Defense Fund, "a non-profit organization dedicated to the vindication of the legal rights of blacks and other citizens," and also supported class actions but he expressed concern that they provide "opportunities for abuse as well as problems for courts and counsel in the management of cases."[54]

Burden of proof.   Both burdens of proof and closely related substantive standards that must be met to prove discrimination, while they may seem arcane to nonlawyers, have significant effects on litigation, particularly on the effort that must be made to prevail. *Keyes v. Denver School District* (1973) was the most important burden-of-proof ruling in school desegregation. Without its rule that once plaintiffs had shown part of a school district improperly segregated, the burden then shifted to the defendant school district to disprove segregation elsewhere in the district, the difficulties of proving discrimination throughout entire large northern school districts would have seriously limited the number of cases that could have been pursued.

The basic framework for burden of proof in employment discrimination cases was established in *McDonnell Douglas v. Green* (1973), under which, after the plaintiff had established certain matters, the defendant employer had to show legitimate reason for not hiring the applicant. Particularly crucial, not only with respect to job discrimination but also for other civil rights issues, was the Court's adoption in *Washington v. Davis* (1976) of a disparate treatment (intent) rather than the disparate impact (effects) test of *Griggs v. Duke Power* (1971). The ruling, foreshadowing the Court's movement to use such an approach in statutory cases, served to make far more difficult the civil rights litigator's task in challenging race-neutral and sex-neutral policies on the basis of disparate impact. The Court's new test is also said to have "dealt a fatal blow" to women's advocacy groups. They had drawn on "the NAACP strategy in going for the easy wins first, thereby building up a momentum of success" before "incrementally bring[ing] more problematic cases." They had proceeded to challenge sex-neutral policies on the basis of disparate impact on women, but *Washington v. Davis* meant that was now clearly insufficient.[55] A more general effect was that *Washington v. Davis* deterred victims of racial discrimination from filing cases, with an effect larger than that visible from overall win/loss figures.[56]

Further effects of the Court's intent standard can be seen in the impact of *City of Mobile v. Bolden*, where the Court ruled that both Section 2 of the Voting Rights Act and the Fifteenth Amendment required proof of discriminatory intent. That ruling made immediately clear to voting rights lawyers that they "would have to spend a great deal of time and money to accumulate the evidence needed to reach an undefineable goal that might satisfy at least a lower court, if not the U.S. Supreme Court"—indeed, a far greater effort than in the past.[57] At least initially, as defendant communities stiffened their resistance, the ruling also halted vote dilution litigation as voting rights organizations held back from filing constitutional challenges and even withdrew lawsuits already filed.[58]

Further impact of the Court's rulings on burden of proof can be seen in the *Wards Cove* ruling in 1989, which seriously undercut *Griggs v. Duke Power*. In *Wards Cove*, the Court ruled both that showing a high percentage of nonwhite workers in one type of job within a company and a low percentage of them in another type was not enough to prove a disparate impact violation of Title VII, and that, instead of considering the employer's practices collectively, plaintiffs must connect an employer's particular employment practice with the disparate impact. However, as we have noted, *Wards Cove* was overturned by Congress.

Attorneys' fees.   Rulings on the availability of attorneys' fees have both assisted and created problems for litigating organizations. After *Newman v. Piggie Park Enterprises* (1968) upheld such fees under Title II of the 1964 Civil Rights Act, "the proportion of public interest law firms' operating budgets derived from attorneys' fees awards" increased in a major way. Although the case hardly was the direct cause of the subsequent proliferation of public interest law firms, in an important indirect effect, the Ford Foundation was led to provide seed money for diverse interest groups which focused on litigation and for litigating components of existing interest groups, both of which could use attorneys' fees to build their own budgets.[59]

The ruling that attorneys' fees were available in cases still pending on appeal when the 1972 Educational Amendments Act became law (*Bradley v. School Board of City of Richmond*, 1974) assisted civil rights organizations that had brought school desegregation cases. Then, in a case brought by an environmental group, the Court severely set back organizational litigators with its 1975 *Alyeska Pipeline Co.* ruling, that attorneys' fees were not to be awarded unless Congress specifically authorized them. That case illustrates that civil rights organizations have to pay heed not only to civil rights cases but also to those in other areas of law with rulings transferrable to civil rights litigation, and must file amicus briefs in such cases to protect their interests.

The civil rights bar and others negatively affected were successful in getting Congress to reverse the thrust of *Alyeska Pipeline* with the Civil Rights Attorneys' Fees Awards Act of 1976 (42 U.S.C. § 1988), so that, in federal court civil rights actions, "the court, in its discretion, may allow the prevailing party . . . a reasonable attorney's fee as part of the costs." Although the Court did not settle important aspects of the statute until a dozen years after its passage, thus preventing litigators from planning on attorney's fee awards as litigation resources, some of its early rulings on the subject were clearly helpful to civil rights lawyers.

Particularly important was the Court's ruling that attorneys' fees could be awarded under Title VII for time in state administrative proceedings and related state judicial proceedings, because Title VII contemplated administrative action through the EEOC or comparable state agencies before litigation. However, the Court was *not* willing to allow attorneys' fees for time in an administrative proceeding not tied to the federal statute under which the plaintiff sued, or for administrative action without litigation to enforce civil rights.[60] Showing the linkage between administrative action and litigation, Justice Brennan objected that the ruling *forced* the filing of lawsuits if that was the only way to recover attorneys' fees for administrative work defending civil rights.

The Supreme Court, however, then made the new law not merely a boon but also a matter of concern for civil rights litigators by ruling, only two years after its passage, that, prevailing defendants (for example, businesses sued for discrimination) could obtain attorneys' fees when the plaintiff's action was frivolous, unreasonable, or without foundation, although fees could not be awarded against plaintiffs simply because they lost.[61] The ruling troubled the civil rights litigation community because it compounded difficulties caused by the tendency of judges and others hostile to civil rights cases to label them "frivolous." Indeed, lawyers had to engage in considerable litigation to determine the basis for calculating fee awards, with some judges then complaining about unnecessary "satellite" litigation in addition to litigation on the merits of a claim. Even Justice Brennan, while supportive of attorneys' fees, observed, in referring to defendants' resistant actions, that "appeals from awards of attorney's fees, after the merits of a case have been concluded, when the appeals are not likely to affect the amount of the final fee" are among "the least socially productive types of litigation imaginable," serving to discourage civil rights litigation.[62]

Litigation to develop the contours of attorneys' fee awards, when successful, often paid for itself, but it nonetheless distracted litigators from enforcing substantive law, and the litigation was not always successful. Particularly significant, and with most serious ramifications for large discrimination lawsuits, was the ruling on attorney's fees in connection with settlements in *Evans v. Jeff D.* (1986), argued by a leading NAACP Legal Defense Fund attorney, in which the Court said that a defendant could demand release from liability for attorneys' fees or costs as a condition of entering into consent decrees, leaving no fees for attorneys.

What does all this tell us about the Supreme Court's impact on litigation? First, lawyers *do* pay attention to Supreme Court decisions. Hindsight suggests that at times they appear to overreact, as later decisions do not follow the ruling's implications fully. Second, Supreme Court rulings can have considerable importance for litigating organizations' ability to carry out their work, and even for their survival. Most Supreme Court rulings affect in some way the resources litigators will have to devote to cases; some rulings either facilitate or hinder obtaining resources; and an occasional, exceptional case deals with organizations under attack, so that their economic viability and effective functioning may depend on the speed with which courts resolve the problem. The need to defend against attacks on the organization is illustrative of the more general proposition that litigating organizations must often respond to other litigators, independent of litigation they would like to undertake.

Litigating organizations must remain concerned about Supreme Court rulings, like those on standing to sue, that affect both their ability to get into court with their cases and the relative difficulty of proving a case, with potentially seriously detrimental effects if a higher standard of proof is announced after lawyers have initiated a case. The longer the litigation, the more likely a Supreme Court ruling bearing on arguments to be made will be decided. Although litigation may continue along the same track after a Supreme Court ruling as before, lawyers are likely to adjust their actions to fit the Supreme Court's opinions, by adjusting their arguments and changing the types of cases emphasized. At times lawyers have virtually no choice but to adjust, although inertia or momentum may keep them moving along "tried and true" paths and continuing to bring cases to the Supreme Court for review, even after making public statements about negatively changed atmosphere.

3

The Major Litigators and

the Proliferation of Groups

An increase in the number of actors invariably increases the complexity of a situation. One element that has made the environment more complex for civil rights groups engaged in litigation is the growth in the number of such groups, coupled with the organization of more and more segments of the population to assert their rights under law. The landscape could be said to be cluttered with civil rights litigators. This chapter provides a look at some of the individual elements of the proliferated set of organizations that came to characterize the civil rights environment. After some general background is provided, first there is an examination of some specific organizations—the NAACP, the LDF (or "Inc. Fund"), the ACLU, and the Lawyers' Committee for Civil Rights Under Law (the LCCRUL), after which backup centers and public interest law firms are described. The chapter ends with discussion of the civil rights bar, which cuts across the individual organizations and serves as a counter to centrifugal forces.

For many years, at least until the mid-1960s, civil rights litigation meant the NAACP Legal Defense Fund, acting as the NAACP's litigation arm. Its dominance continued even when, in response to the lack of progress from judicial rulings, other organizations such as the Southern Christian Leadership Conference (SCLC), Rev. Martin Luther King, Jr.'s organization; the Student Nonviolent Coordinating Committee (SNCC); and the Congress of Racial Equality (CORE), which emphasized activity other than litigation, developed as part of the civil rights movement of the late 1950s and early 1960s. However, development of those organizations decreased the LDF's centrality. At times it seemed relegated to a secondary or supporting, although not insignificant, role, where it served with other organizations that came into being specifically for that support role—the Lawyers' Constitutional Defense Committee (LCDC); the Law Students Civil Rights Research Council; and the Lawyers' Committee for Civil Rights Under Law (LCCRUL), created in 1963 by the establishment bar to provide legal assistance to the civil rights movement, and which has persisted to the present with an expansion of its role. The NAACP Legal Defense Fund further lost its primacy when organizations originated, some with LDF's help, to litigate on behalf of Puerto Ricans, Mexican-Americans, and Native Americans; and for the disabled, children, and gays and lesbians.

A principal cause of this changed picture was that statutes extending the law to protect not only blacks but also other racial, religious, and ethnic minorities and then other segments of society, served to stimulate the development of these groups. This was perhaps most obvious in the case of women's rights, as inclusion in the 1964 Civil Rights Act of the prohibition of sex discrimination required mobilization to implement the protection, and could be seen in the 1970 amendments to the Voting Rights Act, which extended the law's protections to those of Spanish heritage, Asian Americans, and Native Americans. Such an extension led to their engaging in litigation to protect their interests, with the interests of more than one grouping perhaps implicated by, for example, a legislative redistricting. These examples illustrate the reciprocal nature of group development and legislation: groups press for legal protection; the legal protection is forthcoming; the groups seek to implement and expand that protection. It could also be seen in effective use by the disabled of Section 504 of the Rehabilitation Act, more specific legislation on issues like access to transportation, and in the 1990s, the Americans with Disabilities Act (ADA).

Another major reason for proliferation of litigating entities was their support by foundations, particularly the Ford Foundation. This illustrates that "without the influence of the patrons of political action, the flourishing system of interest groups in the United States would be much smaller and would include very few groups seeking to obtain broad collective or public goods."[1] The growth of such groups under the stimulus of foundation funding led to greater competition by the very same groups for those private dollars. This occurred for both liberal and conservative groups, with notable effects: "Competition among like-minded groups for limited resources can be devastating to the creation of a concentrated litigation strategy."[2] Perhaps wanting to avoid putting all their eggs in one basket, foundations funded more than one litigating organization in a particular area of the law, further reinforcing competition. At one point the Ford Foundation was funding four national sex discrimination litigating groups—the ACLU's Women's Rights Project of ACLU, MALDEF's Chicano Rights Projects, the League of Women Voters, and LDF—plus several public interest law firms that handled sex discrimination cases (the Women's Law Fund, the Women's Rights Project of the Center for Law and Social Policy, and Public Advocates, Inc.).[3]

In any area of litigation, there are likely to be many groups litigating. In voting rights litigation, in addition to the Lawyers' Committee and the ACLU, particularly its Southern Regional Office, there were the Voter Education Project of the Southern Regional Council; the Lawyers' Constitutional Defense Committee (no longer extant); the Southern Poverty Law Center; and the Mexican American Legal Defense and Education Fund (MALDEF). For MALDEF, attention to voting, part of a "deliberate forthright campaign" in which the organization did not limit itself to litigation and attempted to "coordinate a number of strategies," came through 1982 renewal of the Voting Rights Act. MALDEF "got a statute enacted, figured out how to use it, and brought cases," in an atmosphere of "much excitement."

In school desegregation litigation, participation broadened, with cases filed by a wide variety of entities—not only NAACP chapters and cooperating attorneys for the NAACP Legal Defense Fund, but also, singly or in combination, by "lawyers from American Civil Liberties Union chapters, volunteer attorneys serving local groups, the Harvard Center for Law and Education, the Mexican-American Legal Defense and Education Fund, [and] the Center for National Policy Review."[4] Although an NAACP lawyer rejected the suggestion that the larger the case, the more likely multiple groups were to be involved, an important local case may involve many national groups. For example, national groups involved in Wilmington, Delaware, included "the NAACP Legal Defense Fund (litigation), the Center for National Policy Review (litigation), the United States Department of Justice (litigation and desegregation planning), the National Association for Neighborhood Schools (congressional lobbying), the Lamar Society (consultation for a community coalition), the Rockefeller Foundation (funding for a study of the effects of desegregation), the Ford Foundation (funding for a community coalition to consult other coalitions), and the Rand Corporation (a study of the role of community groups)."[5]

Participating entities include not only national litigating organizations but also community groups, at times better characterized as informal groupings, and other racial groups which do not see their interests as identical to those of blacks. Because they are often not initially represented in school litigation, these other groups seek to intervene, as do non-minority groupings. For example, "lots of people intervened or tried to" in the Boston school case, both at the violation stage and, particularly, at the remedy stage. The varied "stew" of groups may have been greater than in most other school cases, but is not unrepresentative of the presence of many groupings and of varying and conflicting positions.

In Boston, in addition to blacks objecting to the proposed remedy, the teachers union, Hispanic parents, the Home and School Association, and the mayor "came in," and others wanted to do so—including a "New Left" group of black and white parents interested in school reform, a bus contractor, and an antibusing group. There was a group of Hispanic parents, El Comite; Freedom House; the Dorchester United Neighborhood Association (DUNA), "a coalition of Dorchester neighborhood groups," Better Education Together (BET), "a group of black and white parents" from several sections of the city, all proposing alterations in desegregation plans.[6] The San Francisco case likewise had a wide variety of interests as parties or would-be parties: "Holders of all the divergent points of view—the predominantly white, middle-class parents' groups, who now called themselves Concerned Parents; those blacks who preferred to run their own schools rather than be merged into unenthusiastic white neighborhood schools; and the

Chinatown and Mission communities, reluctant to be drawn into the settlement of what was perceived as a black-white issue—sought an opportunity to be heard at some stage of the proceedings."[7]

The increased number of actors of more recent times diminishes overall control even by a single dominant litigator, which "must worry about the large number of . . . cases that are being brought, some not propitiously, by other organizations,"[8] and decreases any single group's ability to pursue a concerted litigation strategy. No one entity like the NAACP Legal Defense Fund could control litigation under Title VII because, in addition to the Justice Department's enforcement authority, many other litigating organizations and individuals were interested in the area, leaving no one with the monopoly or near-monopoly essential for such control. Similar division could be found in the women's movement's litigation efforts, where one had the Women's Equity Action League (WEAL), created in 1968 by those who saw the National Organization for Women (NOW) as too radical; the NOW Legal Defense Fund, WEAL's own litigation entity, and the Women's Law Fund, created by some who broke off from WEAL. The presence of these other major women's rights litigators affected the ability of the ACLU's Women's Rights Project, "closest to being an LDF-type litigator" among the women's groups, to function consistently.[9] The presence of many groups litigating in an area of law does not, however, necessarily lead to their operating at cross purposes, as each may be able to attend to its own concerns.

In general, the proliferation of interests seeking protection of their civil rights had both positive and negative effects. "In one sense, this expansion of groups under the civil rights umbrella strengthened the movement by providing civil rights advocates with a comprehensive arsenal of legal weapons. Yet, in another sense, it threatened to weaken the movement by pitting interest against interest in the competition for federal enforcement resources and attention."[10] Proliferation of interests can make it difficult to establish working coalitions. Each new ethnic grouping wishes proper recognition and feels the need to make its own decisions, rather than following blacks, who had been at the forefront of the civil rights movement with the NAACP as their lead organization. However, problems resulting from presence of multiple litigators are diminished if groups litigating on a particular area of law have similar goals; if each group litigates in a particularized area, each can have some legal autonomy without intergroup conflict.[11]

Another effect of proliferation was increased competition for protection by the government. One could see this in the Office of Civil Rights going in one decade "from an almost exclusive concern for desegregating southern schools to having responsibility for discrimination against blacks, Hispanics, Native Americans, Oriental-Americans, other national origin students, women, and the handicapped throughout the country,"[12] with the number of claims far outstripping agency resources. Moreover, with the changed atmosphere no longer favoring enforcement of civil rights for blacks, OCR found it "much more feasible and politic to enforce antidiscrimination provisions for these new groups than it did for its original constituency and target—blacks in segregated schools."[13] It was this situation which led the LDF to file the *Adams* litigation to compel OCR to enforce Title VI.

Public Interest Law Practice

Before we examine principal civil rights litigators, in this section we pay some attention to the organizations' internal structure and functioning; these are highly relevant to the making of litigation decisions. All are engaged in public interest law activity, defined as that which "(1) is undertaken by an organization in the voluntary sector; (2) provides fuller representation of underrepresented interests . . . and (3) involves the use of law interests, primarily litigation."[14] Among these, a basic distinction affecting intraorganizational politics is that between membership-based groups and those that have only contributors, not members. The former are further distinguished by the extent to which policy is developed democratically or is instead made by leaders and staff. Such differences may affect positions adopted. A more democratic NAACP might have given less attention to desegregation and more to quality education in the ghetto, and might have accepted the choice by the leaders of its Atlanta branch of more positions for blacks in the educational bureaucracy over desegregation; instead, the national organization put the branch in receivership. Likewise, that the NAACP Legal Defense Fund is an organization without members allowed its director-counsel, Jack Greenberg, to call getting more resources for successful black districts "outrageous nonsense."[15]

And had the ACLU, a membership organization, been more democratic internally and perceived strong internal opposition to its "pure" free speech position, it might have taken a less strong position on the issue of American Nazis' right to march in Skokie.[16]

Also important is the distinction between national organizations with no state or local units and those with local affiliates; for the latter, one must distinguish between those whose affiliates existed before the national organization and those where the national organization established the affiliates. (Most nonmembership organizations, e.g., the NAACP Legal Defense Fund, are likely to be national, but some national organizations do not have members.) Although a national organization's direct control of its local affiliates can be severe, as when an organization's branches must obtain national approval of their hiring choices, the national organization may not be able to control the local unit, as the ACLU learned when its rather independent Northern California ACLU affiliate taught its parent during the challenges to the relocation of Japanese-Americans during World War II.

Another important element is the extent to which the organization has remained flexible or has become bureaucratized, said to be true of the NAACP, even at the local level. Top officials' long tenure and animosities developed over the years decreased the leader's freedom of action. Newer organizations like Martin Luther King, Jr.'s Southern Christian Leadership Conference, which had not developed that bureaucratic style, were able to adjust more quickly, and some organizations, like the Student Nonviolent Coordinating Committee, intentionally abjured development of a bureaucracy.

Litigating organizations without members are generally known as public interest law firms (PILFs). They are financed by foundations and through contributions obtained from mass mailings. Generally functioning as independent entities, they "have more control over the allocation of their time and budgets than do public agencies and private attorneys."[17] The financial situation of many allows them to take unprofitable cases and to handle expensive, complex litigation.

Public interest law firms do not have a single organizational structure. The type most frequently found is the fully autonomous law firm, funded by foundations; other interest groups are its clients. Others are autonomous law offices with cooperating attorneys who handle many cases for the organization. In another arrangement, the PILF is tied closely to a principal client organization which provides resources and policy direction, although there may be other direct funding.[18] Broad policy direction is usually established by a board of directors. Perhaps typical is the Native American Rights Fund, whose Steering Committee of thirteen members has two meetings a year to establish case guidelines, with a four-member Executive Committee meeting more often as needed to "reconsider general policy decisions, develop recommendations to be brought before the Steering Committee, and administer the burdens of finance and fund-raising."[19]

Public interest law firms first developed on behalf of interests, such as the environment and consumer issues, are generally considered liberal. Many, like the Asian-American Legal Defense Fund, took their inspiration and their basic model from the NAACP Legal Defense Fund, which assisted in establishing both the Puerto Rican Legal Defense Fund and MALDEF. Although many serve racial, ethnic, or gender groupings, there are others with issue foci, like the ACLU—or the Public Citizen Litigation Group, initiated as part of Ralph Nader's public interest activities but since 1972 a separate organization. Its lawyer staff litigates on issues like access to government information (FOIA, Privacy Act, and Sunshine Act), labor issues (OSHA and union democracy), health and safety (both OSHA and Food and Drug Act issues), consumer issues like lawyers' minimum fee schedules, prohibitions on advertising of prescription drugs, administrative law, and separation of powers, which led it to involvement in challenges to the Gramm-Rudman-Hollings Budget Act and the legislative veto.

Also drawing on the ACLU and the NAACP Legal Defense Fund as inspirations, the State and Local Legal Center resulted from the perceived need for state and local governments to file amicus briefs before the Supreme Court and lack of specialists to help them. Its purpose is to help attorneys general and city attorneys with briefs and preparation for oral argument and to coordinate amicus briefs. It is funded by the Pew Memorial Trust of Philadelphia and the Academy for State and Local Government, and is operated by umbrella organizations including the National Governors Association and the U.S. Conference of Mayors.

In the 1970s, a number of PILFs were developed to place before the courts an alternative, conservative view of the "public interest" for business and social interests. They did this largely through amicus participation, although they could also initiate litigation, as they were well financed by foundations and major corporations; their trustees are drawn primarily from the ranks of business executives. The Mountain States Legal Foundation has a "board of litigation" of twenty-five attorneys, who, except for a few house counsel, are private law firm partners, while some conservative PILFs, for example, the Mid-America Legal Foundation, have a board and a legal advisory committee.[20]

Some conservative PILFs have had a relatively narrow issue focus. Examples are the National Right to Work Legal Defense Foundation and the Equal Employment Advisory Council (job interests), Citizens for Decency through Law (CDL) (obscenity), Americans for Effective Law Enforcement (the courts' criminal procedure rulings), and Americans United for Life Legal Defense Fund (antiabortion).[21] Among others with broader agendas, primary have been the Pacific Legal Foundation and a set of conservative PILFs that had ties to the National Legal Center for the Public Interest, which attempted to establish a network of such entities,[22] including the Mountain States Legal Foundation, with land and water control its major concerns, Mid-America Legal Foundation, Gulf and Great Plains Legal Foundation, Mid-Atlantic Legal Foundation, Southeastern Legal Foundation, New England Legal Foundation, and Capital Legal Foundation, whose director served as the attorney for General William Westmoreland in his multimillion dollar libel suit against CBS.

Among other types of law firms involved in civil rights litigation are "mixed firms," providing regular legal services to private clients on a fee-for-service basis and then engaging in public interest law practice financed by those earnings.[23] Others are private law firms that engage in civil rights activity as an extension of serving their clients, as they see patterns that need to be addressed with solutions of benefit to their clients. Still other fee-for-service firms, such as those that work with the Lawyers' Committee for Civil Rights Under Law, allow their attorneys to handle some civil rights work pro bono, with the firm, absorbing the lawyer's time and at least some litigation expenses, institutionalizing the pro bono work.

One "mixed" firm with an "income-producing" side received many civil rights cases, which it handled for reduced fees, by referral from local NAACP branches, NAACP General Counsel, and LDF. Indeed, the firm, also a court-appointed attorney in some Title VII cases, received so many civil rights cases that its litigation committee reviewed them to determine whether or not to take them. Because the NAACP had lost a staff attorney handling school cases and because at the time NAACP general counsel Nathaniel Jones had tried no school cases, the firm's principal school litigator accepted Jones's request that it work on one northern school case. Thereafter, as participation in one case led to participation in another, the firm had a continuing involvement in school cases, with several under way at once.

A law firm can be financially successful while focusing on civil rights cases, particularly if it emphasizes class action discrimination claims that carry large attorneys' fee awards. However, a southern mixed firm, established to help provide effective representation to the poor and minorities, with the "new civil rights" an important "ingredient," had to "temper its recklessness" and reject some "potentially good cases" that it would not have earlier rejected "because of the economy and because the courts have not lived up to expectations in implementing the Civil Rights Fee Act."

One mixed firm that illustrated such problems was [former attorney general Ramsey] Clark, [former ACLU Legal Director Melvin] Wulf, and Levine. It was formed to represent those with interests in peace, the poor, criminal justice, education, and the environment, as well as civil rights and liberties. It had a very high proportion (50 to 75%) of civil liberties and civil rights cases, with the rest the "paying stuff." Among its cases were the defense of authors against libel charges made by the Church of Scientology; the defense of Philip Agee against the CIA; and the *Island Trees* school book censorship case. Charging only fees people could afford and doing much of its work free, the lawyers found that increasing rent, a recession in legal business, and the partners' costs of educating their own children were more than the firm could afford, and it lasted only from 1978 to 1983. As stated by a lawyer from another firm handling a significant portion of civil rights cases, because such firms' pro bono cases generate publicity, "Some people think we are the ACLU. But we do have a sizable overhead to contend with, and a great many expenses. We sometimes cannot take on as many charity cases as we'd like." [24]

Working relations between interest group staff attorneys and private law firms that devote a significant portion of their practice to civil rights work often are so close that sharp lines cannot be drawn between group and law firm; at times the law firm is functionally an extension of the group. Few all-black or predominantly black law firms that engaged heavily in civil rights work were not firmly connected with national civil rights litigating organizations. Illustrative of the firms with long working relations with the NAACP Legal Defense Fund is Hill, Tucker, and Marsh, of Richmond, Virginia, a firm of roughly ten lawyers. The firm's focus when it was "coming along" was clearly civil rights, so that "virtually everything had civil rights aspects": jury service, the Railway Labor Act, transportation (the firm had sixty cases pending in Richmond when the Supreme Court ruled on transportation segregation), "everything you did was fighting some form of discrimination." As a result of "economics" as the lawyers "started thinking of sending their kids through school" and of the "difference in thinking of the younger generation," the mix of cases changed so that roughly one-third to 40 percent of its work was civil rights, with the rest "run of the mill legal work (wills, estates, property, bankruptcy) and general practice." Its civil rights cases often came when people "communicate with New York, which will call attention" to the firm, or, "more often," when the firm itself "asks for involvement of a national organization when people don't have funds."

Another firm tied closely to a national civil rights organization resulted from the Legal Defense Fund's internship program, under which the interns established their own law firms in the South while they worked with the LDF on civil rights cases. When Julius Chambers first went to Charlotte, North Carolina, in 1964, there was "no firm, just Chambers operating out of a coldwater flat over a lumber company," but he was joined in 1968 by Adam Stein, who had earlier been his summer intern; James Ferguson; and another lawyer. By 1984, when Chambers became Director-Counsel of the Legal Defense Fund, the firm had grown to eleven lawyers, half of whom were working in the civil rights field, and also had a Chapel Hill office, with the two offices functioning "pretty much" as one firm, with "lots of telephone contact," meetings every month or six weeks, with visits by individual lawyers in the interim. As with other civil rights firms, there was a decrease in the proportion of attention given to civil rights—from 80 percent to 50 to 60 percent, with the remainder noncivil rights work (a "typical general practice: property, business, wills, torts"). The shift came "not from interest: it came from necessity—the cost of doing civil rights litigation and the need to do other cases to sustain the civil rights work."

Some of these firms have had to replace their important first generation of attorneys either because of aging or because those lawyers were successful in achieving important positions. This is illustrated by Adams, Baker and Clemon, in Birmingham, Alabama, which lasted from 1965 to 1978 and dissolved as a result of blacks' increasing presence in politics and government: Oscar Adams became a member of the Alabama Supreme Court; U.W. Clemon was appointed a federal district judge; and James Baker was Birmingham's city attorney when Richard Arrington was mayor.

The Major Players

NAACP

The NAACP, a membership-based organization, with units at the state level known as conferences and local units called branches, operates through an annual convention, a board of directors, and a full-time staff. Its membership was said to be 550,000 in the 1990s. In the mid-1980s, in a situation of declining membership, its executive director claimed 450,000 members, but some critics said the figure was as low as 150,000.[25] The NAACP maintained its headquarters at 1790 Broadway in New York City for many years, moved to Brooklyn for three years, and then relocated to a facility in Baltimore. The last move, which required $4.2 million for building purchase, renovation, and the relocation from New York City, came as part of a mid-1980s reassessment of organizational goals and tactics against a background of weak finances where dues were no longer the organization's principal financial support, foundation and corporation support had become crucial, and the NAACP was said to have been kept financially afloat by the NAACP Special Contribution Fund, its own entity for obtaining tax-deductible contributions for litigation activities.

With policy established by the NAACP's board as a constraint or at least an outer limit, the staff, and particularly the executive director, have considerable leeway to make many key decisions because the staff are full-time and the part-time officers and board members are likely to have only limited involvement. However, officers and board can be very much involved in organizational decision making, particularly in times of conflict or difficulty involving the executive director's authority, which the NAACP, like many other private organizations, has experienced regularly.[26] Roy Wilkins, in office from 1955 through 1977, and who one former staff member asserted "made sure that there was no challenge to his leadership by surrounding himself with lieutenants who are not very strong,"[27] defeated several efforts to remove him.

One such conflict led to a shift of authority to the chair of the board. Yet in 1983, the board did not support board chair Margaret Bush Wilson's attempt to exercise that authority to suspend executive director Hooks, reduced her authority severely, and asked her to resign before her term ended. When Hooks regained control, he asked general counsel Thomas Atkins, whom Wilson had named acting executive director, to leave; Atkins then openly criticized Hooks for the NAACP's decreased prominence. This particular contretemps led noted psychologist Kenneth Clark to say that such "internal bickering and personal conflicts" were among the NAACP's "dominant activities," "reflect a serious systemic disturbance . . . festering [its] national structure," and demonstrated the organization's "increasing impotence."[28] When Rev. Benjamin Chavis, Jr., succeeded Hooks in 1993, he recognized that the NAACP had not sufficiently addressed its financial situation, and openly discussed the need to put the NAACP on a stable financial basis. However, his suggestion—an endowment derived from corporation support—met with opposition from those who saw a conflict between necessary militancy and the conservatism that would be imposed through corporate contributions to the organization. (In 1994, when Chavis was forced to resign and the authority of the NAACP's board chairman was challenged, the NAACP's finances were in far worse condition than when Chavis took office.)

In comparable conflict, in 1984, most of the staff, and eight lawyers, of the Puerto Rican Legal Defense Fund were dismissed as a result of conflict between staff and the board and president over the use of law to aid Puerto Ricans, an action which made funding sources skittish about supporting the group. A few years later, the president-general counsel of the Mexican-American Legal Defense Fund (MALDEF) was ousted by the group's executive committee, apparently for her handling of some cases and for hiring an Asian-American to direct one of the organization's offices. The full board restored the incumbent, but only after the executive committee hired a new president-general counsel.[29]

Shortly after its 1909 founding, the NAACP established a legal bureau and a National Legal Committee, an advisory body which received potential cases from Walter White, the Association's assistant secretary, "screened requests for assistance, summarized the ones worth more attention, and sent them" to committee chair Arthur Spin-garn.[30] The NAACP's efforts at planned litigation date from its receipt of a grant from the American Fund for Public Service (the Garland Fund). At first, cases were handled by attorneys associated with, but not employed full time by, the NAACP; only in 1935 did it gain a full-time staff attorney, Charles H. Houston. After that, there was less consultation of the Legal Committee, on which white lawyers pre-dominated, and a parallel change to greater use of blacks (on the staff).

The NAACP Legal Defense and Educational Fund, created in 1939, was the NAACP's litigating arm, providing a full-time staff of civil rights litigators assisted by the NAACP's National Legal Committee. Later, after the NAACP Legal Defense Fund's separation from the NAACP, a new NAACP legal staff was established under the direction of NAACP General Counsel Robert Carter, who also created the Spe-cial Contribution Fund. However, as Carter wrote in 1961, the NAACP "lost control of its main legal machinery and for a while had an insuf-ficient staff and lack of funds to have a legal program in the pre-1965 sense."[31] When Lewis Steel was fired by the NAACP Board for his *New York Times Magazine* criticism of the Supreme Court's slow progress in race relations, Carter and most other staff attorneys resigned as a result. This again forced the NAACP, without a legal staff for roughly a year, to establish its litigating capacity anew, until Nathaniel Jones was appointed general counsel in 1969.

There was another interregnum of somewhat more than six months when Jones was appointed to the federal bench in 1979, when Theodore Berry served as acting general counsel. Then Thomas Atkins, who had been in charge of NAACP school litigation as special coun-sel during the late 1970s, became general counsel, only later to be discharged by Hooks. He continued to handle some school desegre-gation cases for the NAACP but new general counsel Grover Hankins wanted Atkins completely out of the picture, and removed him from those cases, an action not likely to assist litigation. Hankins in turn was fired by Hooks, and his successor was said to have had "insuf-ficient firepower." The NAACP's legal staff has remained small—in recent years only a general counsel and no more than a half-dozen at-torneys, although earlier lawyers were also on retainer in some of the organization's seven regions. The legal staff must carry out litigation and perform house counsel functions for the organization, including its state conferences and local branches.

These stories tell us that interaction among the staff is an important aspect of intraorganizational politics related to conflict. The presence of a very strong top executive who will not accept disagreement can be detrimental to organizational effectiveness. Particularly important for the organization's litigation program are conflicts of chief executive and chief lawyer. In earlier years, friction with Walter White led Thurgood Marshall to develop something of a "private enclave" within the NAACP. Marshall was "anxious to get out from under the oversight and direction" of Executive Director Roy Wilkins with regard to litigation,[32] although not to cut himself free from the NAACP as such. Wilkins, although not hesitant to lay down the law on many NAACP matters, appears not to have done so to Marshall, perhaps indicating that Marshall, concerned about safeguarding his decisional latitude, may well have obtained the autonomy he sought.

Organizational conflict also affects local units, preventing them from obtaining necessary guidance and direction but perhaps allowing them to obtain greater autonomy if the conflict disables the national organization from taking action.[33] There have always been NAACP branches whose leadership favored more radical purposes or far more aggressive tactics than the national leadership felt it could adopt, as well as branches whose leadership did not, for reasons of will or competence, pursue racial issues as forcefully as the national office desired. This made the problem of authority and control always a significant matter, and national NAACP leadership, with a strong interest in maintaining "the dominance of the National Office as the expositor of policy, with local branches as instruments of action and—particularly—as 'tax-collection' units,"[34] has followed a course of maintaining tight control, even when this firm hand could interfere with the ability of branches and field staff to function effectively in situations with which they were more familiar.

The branches have been superseded and placed under administrators chosen by the national office, sometimes to assure that treasuries are properly managed or that branch officials do not misuse the NAACP name for personal gain. In other instances, it is done to prevent branches from being captured by those averse to the organization's main purposes. In the early years, this meant preventing the allies of Booker T. Washington, whose posture was more accommodative to white dominance than Association leaders could accept, from taking control of branches; more recently, the concern was attempts at penetration by the Communist Party when it wished to show it was taking the side of oppressed racial minorities. Control extended to methods used at the local level, where the NAACP was unwilling to surrender its dominance to others like Rev. Martin Luther King and the SCLC.[35]

Another reason for tight control is to assure that policy sought through "NAACP cases" is uniform. The national organization has even acted to displace branches when their policy diverged from that of the national organization. That happened in Atlanta when local officers accepted administrative positions for blacks in the school system rather than press for desegregation. The branch was ultimately put in "receivership," with national staff believing the organization could "survive negative publicity" from controlling the local branch. More generally, the need for control was sufficiently strong that "if a [NAACP] branch went off with inconsistent litigation" or hadn't precleared that litigation, there would be "hell to pay," with the staff feeling that the organization could survive the negative publicity that would result from overriding the local group.

The NAACP Legal Defense Fund

During the NAACP's increasing emphasis on a litigation program, the Internal Revenue Service refused to grant tax deductibility to contributions to the NAACP because of its lobbying activities. Thus in 1939 the NAACP Legal Defense and Educational Fund, Inc. (LDF, sometimes called the "Inc. Fund") was incorporated both "to provide a full-time civil rights litigation" staff and to allow contributors to make tax-deductible contributions. At that time, the LDF and the NAACP were located in the same building, had interlocking boards of directors and shared staff, and LDF was the NAACP's litigating arm. When Thurgood Marshall succeeded Charles Houston as NAACP's Special Counsel in 1940, from the first he also became LDF Special Counsel. Lawyers entirely on the LDF payroll were considered part of the NAACP's legal department, which "functioned as a single entity without regard to the source of salaries and lawyers' fees."[36] However, with the Legal Defense Fund's lawyers no longer institutionally in the NAACP, psychological distance developed between LDF and NAACP. That the two organizations each now raised funds and that some LDF board members were not also NAACP directors reinforced that separation.[37]

In 1957, southern members of Congress, in the backlash from *Brown v. Board of Education*, prompted an IRS investigation of the NAACP-LDF relationship. Some NAACP officials, Marshall among them, argued for protecting the tax-deductible contributions to the LDF by severing its formal ties to the NAACP, and the two organizations did fully separate in 1957, with interlocking between boards of directors eliminated. However, tax compliance is probably too simple an explanation for separation of the two groups, as complete separation may not have been necessary. For one thing, others in the NAACP contested it, and their view was perhaps vindicated post hoc when Robert Carter obtained tax-exempt status for the NAACP Special Contribution Fund (SCF) in 1964, because the SCF bears the same close relation to the NAACP the LDF previously had. (The Gandhi Society—later the American Foundation on Nonviolence—was established by SCLC as an entity to receive tax-exempt contributions to be used for voter registration and education, but it was not successful, and became a financial drain for SCLC instead of aiding it.)

At first, after the separation took place, LDF did not "move out of the [NAACP's] tent" and remained the NAACP's litigating arm. "There was continuing consultation and interchange," with the LDF and the NAACP remaining functionally one organization for much civil rights litigation, and LDF lawyers still showed concern for the NAACP and "designed the litigation program to satisfy the NAACP membership, as well as liberal supporters of the NAACP's general goals."[38] Indeed, for several years after the two organizations formally separated, the LDF held its conference of cooperating attorneys as a prelude to the national NAACP convention. However, after Marshall, leaving for a federal judgeship, chose Jack Greenberg as his successor, the organizations definitely diverged. Where there once had functionally been one organization, "then there were two." After the 1965 convention the growing competition between the two groups led NAACP Executive Director Roy Wilkins to "disinvite" LDF. Thereafter the NAACP did not have the funds to continue such an annual arrangement for its cooperating attorneys, or to have a mechanism equivalent to the LDF's Airlie House conferences. Similar conferences were not revived until 1982.

Headquarters of the NAACP Legal Defense Fund are in New York City—earlier at 59 Columbus Circle, now at 99 Hudson Street, in a building with many other public interest law organizations. All but a few of LDF's lawyers are in these, with the remainder in the Washington, D.C., office, principally to oversee federal government executive branch performance on civil rights policy; there is now an office in Los Angeles as well. In the 1970s the organization also had offices in four states in the South; they are now closed, as is a San Francisco office, open from 1966 to 1978, that resulted from a bequest to the San Francisco Fund with an indication it should be given to LDF; the Fund's rules required use of those resources in the Bay Area. However, because San Francisco, "relative to other cities, was full of attorneys ready, willing, and able to do civil rights cases," the office was said not to be necessary for LDF. With three attorneys, it operated "more like a functioning law office" in a "pretty autonomous arrangement." (MALDEF is alone among civil rights organizations in having regularly had offices in several cities besides its San Francisco headquarters—Los Angeles, San Antonio, Washington, D.C., and, for a while, Denver and Chicago.)

During the 1970s, LDF had a staff of as many as thirty attorneys, later reduced to approximately twenty, but increasing again by the early 1990s to twenty-eight. Staff attorneys consider these numbers manageable, because they make it "easier for the people in charge to know what is going on." There were also some 400 attorneys throughout the country handling cases in conjunction with LDF. The LDF has a multimillion dollar budget, for example, $5.8 million in 1980 and $5.5 million in 1981. (The 1993 budget was reported to be $9.5 million.) The litigation budget began to expand in the mid-1960s, from roughly $500,000 a year to over $3.6 million dollars in 1975. In 1980 and 1981, respectively, LDF's legal expenses were $2.5 million and $3.2 million, with over $2.1 million from attorneys' fee awards. Ford Foundation grants, which began in 1967, never exceeded one-sixth of LDF's budget for litigation, and year-to-year variations were considerable. For example, in 1975, "with sharply increased litigation expenses and reduced Foundation support, the percentage fell to 8 percent." [39]

Structurally the LDF is a public interest law firm with no members. A seventy-member board of directors, with ultimate formal policy authority, usually ratifies the staff's proposals, perhaps because the staff, through its response to the directors' concerns, has earned the board's trust. As Greenberg observed, "The staff really operates the organization," [40] with most policy discussion taking place among the staff. Serious policy discussion has, however, taken place at the board of directors level, for example, in development of a policy statement when *DeFunis v. Odegaard*, the affirmative action case, reached the Supreme Court. (With *Bakke*, however, there was relatively little discussion by the board, which "deferred to its staff's expertise.")[41] The sixteen-member executive committee and some of its members actively formulate policy and litigation strategy.[42]

Most decisions at LDF are, however, made at the center. The key person is the organization's director-counsel, of whom there have been only four—Marshall, Greenberg, Julius Chambers (1984–1992), and Elaine Jones. "We are a centralized organization, so we can exercise rather strong control over all actions taken in our name." Yet, as in other civil rights litigation organizations, staff attorneys prefer to operate in a collegial mode which allows some flexibility, and the staff is small enough to have daily contact. They dislike a hierarchical mode of organization and do not want "marching orders," instead preferring support and consultation from general counsel. Failure to provide that support can produce severe friction. The effects of a single individual like LDF's Director-Counsel can be overestimated, but in small "law shops," the legal and interpersonal capabilities of the "top lawyer" do affect the litigation unit's performance significantly. Greenberg is said to have shown dislike for staff lawyers who advocated providing legal support to "radicals" or who themselves seemed to be radical, and to have been quite skittish about such connections. Greenberg is also said to have shown distaste for former civil rights lawyers who left LDF to work for establishment firms, evidence of a paternalistic attitude toward staff lawyers' lives.

The Lawyers' Committee

The Lawyers' Committee for Civil Rights Under Law was formed in 1963 after President John Kennedy requested the American legal establishment's leaders to bring the legal community's resources to bear on civil rights difficulties in the South. For many years, the Lawyers' Committee sent lawyers from northern (primarily eastern) law firms to handle cases in the South, but later expanded its range of coverage, operating primarily through participating law firms' donation of pro bono services. Law firms are the organization's constituent units; partners from those firms sit on its board and major committees.

The Lawyers' Committee also engages directly in litigation and related activities through its Washington, D.C., headquarters staff of generalists and others who focus on specific projects, such as employment discrimination, housing, children in poverty, and South Africa, and through local Lawyers' Committees in eight cities. Each unit, which makes its own arrangements for bringing together law firms and cases, is controlled by its own board of directors and is financially independent, except that the District of Columbia unit is funded through national headquarters. The strength of the ties between national office and affiliates varies.

There was also a Jackson, Mississippi office, then the only civil rights law office in that state. A difficulty with maintaining that office was that it lacked backup from experienced civil rights lawyers because of "difficulty in coordinating the short-term visits by attorneys from major law firms on its board of directors."[43] The office was closed because of the difficulty of obtaining funding and the need to allocate funds elsewhere. The office handled voting rights litigation in the state and was the basis for the Voting Rights Project established in 1981 with "new money" from several sources, including the Rockefeller and Ford Foundations and the Carnegie Corporation of New York. The project litigates Voting Rights Act cases, monitors the Department of Justice's enforcement of the VRA, and provides technical assistance to attorneys and community groups bringing voting rights cases or involved in preclearance of voting changes. Its office was relocated to Washington in 1985 because, by that time, Mississippi black attorneys were willing to take cases the office previously handled, available funds were reduced, and there was a need to focus voting rights activities in Washington.[44]

ACLU

The American Civil Liberties Union, the successor in 1920 to the National Civil Liberties Bureau, founded three years earlier by Roger Baldwin, had as its primary activities lobbying and publicizing, and protesting, about violations of civil liberties, but it was also engaged in litigation, for which it is perhaps best known. The ACLU, like other organizations when they first started, was highly centralized, at first, with a few people both determining and implementing policy. This continued even after ACLU affiliates grew, but although some of Baldwin's successors have been strong leaders, there has been no dominant national executive like those in the NAACP, and the organization became both more democratic and decentralized. National

ACLU headquarters are in New York City; a Washington, D.C., office has primary responsibility for lobbying of Congress and contacting executive branch agencies. The American Civil Liberties Foundation (initially the Roger Baldwin Foundation), created to carry out litigation and education activities and to receive tax-deductible contributions, does not operate separately. The group's basic units are its state affiliates, although a few operate effectively in only part of a state and there are three affiliates in California.

The ACLU's first general counsel, Arthur Garfield Hays and Morris Ernst, served on a volunteer basis, and its permanent staff was quite small after mid-century. As late as 1960, there were only two attorneys in New York and a few elsewhere, working primarily on appellate cases for local ACLU units or providing legal resources for the weaker ones. By the mid-1980s, however, the attorney staff increased to over thirty in the national office and a roughly equal number serving the state affiliates (some estimates are much higher), while on the order of 2,000 volunteer attorneys worked on particular cases.

The ACLU's membership, said to have been 275,000 in the late 1980s, has grown in response to government attacks on civil liberties, which the ACLU has effectively exploited, and decreased in the absence of major national civil liberties crises and in response to controversies like the one over the ACLU's support of the American Nazi Party in Skokie, Illinois. ACLU members do not participate directly in choosing the national organization's board, but state boards (chosen by local boards in some states) elect much of the national board (fifty-one of eighty-three seats).

Until 1950, ACLU policy was made almost totally by the national board, but members are now involved as delegates to the ACLU's every-other-year meetings which develop policy positions ("biennials"), although the national board can block, or at least suspend, positions adopted at the biennial session. Within the confines of policy positions, infrequent membership meetings and lack of a requirement that staff consult with the membership mean that national and state staff have much latitude in carrying out directives from the board. However, conflict among board members has affected board-staff relations. Roger Baldwin found, for example, that "political splits and personality conflicts among the board members forced him to tread softly in forging and implementing ACLU policy."[45]

Much ACLU activity is decentralized, taking place through the affiliates, which act independently in deciding which cases to pursue and issues to emphasize. Some affiliates, defining their own policy, are "tied to the national organization largely by a commonly shared ideological orientation," and have "had only the most tenuous ties to the national office."[46] According to ACLU participant Thomas Emerson, "There's always been a problem that the ACLU has never been tightly coordinated. There's always been a problem of coordinating people and not looking foolish." Some national-state linkage is provided by an extensive policy guide, available for the first time in 1966, and an expectation that affiliates' decisions will be "in accordance with" the policy guide. However, only "general unity, rather than absolute uniformity" is sought, and affiliates' policies on issues are likely to diverge from national policy,[47] with national officers often taken to task for local actions they didn't initiate or control. Moreover, there are new issues on which national policy has not yet been developed but on which affiliates wish to act. As the number of potential cases grew, decisions to litigate, made at the national level into the 1950s, were decentralized.

Local ACLU units do not view favorably efforts to rein them in, as one could see in resistance to a proposal to allow removal of affiliate staff and board members, impoundment of affiliate funds, and appointment of a receiver if there were a serious violation of "constitution, policies, procedures or financial rules" that "resulted or will result in irreparable harm to the ACLU." Although the national executive director said it was aimed at financial problems, not policy, affiliate directors said it would negatively affect internal debate and would produce centralization in the organization.

Because national approval is not required unless a case is to go to the Supreme Court under the ACLU name, affiliates have "considerable autonomy" in bringing cases in the ACLU's name. This leads to variation in the extent to which they follow national policy: Los Angeles and San Francisco affiliates, for example, "exhibited marked differences in responding to dictates from New York."[48] Considerable friction between the national and local ACLU units was also possible, and occurred with the northern California affiliate over how to challenge the government's World War II relocation of Japanese-Americans. The ACLU national board was willing to countenance a challenge based on grounds of racial discrimination but was strongly opposed to challenging the president's authority. Orders fired off from

New York City to San Francisco received negative responses or were ignored. The ACLU's name was removed from the brief challenging the president's authority only after the national office threatened to "disaffiliate" the northern California unit.[49]

The ACLU has undergone significant change, so that "as a law reform unit [it] looked conspicuously different from its earlier self."[50] Most important is that it moved away from almost exclusive attention to responding to particular cases, although within a set of goals and general policies, to a greater focus on specific project areas, such as women's rights, reproductive rights, and prisoners' rights,[51] so that the ACLU, being more active than reactive, became much more a direct participant in cases. Indeed, the ACLU became the prototype national test case litigation center, monitoring issues, trying some cases, and also advising other lawyers contemplating litigation. However, despite its shift in emphasis, one of its legal directors estimated that 80 percent of its cases resulted from a potential plaintiff coming to the ACLU, with 20 percent stemming from ACLU efforts to deal with particular issues.

Housing Litigators

In housing, the pattern was somewhat different from that in other areas of civil rights law. There was a predominant, although small, organization, the National Committee Against Discrimination in Housing (NDCH), and a number of other organizations, including major national civil rights litigators handling many cases and small local groups seeking very particular goals in individual cases; however, no single group "was able to provide central coordination and intellectual leadership for open-housing litigators."[52] Likewise, no single group led the efforts to eliminate exclusionary zoning, where organizations were grouped in a relatively loosely structured coalition at times referred to as the Open Suburbs Movement (OSM). It contained the NAACP, NAACP Legal Defense Fund, ACLU, and the Lawyers Committee, in addition to the NCDH and the Suburban Action Institute. Ideological proclivities contributed to proliferation, as some attacking exclusionary zoning felt that there should not be a single overarching organization and did not particularly prefer any greater direction or coordination, adopting instead an ideology favoring a "decentralized, multifaceted approach."[53]

The National Committee Against Discrimination in Housing, created in 1950 and the recipient of the largest amount of funds for open housing from the Ford Foundation, was the largest single private resource for housing discrimination litigation. Litigation was always an important part of NCDH's work, either directly in connection with housing cases or when school desegregation plaintiffs raised housing issues as components of their proof of segregation, although it moved from New York City to Washington, D.C., because "so much of what it was doing was related to federal programs and the legislative process." NCDH's litigation office, only nominally part of the parent organization, and separately funded by Ford starting in 1972, had only four attorneys in the 1980s, an indication of the lesser attention received by housing litigation than by school desegregation or employment discrimination. The litigation staff believed they had "largely autonomous authority to choose case priorities," with their advisory board playing "a relatively small role" in such matters.[54] NCDH, in addition to defending fair housing groups sued by real estate brokers trying to intimidate them for "testing," litigated against federal departments and agencies, such as HUD (Department of Housing and Urban Development) or the agencies regulating lenders, "after trying to persuade them to carry out their duties," and against the private housing and home finance industry, "relatively untouched by housing discrimination laws."

The Leadership Council on Metropolitan Open Housing was initiated in the Chicago metropolitan area in the mid-1960s as a response by the business community (initially including the real estate community), to Rev. Martin Luther King, Jr.'s marches against housing discrimination, and was composed of chief executive officers of major business firms. The Council's lawyers started filing legal actions in 1968, the year of the Fair Housing Act and of *Jones v. Mayer*, but had to contend with the problem that both the minority community and those whites interested in desegregating housing "had no confidence that the legal system would resolve problems." The Council's initial work was mostly persuasion and education, but its major program became litigation, mostly in federal court. Much of its work has been focused in the Chicago area, but it provided technical assistance both in Chicago and elsewhere "to allow other lawyers to do our cases."

Backup Centers

Backup centers, created and funded by the Legal Services Program (later the Legal Services Corporation) but generally independent, are other important elements in civil rights litigation. They have continued to be involved in litigation in their specialties even after they were restricted by statute. Perhaps most important for race relations law has been the Center for Law and Education at Harvard University, the only backup center dealing solely with education. The Center was initially affiliated with both Harvard's Graduate School of Education and its Law School but is now independent of Harvard. Its involvement in school desegregation varied over time, from 25 to 40 percent of its cases and 10 to 15 percent of its resources. Also among its concerns were Title I, tracking and ability groupings, migrant children, bilingual education, exclusion and expulsion of school children, and teachers' rights. The Center's involvement in litigation, a shift from a research orientation, became central only after an evaluation conducted at the request of then OEO Director Donald Rumsfeld concluded that backup centers should be more litigation-oriented. By the early 1970s the Center's litigation capacity had increased to five or six lawyers plus additional summer help and assistance from Northeastern University Law School, and grew further, to ten attorneys, by the early 1980s.

Supervision of the Center by the Graduate School of Education was "light but not neglectful," but Harvard Law School was said to be ambivalent about supporting innovative activities at the Center. Despite a "core of support" for the Center among law faculty, the "Kingsfield component of the faculty" had "gut dis-ease and discomfort" with Harvard-associated lawyering "that might seem radical." This led to continuing law school discussion about withdrawing support for the Center and a continual need to convince the Law School faculty "that the law was not being stretched" and that litigation was being used not to attack the educational establishment but to attack segregation, because tracking was a pretext for segregation. The Center was "never once asked to trim its sails," and the concerns expressed by the law faculty did not lead the Center to take or withhold action in any particular case, but the institutional relationship forced the Center to be "sure it was professionally unquestionable" and to ask regularly, "Does the law have a proper place [in this sort of case]?" and "Is it healthy for law qua law in the long run or should it play a more conservative role?"

A different type of backup center was the Center for National Policy Review, housed at Catholic University in Washington, D.C. The Ford Foundation provided much of its funding; this was supplemented by other foundations and attorneys' fees. Created to provide "research, advocacy, and administrative skills" for civil rights groups, because, with enactment of the major civil rights statutes, "there wasn't any private organization with the capacity to deal with the regulations, cases, and issues, with an advocacy capacity," the Center had a program to obtain enforcement of civil rights laws by lobbying federal executive agencies. Although not established to "do litigation," the Center "always did some," because "administrative initiatives ran into a dead end" and because other litigating organizations sought its assistance in cases. The Center "usually did not litigate on its own, but gathered and analyzed data for legal action," playing clearinghouse and backup roles. School desegregation was the Center's primary litigation focus, in part because its director, William Taylor, was particularly interested in metropolitan area desegregation, and it participated in the Buffalo, Wilmington, and Louisville school cases, among others.

Communication among Lawyers: The Civil Rights Bar

The *civil rights bar* is part of the glue that serves to hold the pieces of civil rights litigation together both at the national level and in particular communities. It serves to restrain the tendency toward fragmentation that could occur with many differing organizations and individual lawyers working on civil rights litigation, particularly if several lawyers not previously associated in litigation work together.[55] Existence of the bar allows lawyers an advantage in developing cohesive strategy, even if they work together on cases only infrequently. Indeed, regular communication among, and meetings of, principal actors in litigation has been central to planned litigation campaigns.

Lawyers working on civil rights matters have long maintained contacts with each other. The antislavery bar that began in the 1830s was a small but "fairly well-defined group of men [who] did the antislavery legal work without compensation." Although they had "different, often conflicting, sectarian affiliations," most "had strong connections with one or another of the groups within the antislavery movement, which had their own contacts"; they also "had a common litigation experience: representation of the fugitive slave and of his friends."[56] In the 1940s, when the numbers remained small, the black lawyers through whom cases came to LDF were "all close friends" of Thurgood Marshall who "either had gone to school together or were very involved in the NAACP."[57]

The presence of a "civil rights bar" among those working for the rights of blacks was not at first matched by a comparable grouping among those seeking to advance women's civil rights, because there was no predominant national women's rights litigator comparable to the NAACP or a single center for legal education comparable to Howard University.[58] However, such a network did develop in the 1970s, as the ACLU's Women's Rights Project devoted much effort to improving methods of communication between women's litigating organizations and to creating a network extending beyond ACLU national-affiliate contacts to community civil rights organizations and women's groups.[59]

Civil rights lawyers "share a real enemy" and "share a conception of that enemy" which allows them to work together regardless of their organizations' formal positions and even when their organizational superiors are at odds, as in the conflict between NAACP and LDF. "Organizational jealousies" might limit "farming out" a case to an attorney for another organization, but major litigating organizations at times ask firms associated primarily with other major litigators to take a case. Thus some lawyers have tried cases, particularly school cases, for both NAACP and LDF, with large, complex cases being handled by only about ten to twelve people around the country who are part of a "network" or "tight little group."

The relatively small number of civil rights lawyers, even today, facilitates communication. Those bringing civil rights cases in federal court are able to stay in contact. They exchange information about the progress of cases, make one another aware of particular cases, and share briefs and copies of decisions. There is less competition between civil rights lawyers than there would be between lawyers in business practice, because the cases the former handle do not have a "commercialized purpose," and the increase in funds during the late 1960s and 1970s also reduced competition. Without communication, there is likely to be repetition of what has been undertaken elsewhere, although, "because each suit comes in a different place, it is often necessary for those involved to learn the lessons again through their own experience."[60]

Interaction in the generally small and relatively cohesive "civil rights bar," quite frequently among lawyers in the same city, produces a partial convergence of perspectives among lawyers. Part of this is that many civil rights lawyers have, at one time or another, worked for the same organization or government agency. For example, J. Harold Flannery, now a state judge, after service in the Department of Justice worked for the Lawyers' Committee for Civil Rights Under Law, the Harvard Center for Law and Education, and then Foley Hoag and Eliot, the Boston law firm most involved in pro bono civil rights work. One of the lawyers on the "floating" team which handled many major Northern school cases had also been at the Department of Justice, while another team member had been at the Harvard Center and then in turn had been Director of the Lawyers' Committee. A lawyer involved in the Boston case, also active in the ACLU, started with the state (not a defendant in that case), then moved to the State Board of Education (one of the primary movers against the Boston School Committee), and then to Foley Hoag. The presence of some individuals in multiple organizations also serves to provide and reinforce ties among them. In Boston, where liberal lawyers "wear different hats on different occasions," the Lawyers' Committee (subsidized by the Boston Bar Association), the ACLU, the American Jewish Congress, and similar groups have overlapping liberal participation.

Communication among lawyers handling civil rights cases may take place at formal sessions and, more important, outside them. Even when direction of litigation is decentralized and a single controlling entity abjured, communication and other forms of coordination among the lawyers have taken place, but the extent of exchange must not be overestimated. For example, in San Francisco, where there was "a civil rights law firm for every group imaginable," not only was there "nothing formal by way of communication" among members of the civil rights bar, but there was "not a great deal of communication—period". Yet there were conferences and other clearinghouse activities, for example, in the "open suburbs" litigation and in litigation on access by the disabled to transportation, where the Public Interest Law Center of Philadelphia (PILCOP) "became an informal consultant to lawyers across the country" who were undertaking or thinking of undertaking such cases, and lawyers from a number of the major cases aimed at increasing access to bus transportation attended a National Center for Law and the Handicapped (NCLH) conference. However, holding a conference did not mean adoption of a unified legal strategy.[61]

At times, meetings of lawyers affiliated with an organization or working in a particular area of the law are held to communicate recent legal developments to them and to increase their litigation ability in civil rights law. This was a principal function of conferences the NAACP Legal Defense Fund held at Airlie House in Virginia. In part because of its financial difficulties, the NAACP has not held such conferences regularly, although it revived the idea in 1988 when, in connection with the University of Missouri at Kansas City Law School, it ran a legal education seminar on developments in school desegregation and voting rights.[62] Specific types of training meetings such as those conducted by the Lawyers Committee under a training contract from the EEOC or by the Exclusionary Land-Use Practices Clearing House, are said to be "conducive to educating those who attend the conferences" but produce "neither close coordination in deciding what kinds of cases to bring nor joint writing of briefs," at least where the individuals did not know each other previously. However, sometimes informal contacts made at these meetings are pursued and "do result in critique of briefs and suggestions for further litigation strategy."[63] While technical information is transmitted at those meetings, the intentional, if at times implicit, purpose of meetings like the Airlie House sessions was cohesion—"to bring the participants [in a litigation campaign] together for a face-to-face encounter" so that they would no longer be working alone and unaware of others' parallel efforts.[64] Contacts made at such sessions facilitate the flow of information from lawyer to lawyer in the civil rights community. More basically, they let those working in a common enterprise meet each other or renew acquaintances because not all members of the civil rights bar saw each other regularly.

Meetings have been held in connection with the campaign against racial restrictive covenants (Chicago, July 1945, attended by thirty-three people),[65] school segregation, and employment discrimination. In 1968, there was a meeting in New York of over 100 lawyers and others interested in abolishing capital punishment. This was not a meeting to discuss "technical" matters but was held to bring together those working in this area of law, and it "gave the movement for legal abolition a cohesion that it had lacked." Because planning a large meeting like that in 1968 used resources and was too large to engage in specific strategy development and because a "small working parley" was thought better when dealing with "pragmatic detail," a smaller conference was held at a later stage. However, to generate publicity, the second conference also had a session for foundation executives and the media.[66] With increasing use of social science in school desegregation cases, some conferences involved social scientists who participated as expert witnesses for civil rights plaintiffs. Judges whose record was pro-desegregation were also present at such conferences in 1975 and 1980.[67] Drawing on just such a mechanism, the Americans United for Life Legal Defense Fund sponsored a 1984 conference devoted to strategy to overturn *Roe v. Wade,* addressed by leading scholars and litigators, to which over 500 lawyers, clergy, and others were drawn.[68]

Larger conferences, although not held as often as small working groups, have been convened particularly when there was a sense that new directions might have to be taken or new conditions confronted. Thus in 1981, stimulated by the need to deal with the Reagan administration's position on school desegregation, LDF brought together cooperating lawyers, education experts, and academics to discuss the shift in administration posture and to develop strategy for counteracting those policies. Important as such meetings are, at times participants think them not terribly productive, even when they are small. Efforts to get lawyers together to plan strategy have seldom produced "grand strategizing," one attorney observed; they produced "petty strategizing if anything." When Jack Greenberg brought six people together in a hotel room to plan, "not much came out of any of that" type of activity, because what results from "sitting around" is "too abstract" for use in actual situations and too divorced from "the grass roots" to be successful. Instead, discussions, over months and even years, both within organizations and outside their bureaucratic structure, may help develop an organizational base to assist in getting work done and may prepare the organization to take advantage of windows of opportunity.

4

Resources

This chapter focuses on resource mobilization—how civil rights litigating organizations *obtain* their resources, which is related to allocation of resources. Resources affect decisions to engage in lobbying, development of public opinion, and litigation; within litigation, decisions to litigate in particular areas of the law; and, within those areas, decisions to pursue particular cases. Resources are certainly necessary if an organization is to have some effective choice of activities in which to engage or cases to enter. What is devoted to one area of the law cannot be spent on another; likewise, within any area on which an organization concentrates, resources devoted to one case are not available for others. With too many lawsuits to be brought in too many different places, organizations have to pass up some because their attorneys are "pinned down" in the trenches elsewhere. The greater the resources, the more different types of activities in which an organization can usefully engage. The extent and type of resources available are also related to the issues raised and thus the scope of cases brought. Lack of resources to finance cases may force organizations to limit litigation activity to amicus curiae participation instead of greater support of cases.

Resource mobilization and resource allocation are often related. Strategies undertaken are also a function of both the amount and types of resources available. For example, "financial considerations frequently affected the pace and direction of the desegregation effort." In mental health litigation, the absence of a network of medical and legal experts served to delay litigation in one state (California) while the presence of a state-funded mental health advocate in another state (New Jersey) facilitated bringing complex class actions.[1] If the need for resources constrains an organization's ability to engage in certain activities such as litigation (mobilization of law), then litigation successes—effective mobilization of law—increase available resources by attracting more contributions and membership dues. For example, one of the first of the contemporary conservative public interest law firms "attracted funds as it became more visible and successful in court."[2] Conversely, membership losses resulting from disappointment not only decrease resources but also require action to forestall further defections. However, an organization can use adversity, like a hostile external environment, as the basis for obtaining resources, as the NAACP did during its attack on lynching,[3] and the ACLU did more recently with Watergate and later with the Reagan administration's record. Indeed, as "contributions . . . increase because their supporters are alarmed," groups like the ACLU and the NAACP Legal Defense Fund "thrive on adversity," being "in good health even though the causes they espouse are in difficulty."[4]

Organizations seldom can simply raise resources and then decide how to spend them, or make decisions on activities to be undertaken and then obtain resources for those activities. Instead, if funds for certain activities are not available, potential contributors, not recipient organizations, may control the latter's actions. If foundations make resources available only for certain types of activities, mobilization determines allocation; thus, to attract funding, organizations must adapt. Organizations that try to obtain resources before allocating them may also be constrained because funds may be earmarked either for particular functions (litigation or lobbying) or specific areas of law. Even if this is not explicit, understandings of members or contributors may be implicit. Uncommitted funds, when available, widen an organization's options, and it may be critical to have discretionary funds so an organization can respond quickly to unexpected civil rights problems.

Mobilization and allocation of resources may be connected in other

ways. Time devoted to mobilization, necessary if there are to be resources to allocate, may itself affect allocation. Staff spending time on
seeking contributions can't engage in long-term follow-up to a legal
victory. Once a particular case has been initiated, that is, once resources have been allocated to it, the case may require more resources
than were originally anticipated. A victory at the liability stage requires
further resources to proceed with the remedy stage and then to monitor the defendant's activities as the remedy implemented, so more
resources must be mobilized if the case is to be pursued successfully.

Organizations invariably seem to engage in activities the expense
of which outruns available resources, so that resources must be constantly mobilized to fund resource allocations to which the organization has committed itself.[5] However, if an organization attempting to
"live within its means" sticks with a few long-drawn-out battles in
the trenches and does not undertake new efforts, incoming resources
may dwindle; thus new projects must be undertaken to generate new
resources, even if such projects do not generate enough to keep all
projects operating. However, dropping some projects in process is to
risk further irritation of one's followers.

Resource Scarcity

In civil liberties and civil rights litigation, that the principal players
have "organization names [which] carry an impressive ring" suggests
they have substantial resources, but "the truth of the matter is vastly
less impressive,"[6] with the actual situation one of scarcity both absolutely and in relation to goals. Resources are always scarce relative
to one's goals and one's reach should exceed one's grasp, but civil
rights litigators lack resources, not only in relation to some ideal goal
but to very realistic short-term needs. The NAACP, although thought
by school boards from which it sought desegregation to be "a large
and powerful organization," has instead been "a fragile and precarious structure that must patch together funds and promises to keep its
existing cases in federal court."[7] (Those problems, said one observer,
had been known "for a long time, but [we] didn't want to talk about
it"—out of loyalty to shared goals concerning civil rights.)

Lawyers' need for resources is always great: "Lawyers attempting
to reconstruct the legal system through litigation need large doses
of money to pay for printing bills, airplane fares, and expert as-

sistance, since without briefs, mobility, and witnesses, the limits of reform are narrow."[8] Even noncomplex cases require significant resources. Thus "relatively simple" cases—requiring only "the drafting of a complaint, marshalling of necessary evidentiary materials, taking of depositions, preparation of motion papers and supporting documentation, and preparation of briefs and memoranda of law on complicated constitutional issues"—could make it difficult for a mid-size Legal Services program to find staff attorney time to complete the work.[9] And the greater complexity of many cases means "the need for extensive lawyering manpower."[10] Class actions, although used to preserve resources, absorb considerably more of them, because of their length, complexity, and procedural requirements such as notification of potential class members. In general, we find "a dramatic contrast between the small size and slender resources of [public interest law] firms, and the formidable resources of their opponents,"[11] particularly when government opponents, determined to resist, draw on taxpayers' money, including taxes of the plaintiffs against whom they have discriminated.[12]

Civil rights litigation does not generate overwhelming amounts of money. It has regularly been true that any "sustained orientation toward law reform will not sell; it requires a subsidy."[13] When fighting lynching in earlier years, "the NAACP found itself in a financial dilemma. Publicizing injustices and generating the resources necessary to combat them cost money the Association did not have."[14] More recently, former NAACP Labor Secretary Herbert Hill said about employment discrimination that "private parties and civil rights organizations did not and do not have the vast resources required for extensive and effective litigation programs."[15] In the attack on exclusionary zoning, Chicago area plaintiffs were "unable to press the[ir] action because of inadequate funds" and a group in the San Francisco area had "to sell part of [its] site in order to meet the financial burdens imposed by the lengthy legal wrangle."[16]

Providing even a sketch, much less a complete picture, of organizational resources in dollar terms is not easy. This is not only because costing lawyers' contributions is difficult but also because organizations with unstable financial situations desire to appear in better condition than they are for fear that knowledge of true conditions will scare away potential contributors. For example, insiders had been well aware of the NAACP's situation for years, but only as a result of conflicts among its officials and two moves of its headquarters in rapid succession did its financial difficulties become public knowledge, with headlines like "N.A.A.C.P. Is Said to Be Facing a Financial Crisis," noting a 1982 deficit of over $825,000, and "Down at the Heels the N.A.A.C.P. Tries to Dig Them In." On the other hand, claims that resources are needed, as long as the picture portrayed is not too serious, may be used as a tactic to raise funds, just as negative external events have been used to the same end.

Yet, despite the possible tactical use of such claims, there is an endemic lack of resources throughout civil rights and civil liberties litigation. In church-state litigation, the three major litigators, including the ACLU, had limited resources, and women's rights groups "frequently [were] unable to raise the large sums of money necessary to sustain any type of meaningful litigation effort."[17] Even when the relatively well-funded LDF sought to obtain a moratorium on the death penalty, it "required men and money which it simply did not have."[18] After winning the Denver school case, it did not bring other northern school cases in part because its resources were already heavily committed in southern school litigation—in places like Richmond, Memphis, Atlanta, Tulsa, Houston, Ft. Worth, Norfolk, and Oklahoma City in the early 1970s.[19] At times, straitened circumstances caused reductions in organizations' commitments.

The lack of resources is likely to be greater at the local than national level. For example, as of 1980, almost half the ACLU's state-level units had budgets of below $50,000, with the figure less than $30,000 for one-third of the affiliates; even after an influx of new members, the ACLU was "far from 'well-heeled'." In church-state litigation, local groups had "chronic" fund raising difficulties and lacked necessary resources such as "legal expertise, the sources of information, [and] the organization skills."[20] Even a single case in one community can dwarf available resources, so that "what begins with a brash confidence of ability to sustain costly litigation often ends in negotiated partial payments to attorneys."[21] Follow-up litigation to a favorable precedent is particularly costly because it involves numerous cases and development of the appropriate facts. An example of difficulties is shown by the Ohio prison conditions litigation, where plaintiffs "lacked funds, personnel, and the means to acquire substantial numbers of experts" or "to support the travel and research needed to prepare a statewide case." Resources were so limited that "some of the pretrial expenses . . . like the cost of stenographic services for depositions were defrayed by donations raised at a wine and cheese party," and the lawyers slept five to a room or stayed in each other's houses when away from their home bases.[22]

Lack of resources both forces choices and limits them. The scarcity of resources limits planning, as an organization may wish to hold back on expending resources until it seems necessary to do so. Although the NAACP could have provided local attorneys with the benefit of its experience about remedies from other school desegregation cases, "because of resource constraints the organization doesn't want to hire an expert to write a plan until they have won a case." At the extreme, it means, that an organization must engage in triage with respect to its ongoing litigation, retaining only the cases most crucial for policy development; retaining a nominal association with some others; and sacrificing still others which are not trivial but for which one does not have the means. Because the substantial resources required by any case will depress the number of cases that are brought, "cases that are 'too close to call' will rarely be brought, except in error or as part of a conscious strategy to extend the legal frontier."[23] If an organization can't afford to take on a case, it may have to enlist other organizations' help or may have to join others' cases as amicus, in either event limiting its control over the litigation. The lack of resources particularly affects the ability to undertake exactly those cases that are at the heart of contemporary civil rights litigation—complex, lengthy, "fact-heavy" cases. In that situation, lawyers may have to resort to pursuing smaller individual cases serially; for example, lawyers without resources to attack the entire Ohio prison system had to challenge conditions in each institution in turn.[24]

National organizations can do a better job than local groups of matching resources to cases, and can alleviate some problems by providing assistance to their local units; such aid is also essential if local units are not to take legal actions that conflict with national litigation plans. Yet, as noted above, major national organizations were not without resource difficulties. What has their situation been? For some, it has not been easy. In the 1919–1920 period, the NAACP incurred monthly deficits, reaching a total of roughly $9,000 when James Weldon Johnson became director, so that retaining an additional attorney for an important case was enough to "impose a burden upon the Association's limited resources."[25] When Charles Houston was the

NAACP's counsel, philanthropists provided some support but could not be relied on to assist in extended efforts, and few blacks contributed funds for the legal program.[26] In the late 1930s, the budget available to Thurgood Marshall was said to be $25,000, but another report is that in 1940, the Legal Defense Fund had income of only $10,000 for Marshall's salary and expenses.[27]

More recently the figures are much greater, but they remained small compared to other organizations' budgets in part because donations had "not kept pace with rising costs in the recession and inflation of the 1970s."[28] The NAACP Legal Defense Fund's litigation expenses were up from roughly $500,000 a year in the mid-1960s, to over $3.6 million in 1975, and were $2.5 million and $3.2 million for 1980 and 1981, respectively, out of a total budget that usually was between $5 million and $6 million, although higher at times.[29] That the NAACP's budget of roughly $8 million before recent reductions was, despite the group's large membership, not significantly larger than LDF's budget was a source of friction between NAACP and LDF. Membership-based litigating organizations like the NAACP and ACLU, which also perform functions beyond litigation, can be seriously tempted to raid their litigation budgets for needed general operating expenses. Assertions have been made that when the Special Contribution Fund had a surplus of almost $350,000 and the NAACP reported a large deficit, portions of the litigation budget were reallocated away from litigation.

The Lawyers' Committee's initial budget in 1963 was $35,000 (over $110,000 in mid-1980s dollars), but twenty years later it was $2,725,000, including the $469,000 budget of its Washington local committee.[30] The matching of cases with law firms undertaken by the Lawyers' Committee also brought a substantial volume of resources—"annually . . . over $4 million worth of volunteer private law firm time"—to bear on civil rights litigation. In the late 1970s, in cities without a local Lawyers' Committee, more than one hundred law firms agreeed to commit at least one percent of the firm's resources to cases the national Lawyers Committee referred to them. In 1982, the Lawyers' Committee "channeled more than 33,000 hours of legal services donated by attorneys in private practice (worth over 2.8 million dollars at market values) to important civil rights cases," with "the contribution of over 31,000 hours of legal services by lawyers in private practice (worth more than 4.1 million dollars)" arranged in 1984.[31] (The ACLU, for whom some 5,000 unpaid lawyers handle over 90 percent of the organization's caseload, estimated that professors and lawyers in private practice donated $15 million of legal services.[32])

Types Of Resources

Although we tend to think of *resources* primarily in terms of money, which can be used to obtain other items, the term should be defined broadly. One catalog of resources contains "devotion to a cause with sensitivity to matters of timing, funds to pay mundane costs, members to serve as parties to an action, lawyers and others to manage long-term pursuit of remedies."[33] To that we should add groups' willingness to cooperate with other organizations.

Lawyers

Lawyers are the "most valuable resource" for organizations engaged in civil rights litigation, "chief among a group's resources" because their availability increases the possibility of involvement in litigation. Lawyers include both salaried staff attorneys and cooperating attorneys willing to pursue cases pro bono, contributing their time without charge or for only a modest stipend or partial reimbursement of expenses. If resources for an adequate number of staff attorneys are lacking, an organization must rely on cooperating attorneys. If lawyers are unavailable where cases must be brought, other lawyers must be sent there. This problem was faced by civil rights organizations as a result of the "small number of blacks at the bar and the even smaller number available to civil rights clients," coupled with the rarity of southern white lawyers being willing to assist with civil rights cases.[34] In the extreme, not having any lawyers means relying on other organizations to supply them and thus becoming the client of those organizations.

Having full-time staff lawyers is particularly important, because they allow groups not only to litigate directly but also to monitor potential and continuing cases. For example, when money for a lawyer was provided, the National Organization for Women could "initiate litigation, or at least to be sufficiently informed to file important amicus curiae briefs."[35] The more active involvement that a lawyer's presence allows is crucial for the control necessary to litigation strategy. Certainly the presence of one or more lawyers reduces an organization's litigation start-up costs; without a staff attorney, an organization must contact a lawyer, persuade the lawyer to find time to take the case and contribute services, and must instruct the attorney about the organization's interests. Not only is this time-consuming, but, done repeatedly, it may lead to lack of continuity in litigation. And lawyers' presence may also change strategic choices. For example, expansion of national NAACP staff, "instead of making more attorneys available for the time-consuming equalization cases, actually increased the pressures for the direct attack."[36]

During most of Thurgood Marshall's tenure, LDF's staff had no more than a half-dozen lawyers, and generally only four or five, although other lawyers were on retainer in Washington, D.C., Richmond, Dallas, and Los Angeles.[37] After 1960, the staff began to grow, to nine lawyers in 1963 (including interns), a dozen the following year, and seventeen a year later. The number rose substantially to twenty-eight in 1967, and then increased to as high as thirty lawyers before being reduced slightly. The higher numbers of the 1970s and 1980s still left LDF "spread thin," as not many lawyers were working on any single area of law. In 1974, only one lawyer was "working full-time on school desegregation"; that lawyer's successor "worked only part of the time on school cases." At the same time, LDF "could only afford to allow two of its twenty-four staff attorneys to work full-time on death penalty cases" despite its major role in that litigation.[38] In addition to staff attorneys, there were roughly seventy cooperating attorneys working with LDF in 1963, 100 the next year and 120 in 1965, stimulated by activity connected with the civil rights movement. The number reached almost 190 in 1966, climbing further to 250 the following year and almost to 290 in 1968.[39]

The Lawyers' Committee for Civil Rights Under Law has had roughly forty staff lawyers in its national office and at its local committees. The Puerto Rican Legal Defense Fund had a staff of more than twenty in the early 1980s, including nine lawyers; the Mexican-American Legal Defense Fund, also assisted initially by the LDF, had a staff of approximately twenty attorneys; and the Native American Rights Fund had a staff of 15 lawyers. At roughly the same time, the ACLU had 35 staff attorneys on the national organization's staff, with its state affiliates collectively having an equal number.

Lawyers' competence—with civil rights, not only general competence—and experience, not merely their numbers, are necessary. One needs lawyers with subject-matter competence, although a litigating organization can help develop appropriate skills, as LDF did with an intern program, and the conservative Pacific Legal Foundation and Washington Legal Foundation attempted to recruit outstanding law school graduates to a one- to two-year internship program. In all these instances, the programs paid off, as some interns stayed on as cooperating attorneys or staff attorneys.

Litigating organizations also must have a reputation for maintaining a competent, effective staff, because lawyers tend to gravitate to those who provide the best performance. That reputation in part is a function of performance, and performance is largely a function of resources. The NAACP Legal Defense Fund's advantage over the NAACP in this regard was evident to lawyers who had contact with both. They found the LDF, an "organization with a long history of experience in litigation," had "competent legal staff" whom local lawyers could call to "get substantive responses." By contrast, the absence of recruitment programs among some of the conservative public interest law firms served to limit the flow of fresh blood into their attorney staffs.[40]

To attract lawyers, litigating organizations must be engaged in work that appeals to them. Lawyers are likely to have particular substantive concerns—civil rights, the environment, poverty—that lead them to one rather than another organization, but their values or orientations, which affect their commitment to their work, may also lead them to seek a particular type or style of litigation. As Cover observed about antislavery lawyers, "the ideologically committed attorney may eschew settlement."[41] Lawyers may be less interested in the individual "test case of the type the ACLU emphasized, perhaps seeing it as "either too traditional or too professionally antiseptic," and more interested in class action-based litigation campaigns like those the NAACP Legal Defense Fund has undertaken.[42]

Lawyers' orientations include whether client, group, or principle is paramount. For one type, the Advocate, the lawyer's "own policy preferences are irrelevant to his activity as an attorney, and the ramifications of his case for others in society are also of little concern, unless they affect directly his chances for winning"; this lawyer, unlikely to be intentionally involved in planned litigation, is "essentially indifferent about whom he represents." Far more likely to be found in planned organizational litigation are Group Advocates who have "long-term commitments" to the client group or to the lawyer's "clientele" (as the lawyer defines it). The Civil Libertarian is also engaged in planned litigation but "views his clients as all of society" and sees a case as "a vehicle by which democratic principles important to all of society may be vindicated."[43] Group Advocates and Civil Libertarians, both of whom view a client's goal "as part of a larger effort to accomplish group or society-wide preferences,"[44] thus share a "social welfarist" orientation, in which "law is viewed not simply as a mechanism for conflict resolution but as a means for accomplishing social change."

Social welfarists are likewise among "activist lawyers"—those who "share a concern for public policy problems and a willingness to use their legal skills in policy-relevant ways"[45]—who may be contrasted with the "entrepreneurial" orientation of the attorney who focuses on service to the individual client. Not all activist lawyers are alike, however. There is the "traditional activist," such as the American Civil Liberties Union lawyer, often affected by the "myth of rights," who uses the "leading case" approach and "engage[s] in what might be termed partially programmatic litigation." By contrast, the "radical activist," at times torn between being a radical and being a lawyer, disavows procedures and constitutional values and most often uses law to advance clients' strongly held political views.[46]

On the other hand, the "innovative activist," including Legal Services attorneys interested in law reform and lawyers representing community groups, chooses plans of action, including combinations of litigation and political strategies, on the basis of pragmatic considerations.[47] The NAACP's legal staff may fit into this category. They were said to have "consisted of political and legal activists, not systematic ideologues or social theorists." Not all were firm believers in planning litigation for social change or considered themselves "social engineers," with some focusing on the particular case rather than on the "larger picture." And because they were pragmatic in their approach, "They tended to use whatever was available in the environment that seemed likely to help with the problem at hand, without worrying too much about whether their actions over the long run could be fit into some rationalized pattern."[48] Whatever the label one might apply, many lawyers involved in civil rights litigation are "cause lawyers" committed to their clients' substantive goals: that is, to more than winning individual cases, and having a broad agenda. "Cause lawyers" are generally "activists" who are likely to have an ideology which includes a critique of oppression to which the lawyer's clients are subject; to be self-conscious about issues of professional policy; and to be connected with a community external to lawyering.[49]

These orientations affect not only the types of cases in which they become involved but also influence factors determining whether to appeal and the relative weights given those factors. "Social welfarists" were more likely than "entrepreneurials" to give the chance of winning greatest weight in deciding to take a case to the court of appeals; "entrepreneurials" gave far less weight to "importance to society" than did the "social welfarists," whose greater overall interest in obtaining a forum from which to make issues known led them to be more willing to file a petition for certiorari in the Supreme Court when the possibilities of its being granted were low. (For both, the timing of a case, an organization's concern, and advice by other attorneys were unimportant factors.)[50]

In any event, ideology is only one factor affecting lawyers' actions, and it is easy to overestimate its importance. Lawyers may also be concerned with enhancing their credibility with other lawyers or with participating in certain cases as learning experiences, and are also likely to be affected by economic needs. For example, in a legal service agency's resource allocation "ideological and political commitments accounted for only 9.7% of the expressed task explanations," although this figure may have been low "because *all* of their lawyering, indeed their becoming legal services attorneys, was rooted in political ideology and commitments."[51]

Other Resources

Another resource crucial for contemporary complex civil rights litigation is other expertise, demonstrated by statisticians or industrial psychologists in job discrimination cases, by demographers and cartographers in the NAACP's self-described "traveling road show" assembled for its northern school desegregation cases, and by the political scientists, demographers, urban planner, and historian used in the Los Angeles County voting rights case.[52] Problems of recruiting experts and of linking their knowledge with lawyers' legal knowledge to make effective use of the experts have been substantial.[53]

Organization itself is a key resource because, without it, one must first assemble and organize people to engage in necessary tasks. Organization makes it possible "to store information, utilize advance intelligence, develop expertise, establish and maintain credibility as a disputant, adopt long-term strategies, [and] coordinate activities in different forums," and provides "support [for] the development of legal expertise, . . . that would be beyond the capabilities of isolated and individual litigants."[54] Organizational structure is also important. An organization that is itself a coalition of organizations may be less likely to engage in action than is a unitary organization, instead leaving litigation to individual member organizations. That a litigating organization's structure is also related to its securing of resources is quite evident in the creation of separate entities to receive tax-deductible contributions.

Law itself, a product of government, is a resource. Without a body of relevant law, true in the employment discrimination area when Title VII was enacted, effort must be devoted to developing that law, but with favorable statutes and judicial precedent, lawyers can focus on implementing them. An example is the administrative preclearance of changes in voting procedures under Section 5 of the 1965 Voting Rights Act, through which citizens can use the Justice Department's facilities rather than having to obtain the relatively scarce voting rights lawyers necessary for enforcement of Section 2 of the Act.[55]

Tax rules also illustrate the importance of law as a resource. In general, rules on tax deductibility are important for an organization's ability to obtain resources. For example, as a result of a 1976 change in the tax rules—from denying exemptions unless legislative activities were "insubstantial" to adoption of a sliding scale based on the organization's income—contributions to the NAACP national office (but not NAACP branches) were made tax-deductible for the first time in 1981. Enforcement of tax laws can also be threatening. In 1988, in connection with the nomination of Judge Robert Bork to the Supreme Court, the IRS took the view that there was no difference between lobbying for legislation and advocating the defeat of a judicial nomination, affecting both liberal and conservative groups.[56]

Support from the government for an organization's positions is another. Groups can shepherd their resources by transmitting complaints to agencies that can initiate civil suits or criminal actions, thus using government administrative machinery effectively against entities discriminating on the basis of race. Moreover, "The existence of government litigation should simplify the [private] plaintiff's task of uncovering and proving a violation by reducing the time that must be spent drafting pleadings, preparing motions and obtaining discovery."[57] The government may also produce resources for the interest group, as when a complaint lodged with the Equal Employment Opportunity Commission "can produce information at public expense to be used for a private lawsuit by the public interest law firm."[58]

To the extent that the government will bring cases, and do so as the private litigator would have done, the latter can utilize its own scarce resources elsewhere, while government pressure is brought on those the interest group would otherwise have to pursue directly. During the Carter administration, the NAACP could refer matters to government agencies (EEOC, the Justice Department's Civil Rights Division, HUD, and Labor), and, "often in contact" with HEW officials, could get HEW "to do things we would otherwise have done." However, limits are imposed on the availability of this resource for private groups by the increasing complexity of situations the government might pursue—which require greater resources, thus decreasing what the government can accomplish with a constant budget—and by increased competition for the government's scarce resources from those seeking to extend their resources by enlisting the government's help. That such competition limits the availability of such resources for any one organization was shown when extension of civil rights from African-Americans to women and the handicapped stretched quite thin the resources of government agencies like the Department of Education's Office of Civil Rights (OCR).

Government can also be a resource drain for interest groups: government action to which they must respond, like the Reagan administration's attempt to undo municipal employment discrimination consent decrees, can tie up considerable resources. Southern officials' prosecution of civil rights workers imposed considerable expense to defend them, limiting groups' activities. More generally, such attacks "reduced both the flexibility of the organization to move into other new areas and also our capacity to sustain, from general revenues, programs which had previously been undertaken with categorical support (usually foundation grants)."[59]

Sources

There are numerous sources of resources for civil rights litigation, including membership dues, contributions from individuals and businesses, grants from foundations and the government, and time and expenses contributed by law firms.

An organization's local affiliates are a potential important resource. Although potential plaintiffs are not likely to fund part of their suits—indeed, someone with the resources to obtain a lawyer is less likely to seek, or to obtain, organizational support—those where a case originates may be expected to provide support before the national organization will enter the case, as in the NAACP's requirement that a branch and conference provide a stated measure of their involvement to show commitment to a case. Although they were seldom used in the pre-*Brown* attacks on school segregation, "Aggrieved blacks could generate individual plaintiffs, conduct investigations of local conditions more easily than could lawyers from New York, and monitor compliance with the day-to-day implementation of settlements and favorable judicial decrees."[60] If a national organization has only limited resources, it becomes more "dependent on its scattered branches for the initiation and funding of test cases,"[61] and when local units are weak, as is often the case, the resource problem can be severe. This was the ACLU's problem in seeking to challenge the relocation of Japanese-Americans, as it had only nominal branches outside Los Angeles and San Francisco, where there were offices and staff—but only minimal budgets.[62]

Dues and Contributions

For organizations with members, membership dues, supplemented by fund-raising drives and additional contributions, provide income on a regular basis, which has supported the activities of some organizations reasonably well over the long run. However, because civil rights organizations produce collective goods rather than selective incentives (material goods), membership dues are not sufficient for financing litigation, and additional sources from outside the membership are necessary. They therefore turn to contributors, like suburban middle-class whites who do not directly experience racial discrimination or who will not benefit from the collective goods the organization achieves, such as desegregation of central city schools or elimination of the death penalty.[63] The LDF's mass mailings to such people have been sufficiently successful to provide principal support for staff and compensation of cooperating attorneys,[64] and contributions have allowed the Lawyers' Committee to continue its national staff's general, non-project activities. For many organizations, however, even considerable activity devoted to fund-raising produces only small amounts from most contributors and the system generally creates "a kind of hand-to-mouth operation."[65]

Moreover, contributions from an organization's contributors, its "conscience constituency" which does not use the organization's services directly, are highly dependent on agreement with the organization's goals because contributors are attracted by the groups' purposive incentives rather than material benefits. Changes in the organization's direction are thus likely to result in a decrease in their contributions,[66] and contributors may shift their contributions to other organizations as their own interests change over time. The relatively few "flush" organizations, however, are not susceptible to contributors' moods or threats. As Jack Greenberg observed about the LDF, "Our support is so broadly based that no contributor can tell us what to do and carry out a credible threat if we refuse"; when, as a result of disagreements with the group's action, contributors have terminated support, the organization had "continued to do what we believe in."[67] Relevant here is that if attorneys have a stable funding source not subject to political pressure, such as the Ford Foundation, they are more likely to be able to "stay the course."

Government

Government agencies now serve as important patrons for interest groups,[68] so that, in addition to the government's own litigation, direct government support has become potentially important for litigating organizations. The most significant direct grants or contractual arrangements between government agencies and litigating organizations were those from the Equal Employment Opportunity Commission, which provided funds for law school clinical programs on employment discrimination law and contracted with the Lawyers' Committee for a private loan fund to pay litigation expenses in Title VII cases; the group's Mississippi office distributed over $141,000 in five southern states in one year alone.[69] Help with direct financing of litigation may also come from government units, such as central city school districts which found that their interests were nearly identical with those of black plaintiffs because desegregation could not occur without a remedy extending beyond the district. The Wilmington, Delaware, Board of Education, for example, voted to finance plaintiffs' lawsuit in which interdistrict remedies were sought.

However, government support can also pose problems. Most obviously, what is given can be taken away, as occurred with EEOC's contract with the Lawyers' Committee. But if an organization receives a particularly high proportion of its budget from government sources, it becomes subject to criticism that it is "less willing to enter cases that have some controversial element in them."[70]

Foundations

Although generally "groups that are heavily supported by a few large patrons are less likely to use the courts than groups that are wholly dependent on membership dues or other diffuse sources of support,"[71] foundations, particularly but not only the Ford Foundation, have become a major funding source for civil rights litigators; it has been claimed that without foundation funds, organizations cannot maintain staff attorneys necessary for pursuing litigation strategy.[72] Reductions in income from other sources, including the government, have led litigators to greater reliance on foundations, and newer organizations— including most of the Lawyers' Committee's local committees and conservative public interest law firms—have found their grants crucial for start-up costs.

Although a grant from the American Fund for Public Service (the Garland Fund) was the basis for the NAACP's systematic litigation efforts, major race relations groups began their litigation programs well before they received regular foundation assistance for it. Initial foundation contributions went to other civil rights activities and did not include major grants for litigation, in part because of the belief that "litigants will come forward to set in motion the necessary machinery to right the wrong," and in part because of "a lingering mistrust of judicial intervention into individual cases as a means of achieving broad reform." There was also the consideration on the part of those who provide interest groups with their resources about the "open hostilities and the full-scale confrontations that are inherent in most lawsuits," leading them to discourage the groups from engaging in litigation.[73] The Ford Foundation's change of mind came from recognition that "natural plaintiffs . . . lack the resources to commission the studies, conduct the investigations, and engage the legal talent essential to an effective challenge."[74]

The first Ford Foundation grants to civil rights litigators, in 1967, were to the NAACP Legal Defense Fund and the Lawyers' Committee. However, the grant to LDF was for creation of the National Office for the Rights of the Indigent (NORI), with poverty as its focus and criminal as well as civil cases among its concerns, and it was not specifically for litigation, although Ford followed it up with grants for litigation. The Lawyers' Committee Voting Rights Project was supported not only by Ford but also by the Carnegie Corporation of New York and the Rockefeller Foundation. Ford also gave grants to MALDEF, the Puerto Rican Legal Defense Fund, the Native American Rights Fund, the Women's Law Fund, the National Committee Against Discrimination in Housing, the Center for National Policy Review, and the ACLU,[75] which was also a recipient of support from the Rockefeller and Carnegie Foundations, primarily for ACLU projects in particular areas of the law.[76] In 1980, the Ford Foundation funded four national litigating groups engaged in sex discrimination cases and also provided support to three other public interest law firms working in the area.[77]

Despite the allegation of increased reliance on foundations, the Ford Foundation claimed that resources from it and other private foundations were "limited," and in a 1977 report stated that "in no year did the Foundation's contribution amount to more than 16 percent of the [NAACP Legal Defense] Fund's total litigation budget," with the proportion falling to half that (8 percent) in 1975.[78] Yet the NAACP's litigation activities could hardly have continued without the Ford Foundation's $4.35 million grant to the Special Contribution Fund in the decade starting in 1967, much of which, including grants for northern school litigation, went to the NAACP's Legal Department.

The high level of foundation grants, in the early 1970s, led to a problem for the foundations because they wished to shift resources to other activities such as the attack on poverty. However, if they did so, they risked injuring continuing activities they had been supporting and which continued to be necessary, the more so in the 1980s when civil rights groups faced the Reagan administration. The foundations were aware that, without their support, many of their beneficiaries lacked a sufficient fiscal base because they had been unable to obtain core funding elsewhere. Foundations nonetheless made efforts to reduce support for litigating organizations and thus to lessen their dependence on foundations; in the process, they helped them to improve and diversify their financial base. The Ford Foundation provided one-shot grants to help develop more effective fund-raising and to show confidence in a recipient, leading others to provide additional grants. Foundations also made clear that willingness to continue funding depended on others' increasing their commitments.

Despite these efforts, substantial foundation support continued. For example, 1983 grants from the Carnegie Corporation of New York included $390,000 for the Puerto Rican Legal Defense Fund, almost $220,000 for the Native American Rights Fund, $200,000 each to the ACLU Foundation and the Lawyer's Committee for voting rights litigation, and almost $200,000 for the Southwest Voter Registration Education Project. In 1984, the Ford Foundation gave a $1,365,000 two-year supplement to MALDEF for research, public education, and litigation in the fields of education, employment and immigration; $750,000 to LDF for litigation, advocacy, and public information activities in such areas as education, employment, and voting rights; and $400,000 to the National Committee Against Discrimination in Housing, plus another $400,000 for renovation and sharing of office space at the Public Interest Law Center (99 Hudson Street) in New York City where LDF, the Asian-American Legal Defense Foundation, the Puerto Rican Legal Defense Fund, and NOW Legal Defense Fund, among others, are now located. Ford gave another $6 million for five years to the LDF in 1987, to serve as a permanent matching fund and to serve as reserves for litigation, education, and advocacy programs on the major civil rights subjects.

Apart from possible dependence on them, what have been organizations' relations with foundations? Some have had almost completely beneficial ones. Jack Greenberg's ability to deal with foundations was said to have them "pretty well tied up" as a source of funds for LDF, which was thought quite persuasive in getting foundations to support what LDF wanted to do.[79] Some other organizations, such as the ACLU's Women's Rights Project, also had superior access, perhaps because of their achievements and because the foundations were accustomed to working with them.

However, there were also problems in relations with foundations. A potential one was dependence. One element is that considerable disruption could occur if the full amount pledged by a foundation was not received, as occurred at the beginning of the NAACP's litigation activities when the Depression meant severely decreased returns on the investments of the American Fund for Public Service, which had voted in November 1929 to provide $100,000 to the NAACP's legal efforts. Because the anticipated grant was a significant portion of its budget, the NAACP had to reduce the budget when it did not receive the entire $100,000.[80] Another aspect of dependence is that the desire to please the foundations, or at least not to alienate them, may influence organizational decisions. This is said to explain the NAACP's action in firing Lewis Steel for his article critical of the Supreme Court, even though Robert Carter and the remainder of the legal staff also left the organization. In this "better of a bad set of choices," the NAACP may have been unwilling to bite in public the hands that fed it—either the Supreme Court or the foundations, which would not have wanted to be seen as subsidizing criticism of the Court.

Foundation grants for specific project areas—and much of their contribution is so designated—limit an organization's ability to maneuver, either to choose between litigation and other means of attacking a problem or to make choices within litigation, particularly as unrestricted funds are never in great supply; indeed, foundations realized that project-based funding made it difficult for recipient organizations to address a broad range of issues by limiting their flexibility. Funding sources, by favoring activities in pursuit of traditional rights or which entailed "due process" and created access to the system and by being particularly unwilling to encourage redistributive activities, have influenced areas in which organizations litigated. Thus, foundation dollars went to lawyers, not to community organizations seen as less system-supportive; this was true even when lawyers recognized the need for community organization.[81] Radical associations were also discouraged: although some objects of foundation support may seem left-of-center, foundations are mainstream organizations. Association with the National Lawyers' Guild by those receiving Ford Foundation money was discouraged, with foundation resources "openly tied to eliminating the influence of the 'Guild lawyers'."[82]

The influence of foundation grants can be seen in the question said to present for any civil rights organization: "Do you undertake work in an area because the money was available or because you want to do it anyhow?" and in a civil rights lawyer's comment that one factor in his organization's choice of cases is "what there's money for, you tend to do." You "can write a report to a foundation saying what we've done, and so get more money." Foundations are said to have affected even LDF, although it apparently could choose where to seek funding on the basis of foundations' interests. LDF "solicited for specific issues," with choices made by the LDF among available sources "to help bring about a balanced program," so that, "to the extent the funds are ear-marked, we play a part in the earmarking." One LDF attorney even observed that "it could even have been the case that we would say to a source not to give LDF money because LDF couldn't do the case," although he couldn't remember such a situation.

However, some foundations were willing to give general support; for example, Ford Foundation grants to LDF were "essentially 'free' money, to be used where the litigation needs were great but not other-wise sufficiently funded." [83] And strings on earmarked grants were not always drawn very tight, with some organizations, at least strong ones like LDF, using funds provided for one purpose for another through redefining the original purpose. Thus LDF used its first Ford Founda-tion, for NORI, for its campaign against capital punishment, for which resources were needed. This use was thought justified because many thought the discriminatory application of the death penalty against the poor was more obvious than its discriminatory application against blacks.[84]

Attorneys' Fees

Attorneys' fees, awarded under specific civil rights statutes and the Civil Rights Attorneys Fees Act of 1976, became an important source of funds for civil rights litigators. After the Supreme Court upheld at-torneys' fee awards under the Civil Rights Act of 1964, attorneys' fees as a proportion of litigating groups' budgets did increase. By 1975, the NAACP Legal Defense Fund received $500,000 in attorneys' fees, one-sixth of its $3 million budget.[85] LDF lawyers commented regularly about the organization's receiving $1 million in fees a year "more or less." In 1980, the organization's $5.8 million budget included $1.5 million in court-awarded attorneys' fees and expenses; the following year, the figures were $5.5 million and $653,000.

Some attorneys' fee awards are extremely large, even when the judge does not grant all that was sought. In the lengthy St. Louis school case, plaintiffs requested over $520,000 and the NAACP claimed another $1.6 million for 20 attorneys (from Memphis, New York City, St. Louis, and the District of Columbia), who had to drop other work and lost private business because the case was controversial; the school board, which had used a civil rights lawyer from a major Washington, D.C., law firm, sought $1.58 million in attorneys' fees and an additional $500,000 in expenses for its efforts to obtain a metropolitan remedy. In the Kansas City, Missouri, school case, the judge had awarded $1.7 million to the local attorney who devoted virtually his entire time to the case and had to borrow over $600,000 because he could take no other employment, and $2.3 million to the NAACP Legal Defense Fund, including fees for post-judgment monitoring.[86]

Certainly failure to receive awards discounted from the figure requested can create problems for an organization. The ACLU's New York affiliate found that a fee award for its participation in the Willowbrook litigation (on conditions at an institution for the mentally retarded) that was far less than expected strained its budget, although it disclaimed dependence on attorneys' fees. Defendants' resistance requires litigation to obtain the fee award and judges' lack of generosity makes appeals necessary. Thus attorneys' fees do not come into the lawyers' hands for a considerable time, usually not until the often lengthy litigation is completed, because judges will only infrequently grant an intermediate fee award if a lawyer's availability to handle other fee-generating business has created a precarious financial situation.[87]

Often the fees are not forthcoming until after further "satellite litigation" over the amount of the fees. (This may explain why at least one group considers them a "windfall.") For example, in Dougherty County, Georgia, school case, initiated in 1963, full desegregation did not occur until 1980–1981 because of the district judge's delays. The judge first claimed that appellate rulings had affirmed his earlier denials of fees, and then, after the Eleventh Circuit reversed him, awarded only $50,700, including $5,100 for costs and expenses, of the almost $144,000 in attorney fees claimed for over 1,000 hours of work.[88] In other instances of severe delay, some Title VII cases begun in 1965 did not produce fees until the mid-1970s. In 1982, public interest groups won an appellate court ruling allowing them over $375,000 in fees in the *Gautreaux* housing case, which extended back beyond

1969. This award did cover the entire period of the case, even though the early years of the case predated the 1976 Fees Act, because the court took into account the case's continuing nature and the defendant housing authority's resistance.[89]

As Justice Blackmun remarked in a recent case, litigating organizations have made it "clear that we can expect many meritorious actions will not be filed, or, if filed, will be prosecuted by less experienced and able counsel" if adequate attorneys' fees cannot be recovered.[90] Thus policy about attorneys' fees—in statutes, the Federal Rules, and court interpretations of both—demands constant attention from litigating organizations. National civil rights organizations have sought to facilitate getting cooperating attorneys their attorney fees, although their own internal mechanisms can also be a cause of the delay in lawyers' receiving fees and expenses. The Lawyers' Committee, which was among those in the successful effort to overturn the *Alyeska Pipeline* ruling, provided a memorandum on attorneys' fees to some 150 lawyers working on civil rights and poverty issues, in which it urged them to be more assertive concerning fee awards; after receiving a large number of inquiries about attorneys' fee issues, the organization developed a guidebook on attorneys' fee laws; and, in 1972, took a further step by creating an Attorneys' Fees Project as a clearinghouse and backup center.

Attorneys' fees can be a strong incentive to initiate a case and can incline groups to pursue cases in which attorney fee awards would be available rather than other cases. This is said to explain emphasis on employment discrimination cases, where attorney fees are available,[91] and on class actions because they provide substantial attorneys' fees. Another possible distortion is that, with lawyers paid only for successful litigation (and certain litigation-related activity), attorneys' fees may discourage the pursuit of legislative initiatives and innovative legal theories.[92] Examination of Section 1983 cases, however, shows no "burst of civil rights litigation" under the Civil Rights Fees Act and "no evidence that fee awards in civil rights cases are higher or more common than in non-civil rights cases," thus challenging the idea that fee awards drive certain types of civil rights litigation.[93] And civil rights lawyers take cases like protracted death penalty cases where attorneys' fees are not available even though they will lose money.

5

The Use of Litigation

In this chapter, we examine litigation and its relation to other political activities such as legislation and administrative proceedings. We do so to learn *why* people turn to the law, and, in particular, why they turn to litigation. Among the reasons offered for interest groups' involvement in litigation to which attention will be given, some are related to access to courts or incentives to engage in litigation; others relate to the legal profession's mindset; and another, powerful argument is that our belief in rights propels us toward litigation.

Talk of race relations often begins with, or soon includes, court cases, perhaps because much race relations policy has been developed in the courts, with contemporary civil rights policy dating from the Supreme Court's landmark 1954 school desegregation ruling in *Brown v. Board of Education.* Through the vision it embodied and the success it represented, *Brown* created the impetus that led lawyers to persist in litigation efforts and served as "the principal inspiration to others who seek change through litigation,"[1] the paradigm of planned litigation for social change. In part for these reasons, the prevailing view became one that "race is peculiarly the province of the judiciary," with "racial questions . . . routinely defined in constitutional or ideological terms, with principle and precedent substituted for bargaining and brokering."[2]

While *Brown* invariably begins talk of civil rights litigation, it has a much longer history. The NAACP did not have a full-time staff attorney until Charles Houston was hired in 1935, but it had had a concerted focus on litigation since the late 1920s and had been involved in litigation even earlier. Even before then, in the early nineteenth century the Quaker-initiated New York Manumission Society had a strong legal arm which engaged in at least two hundred cases as it "represented Negroes claiming freedom, prosecuted actions to prevent export of Negroes from the state, and tried to prevent importing slaves."[3] In the late nineteenth century, Booker T. Washington proposed a test case attack on the Louisiana "grandfather clause" (barring voting by those whose grandfathers had been ineligible to vote), raised funds for the case, and influenced its strategy.[4] This took place at roughly the same time as the challenge to laws requiring that blacks ride in separate train cars, resulting in the Supreme Court's "separate but equal" pronouncement in *Plessy v. Ferguson*.

Controversy over the appropriateness and effectiveness of civil rights litigation, and whether it has been used without adequate consideration of alternative political modes of mobilizing for rights, also is not new, being evident as early as the formative years of the NAACP's legal efforts. The question arose again in *Brown*'s aftermath, the more so as it became clear that the ruling, while a crucial symbolic victory, brought few results, particularly in the Deep South. This failure led many blacks, while not rejecting litigation entirely, to turn to more direct methods such as sit-ins and demonstrations. In the struggle to obtain equal access to public accommodations and to achieve voting rights, the prominence of newer civil rights organizations, such as the Southern Christian Leadership Conference (SCLC), the Student Nonviolent Coordinating Committee (SNCC), and the Congress of Racial Equality (CORE), stemmed from the feeling that the NAACP's reliance on litigation was both unsuccessful and too oriented to the status quo.

Although the new groups' success prompted the NAACP to move closer to its constituents, it neither changed its major emphasis on litigation, which "comparative advantage" led it to continue, nor eliminated the reservations about litigation. Those views were held even by those engaged heavily in it. Although they might not reveal their concerns because they were fully committed to their work, did not wish to appear to weaken efforts in which they were engaged, or were simply too busy "in the trenches" to be reflective, at times they stated their ambivalence. NAACP Legal Defense Fund director-counsel Julius L. Chambers did so thirty-five years after *Brown*, when, while asserting that the Supreme Court had in *Brown* provided a standard and an ideal on which a dialogue can be based, and arguing that with limited resources the courts and constitutional cases are the best way to proceed, still conceded the force of arguments that courts do little more than issue hortatory statements and render decisions only in whites' interests. Others are more hesitant about the emphasis on litigation. Writing after his long ACLU service, Aryeh Neier said that "it may be that concentration of energies and resources on the ordinary political processes is in the best interests of racial minorities," but he asserted nonetheless that in race relations, "Most gains could not have been achieved at all, much less enduringly, in any other way" than through litigation."[5]

Why Litigation?

"Law on the books" does not become "law in operation" by some immaculate process but as a result of choices in a process in which someone—individuals, or groups, or the government—seeks to mobilize the law. Mobilization of law—"the process by which a legal system acquires its cases" through actions by individual citizens or the state, or "*how* the law is set in motion"[6]—like any political mobilization, requires not simply feeling or belief; although ideology is often crucial, organization, resources, and events present and past also play a part in decisions to mobilize the law. Law is mobilized in courts and also in administrative tribunals, to which in some instances cases must be taken before courts will hear them. The presence of multiple legal actors produces "uneven movement of cases into the legal system"[7] and multiple patterns of mobilization. Citizen mobilization of the law can be seen in efforts to allow individuals, often assisted by groups, to enforce civil rights law. Group mobilization of law occurs when interest groups or their lawyers "actively seek to assure that their view of the legal good is imposed on the society at large."[8] Lawyers who bring civil rights cases most often focus on mobilization *of* law, not on mobilization *by* law, although cases can produce political mobilization.[9]

Most frequently cited among reasons for use of litigation is that it is a *last resort* when elected political officials do not respond or goals cannot be achieved in other arenas. Indeed, the Supreme Court recognized this reason for litigation when it upheld the NAACP's right to initiate civil rights cases. "Groups which find themselves unable to achieve their objectives through the ballot," wrote Justice Brennan in *NAACP v. Button*, "frequently turn to the courts," which "may well be the sole practicable avenue open to a minority to petition for redress of grievances." [10] A strong case can be made for the assertion that going to court "usually arises out of an interest group's frustration at its inability to secure the relief it seeks from those branches of government charged with the responsibility for weighing its interests against competing interests." [11] Examples can be found in many civil rights topics, including the NAACP's early efforts to prohibit lynching; housing discrimination and exclusionary zoning; and school segregation, where the Boston case produces a contemporary instance: When public officials refused to support any desegregation proposals of substance, "pro-integration forces relied increasingly on the courts to resolve the conflict." [12]

Closely related to the "last resort" explanation is one related to the notion that law can protect those otherwise weak and redress their harms: groups turn to court when they lack political resources that make them effective elsewhere or are seriously disadvantaged relative to other interests, that is, they litigate "because they are temporarily, or even permanently, disadvantaged in terms of their abilities to attain successfully their goals in the electoral process, within the elected political institutions or in the bureaucracy," because "in the judicial branch legal resources can sometimes offset political resources." [13]

The "political disadvantage" notion explains why interest groups use the courts in pursuit of their goals even if they do not expect to be particularly successful; they believe they will be *more* successful than in the legislature or executive branches. With the legislature and executive branches inaccessible to groups, they have little choice. Groups combating exclusionary zoning, like the Open Suburbs Movement (OSM), were forced to use litigation because they had little popular support and thus could not obtain results they desired from the political process.[14] In this circumstance, the courts may seem promising. Thus even groups which distrusted law went to court not so much because of "strong faith in state institutions but rather because, compared to other alternatives, litigation has some possibilities."[15] And in seeking support for civil rights, people can often do better in court than in the other branches. Thus, for example, federal appeals courts showed a greater, more persistent commitment to school desegregation than did executive agencies, and their orders reduced segregation more than did school board or federal agency action.[16] More generally, at least starting with the Warren Court, courts were "the most accessible . . . instrument of government for bringing about the changes in public policy sought by social protest movements," and federal courts "reflect[ed] less a local than a national legal culture" in which more weight was given to protection of rights.[17] Indeed, the Warren Court's civil liberties record, reinforced by its easing of access to the courts for those wishing to challenge government action, increasingly led groups to turn to the courts, not as a last resort, but first for redress of their grievances, with litigation becoming the principal, or even exclusive, means of redressing grievances.

The political disadvantage argument explains in some instances why groups turn to litigation, but it does not explain sufficiently participation of some interests that have considerable strength in other political arenas, and thus the argument should be expanded.[18] Although at times groups participate in the judicial arena because they are *temporarily* disadvantaged elsewhere, in other situations they obtain legislative victories but meet with judicial resistance—and so must focus on the latter, as "pro-decency" groups, seeking to limit obscenity, had to do.[19] Interests with strength elsewhere but lacking advantage in the judicial forum may intervene there to try to right the balance in perspectives presented to the judges, as contemporary conservative litigators have done.[20] As "repeat players," dominant social interests such as large corporations have long invested effort in the legal system not only to resolve disputes but also to create rules for their future advantage,[21] and wealthy, established groups are more likely to be found in court pursuing their goals than are organizations seeking liberal policy. These situations make litigation of rights claims "not the largest part of the picture of interest-group litigation."[22]

Some civil rights groups, like the LDF or the Lawyers' Committee, have also become "repeat players"; as large-volume litigators, they can obtain advantages in choice of forum, cases to pursue, and the pace at which they move different cases. This makes a group's longevity a resource of particular importance; with some lawsuits taking much time, groups must adopt a "long view" to be able to stay with lawsuits to their conclusion—and thus to think of using them as a means of pursuing goals.[23] An organization with longevity may also be better able to absorb a negative ruling than a new organization seeking to establish itself. However, even a newcomer to civil rights litigation, bringing cases to achieve publicity, may be able to profit from such adversity, particularly when a ruling, even if negative, gives some legitimacy to its stance. This suggests why groups' use of litigation is related to the *courts'* requirements and institutional characteristics, and how those fit with groups' interests and goals; the goals of affecting public policy, producing social change, and contributing to development of civil rights doctrine are thought especially suited to adjudication.[24]

An organization's relative political and judicial advantage is one factor in its litigation activity. Litigators' strength at the appropriate level of government is another that helps to explain organizations' effectiveness. For example, major housing litigating organizations, highly centralized national organizations, were disadvantaged, for they lacked local political strength to deal with suburban planning commissions and city councils.[25] This is also illustrated by the efforts of "defensive litigants," whose strategy is to convince judges "that prevailing constitutional norms, already favorable to his interests, should be applied." While they were effective in invoking precedent and custom before local judges who shared their views, they were not prepared to cope with more nationally oriented values which "aggressive litigants," "seeking innovative interpretations of the Constitution" and social change, invoked in the Supreme Court. The defensive litigants could not defend their positions either in terms of the latter values or through support from an appropriate organizational network, which they lacked.[26] If in that situation, defensive litigants had conservative values, later, as the Supreme Court became conservative, the reverse became true. Indeed, earlier aggressive litigants became the "defensive" ones as they tried to uphold now-older liberal precedent and at times turned to state courts when those courts were seen as providing favorable results.

As this indicates, another element to be considered when deciding to use litigation is whether available precedents can be adapted for the group's purposes or new ones will have to be developed. When it was trying to eliminate racial restrictive covenants and school segregation, the NAACP Legal Defense Fund "had to create its own favorable precedents to counterbalance earlier negative decisions" and, moreover, had to do so when the environment was only beginning to accept changes in race relations. On the other hand, Legal Services Program lawyers later "were able to invoke prepackaged precedents" and to do so at a time far more hospitable to their claims.[27] Where precedents are ambiguous, the resulting legal uncertainty may increase the likelihood that interest groups will litigate to establish new precedent.[28]

Litigation appears to have some intrinsic advantages as well as relative ones. Judicial decisions, particularly Supreme Court rulings on constitutional matters, are difficult to dislodge. Thus a victory there is more permanent, decreasing uncertainty and stabilizing the environment, than one in Congress or in presidential administrations, which will be affected by election shifts. Litigation to obtain favorable judicial interpretations of a new law may also nail down and protect a legislative victory against opponents' continuing efforts to weaken it, thus helping to produce the benefits the legislation promises; this has occurred with respect to both employment and voting.

If groups are drawn *to* litigation by its benefits, they are also drawn *into* litigation by others' initiatives; for example, when civil rights groups had to respond to white males' "reverse discrimination" cases challenging affirmative action programs. More generally, involvement in litigation to protect interests is forced when others bring cases impinging on an organization's concerns; such activity must be undertaken even when resources are scarce. Thus organizations "get dragged kicking and screaming with the budget people saying there was no money." Government litigators have put civil rights groups on the defensive and drawn them into lawsuits by taking action against policies the groups have won earlier. Thus a group's entrance into litigation, as well as its posture in a particular case, may be reactive or responsive rather than planned and self-initiated. Government litigators likewise can be put on the defensive. For example, the Agricultural Adjustment Administration found it had to respond when others asked the courts to reject government tax claims, and the National Recovery Administration's top officials "were finally stung into action . . . by an unexpected decision in a case in which the NRA was a bystander and of which it was totally unaware."[29]

Another set of reasons for participation in litigation concerns the absence or presence of resources, which become part of a rough assessment of costs and benefits in the decision to litigate, even if no formal cost-benefit calculus is undertaken. Availability of resources such as attorneys' fees may serve as an incentive to engage in activity necessary to obtain them. Lawyers are particularly important in this regard. If an organization has salaried attorneys on staff, even if they were not initially hired to litigate, "start-up costs" of entering litigation are diminished. Staff lawyers' desire to demonstrate their worth is one noneconomic pressure to litigate. Professional pride and a feeling of having been relegated to lower status by demonstrations and other 1960s civil rights activity help explain the NAACP Legal Defense Fund's involvement in the death penalty campaign.[30] When young lawyers with a positive orientation toward litigation rather than, for example, lobbying, join public interest law firms, which are formed specifically for litigation, that self-selection reinforces the organizations' orientation. Also relevant, and serving to develop pressure for litigation, is "the desire of each litigator to be the first to persuade a court to make new law" and "the realization by each litigator that if he doesn't push for the development of new doctrine other litigators will."[31]

Lawyers' desire to litigate is related to perhaps the most important factor explaining contemporary group-related civil rights litigation—ideology or mindset, not only ideology with respect to policy goals sought but also ideology about the propriety of litigation itself. For example, conservative public interest law firms were constrained from litigation by conservatives' division over how the courts are to be used and by reluctance "to advocate judicial activism, regardless of ideological bent."[32] Lawyers entering litigation do not invariably do so for ideological reasons but may treat litigation "as a practical necessity, not as an ideological opportunity," as in cases brought to help fugitive slaves.[33] Lawyers' ideologies affect the focus of their concerns—on client, group, or principle; their orientations toward the law and toward clients; and their decisions to initiate litigation and to proceed with and appeal cases already initiated.[34] In examining civil rights litigation, we may assume all lawyers value litigation for its own sake, but some others seem predisposed against it, preferring negotiation and persuasion; at times, they see litigation as an embarrassment which demonstrates their failure to reach agreements with opposing parties. They may also see litigation as inappropriate if they view legal change as best coming from legislators, not judges, a view which "precludes the possibility of innovative litigation." [35]

Civil rights interest group lawyers' preference for litigation is quite clear. Indeed, civil rights groups, and others such as environmentalists, turn "almost reflexively" to the courts [36]—and almost invariably to the federal courts. As Jack Greenberg observed, "Despite the occasionally greater ease or effectiveness of legislative or administrative law making, lawyers still love most the judicial forum." [37] Litigation becomes part of a mindset, which creates a momentum, in which, having started litigation for whatever reason, litigants continue even when the situation changes; thus the mindset hinders prompt response to changes in a group's environment.

Many, perhaps most, civil rights interest group litigators seem to embrace an ideology, *the myth of rights,* according to which litigation, the "principal institutional mechanism," can produce both statements of rights and their implementation, which in turn will produce change.[38] As with most rights-based language, the myth involves heavy dependence on lawyers, although mental patient liberation groups' use of a "liberation ideology," in which individuals seek political involvement without the assistance of professionals, has demonstrated that ideology can focus on rights without heavy reliance on litigation.[39]

The myth of rights, in exaggerating the change lawyers and litigation can accomplish, interferes with allocation of resources to techniques of *political* mobilization that might more effectively achieve rights.[40] This concern was expressed by the civil rights lawyer who asked whether anyone had said that litigation killed the civil rights movement. Saying, "Of course, perhaps it was only manslaughter, not murder, because it wasn't intended," he said the effect was the same because the lawyers were saying " 'Concentrate on what we're doing and don't make waves' when it was only the waves that would accomplish anything." Another civil rights veteran suggested that the Supreme Court's conservative movement may be a "good thing" in forcing people to get away from litigation—indeed, as the conservative justices themselves have at times suggested, to use the political process instead of the courts.[41]

Is Litigation Successful?

With propensity to litigate depending in part on expecting success,[42] and others' litigation success increasing litigation's attractiveness and prompting more litigation, we need to know whether litigation has been successful. Success can be defined as winning, but that may be too limited, because litigation can give "hope, encouragement, psychological sustenance and support"; may produce leverage through which a group can, for example, extract a statement from a school board of its commitment to desegregation and increase its bargaining power with private entities and in other political and governmental arenas; and, perhaps most important, may provide legitimacy by reassuring elites that the litigating group has moral worth, thus prompting their support.[43]

Litigating civil rights interest groups seem to have had success in some instances but poor records in others. The Supreme Court accepted the position of groups litigating prisoners' rights only one-fourth of the time; the ACLU's National Prisoners Project lost every case from its 1972 inception through 1982, with including several that were "quite devastating."[44] On the other hand, women's rights organizations acting as direct sponsors of litigation or as amicus curiae in the Supreme Court's 1969–1980 Terms won almost two-thirds (63%) of their cases with gender-based claims, with the ACLU's efforts increasing chances of success 16 percent.[45] The NAACP Legal Defense Fund won 70 percent of its directly sponsored race discrimination cases in the Supreme Court from 1970 to 1981, doing only slightly less well (61.5%) as amicus; the Lawyers Committee's success rate also exceeded 60 percent.[46] Roughly one-sixth of a broader range of appellate equal employment opportunity decisions through 1984 could be considered "victories," defined as "final victory for plaintiff, with remedy substantially as sought." Defined "as any victory—final or nonfinal, with full or partial remedy," victory rose to close to three-fifths (58.1%); for final rulings alone, over two-fifths of cases (41.8%) were full or partial victories.[47] Yet these findings may be overstated because success is attributed whenever the group participates. If cases in which groups were involved are matched with those in which they were not, groups appear *not* to do better than individuals, although national groups do better than "subnational" groups and also do better on constitutional cases.[48]

Critics suggest that litigation is not effective in achieving rights. Why? For one thing, because of lack of knowledge of the law and failure to see problems as ones for which the law can give protection, laws are often not invoked by those they are supposed to protect, perhaps because they do not see the laws' direct meaning unless and until the laws are implemented for them. When the law *is* invoked, victory is by no means guaranteed, either for individuals seeking redress or those seeking precedents to assist others. And courts may produce negative rather than positive precedents, including rulings that make achieving rights more difficult, such as decisions limiting standing to sue. Thus those seeking advances can set back their own causes and the use of litigation generally by failing to be aware of such limits.[49]

Nor do apparent victories necessarily translate into gains for intended beneficiaries. Courts decide in someone's favor, but, as a result of evasion, resistance, or neglect by those who lost in court, nothing happens. The ingenuity of those seriously committed to a longstanding practice can be considerable, so that after one knocks down the first target, several more appear, leaving the litigator to hack away at more of the hydra's heads. Litigators' habit of incrementally attacking only one aspect of a problem at a time allows opponents to adopt one fall-back position after another. This was true with efforts to eliminate school segregation or to secure a woman's right to obtain an abortion, where each invalidated restriction was followed by several others. Thus "litigation begets litigation" because victories won in court can be sustained only by more litigation.[50] Indeed, initial litigation victories may up the ante as demands must be increased to achieve realization of what judges have declared. The lack of gain for potential beneficiaries is exacerbated by giving more attention to developing new precedent and by failing correspondingly to follow up broad rulings in order to provide the ruling's practical benefits for the many individuals who could obtain them if someone were to take legal action on their behalf.[51]

Case-by-case litigation has also been called "totally inadequate to eliminate unlawful discriminatory systems," with even class actions aimed to help many or government "pattern or practice" cases "limited to a comparatively small percentage of the workers employed by major multiplant corporations."[52] This validates the early fear of NAACP officials, who, while favoring litigation, thought the litigation approach "too cautious to help segments of the black community needing immediate protection."[53] Group-based litigation may also be quite limited in dealing with redistributive policy. Litigation was tried, seriously and with a clear plan, to alter the welfare system, and some headway was made, but, at least in retrospect, on balance "the idea that poverty in America might be ended through litigation seems hopelessly naive," because it is "too puny an instrument with which to undertake a task of such magnitude."[54]

Whether or not external observers believe litigation to be effective, organizations continue to use it as a primary mechanism if leaders believe that the courts are effective. Perhaps as part of adherence to the myth of rights, they believe the myth of their own success. Thus the recently advanced empirically grounded argument that courts have not accomplished much in major areas like school desegregation or abortion[55] may be beside the point because litigators believe they can make a difference; and, although science by anecdote is not good social science, the lawyers' views, based on their immediate experience, is that litigation does work, so they continue to use it. Yet in doing so out of inertia, they may hurt themselves, by assisting in the generation of other organizations based on the same model, which then compete for the same resources; and by focusing on issues like school desegregation that are more nearly subject to remedy by litigation, instead of attacking redistributive problems which may be more important for the people they believe they serve.

What about Administrative Agencies?

Because administrative agencies, once they have accepted a complaint, undertake to prosecute a case and bear the cost of doing so, administrative proceedings, closely related to litigation, may be a viable, perhaps more effective, alternative, at least in certain circumstances. However, this belief was not shared by civil rights advocates on the basis of their experience prior to the 1964 Civil Rights Act. State fair employment or fair housing agencies, which had few powers and were not particularly assertive in using them, accomplished little.[56] The National Labor Relations Board had greater powers to issue cease-and-desist orders and to petition courts for affirmative relief such

as back pay. Yet, while acknowledging minorities' right to file discrimination complaints, the Board had resisted charges that a union
had breached its statutory duty of fair representation when it discriminated against blacks. Even after it ruled in 1964 that it would
consider a union's race-based refusal to process a worker's grievance
an actionable unfair labor practice (and then decided that unions had
an affirmative obligation to eliminate racial discrimination), the NLRB
was unwilling to act against employers who discriminated. That left
the NAACP, while attempting to press forward with favorable NLRB
rulings, having to initiate litigation against unions based on the duty
of fair representation in litigation that was "costly, time-consuming,
and unpredictable."[57]

With such negative experience, it was no wonder that civil rights
groups viewed new administrative devices in the civil rights field
skeptically. The absence of past experience with the agencies meant
civil rights groups lacked sophisticated understanding of operation of
government agencies when it became important to deal with them,
for example, in connection with the development of desegregation
guidelines in the 1960s. Yet the pursuit of civil rights through the
administrative process was very important, not only for school desegregation but also, and more so, for employment discrimination, because Title VII required filing complaints with the Equal Employment
Opportunity Commission or a comparable state agency in so-called
deferral states before one could sue in court.

Administrative enforcement of Title VI by the Department of
Health Education and Welfare in school desegregation did produce
effects. Although many school districts did not desegregate until
threatened with loss of their state education aid or with loss of both
federal and state funds,[58] some districts did comply when their federal
funds were impounded, and federal administrative action achieved
far more than did state and local officials' actions. Somewhat less was
achieved through judicial action: one and one-half times as many students were reassigned by HEW as by state and local officials, while the
courts reassigned twice as many as state and local officials.[59] The interplay of administrative and judicial action, however, at times worked
against achieving desegregation, as school districts under court order
were considered in compliance with HEW's Desegregation Guidelines even when their desegregation was less than the guidelines
demanded.

Even when the administration was supportive, there were some notable failures to follow up on threatened withdrawal of federal education funds to school districts, most notably in Chicago, where political pressure led to reversal of agency action.[60] Of course, when administrative agencies were headed by appointees of a presidential administration unsupportive of civil rights, they could act to drain resources that groups expended to counter the agencies' actions.[61] Nor were agencies charged with enforcing Title VI and Title VII seen as strong or particularly aggresssive: the EEOC's most important contribution may have been the guidelines it developed to interpret the law's provisions.[62] Although empowered in 1972 to file suits seeking injunctions and to bring "pattern or practice" suits, the EEOC initially did not have authority to issue "cease-and-desist" orders and it was expected to rely on conciliation before issuing the complainant a "right to sue" letter. Also, rather than pursuing its own investigations, the EEOC tended to rely on complaints. However, Title VII was said to be administratively workable because of the threat of private court action,[63] because once a complainant filed an administrative complaint, the person could go to court even if the EEOC thought the claim lacked merit or did not act within a specified time. Indeed, litigation came to be the primary engine of enforcement for Title VII as the very lack of EEOC enforcement power led the civil rights bar to develop litigation efforts.[64]

That the effectiveness of administrative mechanisms is intimately related to and reinforced by litigation is also seen in the linkage of administrative and judicial action in voting rights. The basic process for dealing with changes in election procedures was administrative (preclearance by the Department of Justice); jurisdictions disagreeing with DOJ's refusal to approve a proposed change could seek to obtain declaratory judgments from the federal court in the District of Columbia; and litigation was used to force local jurisdictions to submit changes.

Litigation and Other Political Activities

Litigation's prominence may obscure other political activities in which civil rights interest groups engage, although lobbying of legislators and executive branch officials and litigation to produce social change are all types of political activity. Yet they may occur simultaneously, as we can see from civil rights activity in Mississippi, where the presence of litigation was correlated with mobilization of blacks into electoral politics.[65] They may also be linked, as when Common Cause used litigation to obtain publicity for its legislative concerns on campaign finance reform, and when those opposing Army surveillance of the military used the *Laird v. Tatum* litigation both for publicity and, through discovery, to obtain information for use at legislative hearings.

Separation of litigation from other political activity in the field of civil rights has been more striking than in other policy areas, but groups devoting a significant portion of their activities to litigation do engage in other activities. Most obviously, the NAACP has long engaged in lobbying and litigation simultaneously. For example, in attacking housing discrimination, the NAACP "challenged suburban zoning in the courts, lobbied for open housing in Washington, and conducted educational efforts,"[66] and the name of Clarence Mitchell, its long-time and highly regarded lobbyist, ranked as high in the organization as that of Thurgood Marshall, the premier litigator. The Lawyers' Committee likewise often "uses a blend of several different techniques to approach an issue or attack a problem," engaging in "monitoring administrative agency actions, participating in agency proceedings, analyzing and drafting legislation, writing research reports, and keeping client groups informed about their legal rights and remedies."[67] The linkages between litigation and lobbying can also be seen in government efforts to constrain advocacy, such as the Reagan administration's rules under which recipients of federal funds would have had to separate office space in connection with lobbying from other facilities.

Combining litigation and other activities is not new. In its efforts to combat lynching, the NAACP "resorted to investigations, disclosures, conferences, publicity, negotiation with influential persons in government and business, lobbying, and litigation to achieve their objectives." Activities other than litigation, particularly lobbying, had initially been more prominent; linking litigation with them showed the growing importance of the organization's legal staff.[68] Even in the civil rights movement, which is associated with direct action, political action and litigation were combined. Although the lawyers' task of getting demonstrators out of jail quickly to continue their activities was clearly secondary, the place of litigation in "direct action"

should not be underestimated. Indeed, in the Montgomery bus boycott, which many see as the prime instance of direct action, "The legal
system—more accurately federal law and federal judges—played a
pivotal, indeed controlling, role in integrating Montgomery's buses."[69]
A particular linkage can be seen in the attention interest groups have
long paid to the Senate's confirmation of federal judges, to try to produce a more favorable—or at least less hostile—reception for their
cases. This dates at least from the NAACP's central involvement in
defeating the nomination of Judge John Parker in 1930, with such activity more visible in connection with the Haynsworth and Carswell
nominations. However, the NAACP and other groups did not systematically monitor and combat judicial nominations until the late 1980s,
when the Leadership Conference on Civil Rights played an important
part in the defeat of the Bork nomination.

Litigation and other political activities often follow each other in
clear sequences. Most obvious is that litigation occurs only after political activities appear to be failing or fail. At times, the shift from
legislation to litigation is quick: the ink may not be dry on certain
new statutes, such as those imposing conditions on obtaining abor-
tions, before there is a rush to the courthouse for an injunction. At
other times, as in northern school cases, there was a lengthy sequence
of bargaining, position-taking, and rights-claiming before black complainants went to federal court.[70] This pattern has been described in
greater detail as entailing pressing of claims to school officials, school
board appointment of an advisory study committee, release of the
committee's report followed by the board's adoption of some of the
recommendations, an election to recall school board members who
supported desegregation, and election of a new board which revokes
the earlier desegregation plan before adopting a more limited one, at
which point litigation ensues.[71] In school desegregation, where most
school board action resulted from political bargaining, not from litigation, the filing of a lawsuit, as "essentially another move in the political
chess game,"[72] makes us forget the considerable prior political activity.

Political activity may also follow litigation, when efforts are made to
implement court victories in a community. Some school desegregation
lawyers found that using litigation to circumvent the political process
was a strength—but it was also a defect because, after going to court,
the lawyers would have to deal with those they had sued, the very
people with authority to convert a judge's ruling into practice.[73] Once a

defendant's liability for discrimination has been established, the most complex part of the case—crafting and agreeing on a remedy—is yet to come. Once consent decrees or judicial orders are obtained, monitoring is necessary to ensure proper implementation, which requires paying close heed to the political process. Treating litigation as separate from political efforts may hinder the implementation of judicial victories.

Legislative interest may also have been stimulated by litigation, or experience with litigation may show litigators the need for legislative activity, particularly to retrieve rights limited by the courts, as in the Civil Rights Act of 1991 and earlier reversals of Supreme Court decisions. When, as in the effort to rewrite Section 2 of the Voting Rights Act to overturn *City of Mobile v. Bolden,* litigators developed expertise useful in the legislative arena, much legislative work will have been completed before the legislative campaign starts.

Turning to legislation when all else is lost may not be any more successful than the litigation which prompted the legislative initiative, and it suggests the need to have a strategy in which litigation is "more integrated conceptually and practically with nonjudicial political strategies for achieving social change."[74] Those attacking capital punishment were unsuccessful in persuading the Supreme Court that the death penalty discriminated against racial minorities. Saying that they would turn to Congress or to the state legislatures perhaps was an ironic choice because the effort to eliminate the death penalty started in legislatures, and lack of success there drove these same groups to litigation to fend off state death penalty actions. Yet the chances for a legislative victory were slim despite the Court's concession in *McClesky v. Kemp* that race affected the criminal justice process on the death penalty. This concession was a "powerful statement" that could serve as a basis for a legislative challenge. In this situation, just as in the abortion controversy, with defeat in the Supreme Court highly likely, death penalty opponents (like pro-choice supporters) should have linked litigation with legislative efforts earlier rather than suffering a major judicial defeat before focusing on the legislative arena. Instead it took defeats like *Webster* and *Casey* to produce a significant increase in legislative action.

Uses of Litigation

Despite disputes over emphasis to be placed on litigation, it is well established as a principal tool in the quest for civil rights. How to use that litigation, for what groups in the minority community, and with regard to what subjects, remains a major issue. Does one initiate a lawsuit to attract the attention of an adversary who had previously ignored you, or use a lawsuit primarily as a bargaining chip? Does one settle or go to trial? Or does one pursue the case "all the way to the Supreme Court"? Decisions must be made on how frequently to use litigation and how far to pursue it. Frequent, systematic use of litigation increases litigation effectiveness as participants become "re-peat players." Trial and appellate proceedings are essential if litigating groups are to "make law," and civil rights cases may be more likely to go to trial than some other types of litigation because where an entire institution is challenged, resolving complaints short of formal proceedings is difficult: employers will resist when faced with class action cases affecting their hiring and promotion practices, and elected school board members are not likely to accept demands for school desegregation.

What goals should be achieved through litigation? Interest groups with a Washington, D.C., connection supported statutory interpreta-tion as a litigation objective most strongly, with constitutional litiga-tion given slightly less emphasis. Given a lower priority was "securing legal relief for the immediate parties to the litigation." However, civil rights and social welfare organizations, along with labor unions and public interest law firms, ranked achieving immediate relief "the most highly on average." Overall, publicity received the least support.[75] Some goals sought through litigation are "outcome-oriented." These include establishing new constitutional rights through precedential rulings, developing favorable guidelines under statutes, and crafting appropriate remedies.[76] Goals for the longer term include establish-ing the litigator's credibility or producing a favorable environment for later endeavors. Other goals, such as generating publicity to as-sist in attracting contributions, are more closely related to organiza-tional maintenance. If litigants focus attention on their cause, they can achieve some of these goals even when undertaking litigation with low expectations of success as conventionally defined. Thus even when courts are hostile or "infused with the spirit of *Plessy*," litigation can draw attention to the organization, demonstrate injustices, and rally support.[77]

Groups seldom direct all activity to one primary goal. They are likely to seek more than one simultaneously, perhaps through several activities, including agenda setting and balancing competing interests.[78] As a former civil rights litigator put it, "legal strategists I have known never viewed lawsuits as ends in themselves" but instead "saw them as means to embarrass, for publicity, and even to produce hostility."[79] Indeed, while most groups remain concerned about achieving victories, "they also use the judiciary to achieve other, more subtle ends."

6

Litigation Complexity
and Choice of Forum

In this chapter, we examine two further crucial aspects of civil rights litigation. The first is its increased complexity, which has considerable effects on organizations' ability to plan litigation and to pursue it over time. Here we focus on several elements of litigation complexity, including community demographics, changes in the discrimination to be attacked, and the length of cases. Then we turn to civil rights litigators' choice of federal or state courts in which to bring cases.

Litigation Complexity

Beginning in the 1960s, civil rights advocates contemplating litigation had to take into account that civil rights litigation itself had become more complex, increasing resource mobilization and resource allocation problems and affecting the likelihood of success.[1] Most obviously, complexity affected the conduct of litigation, both increasing courts' workload,[2] perhaps affecting judges' willingness to hear such cases, and making the type of strategy used in *Brown v. Board of Education* difficult to pursue.[3] Facing labor-intensive, evidence-heavy cases, civil rights litigants found it necessary to shift from volunteer cooperating attorneys to greater use of staff lawyers and to become involved from the beginning to exercise control, forgoing the strategy of entering cases at the appellate level as amicus curiae to address a constitutional issue. At the same time that complexity could hinder control, increased complexity of cases could increase an organization's control of litigation to the extent there were fewer cases outside of organizational litigators' purview. Here the complexity of individual cases receives our attention. That complexity, which includes greater complexity of legal issues, increased complexity of evidence, and a higher volune of evidence,[4] should not be confused with the complexity a litigating interest group faces when it engages in a campaign involving a large number of cases. Bringing cases in a multiplicity of communities increases the diversity, and thus the complexity, of the situation any litigator faces, as does the presence of litigation others have brought.

Civil rights litigation's increased complexity has been evident in all areas of law. It can be seen particularly in "public law" cases—polycentric controversies involving multiple parties, cases often entailing detailed and continuing relief and thus prolonged involvement by the judge hearing the case[5]—many of which are institutional reform cases aimed at public entities like mental hospitals and prisons.[6] Some employment discrimination suits, even if brought by and against private parties, are polycentric, with multiple parties—not only worker and employer, but minority workers, nonminority employees, and unions in addition to management—and complex remedies sought for classes of individuals, entailing changes in hiring, promotion, and layoff policies.

School desegregation cases are said to "remain the paradigm" for institutional reform litigation because they "undertook to accomplish no less than the remaking of a system of education and the social order in which that system was embedded," and thus required remedies like "revamping of student and teacher assignment practices, new school construction policies, and reallocation of resources."[7] Desegregation cases, which have been likened to "a whirlpool which pulls into itself all sorts of disputes," became still more complex because, once they are in court, political participants have been tempted to ask the judge to deal with their problems, stated in terms of education for purposes of the case.[8] In the *Adams* litigation to make the government enforce antidiscrimination laws, addition of parties and related cases "developed into a web of collateral actions" by national organizations representing other civil rights interests (women, the handicapped, and language groupings).[9] This illustrates that what may appear to be, and may have started as, a single lawsuit may in reality be a set of lawsuits—with multiple parties, some of whom are intervenors—in which different issues are raised, with the number of issues growing and thus, although no one matter may be at issue for the lawsuit's entire life, extending the litigation's life. At the remedy stage, matters may become especially complex, not only because the issues are complex but because even more parties intervene at that stage.

The Omaha and St. Louis school cases illustrate the extent to which additional party intervention can expand the range of interests in a case. The Justice Department brought the Omaha case but black plaintiffs—wishing to prevent the Justice Department and school board from settling the case without dealing with their concerns—intervened; they were represented by the Legal Aid Society, funded by Urban League efforts, and were provided further assistance by the Harvard Center for Law and Education. Added to private plaintiffs and the defendant school board in the St. Louis case were numerous suburban entities, the Justice Department, "the NAACP (which sued to intervene in the suit over the original plaintiff's objection because it opposed a potential settlement of the case), the city of St. Louis and the state of Missouri (concerned with who would pay for any court order, and one 'white parents group' (resisting the alteration of neighborhood schools)."[10]

Further "complexifying" school cases, adding evidentiary difficulties, and posing questions of manageability is the injection of housing problems to show that residential patterns, which defendant school boards claimed adventitious or accidental, in fact resulted from government action. Some judges (Weinstein in the Mark Twain Junior High School Case from Coney Island,[11] and, more recently, Judge Sand in the Yonkers case), dealt with both housing and schools, but most judges have kept them separate, reinforced by the Supreme Court's refusal in the Detroit case to deal with them together.

All this helps explain why proving a school district in the urban North, with thousands of children and many schools, to be actually segregated de jure, the result of official action, requires extensive work developing an "evidence-heavy" case even before developing the remedy is begun. And obviously support from an interest group was essential, as individual plaintiffs could not have mustered the necessary resources. In general, complex civil rights litigation, like institutional reform litigation, saw "the emergence of organizational and group plaintiffs . . . capable of the new kinds of systematic analysis and evidentiary presentations demanded by these suits."[12]

Many contemporary civil rights cases are quite different from earlier cases in which constitutional precedent was sought on the basis of affidavits without significant presentation of evidence. They were " 'clean' in the sense that time-consuming problems of investigation, proof, and attendant courtroom delay are not involved."[13] A civil rights lawyer from southside Virginia recalled that he could once put on a school desegregation case in fifteen minutes by calling the school superintendent and school board chairman as witnesses and reading school board minutes into the record. But instead of facing clear, statute-mandated de jure Southern segregation, one must contend with allegedly "de facto" segregation, explained by school officials as the result of individuals' residential choices. Instead of moderately populated or rural counties, litigators face increasingly decentralized metropolitan areas seventy to eighty miles wide. For example, the Kansas City, Missouri, case consumed sixty-four trial days, with 140 witnesses, 2,100 exhibits, and approximately 10,000 pages of depositions, all "brought in" by plaintiffs.[14] This is part of what is said to be the change in race relations litigation from pursuit of moral principle into a "technical enterprise,"[15] requiring heavy use of discovery and lengthy preparation before one approaches court for what may be a lengthy trial.

Lawyers must study information often not easily accessible—"hundreds, even thousands, of school board decisions made over many years," including "school board minutes, public statements by board members or school administrators, the historical pattern of school construction and attendance zones, the evolution of residential segregation, and the selection of sites for public housing" (as well as sites for schools themselves); the discovery process is not likely to produce evidence of violation.[16] However, in Boston, School Committee records "provid[ed] a clear record of resistance to desegregation, as well as hints of its motivations."[17]

Housing discrimination cases can be relatively straightforward, not requiring as great an "extent of proof" in terms of number of witnesses and time as for school and employment cases. While they may "look less complicated" because of the lack of a monitoring capacity equivalent to those for schools and jobs, cases under the Housing and Community Development Act are quite complex. So are cases challenging exclusionary land use, which are complex because "you must prove everything" and because defendants have opportunities to stall and to frustrate judicial orders.[18]

As Voting Rights Act cases shifted over time from denial of the franchise to vote dilution, they, too, became more complicated and also became "evidence-heavy." The first Voting Rights Act case involved a one-day trial, in which no expert witnesses were used, and generated an eight-page transcript. The 1990 Los Angeles County case, by contrast, entailed a forty-two-day trial, with fifteen expert witnesses (eight for one side, seven for the other), and generated several thousand pages of transcript.[19]

Remedy elements make matters still more complex. In Northern school cases, as a result of "dense urban settlements, multiethnic student populations, and diversified curricular programs," along with "transportation logistics," problems of remedy were extremely difficult, and it is no wonder that a principal LDF litigator felt that the Denver case was "almost unmanageable."[20] In cases involving large bureaucracies, whether big-city school districts or large corporations, the range of administrative activity that must be covered by remedy proposals, which must reach to lower levels of management, often required procedures like use of special masters to monitor compliance. And the implementation process, often itself complex and extended, may entail "continuing interactions among the judge, counsel for the parties and amici, affected administrators, and other individuals and organizations involved in the implementation process."[21]

The difficulty of some civil rights cases can perhaps be seen in the number of hours needed for them. The *Griggs* Title VII case required over 1,000 lawyer hours; the effort to cut off federal funds to the City of Chicago because of its police department's job discrimination "required thousands of hours of time from the two government attorneys, five law firms' attorneys, and two Lawyers' Committee attorneys."[22] And after the Supreme Court's ruling in *City of Mobile v. Bolden,* "at least 6,000 hours of lawyers' time, 800 hours of paralegals' time, 4,400 hours of expert witnesses and research assistants' time, and eleven and a half days of trial" were needed to prove that the city's election plan had been adopted with the intent to disfranchise racial monitors.[23]

A look at funds rather than hours shows that in the mid-1960s, before double-digit inflation, "a suit involving a trial in a district court, an appeal to a circuit court, and a petition for certiorari to the Supreme Court costs between $15,000 and $18,000," and plaintiffs in *Griggs*, which consumed $100,000 to get to the Supreme Court, were awarded "over $65,000 in costs, expenses, and attorneys' fees."[24] In the Dayton school case, which went to the Supreme Court twice, the NAACP's application for fees and costs for itself and retained counsel was $1.8 million—a figure which, if corrected for inflation to the late 1980s, would be closer to $3.0 million. Expenses for the Detroit school case, also twice in the Supreme Court, were just under $4 million; even with "extensive free legal counsel" from the Harvard Center for Law and Education, it cost the NAACP "several hundred thousand dollars" and was "a financial morass" for the group.[25]

Demographic Elements

Adding to the complexity of school litigation is its demographic environment. One element is racial separation (segregation). Once a desegregation order was handed down, the distances which children had to be transported to bring about desegregation were no greater, and perhaps less, than they had been when children were bused *to* segregate—at least until southern metropolitan areas began to take on their northern counterparts' residential characteristics, with residential separation between the races. In the North, greater residential segregation required longer bus rides to bring black students to previously all-white schools, or, less likely, vice versa. And fewer white students remained to participate in central city desegregation—in 1980, "only 4 percent of the public school enrollment in Washington, 8 percent in Atlanta, 9 percent in Newark, and 12 percent in Detroit."[26] This produced pressure for interdistrict remedies, where was also less of a problem in the South, with its combined city-county school districts including the suburbs, than in the North, with its separate suburban school districts.

African-Americans were also no longer the only "minority." The presence of Latinos—in 1982, 49 percent of the students in the Los Angeles Unified School District—posed somewhat different issues.

Some school boards treated them the same as blacks for desegregation purposes, considering a school integrated when it contained only blacks and Latinos. Native Americans were also combined with whites, for example, in the Omaha case.[27] That practice ended after rulings in the Corpus Christi and Denver school cases that Hispanics were an identifiable ethnic minority whose interests had to be considered separately. A major issue was whether to recognize special language needs, which would require Spanish-speaking teachers and might require concentration of Hispanic children in a few schools rather than spreading them throughout the school system.[28]

In the Denver case, the Court had seemed to say that Chicanos were a minority whose deprivations were to be remedied through integration, but in *Lau v. Nichols,* involving English language training for Chinese-speaking students, the Court, while saying the primary problem for these students was linguistic, left to education officials to choose the type of language training. These two messages gave no clear guidance to school officials as to whether Hispanics' language concerns were to be addressed through bilingual programs.

That blacks at times initiated desegregation cases without consulting Hispanics exacerbated friction that underlay the absence of Hispanic-black political coalitions; in Milwaukee, black plaintiffs (and the defendant school district) actively sought to prevent Hispanics' intervention.[29] At least outside the Southwest, a common pattern was for a school case to be initiated by black parents without either Latinos or a coalition of minorities; sometimes, when the case was initiated, the number of Hispanic students was small. Only later, at the remedy stage of the case, after desegregation planning had proceeded on the basis of black-white student ratios without Hispanic groups' input, the significant increase in numbers of such students led to Hispanic involvement in the case.[30] In the Boston school desegregation case, the first such major federal court encountered after recognition of Hispanics' concerns in the Denver case, the judge accepted El Comite as intervenor. However, recognition of its special concerns meant the likelihood that it could not speak "for the Chinese Education Association, for American Indians, for Cape Verdian Islanders."[31]

Changed Discrimination

A major reason why litigation became more complex was the changed nature of the discrimination. For example, by the time Title VII went into effect, "overt discrimination on the basis of race was not fashionable," and thus earlier, more blatant methods had been replaced by more subtle kinds, in which discrimination was camouflaged in practices, like testing, education requirements, or seniority plans, that seemed "facially neutral or color-blind but operated to perpetuate the effects of past discrimination."[32] This type of institutionalized discrimination required litigators to penetrate volumes of information and to know about differing patterns of discrimination in each plant and industry. This was among the reasons why a "*Brown* model" might not be directly applicable in that area of the law. To it one should add the requirement that administrative proceedings at the EEOC had to be exhausted before one could turn to court, and the large numbers of governmental and private players in the litigation, as a result of which no one could have "exclusive control over the sequence and pace of litigation," so that there was a greater likelihood settlement would end cases in which precedent was sought.[33]

In schools, discrimination likewise became "substantially more subtle and sophisticated in its origins, structure, and operation" than before Title VI's enactment, so that, where school systems appeared to be desegregated, "second generation" discrimination existed *within* individual schools. This took the form of faculty hiring practices, "discriminatory disciplinary practices, disproportionate assignment of minorities to special and vocational education classes, competency testing, ability tracking, and segregation within the school and classroom."[34] Even the Reagan administration's Assistant Attorney General for Civil Rights, William Bradford Reynolds, conceded that instances of "flagrant discrimination" were replaced by "subtler forms of discrimination," so that it "cost[s] more in terms of effective enforcement."[35]

Showing that increased complexity of litigation is not solely a contemporary phenomenon is that somewhat the same pattern, in which complexity increased, could be found in the NAACP's earlier cases seeking equalization of teacher salaries. Faced with attacks on salaries that explicitly discriminated on the basis of race, "School boards abandoned salary schedules that were overtly discriminatory, only to adopt schedules that reproduced discriminatory results by seeming to rely on nonracial factors." After the Court in the *Gaines* case required that "separate but equal" graduate education be made available within the plaintiff's state, the obviously unequal programs estab-

lished by the states also forced attorneys to litigate the issue exten-
sively to demonstrate that seemingly objective measures embodied
unequality. The salary cases in particular showed "how serious a drain
on the NAACP's limited resources one fact-laden case could be," just
as "substantial investments of attorney time" were necessary in cases
on inequalities within school systems.[36] However, despite parallels between the patterns of increasing complexity then and now, the earlier
evidence-heavy cases were likely not as complex as their current-day
cousins, and it is likely "that modern civil rights litigators would regard the equalization suits as relatively small-scale."[37]

Length of Litigation

Also related to litigation complexity is its length, with lengthy cases
requiring expenditure of additional resources. A former welfare litigator observed that some "resource-intense" cases are "compressed
into a short time frame," but others "last the better part of a decade
and require a long-term commitment of costly resources."[38] One case
in the housing area, such as the *Contract Buyers League* case, could
absorb large amounts of resources not only because "the transactions
involved in each case were complex and difficult to unravel and document" but because lawsuits to achieve the plaintiff's goals of remedies
for numerous house-buyers were "likely to be . . . extensive and protracted."[39] Even in more traditional areas of civil rights litigation, "One
school case could tie up a staff lawyer for months. It took a thick slice
of lawyer time and an outrageous amount of money to desegregate
a hospital, a lunch counter, or a public park."[40] Bringing a case as a
class action is likely to lengthen it, both because of the time necessary
to obtain class certification and to carry out the notification required
by the rules and because such a case is likely to be more complex than
one based on an individual complaint.

The length of cases is important beyond the additional expenditure
of resources required because it affects the conduct of the litigation
itself. For one thing, the longer the case, the more likely that a higher
court, and particularly the U.S. Supreme Court, will hand down decisions that will affect it in midstream, perhaps requiring relitigation
under a new standard. For example, the Dougherty County, Georgia, school case was twice remanded for consideration of new rulings—the Fifth Circuit's *Jefferson County* case and the Supreme Court's
Swann opinion. Lawyers in a case may also change, perhaps because

a private attorney may find it impossible to handle a major school or employment case along with a regular practice, forcing the lawyer's withdrawal from the case. At times this can produce shifts in litigation posture.

A litigator of school cases has estimated that urban school cases "may take five years or more between the filing of the action and the actual implementation of a plan," and the five-year figure is also said to apply to housing cases.[41] Employment discrimination cases are also lengthy. *Albemarle Paper Co. v. Moody,* initiated with complaints to the EEOC in 1966, resulted in a major Supreme Court Title VII case nine years later, and other employment discrimination cases did not receive lower federal court rulings until close to ten years after their initiation.[42]

School cases lasting a decade or more were not unusual. The initial busing order in the Prince Georges County, Maryland, school case came in 1972, but the parties were back in court ten years later because the school district had allowed some schools to become 90 percent black. Parts of the Buffalo school case, filed in 1972, were being decided on appeal in the Second Circuit in 1984. Other civil rights cases have been in litigation, either sporadically or continuously, for more than twenty years. There were rulings as late as 1984 in a suit filed in 1968 to desegregate Tennessee's institutions of higher education. The Dougherty County, Georgia, school case, initiated in 1963, did not produce desegregation until 1980–1981, but attorneys' fees issues remained, leading to an appeals court ruling in 1985.

The Dallas, Texas, case, like many initiated after *Brown,* was twenty-six years old in 1981. The Norfolk, Virginia, case, one of the vehicles in which the Reagan administration sought to assist ending mandatory desegregation remedies, had been in court since 1956, with busing implemented in 1971; in the 1980s, after the court had ruled the city had a unitary school system, efforts shifted to elimination of cross-town busing and a return to neighborhood schools. Some cases seem never to end. Fifth Circuit Judge Patrick Higginbotham, writing in 1987, observed pointedly, "We are reminded of just how old this case is, and just how fragile its holding, by the related circumstance that Chief Judge Clark, the most senior active member of this court, is recused because he was counsel in the case."[43] Most important symbolically is that twenty-five years after *Brown I,* a new school desegregation case against Topeka was filed. It was still pending on the thirtieth anniversary of the ruling, and received a ruling from the Tenth Circuit more than thirty-five years after *Brown I*. Three generations of the Scott family had served as local attorneys in that case, although the American Civil Liberties Union rather than the NAACP helped with "*Brown III*." As this illustrates, even when a particular case appears to have a measurable termination, the litigation against a particular school system may continue almost indefinitely. That is, the length of the controversy resulting in litigation is far longer than the length of *litigation* as measured from filing of a lawsuit to a judge's decision and the completion of appeals.

Choice Of Forum

One can can find consideration of the choice of forum as early as the *Plessy* litigation. There, before the lawyers decided to pursue a petition to the state supreme court, then seen as a "more expeditious" route to the U.S. Supreme Court, attention was given whether to proceed initially in state court or to prompt the state into a criminal case so that habeas corpus could be obtained from the federal court.[44] For many years, beginning in the mid-1950s, civil rights litigators would not have tarried long over whether to bring cases in federal or state courts. Not finding the answer difficult, they would have easily responded, "federal." All the civil rights lawyers interviewed for the present project chose the federal courts as their preferred forum. Because civil rights lawyers have been and are "more comfortable" in federal court, observed one, "It is unusual for us to be" in state courts. They saw the federal courts as having "greater sensitivity . . . to novel constitutional claims." However, as federal courts became more resistant to civil rights claims, the answer would not have been so easy, and the choice of forum, requiring considerable skill, would have become part of the increasing complexity of civil rights litigation.

Preference for Federal Courts

One of American federalism's most significant parts is its dual system of federal and state courts, with their concurrent jurisdiction over many matters while each retains some exclusive jurisdiction. Those who seek policy goals through the courts have a choice, within limits imposed by jurisdictional statutes, as to whether to proceed in federal or state courts. Preference for use of federal courts might be affected by the type of argument to be made, procedural concerns, courts' effective case-processing, and, particularly, the courts' *product,* as well as federal courts' inertial pull on civil rights litigators; state courts are preferred because of their more favorable positions on some issues. Although it does not necessarily explain why federal courts are chosen, federal litigation is said to involve greater stakes, to be complex, and to have more frequent participation of "repeat players."[45] It also is purported to have a higher ratio of external benefits (for those other than the immediate parties) to internal benefits (for the immediate parties) than does state court litigation; this resulted in a regular increase over time in federal education litigation in proportion to state litigation.[46]

Perhaps the best-known argument for using the federal courts was made in 1977 by ACLU attorney Burt Neuborne as part of his argument against the "myth of parity," the idea that federal and state courts are equally preferable for handling civil liberties and rights claims. Neuborne found that because of the importance of the fact-finding process at trial, and expense, delay, and uncertainty in appeals, the proper comparison was between the two levels' trial courts. He asserted: "First, persons advancing federal constitutional claims against local officials will fare better, as a rule, in federal, rather than a state, trial court. Second, to a somewhat lesser degree, federal district courts are institutionally preferable to state appellate courts as forums in which to raise federal constitutional claims."[47] Although conceding that incompetent or insensitive state trial judges can block exercise of federal constitutional rights, Paul Bator found that federal courts and the entire hierarchy of state court systems, including their high courts, should be compared, and that "once the state appellate system is folded into the consideration of the argument, claims for a clear federal superiority become greatly attenuated."[48]

Such are the arguments. What about reality? Comparison of constitutional claims in federal district courts with those in state appellate and supreme courts showed that, for the 1974–1980 period, the federal courts upheld 41 percent of the claims and the state courts 32 percent, a statistically significant but not important difference. Differences were greater in civil cases (44.6% of constitutional claims upheld in federal court, 33.2% in state court) than in criminal cases (33.9% v. 30.2%). There was no pattern by subject type, and there was statistical parity between the two sets of courts in equal protection claims in civil cases.[49]

Empirical studies do not dictate litigators' actions. What has been true of church-state litigation, that "the majority of attorneys and groups, but by no means all, would appear to prefer the federal courts,"[50] applies to civil rights litigation. Civil rights lawyers' tendency to gravitate to the federal courts was reinforced by the Warren Court's support of civil rights claims and assisted by its easing of federal standing requirements. It was further reinforced by an attitude toward federal courts communicated to lawyers during their law training. As a result of the Warren Court's rulings, a federal judge observed, several generations of lawyers were taught to "seek ye first the kingdom of the federal court," a teaching that led to an almost reflexive preference for the federal courts.[51] Indeed, civil rights lawyers have often preferred federal courts even when federal judges were conservative, as in Mississippi in the 1960s, because of the belief that appellate courts could overturn federal trial judges' unfavorable rulings. State judges themselves perhaps unwittingly contributed to the federal court preference by drawing on federal constitutional law to deal with state civil liberties claims, and by giving insufficient attention to possible differences between state constitutional provisions and the analogous federal ones, even when the former are at least as strong as if not stronger than the latter.

A principal reason for the federal court preference is that because civil rights lawyers' goal was constitutional precedent, federal courts were "the surest and fastest route to the Supreme Court,"[52] particularly when three-judge district courts were necessary to challenge the constitutionality of and enjoin enforcement of state laws, because cases went from them to the Supreme Court on direct appeal. The Supreme Court was both civil rights lawyers' ultimate goal and the only place they felt they had a chance. As Greenberg remarked about bail cases, it was "the only judicial forum sufficiently detached to see the issue as more than opening the jailhouse doors, the one forum where the issue would receive a hearing on the merits."[53]

Why State Courts?

The preference for federal court may be time-bound. Indeed, the argument for federal court superiority may "derive primarily from a special historical experience, involving the division of the country on the issue of racial segregation."[54] In earlier days, the NAACP saw little difference between the two sets of courts because federal and state judges "were very similar sorts of people, drawn from the same segments of the white bar and white society. There could be no systematic advantage, but only random variation, in choosing one forum over the other."[55]

With the realization that the "go-to-the-federal-court strategy holds only so long as the Supreme Court is a hospitable forum for the cases,"[56] and with the U.S. Supreme Court becoming more restrictive, the preference for federal courts diminished. The Burger Court's decisions made those state courts that granted individuals greater protections under state constitutions appear more favorable.[57] Indeed, the Court's decreased support for civil rights and civil liberties claims led Justice Brennan to suggest greater use of state courts,[58] which were getting better. In the words of one civil rights litigator, "there is a recognition that state courts are viable—and perhaps more effective, depending on the state." In southern civil rights cases, they became more so with the departure of staunch segregationists and their replacement with moderates and at least a few blacks, with the newer judges more likely to have been trained on decisions upholding civil rights. ACLU lawyers began to move away from "nearly instinctive reliance on the federal Constitution and the federal courts" as a result of "the demonstrated willingness of many state courts to recognize individual rights that go beyond the protection afforded by the United States Constitution, as interpreted by the U.S. Supreme Court."[59]

The possibility of achieving civil rights goals through state courts was opened up, first, by the ability to bring civil rights cases in state court under 42 U.S.C. §1983, so that civil rights lawyers were no longer restricted to federal courts, and, more particularly, by the "new federalism," that is, "the renewed willingness of state courts to rely on their own law, in order to decide questions involving individual rights,"[60] as state judges learned that making a "clear statement" that they were relying solely on state law could insulate their *state* law decisions from federal court review. However, state courts were attractive only in some states and for some subject matters, such as gender discrimination, defendants' rights, prisoners' rights, and altering the state system of financing education.[61] State court treatment of some subjects, such as defendants' rights, has not provided a picture of liberal state court outcomes but instead "evidence of moderate postures on the part of state appellate courts" and "some evidence of state court conservatism as well." Indeed, state courts were far more likely to adopt the conservative criminal procedure rulings of the Burger and Rehnquist Court than to develop different positions based on state law.[62]

A definite reason for change is that Supreme Court rulings directed litigators to state court. When the Supreme Court cut off access to federal courts, if lawyers were to proceed, they had to do so in state court. Thus *San Antonio School District v. Rodriguez* (1973) forced later challenges to property tax financing of public schools into state court, where lawyers won cases in a number of states[63]—ironically including Texas itself, although not until over a dozen years after *Rodriguez.* In particular, the *Warth v. Seldin* ruling focused attacks on exclusionary zoning in the state courts, some of which decided for the plaintiff. Mental health litigation also was directed toward state courts by the Supreme Court's refusal in *Pennhurst II* to expand the rights of the mentally ill. For example, plaintiffs' lawyers in a federal case pending in the Supreme Court rescued their case by trying to shift it to state court. They did so by pointing to a recent Massachusetts state court decision on a state constitutional basis for a right to refuse treatment, and the Supreme Court remanded for consideration of the Massachusetts law.[64]

Both limits on federal causes of action and favorable state law are necessary for lawyers to use state court. The strong rights orientation of Colorado state mental health law led lawyers there to deal with their clients' concerns through state law in state court.[65] Favorable state school desegregation policy helps explain why the Los Angeles school desegregation case was initially a state case, and why the Mount Vernon, New York, school plaintiffs initiated state administrative, then judicial, proceedings. (However, NAACP lawyers were not able to extricate themselves from that situation when the school board significantly delayed matters.)[66]

Use of state courts allows lawyers to avoid the political friction that results from "the feds" ordering state or local governments to act; the potentially unpopular decisions they want, controversial in the local community, have a better reception if issued by a state judge.[67] Yet lawyers are also aware that many state judges are elected, making them potentially wary of upsetting the voters. Although appointed federal judges are affected by public opinion,[68] their insulation may be useful under some circumstances, particularly if it can help sustain making unpalatable rulings. (It may not be beneficial in others, however. An example is the remedy stage of a civil rights suit, when "an insulated federal judge may be less sensitive to the social milieu into which his decisions must fit and thus less successful in shaping decision and remedies to the reality of that milieu." [69])

Whether in fact civil rights lawyers shifted their forum much is open to question, although major change is indicated even in the statement that, instead of an automatic use of federal courts, it was "now a matter of predicting, and deciding to use state or federal court depending on the case." One lawyer said the "upshot was that there wasn't much change" despite "talk of greater use of state courts" and Brennan's suggestion. Even the presence of numerous federal judges appointed by President Reagan did not noticeably diminish civil rights litigators' use of federal courts in the early 1980s, despite their statements of increasing unhappiness with the courts. Prior preferences, a result of negative experiences, create a considerable drag limiting change, and attorneys continue to view state courts skeptically, continuing to believe that "many state courts remain terrible" so that the lawyer cannot obtain the "practical results" they seek "even in states with favorable policies."

Use of Federal and State Courts

At times litigants are in both federal and state court simultaneously, pursuing separate causes of action in the different forums; at other times, and somewhat more often, they are in the two sequentially. The extended Boston school litigation illustrates state court action interwined with federal litigation. Considerable initial state court litigation, including appeals to the U.S. Supreme Court, came first under a state racial imbalance law which provided the basis for state withholding of funds. This was followed by both state (Massachusetts Commission Against Discrimination) and federal (Department of Health, Education, and Welfare) administrative action. The NAACP's federal case against racial imbalance in the schools and other violations caused by placement of new construction and pupil assignments was deferred during state proceedings. Plaintiffs filed the primary federal court suit against the Boston School Committee only later, as state court proceedings continued, and indeed most were still to come.[70] The intertwining of state and federal proceedings allowed U.S. District Judge Arthur Garrity the hope that if he held back a major decision while awaiting state appellate court action, he could fuse state and federal strands of litigation to reinforce the other; at one point, a state court ruling eliminated his need to issue a ruling, which stood a strong likelihood of being appealed.[71]

The Port Gibson, Mississippi, boycott case that produced the Supreme Court's *Claiborne Hardware* ruling also took place in both federal and state courts; the state court action was primary. Trial in state court of the white merchant plaintiffs' claims was enjoined under a federal court order obtained by the black defendants, but the Fifth Circuit reversed and the state trial proceeded. When that led to a massive judgment against the NAACP and the requirement that a bond equal to 125 percent of the judgment be posted pending appeal, defendants quickly returned to federal court for emergency relief, and they successfully challenged the bond requirement there in both federal trial and appellate courts. At one point, two teams of lawyers, one from each of two cooperating Washington, D.C., firms, were in Mississippi, one in Jackson at the state high court, the other in Oxford at federal court.

There was also simultaneous federal and state court action in the Contract Buyers League case. While the primary case was proceeding in the federal courts, the plaintiffs were also in state court, challenging eviction proceedings against buyers who were involved in a strike against making payments. When they failed in their state court effort to test the constitutionality of the eviction law, they tried unsuccessfully to go to federal court to invalidate the eviction law, and then appealed to state supreme court.[72]

Involvement in both state and federal courts results in part from certain Supreme Court rulings. *Edelman v. Jordan,* the 1974 ruling that the Eleventh Amendment bars obtaining retroactive payments from the states, caused an instance of sequential litigation in which follow-up cases are brought in state court after relief is not obtained in federal court: plaintiffs who could not obtain full relief from federal judges split their claims and went to state court with their demand for retroactive payment. Because of the 1984 *Pennhurst* ruling that federal courts cannot enforce state law, civil rights plaintiffs also had to bifurcate claims or had to leave federal court for state court if they wanted federal and state claims decided together.[73]

The doctrine of abstention, that federal judges should not decide issues that state courts could decide or need to decide to clarify the meaning of state law, is another basis for sequential use of state and federal courts, operating whether or not state court litigation has been initiated before federal lawsuits are commenced. In the Prince Edward County school closing litigation deriving from *Brown,* for example, the federal judge withheld decision as he waited the state courts to rule on the claim that the state constitution required that schools be kept open throughout the state. Only after the black plaintiffs had lost in state court did they obtain the federal ruling they sought, which the U.S. Court of Appeals then reversed.[74]

Sequential use of the two forums is not infrequent. Civil rights litigators, particularly when seeking rulings of national import, may prefer to try federal constitutional issues first in federal court and then turn to "smaller, state 'universes' " to try state constitutional issues.[75] Alternatively, litigation begun in state court may be removed to federal court. Major Supreme Court rulings in the 1960s limited the situations in which civil rights plaintiffs could remove cases with racial claims, but removal has become quite attractive to civil rights *defendants* faced with state cases that plaintiffs could have filed initially in federal court under general federal question jurisdiction.[76]

There are other situations in which litigation moves from state to federal court. The Pasadena, California, school case, initially a state case, was refiled in federal court after a state trial judge refused to order implementation of a proposed plan.[77] The Los Angeles school litigation was initially a state case until the Los Angeles school board discontinued mandatory busing after a state referendum limited busing permitted under state law. At that point, plaintiffs took federal court action to overturn the referendum and also tried to go to federal court with their underlying school case, claiming a new right not previously pursued. However, illustrating the difficulties that can be created when a shift of forum is attempted late in litigation, the en banc Court of Appeals for the Ninth Circuit limited the federal case to events after the 1969 state court trial.[78] More generally, there may be a complex sequence in which "the frustrating merry-go-round process of victory in the federal arena, then retrial in the still segregated state system, followed by victory again in the federal courts, and back to retrial in the states."[79]

The Basis of Choice

Despite the preference for federal court, the choice of forum should be treated as problematic. An NAACP lawyer observed, "We seldom had the luxury of determining" where cases would be brought: "by being reflexive we had to take the game where it was being played." In short, he said, "we had to shoot the ducks where they were." And as Cover commented, "In the jurisdictional world of complex concurrency, it is usually possible for one of the parties in a law suit to choose the most favorable from among two or more forums in terms of expected return. . . . The fifty-plus state jurisdictions reenact the international order in many respects, while the potential choice between a state and a federal forum squares the difficulties or opportunities."[80]

In general, the side taking the initiative will at least initially choose the forum, subject to the possible removal of the case from state to federal court or remand from federal to state court. This may make choice illusory because the forum may be chosen for them: defending civil rights workers from assault charges and traffic violations brought to harass them put a lawyer in state court,[81] explaining why, during the 1960s, major civil rights litigators in Mississippi were not solely or even primarily in federal court. Although nearly 80 percent of the NAACP Legal Defense Fund's cases were in federal court, 71 percent of the Lawyers Committee's cases were in state and local courts, with Lawyers Constitutional Defense Committee activity divided more evenly.[82]

Another situation in which choice was lacking was posed by a state court injunction against civil rights marches in Birmingham, Alabama:

> Even though it was clear that we could not expect relief from the Alabama state courts, . . . the law with respect to the right to remove a state proceeding of this nature to a federal district court was unclear but seemed to be against us. Even if the injunctive proceeding was removed, there was scant likelihood that we could get any relief from the local federal district court either, and at that time, an unfavorable decision in a case removed from a state to a federal district court could not be appealed. The other possibility for federal court relief from the injunction, an affirmative action seeking to enjoin the state proceeding, seemed also not to hold much promise of success. Consequently, we decide to defend the injunctive proceeding in the state court even though we realized that we would lose there and at every appellate level in the state judicial system.[83]

When litigators do have a choice of forum, a variety of factors may play a role in their decisions. One is the type of argument to be made.

In the attack on housing discrimination, equal protection arguments were more likely in federal courts, substantive due process arguments in state court. Equal protection arguments were not used frequently in school desegregation cases in state courts.[84] Cases are brought in federal court when there is a federal cause of action, in part because those courts, with more experience with laws, are likely to interpret them favorably. The remedy sought is a related factor. Nathan Margold, recommending to the NAACP a litigation campaign against segregation, noted that different remedies were required depending on the particular statutory scheme being challenged, with mandamus to be obtained from state courts and injunctions from federal courts.[85] Doctrines limiting federal courts' ability to grant complete relief might also lead lawyers to find state courts preferable.[86]

Procedural matters, and particularly federal-state differences, also affect choice of forum. For example, California state courts "routinely grant[ed] stays in civil rights litigation" whereas the federal courts did not. Thus whereas the San Francisco desegregation plan went into effect while the federal court case there was appealed, the Richmond, California, school desegregation plan did not go into effect while the school district appealed the state court case.[87] Major procedural elements which make the federal court a desirable forum are that liberal discovery is available in the federal courts and that the Federal Rules of Civil Procedure are simple; because the rules, including federal class action rules, are the same nationwide, "Once the basics are mastered, the same rules apply in Oregon as in Mississippi." This is an important organizational element: if civil rights organizations' staff attorneys know the Federal Rules, when "called upon to litigate constitutional cases in numerous states, often simultaneously," they can avoid the "bewildering array of state procedures," mastery of which would consume scarce time, and they also supervise and coordinate local attorneys more effectively.[88] However, state rules are now more nearly uniform from one state to another, as many have adopted some variant of the Federal Rules of Civil Procedure; this makes it easier to bring cases in state court.[89]

Other elements of choice, which are less a matter of law, relate more to courts' functioning. These include how efficiently and effectively cases are processed. For example, all lawyers considering whether to take diversity-of-citizenship cases to federal or state court take into account the courts' competence and judges' quality.[90] Civil rights lawyers see federal judges as having "usually higher intellectual calibre" and to be of a higher "level of technical competence," better able to handle complex cases, and "more likely to produce competently written, persuasive opinions."[91] Federal judges are thought to be less likely to commit reversible error, but, if they do, the lawyers will have had a better chance to develop a record on which an appeal can be based.

Also relevant are the length of time a lawyer has to wait for a trial because of court backlogs and whether judges write formal opinions that will be published. On these matters, despite heavy caseloads which might lead to a failure to enforce civil rights in some instances, federal courts are thought to operate more efficiently.[92] Surveys in 1980 and 1981 indicated that lawyers with cases eligible for federal diversity jurisdiction, who "may be willing to risk trying a matter in a potentially less sympathetic forum" if trial will be prompt,[93] pick the court, state or federal, that will most expeditiously process their cases.[94] The ability to get to trial promptly is particularly important for plaintiffs' lawyers seeking damage awards for clients who have been discriminated against, for whom "delay can make [their] cases more difficult, can result in relief coming too late to be of benefit, and can reduce the present value of final awards."

Still another factor in lawyers' forum choice is a court's location. If a federal court is nearby, lawyers "are more likely to choose federal court than lawyers in cities without federal courts." However, choice might also be affected by a desire to force an adversary to some inconvenience, a desire that will be reinforced if one lawyer has practiced more than the adversary in a particular court[95] and thus is more familiar with it. The "local boy" aspect of state courts is a particular problem for civil rights lawyers who appear there only infrequently while their opponents "deal all the time with that judge." This is a reason that civil rights organization staff lawyers need contacts with lawyers in the local community, to make appearances before local judges and to "interpret" the court.

These procedural and institutional considerations for forum choice, Neuborne argues, are likely to be at their strongest when federal and state courts are seen as equally likely to produce the same substantive result. However, where controlling precedents are clearly more favorable in one court, lawyers are not likely to shift away from such substantive advantages for better procedures. Courts thus are chosen on the basis of what they will *deliver,* that is, the values to which they give the greatest weight. Thus it is "the sympathy and philosophy of judges," not their abstract quality, that is crucial in forum choice. The views of civil rights lawyers that state courts' "parochialism, which makes them still predisposed against LDF in many parts of the country" and "not hospitable to civil rights claims," would thus help explain LDF's federal court preference.

When, however, federal judges are resistant, civil rights lawyers may turn to state court. A North Carolina litigator commented, for example, that "some state court judges were more sympathetic and concerned" than President Reagan's judicial federal appointees. If one were faced with "one of the most conservative federal courts of appeals in the country," "more concerned" state appellate courts might look better. Nor did the problem occur only with recent federal judicial appointees. As a former Legal Services lawyer observed, some federal judges, by delaying rulings, "wouldn't even give the attorneys what the Supreme Court rulings directly compelled." In that situation, lawyers learned quickly not to go to federal court and to consider shifting their efforts to state courts. As one put it quite clearly, "If your choice is Harold Cox [a Mississippi federal judge openly hostile to blacks], you shouldn't overlook state courts." If lawyers faced state judges who "didn't want to hear the specifics" of a housing discrimination case or who had serious docket problems "so that the lawyer doesn't get to see the judge and the judge doesn't write an opinion," they would not hesitate to make further efforts in state courts.

The focus of forum-shopping is usually on the specific court within whichever system, federal or state, is preferred. For example, in its 1970s Northern school cases the NAACP "concentrated on the Midwest because the Sixth Circuit Court of Appeals was more favorable than other appellate tribunals"[96]—a choice also affected by NAACP General Counsel Nathaniel Jones's familiarity with that court because he was from Ohio. Particularly important are the attitudes of trial judges, which explains why, however much the argument may be stated on other bases,[97] "familiarity with the trial record of the individual judges in his area is a must for the test case lawyer." Thus lawyers who proceeded with diversity cases in state courts did so because they thought those courts "friendlier" to attorneys, and state judges more "down to earth" and more acceptable.[98] This "forum-shopping," hardly restricted to civil rights, basically is undertaken to find judges who will not look askance at the values underlying one's legal claims. While litigants may be drawn to a court, conversely they may seek to avoid a court or a judge. Although assignment of cases to judges by a random process makes this difficult, it may be possible to get one's case before a desired judge who has already been assigned related cases.

7

The "Planned" in
Planned Litigation

To speak of planned litigation is to assume, at the least, that such litigation exists and that some organizational litigators make efforts at planned litigation; it is not to say how thorough or successful those efforts are. According to conventional wisdom, civil rights litigation of the 1940s and early 1950s consisted of organized campaigns to produce social change, as did more recent civil rights litigation. The exemplary civil rights litigation campaign is the one that produced *Brown v. Board of Education*.

The *Brown* campaign, however, certainly was not the *first* litigation campaign. There had been the NAACP's protracted attack on devices that disfranchised blacks, extending from *Guinn v. United States* (grandfather clause) through *Smith v. Allwright* (white primary); the effort directed against restrictive covenants in housing also was well planned. Still earlier there were instances, involving not one litigating organization but a number of individuals acting in concert, that could be considered campaigns. One was the litigation to protect fugitive slaves, which involved a number of cases brought by lawyers of relatively like mind; Albion Tourgee's attack on Jim Crow laws, which included *Plessy*, is another instance of several cases brought by one principal litigator, without group affiliation, although the railroads, required to provide separate cars for Negroes, were not far in the background.

There was also planned litigation in the sphere of economic regulation, including that aimed at child labor laws[1] or at New Deal legislation. The latter was organizationally supported and well planned and was matched by efforts on the government side. The lawyers at the National Labor Relations Board in particular relied on "an aggressive litigation campaign," which started with their looking for test cases and "thinking in terms of preparing cases to be presented in sequence to the Supreme Court, with the strongest cases first." Even before the Wagner Act was passed, they even had "a 'master plan' which specified in detail the types of test cases best suited for eventual submission to the Supreme Court."[2] More recently, there has been a resurgence of planned litigation by conservative groups on issues like obscenity, criminal procedure, and abortion, that came with development of conservative public interest law firms in the late 1960s and 1970s. In litigation attacking *Roe v. Wade*, the Americans United for Life Legal Defense Fund used "an 'NAACP-type strategy'—the gradual, unrelenting, continuous, whittling away of negative precedent."[3]

In this chapter, we first examine what planned litigation is—both the model and the reality, including a look at the paradigm provided by *Brown v. Board of Education*. We then turn to examine in greater detail elements of planned litigation. These include goals sought in such litigation, the extent of control exercised over the litigation, and internal networks that are a basic part of carrying it out. We also look at responsive litigation and at two dimensions of the reality of planned litigation: litigation that is a response to others' actions and the flexibility that accompanies planned litigation and the momentum (or inertia) that impedes flexibility.

What Is Planned Litigation?

The activity by the NAACP and the NAACP Legal Defense Fund in the school desegregation area in the late 1940s and early 1950s is said to be "probably the most ambitious undertaking of law-reform activity by social-reform groups"[4] and is the model of a litigation campaign by which civil rights litigation activity is measured. What might be called "the *Brown* paradigm" has been "the principal inspiration to others who seek change through litigation" and became "the single most important influence in the development of OEO Legal Services, consumer and environmental law, and public interest law.[5]

On close inspection, the model turns out to be less than the myth it has become, and its utility has been diminished in more recent times because of the increased complexity of litigation and its environment. Whether even the *Brown* litigation itself involved a strategy has been questioned. Within a broad commitment to eliminate racial subordination, the NAACP dealt with several "broadly defined evils" such as school segregation, Jim Crow laws, and lynching; the litigation goal was not initially to eliminate school segregation in particular. In the pursuit of litigation to remedy those situations, there was discussion of a plan, but "the contents of that 'plan' changed with some frequency," and one regularly found "proposals made by planners who were removed from implementation of the plans, the abandonment of those plans in favor of others that reflected the NAACP's internal organizational constraints, decisions altered because of preferences of the staff, and negotiations over plans with constituencies having diverse interests."[6] In fact, prior to *Brown,* only in the 1940–1945 salary equalization litigation could one find "an extended period of relatively consistent strategic activity," but the nature of the equalization suits changed as the stable environment on which "planners had relied . . . proved to be lacking," in part because of changes in state law, requiring repeated changes in tactics.[7]

One view is that Thurgood Marshall believed that, for school desegregation, there was "a general plan whereby the NAACP/LDF would attempt to induce the courts to develop a relatively empty area of law into a coherent body of jurisprudence." However, Marshall appears to have believed it impossible to develop a blueprint because of "the impossibility of obtaining plaintiffs according to any prearranged plan," with "pressure to litigate . . . always from the bottom up," as the membership-based NAACP found it "necessary to respond to the demands of its constituents."[8] Thus the NAACP had to proceed with cases in Prince Edward County (Virginia) and South Carolina despite believing them less ideal locations in which to challenge "separate but equal" than were border states like Kansas and Delaware, which had less racial tension and a smaller proportion of racial minorities.

A lawyer familiar with both pre- and post-*Brown* NAACP activity has warned that one "must be careful not to make things [look] too overly determined." The desegregation litigation ending in *Brown* can be seen as a progression, but lawyers must be careful not to "get fooled" by such an idea, because one "gets overconfident as you watch things build up." Before *Brown* "there was a *zeitgeist*," and "an internal logic, an overall logic to the campaign leading to *Brown*," but "on a day-to-day basis" things were not so well organized. Thus it was "true but not true" that there was a program. The written record makes matters look organized, especially when one "presents it in an orderly sequence," but there was "a tremendous amount of matter extraneous to policy which determined whether a case was brought in one state rather than another or one place rather than another." Policy was made primarily "around Thurgood Marshall's desk" rather than in board of directors resolutions, and things often happened when someone made a suggestion and others responded, "You're crazy but if you want to go ahead and try, go ahead." Thus, there was a "lot of improvisation, a lot of impromptu," and much movement was unpredictable. "Cases were taken from many available, starting with the idea that a direct attack on separate but equal was 'crazy,' a case was won, confidence grew as a result, and lawyers moved to the next step."

A 1973 statement by LDF Director-Counsel Jack Greenberg is particularly instructive. Arguing that "litigation programs pose practical, political, and jurisprudential problems, large and small," he discounted the image of a planned litigation "campaign" as one of "military precision" because "time and again, cases take on lives of their own and mature along unexpected lines." There are difficulties in developing and maintaining cases to produce necessary precedent, and those difficulties recur in the development and maintenance of follow-up cases aimed at applying the precedents to other parties. Generally, one faces an extensive set of potential difficulties: "Too much that occurs in court is not subject to control, such as the chance occurrences of any lawsuit, the defection of plaintiffs or capitulation of defendants, disagreement among counsel, the vagaries of legislation, unanticipated precedents, and the effects of public sentiment and political currents on constitutional adjudication."[9]

What then, is planned litigation? At the heart of planned litigation is said to be the litigation campaign, which entails focus on a particular area of law; pursuit of many cases in sequence and thus the choice of cases to bring; control of development and progress of those cases; and strategy, at least in a general sense. Although some strategy for planned litigation develops inductively after the fact, if there is to be a campaign, strategy cannot develop only as it proceeds. The number of planned campaigns is not large, but the number of cases within each is, as is the number of people affected. Despite the risk of dispersion of resources and energy, several campaigns may be under way simultaneously, although perhaps at different stages of development. The NAACP, for example, dealt simultaneously with education (equalization of teachers' salaries and admission to higher education), restrictive covenants in housing, and voting rights (attacking whites-only primary elections)—at the same time it was lobbying against lynching.

Development of litigation strategy, which is a connotation of the idea of planned litigation, can mean several things. To many lawyers, litigation strategy is equivalent to trial strategy, consisting of actions taken within a particular case, including decisions on which witnesses to call, what types of evidence to introduce, and what procedures to follow. Or it can have a far broader meaning, entailing "a strategy of strategies, an overall priority of concerns."[10] Strategy, "the over-all planning and direction of large-scale projects," has been distinguished from tactics, "the actual processes involving in executing the strategy," including "selection and initiation of cases in a particular issue area" and specific "techniques" like "use of class action suits, expert testimony and research by social scientists, and filing of amicus curiae briefs."[11] However, as used here, litigation strategy subsumes both strategy and tactics as just defined, except that use of expert testimony and social science research is trial strategy outside the focus of this study.[12]

As found in planned constitutional litigation (and the sense in which it is used in this study), litigation strategy includes identification of goals to seek and institutional targets to attack, the areas of law in which to become involved, and then the cases in which to become involved. Having only some of these elements is not sufficient. For example, although a number of cases have been brought to prove the tobacco industry's liability for deaths from lung cancer and although the litigation "is motivated, at least in part, by its potential contribution to a critical public health goal," one cannot talk of a planned litigation campaign because efforts at coordination "have been, at most, limited to a modest pooling of resources in individual cases." Most important, "Strategies of refined test case selection are not consonant with the structure of the personal injury bar." [13]

A broad sketch of what is meant by "planned litigation" is found in a list of elements identified from studies of interest group litigation:

1. longevity
2. full-time staff and attorneys, or skilled and dedicated volunteers
3. sharp issue focus
4. financial resources including foundation support
5. technical data
6. ability to generate well-timed publicity
7. close coordination between national headquarters and local affiliates
8. coordination and cooperation with other interest groups
9. ability to persuade the Justice Department or Solicitor General to enter the dispute on the sponsoring organization's side [14]

By definition, any "planned litigation" has a fairly broad scope, although the broader its scope, the more is planning needed. A planned litigation campaign is broad because it requires bringing numerous cases so that more will be available to reach the Supreme Court, from which the case or cases with the best record can be selected.[15] That a litigation campaign is by nature broad usually requires a national-scope organization to deal with cases arising in differing local circumstances and to understand implications of action in one case for cases brought elsewhere, as settlement of a case in City A may affect how cases are pursued in Cities B and C. Planning also requires organizational longevity, which allows a group to be a "repeat player," developing the law for use in subsequent cases. Longevity allows an organization to chip away slowly at adverse precedent and to pass up some cases to wait for others in which issues can be better framed; to engage in backup or emergency planning in the event some cases "fall out" and a sought-after precedent does not materialize; to reduce or suspend litigation efforts in a less receptive political or legal environment and thus wait until the situation is more propitious; and to handle complex cases through trials and extended appeals.

The "programmatic law development" [16] of planned litigation may also entail concentrating on "leading cases," which "provide particularly striking illustrations of the shortcomings of current constitutional doctrine or underscore the gap between constitutional doctrine and real world behavior," and in which a definitive Supreme Court decision is sought; it is only "partially programmatic litigation" because it does not lay out a full set of activities to be pursued. This approach, used by the NAACP from 1910 through 1930 before its better-known later sustained litigation activity, may be necessary in the absence of resources for more extensive action. When the NAACP did obtain external funding for a litigation program, receiving the Garland Fund contribution as a result of serious self-study about the organization's directions, it moved toward a more complete plan that included preparation of blueprints for a broad litigation attack on segregation and discrimination, initiation of several cases with respect to each issue, and the undertaking of action on certain issues prior to action on others.

Planned litigation often proceeds incrementally, a step at a time, much as the common law has developed. For the NAACP, this stemmed from the approach taken by Charles Houston, who felt the organization's litigation program should be to "lay a foundation for subsequent frontal attacks against racial discrimination and segregation," thus developing precedents on which he could then build. Unlike Nathan Margold, who would have proceeded more quickly to attack "separate but equal," "Houston believed the step-by-step process would have greater long-range effects."[17] Thurgood Marshall, carrying on this approach, continued to move the law ahead a bit at a time, distinguishing past cases, and did not focus on attacking "separate but equal" frontally until after *Sweatt v. Painter* suggested the possibility. This approach was also followed later, for example, in the school desegregation area after *Brown*, when the NAACP Legal Defense Fund "nudged the law along a bit at a time." And the Women's Rights Project of the American Civil Liberties Union, as the only women's group to pursue litigation systematically, brought a series of cases, each serving as a foundation for the next, and each moving closer to the doctrinal goal being sought.[18]

In this "case-by-case, building-block strategy," each successive case is not a step specified by a prior blueprint, with an "inevitable and orderly march toward progressive reform." Instead, in a "halting and thus unpredictable" tempo, because "judicial policy initiatives emerge erratically and unpredictably" and because of "built-in frictions,"[19] theory is deduced from individual cases in a "pursuit of the possible," or, as one observer noted, "We have a route but we're firefighters to get there." The ultimate goal—for example, desegregation of public education—is not sought immediately; cases are brought and won; and then a goal that "seems crazy one year is reached as intermediate points are filled in." Thus even when an organization has an overall national strategy for litigation on a particular subject, the results may be local and piecemeal, as "Victory in one case or one locale does not guarantee victory in another."[20] For example, school desegregation litigation tended "to 'grow' rather than to develop in logical fashion," and "accidental factors" were often decisive.[21] Recognizing this, litigators develop fallback positions in the event cases do not proceed as expected.[22]

That an organization escalates its demands from one case to the next does not, however, necessarily mean it is engaged in a litigation campaign. An illustration is LDF's activity in the sit-in cases; they were not "part of a long range plan since few people foresaw the importance which the sit-in cases would come to assume," so that "legal strategy had to be improvised along the way."[23] Thus even the presence of many cases in an area of the law, brought in the name of one entity, does not necessarily mean a litigation program. The Legal Services Program (LSP), through its many offices and with the assistance of its backup centers, initiated many poverty law cases. However, a large number of cases deal not equal a litigation plan, or mean that a national organization like LSP is in general charge of the litigation or that test cases were planned by a central unit and then brought at the local level. Instead, most test cases were brought by attorneys from individual LSP projects as a result of service to individual clients, including the many LSP cases that reached the Supreme Court.

This situation was typical of the planned litigation effort to change the welfare system through litigation. That effort was the brainchild of Edward Sparer through the LSP's Center of Social Welfare Policy and Law at Columbia University. Many of the issues that Sparer wanted addressed received Supreme Court rulings, but that did not necessarily happen because of the LSP's litigation program. Indeed, most of the cases the Supreme Court decided "were brought 'out-of-order' and without the direct assistance of the Columbia Center." Local LSP lawyers' autonomy affected—and even got in the way of—Sparer's attempts to plan, in part because they brought cases in states that had statutes that were not the best to litigate.[24] *Shapiro v. Thompson,* the Court's major ruling on durational residence requirements for welfare benefits, arrived at the Court from among the many challenges to residency rules brought by local LSP lawyers. Although striking down such requirements was a goal of those planning challenges to the welfare system, litigation planners had discouraged tests of durational residency requirements because they were complex and precedent was not favorable; thus *Shapiro* and cases like it were brought against their wishes, probably because LSP lawyers thought "the issues were easy to understand without mastery of the technical complexities of welfare law."[25]

Although cases in which efforts are made to extend precedent "are likely to be brought by experienced litigators working for [and] in conjunction with major litigating groups,"[26] the welfare litigation example suggests an important point about planned litigation: "Litigation was not executed as the original memorandum suggested because other lawyers had their own ideas of how and when to proceed; cases tended to arise where poverty lawyers were, appeals often were controlled by opponents, not allies, and the courts were influenced by forces other than the argument."[27] Likewise, in sex discrimination cases, instead of cases being brought in an orderly, sequential fashion, often "individual plaintiffs have brought and shaped issues in the courts by chance," which has "frequently harmed what litigation strategy there has existed."[28] More generally, constitutional questions are brought to court, but in "a sporadic, even haphazard way," as "[p]laintiffs come to the court to seek redress or to enforce a law, and in doing so . . . raise, more or less in passing, the broader questions of public law."[29] One might even speak of an "accident theory of litigation." For example, the leading mental health case, *Wyatt v. Stickney*, stemmed from a backyard barbecue in which a lawyer visiting a neighbor met someone upset about staffing at Alabama mental hospitals.[30]

Shapiro likewise indicates that we must not assume that when major doctrine results from the Supreme Court, it results from a litigation campaign. Thus in criminal procedure cases, where the Warren Court was ready to incorporate provisions of the Bill of Rights into the Fourteenth Amendment Due Process Clause as prohibitions against the states, "many of the important decisions were the unintended byproduct of attorneys who provided the Court with occasions to make policy but who were themselves relatively uninterested in policy."[31] They offered constitutional arguments along with other arguments.

The cases were not even brought as test cases, as the challenge to the law was merely coincidental to the goal of winning reversal of a criminal defendant's conviction.

Major rulings thus do not even necessarily result from a test case and may even result from defensive activity, which is certainly not part of litigation campaign. *New York Times v. Sullivan,* in which the Supreme Court constitutionalized the law of libel, provides an example. Initially it "showed little promise of a landmark Supreme Court case."[32] It was undertaken to protect the finances of the SCLC leaders who had been sued, so that there really was no choice about whether to get involved in the cases, and considerations of whether the case would go to the Supreme Court were not likely to have entered into that decision. Making management of even this one case more difficult were elements that made it "a very hard case for the plaintiffs": "preliminary stages of bluster and petty bickering" and "extrinsic circumstances over which the lawyers in the case had no control—including the amount of the verdict, the unfortunate social and political climate and the proliferation of contemporaneous lawsuits brought by others."[33]

Even when organizations handle many cases in an area of law, as the ACLU did with obscenity, and have goals in mind, they may proceed without having "developed a formal litigation strategy designed to bring these issues systematically before the courts to realize its goals or without a preconceived plan tying its goals to a series of 'test' cases."[34] Thus the three organizations at the forefront of church-state litigation (American Civil Liberties Union, American Jewish Congress, and Americans United for Separation of Church and State), because they had done little to develop priorities in that area, had "more or less taken the issues as they came," with "the flavor of the ad hoc" and "a strategy that sees no further than the case at hand."[35] However, particularly if interest groups are involved, even if they are not a result of planned litigation campaigns, important cases "don't just happen." Organizations may engage in "an ad hoc search for targets of opportunity"[36] so that group involvement does not necessarily equal "planned litigation," but the groups do not operate randomly or pursue every target that presents itself. Organizations are likely to have determined some basic areas on which to focus, thus imposing at least a very loose program—what we might call "organized litigation" rather than planned litigation.[37] And once an organization has begun to litigate in an identifiable area of attention, for example, the ACLU on obscenity, it would likely take on more such cases, further prompting development of a more coherent approach for dealing with them.

Even without a long-term strategy linking individual cases, those cases may be undertaken with specific intentions. In particular, they may be test cases, that is, cases brought intentionally to challenge a particular statutory interpretation or more usually, to challenge the validity of laws under the Constitution. If a challenge to a statute is, or becomes, central, a case should be considered a test case regardless of its provenance and regardless of whether the plaintiff was chosen by the litigating organization or simply came to the organization.[38] Although test cases are an essential part of planned litigation strategy, not all test cases are part of such a strategy, and not all groups bringing test cases engage in broad litigation planning. Indeed, the ACLU's work for many years was quintessential test case litigation without planned litigation. Therefore, pursuit of a case as a test case does not mean it is part of a larger plan or even that it is chosen from among several possibilities: it may be seen, when it arises, as an appropriate vehicle according to some (more or less clear) criteria, or may also be part of responsive litigation.

Yet when several cases are each started separately for different reasons, they can become the basis of a larger strategy. Or the need for strategy may be recognized after fortuitous participation in several cases in which the organization's participation had been sought, as more cases signal the need to do something more than handle those cases individually. At that point, the organization engages in a "shift in emphasis from defensive to offensive measures."[39] And a sequence of individual test cases, viewed after the fact, can take on the *appearance* of planned litigation strategy, as participants reconstruct past events, although at the time the cases were initiated no one intended to link them. This was true of the NAACP's Charles Houston: "In the retelling, the progress of precedent in a particular line of cases tends to take on a misleading gloss of certainty," covering up "extraordinarily long periods of indeterminacy."[40]

This discussion should indicate that we must be careful not to assume that a set of cases bearing the label "planned" is thoroughly or fully planned, with litigators in control of the areas of law in which they focus their efforts, the particular cases they undertake, and their sequence, although the tag can be attached to some litigation. Even in areas where we have come to assume that litigation activity was planned, that may not have been so. While individual organizations may have had a strategy, collectively they did not, so that civil rights groups were not able to mount a "coordinated, adequately financed drive" to bring about school desegregation.[41]

Civil rights lawyers—lawyers with definite goals, working for organizations that have clear statements of purpose—have, without prompting, often volunteered comments about the less than fully planned nature of their enterprise. Instead of reinforcing a textbook view of fully orchestrated litigation campaigns derived from a blueprint, or attempting to picture civil rights litigation as a series of neat, preplanned steps, they unhesitatingly stressed the difficulties of keeping litigation strategy under control and underscored the lack of grand strategy. Litigation, said one lawyer, is a "responsive posture" inhibiting one from anything; it provided "some room for maneuver" but was "not a strategic tool." In the words of another observer, it may well be the case that "whatever gets done, gets done, rather than by design." Particularly on point is the observation of a civil rights litigator: "The vagaries of litigation are such that if you bring a case solely to go to the Supreme Court, there are 100 ways not to get there, and if you try to play cute in order to stay away, you end up there."

Indeed, the key words in connection with supposedly planned litigation strategy are *problematic* and *contingent*. While much may be done to try to plan, planning is only a possibility, not a strong likelihood, and most assuredly not a certainty. Being able to carry out efforts to plan with even a fair degree of success is contingent on a wide range of matters, many of which are not under the control of the planners; there are elements of serendipity in the process, including when particular cases come to an organization. What happens during the planned efforts is problematic and "fortuitous," with the presence of "chance" and luck, of "unexpected turns" of events. Nor is this new: it can be found in the efforts to mount a test case to challenge requirements for racially separate transportation in Louisiana.[42] An organization may be capable of developing "offensive" strategies, but "circumstances control," making it "reflective and responsive to events and developments." This was true as early as Houston's work for the NAACP: "Although Houston was responsible for the conduct of what at some points had been thought of as a systematic and coherently organization litigation campaign, he was more comfortable with pinpoint activities, frequently responsive more to the demands of the moment than to those of the plan."[43]

The speed with which cases arise may make control of litigation difficult; it presents a major obstacle to following strategy that has been developed or even to developing one, as was the case with the sit-in and demonstration cases during the height of the southern civil rights movement's activity—cases the LDF took to the Supreme Court but which it had not anticipated. If at times in civil rights litigation, it seemed "as if there was a grand strategy applied from New York, the opposite was true": matters "arose in the countryside" and then moved to the national level.

Planned litigation, suggests a former government litigator, is possible only if one is litigating for a government agency. However, this seriously overstates a government agency's ability to control litigation. A government agency can pick cases to pursue, dropping its losses in order to build a progression. However, in addition to shifts in direction resulting from changes in administration, there are the glitches common to any litigation. Nor can government attorneys control judges' or opponents' responses to government-initiated cases. And some government litigation is responsive, coming only after someone else has initiated the process, just as it is for interest groups. If an adversary files suits against a government agency, its lawyers have to concentrate on the "trouble spot," and government lawyers must guard against "a precipitate test case" brought by opponents.[44] A particularly determined adversary can drain an agency's litigation budget. In an example of such situations, the National Labor Relations Board, before its lawyers could even begin the orderly processing of cases filed with the agency, found itself with the more serious problem of having to respond to litigation planned by management, particularly "a barrage of injunction suits brought in the district courts" based on a standard brief provided by the American Liberty League which was "a well-coordinated diversionary assault."[45] It is also the case that an agency with the opportunity to plan its litigation may not do so. For example, the Department of Education's Office of Civil Rights, instead of engaging in "a careful assessment of priorities and a disciplined concentration on feasible undertakings," necessary "if its limited resources were to have any significant impact," was said to have been "mismanaged in larger strategic terms as much as in smaller aspects of its operating routine." [46]

Elements Of Planned Litigation

For planned litigation to work with even a modest degree of success, a number of elements must be present: goals, both particular *substantive* goals and *process* goals; control of litigation; the availability of resources; and an organizational base.

Goals

Organizations undertake planned litigation to achieve a variety of goals. There must be some goals for planned litigation to exist,[47] and disconnected individual cases are likely to accomplish more if they are related, even loosely, to some end in view. More important, particular goals may necessitate certain types of strategic litigation action, although we cannot systematically specify conditions for specific strategies.

Substantive goals, the particular legal policy or social result being sought, may be found in formal statements, at times adopted after debate following staff work. For example, after the decision to seek to end "separate but equal" was adopted at an NAACP conference of lawyers along with branch and state conference presidents in June 1950, Thurgood Marshall persuaded the NAACP board of directors to adopt as the organization's official policy that education cases would only "be aimed at obtaining education on a non-segregated basis and that no relief other than that will be acceptable." [48] At other times, particularly when an organization has become involved in an area of law somewhat unexpectedly, as was true with the Legal Defense Fund's sit-in and demonstration cases, goals develop implicitly from pursuit of cases.

Process goals are perhaps more important for strategy, although if litigators emphasize an organization's strategy, that may lead to a loss of the sense of goals and values.[49] The broad goal most often associated with organization-related litigation is achievement of precedent, particularly constitutional precedent, which requires a trip to the Supreme Court and a national organization's relatively centralized control of a litigation campaign. Getting a couple of students into graduate school did not have "marginal consequences . . . of sufficient immediate practical importance to warrant the effort"; what made the early graduate and professional education segregation cases "litigation campaign law making cases *par excellence*" was the long-term law making that came from the Supreme Court rulings in them.[50]

With a Supreme Court ruling the goal, negative lower court outcomes are not unexpected and may indeed assist strategy because they leave the decision to appeal in the hands of those seeking a ruling from the high court—known as "losing one's way to the Supreme Court." The alternative is being dragged there, the disadvantage of winning in the lower court, as Legal Services Program attorneys and welfare litigators learned when lower court victories allowed their opponents to control the decision to appeal.[51] In contemplating a Supreme Court precedent as a goal, lawyers may misjudge either what the Court may do or some consequences of Supreme Court rulings. In Title VII litigation, lawyers did not think their argument about the effects of tests, central to their efforts, was "winnable." They won on the testing issue nonetheless when the Supreme Court adopted their position in *Albemarle Paper*. The lawyers then thought the test element in *Washington v. Davis* easy, but the Court "came out the other way," because lawyers had forgotten the difference between obtaining jobs for blacks at a private company and having "blacks as cops on the street."

Not all litigators seek new precedent. The *aggressive litigant*, "one who finds the prevailing constitutional policy unfavorable," will be likely to seek "innovative interpretations of the Constitution from the Courts." At least until the Reagan administration, many civil rights organizations were "aggressive litigants" in these terms. A *defensive litigant*, however, instead of having such an aim, will "pursue a strategy which will succeed in convincing the courts that prevailing constitutional norms, already favorable to his interests, should be applied. Such a litigant seeks stability, not change, in constitutional policy;"[52] as was true of civil rights groups trying to protect favorable precedent.

Whether or not they take the initiative to create favorable precedent, litigators seek to avoid negative ones. This forces them to pay attention to "non-landmark" cases, into which "some of the most difficult, creative work" has gone, both "to get something for someone and to keep them from being bad precedent." This also indicates that a short-term process goal is remedy or result, successful short-term outcomes in the particular case. This was the focus of litigation by the disabled for access to transportation. Here the goal facilitated a decentralized approach to litigation and made settlement often an acceptable outcome.[53] Outcome goals were also said to characterize employment discrimination litigation under Title VII and the LDF's employment discrimination law campaign did win jobs for particular individuals. However, the campaign, based heavily on class actions, focused primarily on law development and "in the initial years . . . setting the tone and direction of Title VII enforcement was more important than the exact number of jobs gained." [54] Still another goal, although not explicitly proclaimed, is an organizational one—publicity which is closely associated with participating in cases as an amicus curiae to make a group's views known. Although possible publicity benefits may be factored into a litigation decision, at times publicity is an unintended byproduct, not a consciously intended goal.

To talk about *a* goal is difficult because more than one may be sought simultaneously. Goals may also operate serially, with relative emphasis among them varying over time. For example, as a case gets closer to the Supreme Court, obtaining constitutional precedent gets greater emphasis. Multiple goals are likely to be operative when an organization proceeds without specifying what it is seeking or lacks internal consensus, because seeking multiple goals is a way of satisfying diverse interests or constituencies. More than one goal may be sought in a single case. Lawyers may try both to implement precedent and to advance it. Despite considerable apparent tension between the two, some say that the distinction between seeking new precedent and enforcing existing rules, associated with emphasizing particular outcomes, "often breaks down in practice," [55] with both invariably being affected simultaneously. However, greater emphasis on precedent generally is thought to mean less attention to remedy. Thus achieving "viable compromises regarding race relations and the quality of the educational system in a particular city" [56] may require giving up the effort for precedent. The Detroit school case seems to provide another example, because the NAACP "appeared reluctant to jeopardize [its] victory by pressing for a remedy of unprecedented size and scope," such as the metropolitan busing remedy sought by the school board, and instead sought a desegregation plan limited to the central city. However, because the NAACP was concerned about "precedent and the effect of the decision on national developments," it was looking at the case as a precedent—perhaps for remedy achieved rather than for an innovative legal doctrine.[57]

At times, more than one goal can be satisfied simultaneously. An example of "perfect convergence" of an organization's programmatic goals and members' demands, which are not always congruent, is *Ethridge v. Rhodes*,[58] a case that "arose out of the rank and file" to challenge employment discrimination in state-funded construction. In other cases, however, differing goals may diverge or even conflict. For example, short-term victories in individual Title VII cases are necessary to "show the flag" and to mobilize resources, but such cases may tie up resources needed for major, longer-term class action cases. In other instances, observers believe that with more effort, the NAACP could have obtained more than what it obtained in settling a case but that long-term concerns did not permit investment of resources necessary for pressing cases that lacked apparent potential precedential value. Thus emphasis on precedent and long-term concerns over the series of individual cases necessary for a litigation campaign can lead to a conservative short-term result, with less done in almost every single case litigated.[59]

Control

At the heart of planned litigation is control, "the cornerstone of successful implementation of the Legal Defense Fund's goals" in the *Brown* model of litigation,[60] because without control, one cannot plan, or, if one has planned, effectively implement. Thurgood Marshall, finding restrictive covenant cases "bubbling up all over the country, not really under any central control, understood instinctively that it was important to take charge of them."[61] The importance of retaining control is shown in organizations' unwillingness to fund cases unless they could control them. Control over litigation is, however, "far from automatic" or complete, even for dominant civil rights litigators like the NAACP Legal Defense Fund. In earlier times one could talk at best of "a large measure of control, a substantial ability" to affect how a set of cases proceeded. However, by the early 1970s that measure of control "did not exist with many other efforts to make law in the courts."[62]

Control involves activity both within individual cases and sets of cases. At one extreme, with cases unavailable, there can be no control. One reason the campaign to attack bail practices failed is that "[d]espite conferences, meetings, circulation of literature, and so forth, it was extremely difficult to find reviewable cases."[63] On the other hand, too many cases means little control. One reason "Title VII law fell apart," we are told, is that "too many lawyers brought cases." LDF won the major cases but "others jumped in," which "made it difficult to retain control of development of the law."

Among the many problems in trying to exercise control in individual cases are "assignment of judges, the argument of lawyers on the other side, the rulings of judges on points of fact and law during trial, and the timing of judicial decisions," all of which are "vagaries that may suddenly uproot a promising test case."[64] Control is difficult when cases in which an organization becomes involved have been initiated by lawyers "who may not have shared the same goals,"[65] as occurred in the welfare litigation campaign. Control requires that cases "should be managed from the outset because choices of forums, type of action, pleadings, appeal papers and the like affect the outcome,"[66] and thus requires a shift from an amicus role to sponsorship of a case. This was learned by conservative public interest law firms such as the Citizens for Decency Through Law and the Pacific Legal Foundation; when they financed the defense in a case brought by liberal plaintiffs, they put the liberal plaintiff groups on the defensive.[67]

Early involvement is vital for making a good record and for properly framing issues and preserving them for appeal,[68] as well as for influencing as many aspects of the case as possible. Lack of involvement in the first stages of a case means not only that a litigating organization cannot develop and shape the record but also that it cannot make key legal arguments to the trial court or propose remedies that would extend case law. (However, even if cases are planned, with group involvement from the beginning, the organizations do not always think the cases through to the end before they are commenced.[69])

Control is also important so that if the case is lost at trial, appeals are taken only when appropriate: "there is no more powerful argument on the side of a full sponsoring role . . . than the argument that only in that way can the group make sure an unwise appeal will not be carried." If local attorneys make the decision to appeal, those at the national organization can only "climb aboard and try to prevent the worst from happening."[70] Only one attorney spoke of advantages of getting into a case at the appellate stage: discovery and trial, "which can be interminable," are avoided and the group gets "free court of appeals argument," important when the lawyers enjoy brief-writing and oral argument. And if an attorney who started a case without the organization's resources "has not build a substantial record," there is a "chance to resuscitate the case on appeal." Thus some national litigating organizations have "attempt[ed] to establish relations with the local lawyers that will permit them to shape and argue much of the appeal," but such a situation poses "a delicate and not always soluble problem." Yet even this lawyer recognized the drawback of not being able to shape the record.

Organizations do "prefer to get into cases at the ground floor, but the world doesn't work that way," and thus they will enter cases where control is lacking or not complete. Lack of control "doesn't necessarily preclude" an organization's becoming involved in a case, said a voting rights attorney; it "can affect the decision but will not preclude" participation. There are instances in which groups "get into cases already started by others" because the cases are important and those who have initiated them "get in over their heads and don't know what they are doing" or don't have the finances to continue. According to a lawyer for a civil rights organization, at times, a lawyer who has started the case will "consult with us or associate us in a case," particularly if the original attorney "isn't familiar with civil rights work." The local lawyers, however, may not want to give up the case, while they may also not wish to do much with it even with national organization assistance. That appears to have been the situation with the Indianapolis school case, where local NAACP-affiliated lawyers would not communicate plans even to allies in the community.[71]

For a set of cases, control allows litigators to influence their development and sequence so that they can "produce cases which presented the issues they wanted decided, where and when they wanted them," "to assure that only the *best* cases—in the most advantageous order— reach the High Court."[72] A particular difficulty in efforts to control cases moving toward the Supreme Court is that important cases develop and arrive there without the knowledge of major civil rights litigators. Although the NAACP Legal Defense Fund was the primary employment discrimination litigator, it was not aware of *Washington v. Davis* (1976) reaching the Supreme Court until after review had been granted, leaving it only the option of filing an amicus brief.[73] Because of its limited contacts on the West Coast outside California, the national ACLU learned of the first legal challenge to the curfew and exclusion orders only months after it had been initiated, with the ruling in the case escaping its notice.[74] Despite the ACLU's policy that jurisdictional statements were to be filed with the national office before being submitted to the Supreme Court so they could be monitored, "through some mix-up this was not done" in the sex discrimination case, *Kahn v. Shevin,* which thus "got to the Supreme Court before the ACLU was even aware of it."[75]

Control over the sequence of cases is particularly important for gradual erosion of adverse precedent. Such control requires coordination of cases brought by staff attorneys, cooperating attorneys, and nonaffiliated counsel, and is more difficult in proportion to the number of actors. The more cases a litigating organization can handle directly, the more control it can exert over sequence. The absence of a single dominant group in an area of law makes it "almost impossible for a single group to bring cases in a well-ordered manner."[76] Likewise, not having possession of a significant proportion of funds available in a particular area of law makes it extremely difficult to exercise any significant control over litigation.

Control is hindered when lawyers act without coordinating their activities with principal litigating groups. Such action occurs even when they have had contact with the groups. Although there was a "cooperative spirit" among the attorneys in the three cities from which restrictive covenant cases came, only one of the four cases to which the Court granted review "was an NAACP case in the strict sense," as "the lawyers managing the cases planned their work differently."[77] A more striking instance which caused more difficulty came in the campaign against racial restrictive covenants. Although *Sipes v. McGhee,* from Michigan, was the NAACP Legal Defense Fund's preferred case, and although George Vaughn was present at planning sessions, he filed a certiorari petition in *Shelley v. Kraemer,* forcing NAACP leaders to file a certiorari petition in *Sipes.* In women's rights litigation, because individuals and groups went to court on their own with different goals and varying resources, the courts received a haphazard collection of issues. The absence of intergroup coordination interfered with achieving the groups' goals by threatening step-by-step legal development, as both "friends of the movement" and "unsympathetic and opportunistic plaintiffs" created the possibility of negative precedents and impeded the predominant women's rights litigator, the Women's Rights Project.[78]

While most litigating groups consider control of an area of litigation to be an advantage, indeed an imperative, some civil rights litigators have eschewed it. For example, in the efforts to strike down suburban exclusionary zoning, the central coordination that is part of control was thought to "curtail . . . creativity" and "dampen . . . competitive excitement among activists" and decentralization was more highly valued.[79] Mental health client groups and those with disabilities seeking increased access to transportation also valued reduced central authority because they felt it helped decrease reliance on attorneys.

Individual organizations' decentralization, including their use of cooperating attorneys, also affects control, but if the national organization fails to support locally initiated litigation, it may be hurt later when it wants local lawyers to listen concerning cases important to its overall strategy. ACLU-affiliated attorneys did represent Gordon Hirabayashi and Fred Korematsu in the Japanese-American Exclusion Cases, but the ACLU's control was diminished by the independence of some of its affiliates—in particular, "a San Francisco branch that resisted dictation from ACLU headquarters in New York"—and of lawyers who had taken some of the cases. For example, when the national office was faced with reports that Hirabayashi's lawyers had done a poor job in the court of appeals, it also faced the defendant's supporters, who didn't want to change lawyers—and who were unhappy with the national organization for not filing an amicus curiae brief in the court of appeals.[80] And because Minoru Yasui's lawyer lacked ties to the ACLU, "which had refused in any event to support his client" in his challenge to the curfew, he "would not be constrained by the ACLU resolution limiting the grounds of . . . an attack," and thus proceeded "without any connection to the other test cases."[81]

Responsive Litigation

In attempting to conduct planned litigation, litigating organizations—whether rights groups or conservative public interest law firms—often find themselves in a responsive or reflexive mode. The NAACP shifted from crisis response to litigation planning at a relatively early date, but other organizations continued a reactive posture until much more recently, and now some litigators intentionally limit their work to responsive litigation. A central tenet of being a "people's lawyer" is responsiveness to clients, with "one of the most important abilities of a people's lawyer in the southern struggle the ability to jump on a plane and get where you had to be fast."[82] The ACLU did not begin more consciously planned litigation activity until roughly the last twenty-five years, when, as its focus expanded from traditional concern with First Amendment and criminal procedure issues to a much broader set of issues, it established special project areas like women's rights, rights of the mentally ill, and prisoners' rights. That much remained responsive even after initiation of the project focus is typical even when an organization seeks to plan litigation. Once a litigation campaign begins and is known, individual cases come to the litigators, who often must take some of them. If test cases initiated as part of a plan are lost in the trial court, further action results from having to respond to the defeat. Another reason is that "Organizations committed to minority-group rights seldom have the luxury of picking their targets before the fact," with much effort devoted to "reacting to conditions beyond their control."[83] The result is a combination of planned and responsive action.

One aspect of responsive litigation is that organizations often become involved in it as a result of someone else's plan. The Equal Employment Advisory Council and the National Chamber Litigation Center, for example, instead of planning their litigation, took cases from those already placed on court dockets by others' actions.[84] When a law cannot be challenged until a prosecutor acts, control is in the prosecutor's, not the litigating organization's, hands. That was true in *Plessy*, where "timing of the case, not to mention aspects of two attorneys' legal strategy . . . depended crucially on decisions by the District Attorney for the Parish of Orleans."[85]

Those wishing to challenge the death penalty or its application obviously cannot proceed until someone has been convicted of a capital crime and sentenced to death, although there are many such cases from which to choose. The Supreme Court's greater openness to prosecutors and other state officials has meant that if organizations representing civil rights and civil liberties claimants win in the lower courts, they must act responsively in the Supreme Court. Instead of being primarily a petitioner in the Supreme Court, said an ACLU lawyer, "Now we are the respondents 80 percent of the time, dragged into the Supreme Court to be reversed."[86]

Perhaps the most important type of defensive litigation is that which responds to attacks on the organization itself. The most obvious example is the post-*Brown* southern counterattack on the NAACP, with more than two dozen lawsuits by states and cities seeking to prevent the NAACP from operating taking place at one time. Other litigating organizations have found themselves in the same situation, as when the National Right to Work Legal Defense Foundation had to respond to union charges that the Foundation was violating the Landrum-Griffin Act by serving as a conduit for employer funds to attack unions. Just as in *NAACP v. Alabama*, the unions' lawsuits took their toll in money and diversion of other funds for security at headquarters.[87]

Instances of litigating organizations responding to others' actions are frequent. The NAACP's campaign against racial restrictive covenants in housing, although a planned campaign, was a response to white property owners' enforcing the covenants and ousting blacks from property or preventing them from taking occupancy. Many Northern school desegregation cases were responses to local school board or state legislative action reinforcing segregation. The Boston school case was initiated in large measure because the Boston School Committee reneged on its promise, made to obtain state funding, to obtain a new school on an integrated basis, and the Detroit case was largely a response to state legislation that undid a desegregation plan.

In the mid-1980s, civil rights groups were forced to respond when, after *Firefighters v. Stotts*, the Reagan administration Department of Justice moved to reopen consent decrees with affirmative action components that had been reached in employment discrimination cases in thirty cities, presenting civil rights litigators with "the most severe challenge of the decade,"[88] and the NAACP, the NAACP Legal Defense Fund, and the Lawyers' Committee entered a number of those cases as attorneys for plaintiff-intervenor organizations of black police officers and firemen. When the Justice Department announced plans to seek dismissal of several hundred school desegregation cases, on the grounds that the systems were now in compliance with desegregation orders, the reopenings had to be fought on a case-by-case basis, creating a heavy drain on organizational resources.

Defendants' use of the revised Rule 11 of the Federal Rules of Civil Procedure against civil rights plaintiffs has reinforced civil rights lawyers' defensive posture. In 1983, Rule 11 was amended to permit sanctions to be imposed against lawyers who do not make a "reasonable inquiry" into the foundation of a case they file; that they have made such an inquiry is attested to by their signing the papers in the case.

Civil rights attorneys claimed that Rule 11 became a weapon in the hands of judges unsympathetic to civil rights claims: because many of the claims were at the cutting edge of the law, hostile defendants could argue that claims were without an adequate legal foundation. That perception was reinforced by some significant monetary sanctions imposed against civil rights lawyers and in one case against NAACP Legal Defense Fund director Julius Chambers, and it put civil rights lawyers in a defensive posture. Their concern was not removed by research findings that "The imposition rate of sanctions in civil rights cases was not out of line with that in other types of cases," and that "Rule 11 has not been applied disproportionately against represented plaintiffs or their attorneys in civil rights cases, nor has it been applied to reasonable arguments advanced by plaintiffs' attorneys in civil rights cases." [89]

Flexibility and Momentum

Litigation strategy implies flexibility or adaptability. Lawyers' willingness to rethink problems indicates the flexible adaptation we might best associate with strategy. Flexibility can take place in the very use of litigation itself, so that one would "be able to commit resources to lawsuits, administrative complaints, publicity seeking, or to informal negotiation," [90] in choice of cases to pursue, or in choices within a case. Flexibility has been an important element in anti discrimination litigation from the earliest NAACP planned litigation, because Charles Houston saw it as an important part of the organization's efforts. Houston has been seen as engaged in a "consistent pattern of defining the problem, setting a goal, analyzing the situation, assessing the available options, developing the appropriate strategy and tactics, and implementing the planned strategy." [91] However, a closer look shows that he was "reasonably self-conscious about his refusal to stick to a preordained plan; the litigation he conducted would be sensitive to pressures of the moment, the opportunities provided and foreclosed by shifting local circumstances." [92]

Adaptability can be seen in shifts in position over the course of school desegregation litigation. The NAACP's position at the time of *Brown* was support for "color-blindness"; race-based remedies, including "racial balance," were not contemplated and Jack Greenberg, who was to succeed Thurgood Marshall at LDF, supported "freedom of choice" plans in his 1959 volume, *Race Relations and American Law*.

Illustrative of the proposition that maintenance of the organization "may depend on choosing purposes inconsistent with its earlier purposes,"[93] the failure of such plans to bring about desegregation led LDF lawyers, Greenberg at their head, to turn to racial balance remedies. In another shift, LDF lawyers who did not at first protest the closing of some black schools later did so when the schools closed were physically better facilities or ones about which parents had sentimental feelings particularly where the closings meant that black students would have to absorb much of the burden of busing while white students could stay in "their own" schools.[94]

If flexibility aids strategy, the inflexibility which can accompany it hinders responding to changes in environment. Important aspects of inflexibility are momentum, impetus to continue in a certain direction once action of a certain type has been started, and inertia, the resistance to changing one's means of operation or fixation on a certain position. This could be seen in the mid-1930s, when the NAACP was already committed to litigation as a principal activity. Efforts to shift program emphasis from litigation to greater attention to economic matters, including black labor, were resisted by NAACP leaders, whose continuing commitment to law made it difficult for them to reorient their attention.[95]

More recently, lawyers are said to have persisted in seeking racially balanced schools despite changes in judicial outlook, defeats in efforts to achieve school desegregation, and membership demands for more attention to quality education.[96] The NAACP has been criticized for having become "so committed publicly and ideologically" to school desegregation that the organization "locked itself in," allowing itself "no margin" to move resources to other activities of importance to the black urban community. A former staff member has said the NAACP "stopped thinking, stopped any analysis; it became fixed on a particular historical point," and was "just repeating" although the world had become far more complex, and litigation, "placed in contemporary social context, was not adequate and may even be disadvantageous." Instead of "rethinking about better strategies" and "attacking in other, new ways," NAACP's view is said to be: "We have the magic key and we have to keep attacking."

Momentum can be seen in the pursuit of litigation as the principal means to achieve civil rights goals; the use of litigation was reinforced by success as the spirit kindled by continuing success is likely to pro-

pel continuing litigation. In the pre-*Brown* period, the NAACP's success with salary equalization litigation in Maryland "encouraged the
national office to pursue equalization cases with some vigor," while
more recently, public interest law firms have been in a "cyclical pattern . . . in which the more they went to court, the more cases they
won. And . . . the more often they won, the more often they sought
to litigate."[97]

What are the reasons for inflexibility and inertia? It can result from
a lag in learning, as time is necessary for lawyers to shift their focus
after courts and Congress reduce their receptiveness to civil rights
claims. Thus once organizations, prompted by favorable Warren Court
rulings, set off down the litigation trail, they did not quickly turn away
from such activity even when the Court's composition and approach
changed. Inertia also occurs because organizations, like armies, fight
the last war. Past struggles, which affect lawyers' present litigation
posture, force them to bump their heads before changing. In addition,
like others, they are prone to want to continue doing those things
that have worked in the past,"[98] and they may "steadfastly refuse to
recognize reverses . . . which, to some extent, have been precipitated
by their rigidity," as was said about school desegregation litigation.[99]
Abortion litigation also illustrates this. Arguments and strategies by
pro-choice advocates should have changed, as a result of change in
the political and legal environment, including "the vigor of their opponents, . . . the entry of the solicitor general, and . . . their narrowing
margin in the Court," but they continued to believe that *Roe v. Wade*
would be sustained. As a result, "they never seriously raised alternative arguments" that might have preserved more of their position.[100]

Inflexibility can also result from the goals and expectations of a
litigating organization's constituency. Once involved in a case, after
they "have been rallied and solicited for funds," they have a "disposition . . . to total victory and vindication."[101] In the NAACP's litigation,
"the grassroots origins of and support for specific lawsuits . . . inevi-
tably diminished the degree to which a coordinated campaign could
be conducted."[102] Other constituencies, particularly those attracted to
civil rights groups by principle rather than material incentives, make it
quite difficult to alter an organization's position without losing the constituents' support.[103] Likewise, for an organization that has received
significant support from foundations, another constituency may en-

danger that support if it shifts position. Thus organizational imperatives lead to maintaining positions even if they are not productive for litigation strategy. Indicating adaptation to internal organizational concerns that produces inertia vis-à-vis the outside world, in earlier NAACP litigation one frequently could see "proposals made by planners who abandon rational plans made by those more removed from decision in favor of those that reflected the NAACP's internal, organizational constraints, decisions altered because of preference of the staff, negotiation over plans with constituencies having diverse interests." [104]

Success might encourage flexibility—having won, one would do what was necessary to win again—but it may instead produce inflexibility. Victorious litigants do not wish to give up, or be seen as giving up, what they pressed hard to achieve. Defeats, even when conveying "the difficulty of traditional litigation as a way of protecting . . . rights," do not easily change habits.[105] Some persistence is valuable, as new law is not likely to be made on the first try and the Supreme Court is not likely to take the first case raising a particular issue, so that nothing would have been accomplished if initial failure prompts withdrawal. Thus an organization that has begun to use a new legal argument may not be willing to cease its efforts with the first loss. However, it may "throw good money after bad" and persist even while accumulating more losses. The NAACP did this in its attempt to convince courts that segregation of races should be found to violate the Constitution even where statutes did not mandate the separation, as "the effort to breathe life into this doctrine tended to divert resources from the more promising (at least in retrospect) approach of proving deliberate, and therefore illegal, Northern segregation." [106]

Momentum also occurs in the pursuit of individual cases even after the legal environment changes subsequent to initiation of the case. With time and energy already invested in a case, litigators, perhaps reinforced by clients' demands, are unwilling to stop before getting to the top of the appeals ladder. The pressure of past positions can become quite substantial, and adherence to the past, born of pragmatism, can overcome pragmatism itself, as lawyers "become straitjacketed in how they viewed a . . . case." And altering legal theories in midlitigation may be particularly difficult if opponents, and Supreme Court justices, call attention to changed positions.

Although some lawyers are "more adventurous" and thus "willing to lose a few" in their attempts to implement innovative approaches, pragmatic attorneys who don't want to lose cases at times become conservative in their approach in litigation.[107] Because lawyers have to argue to judges that they are simply extending the past, not advocating a new theory, it "gets you thinking that way" and "innovation becomes the strategy of desperation." As another lawyer put it forcefully, "Litigation is not a process giving one time to think." Lawyers themselves often say that past rulings "make them do it." Thus, in the Boston school case, when some black parents wished greater emphasis on their concerns about educational quality, the lawyers trying the case "made clear that a long line of court decisions would limit the degree to which those educational priorities could be incorporated into the desegregation plan the lawyers were preparing to file."[108] The lawyers may, however, only be engaging in rationalization, using doctrine to resist change when their views of what the law should be are congruent with judicial rulings.[109]

A particularly important reason for momentum is *the myth of rights*— the collection of ideas that rights exist, that courts can define rights, and that those rights can be enforced in the courts, which leads lawyers to continue to turn to the courts to seek new precedent even after they sustain defeats or when rights "won" in court are not implemented.[110] This is related to the idea that litigation itself may entail inertia. The idea of progression, that one would be able to progress from one case to the next and from one victory to the next, can prevent lawyers from focusing on a central issue like ending school segregation because they did not think they could win it immediately; they focused on the next case rather than the ultimate goal. On the other hand, the progression made lawyers "get overconfident as they watch things build up."

As we contemplate civil rights litigators' inertia and momentum and the increased complexity they face, an interesting question is whether litigating groups are more clever than they once were in dealing with litigation. That is, do they have a more sophisticated understanding of what is involved and of the difficulties involved in pursuing a litigation campaign than they may have had earlier? For example, do groups that enter litigation after others have been involved in it avoid the earlier groups' mistakes? Do groups set up by the model litigators, the NAACP Legal Defense Fund, begin with a higher level of knowledge than groups that enter litigation without such assistance? There is the possibility that litigating civil rights groups have moved along a learning curve, but whether each group does it individually or the groups learn from each other as part of the civil rights bar is unclear, and there certainly appear to be severe limits on such learning.

8

Choosing Areas of Law

In this chapter, a crucial part of litigation planning, groups' choices of areas of law in which to concentrate their efforts are examined, with attention to both the process by which particular organizations make those choices, with especial attention to NAACP and LDF, and the criteria brought to bear in choosing some areas rather than others. The focus here, and in the following chapter on the choice of particular cases to be pursued, is on decisions by lawyers associated with organizations.

Basic Aspects

Some areas of law in which organizations litigate, for example, Title VII and capital punishment for the NAACP Legal Defense Fund, are chosen with care, with constraints imposed mostly by limited resources, and with organizations bringing criteria to bear, at least implicitly, in a process of selecting and emphasizing issues for litigation. This is not unlike the process for groups' selection of topics for their legislative lobbying, where among key criteria are "the probability of success," whether and how the area selected "will contribute to the group's internal agenda," and whether a victory will have "precedential or symbolic value" to the organization.[1]

Other areas are said "simply [to] arise naturally," perhaps evolving because many cases on a topic are brought to the organization, as with sit-ins and demonstrations. In choosing particular areas of law in which to focus litigation activities as part of their pursuit of strategy (really the selection of issues), litigators must choose areas of law in which a sufficient number of potential cases can be generated to provide a choice of those appropriate to pursue. This leads, as one lawyer put it, to a preference for choosing "a subject with broad interest and appeal through which branches and attorneys could get a feel for what they could do to implement law on the books."

Areas on which particular organizations focus are not static. Most obvious was the ACLU's shift, roughly congruent with its adoption of a project-centered approach, to a range of concerns much broader than its traditional attention to freedom of expression, church-state relations, and criminal procedure. Its new agenda, under which 50 to 85 percent of the cases on its docket in 1983 would not have been there fifteen years earlier, included rights of women, prisoners, and children, as well as increased involvement in civil rights–voting rights, enforcement of Title VI against city police departments, and school desegregation, where it became a major player in important school desegregation cases, including Atlanta, Los Angeles, Pasadena, and *Brown III*, the reopened Topeka case.

The ACLU also provides an example of change through a group's abandoning a litigation area, an option more likely if an organization's internal situation provided latitude to its leaders. Obscenity's apparently low salience to the ACLU's members, coupled with other issues' perceived importance and resource demands from other litigation areas, allowed the group's leaders to shift their attention elsewhere. That decision was reinforced by the presence of other organizations to protect the "libertarian" position concerning obscenity, even if through material motives.[2]

Resource availability and geography are two major elements in choice of areas in which to litigate. Selecting areas and obtaining resources are closely related, although it is unclear whether, or to what extent, the availability of funding affects choice of areas, or the extent to which funding sources serve to constrain organizational choices. An organization, in "sending out proposals for funding," "tries to get funded what is important but to some extent what foundations will fund." One organization official said his organization "never did anything it didn't believe in," but he conceded that "some things less important are done, some things more important are not done because of funding." Geography is another element. Most early activity to achieve civil rights took place in the South where segregation was mandated by statute. Later, increased recognition that segregation and other forms of racial discrimination were prevalent in the North prompted, if not forced, organizations to begin efforts there. However, that did not take place before debate in the civil rights community and not without criticisms of organizations, including LDF, for failing to shift their attention and for continuing to focus much of their efforts in the South.

The importance of process in selecting areas on which to focus is also important, and it can be seen in an organization's consultation of its members, either individually or through their representatives such as delegates to a national convention. An important part of this process is the extent to which choices by organization staff, particularly lawyers, are constrained. Staff prefer having discretion to make choices without having to obtain advance approval, even if they report afterwards on their stewardship. The likelihood of staff discretion is high in an organization, whether or not membership based, that has centralized control,[3] although ideology or principle may well limit such discretion. Major civil rights litigating organizations have relatively high centralized authority structures, and both central staff litigators and observers report considerable staff discretion; however, they may well have less discretion in the choice of areas in which to focus their efforts or choice of positions adopted than in the choice of particular cases.[4]

Whether or not the views of an organization's membership *are* taken into account, whether or not their views were directly solicited, is an open question. In the choice of areas on which to concentrate or on positions taken, there appears to be no focus on membership involvement. Few of the lawyers interviewed indicated that members, or others in equivalent positions outside the staff, were consulted in such choices, even if the issue is as important as affirmative action. Typical of the process in civil rights organizations is selection of issues within the Native American Rights Fund (NARF), the predominant litigating entity working on behalf of native Americans' rights. There the issues were selected not by the clients themselves but by a small group differing in socioeconomic status from the group's clients. This led to criticism for setting of goals that did not always match the needs of its clientele and for detachment from that clientele.[5]

Membership-based litiating groups such as the NAACP, because they are expected to heed membership concerns closely, have been hypothesized to be more likely to litigate concerning issues of immediate concern to large numbers of individual clients and potential members than nonmembership-based public interest law firms such as LDF.[6] However, counter to this hypothesis is that LDF was far more involved in Title VII litigation, of "importance to the people," than was the NAACP. That, despite different organizational structures, both NAACP and LDF gave attention to employment issues counsels delay in accepting the hypothesis and leaves open the empirical question of the extent to which membership- and nonmembership-based types of organizations differ in case selection.[7] Pressures on both types of organizations to litigate certain types of cases may be similar; or a membership-based organization's litigation unit with autonomy may be able to focus its litigation in the same way as do nonmembership-based public interest law firms. With cases coming to the NAACP as well as to LDF through lawyers, neither organization's national legal staff feels direct client pressure. Or, alternately, both feel it—through client contact with local lawyers. As a Title VII attorney said of LDF, the organization doesn't feel client demand directly, but does feel it through cooperating attorneys: "When there is a civil rights problem, clients will knock on their doors."

Interorganizational Elements

In an interorganizational element in the choice of areas of law, organizations have "to consider that other organizations were considering some issues." Clear patterns develop that decrease the "potential for legal chaos" when a number of groups litigate issues in a major area of law, so that instead of "fragmentation," there is some "order and stability." The stability stems in part from LDF's litigating dominance, NAACP's major involvement, the regular presence of the Lawyers' Committee and specialized litigating entities, and the important glue provided by the civil rights bar. There seems to have been little battling over turf, perhaps because there has been so much work to do in aid of civil rights. If, as one attorney said, LDF was "not out to get into other organizations' turf," thus improving relations with them, there could be turf-*protection*, as when an "extremely insecure" LDF protected its territory in the early 1960s: "Jack Greenberg didn't want anyone treading on his turf."

At times, division of labor, while not providing a completely and neatly divided pie, resulted from "both formal and informal discussions" and "constant contact and dialogue." However, it generally remained more a matter of "we saw what they were doing" and of "trying to stay out of each other's way" than of explicitly "carving up the territory": one organization concentrated on an area of law and other organizations devoted efforts to other areas. For example, because other national groups already were investing efforts in the campaign against exclusionary zoning, LDF did not initially direct its resources to that cause. Likewise, "If the ACLU is involved, the NAACP need not be." With the ACLU ready to step into criminal justice cases and public defender organizations charged with protecting defendants' rights, the NAACP could refer cases to them. However, "notwithstanding, the NAACP needs to be involved to cover some of the issues." The operation of subject matter comparative advantage in interorganizational relations could also be seen in an agreement under which the Lawyers' Committee specialized in criminal defense, the Lawyers Constitutional Defense Committee (formed by civil rights and civil liberties organizations to protect people during the 1964 Freedom Summer) took the lead in cases involving brutality by police or guards, and LDF, better equipped to seek groundbreaking precedent, left day-to-day litigation to other organizations but was predominant in education cases.[8] This arrangement functioned in part through referrals of cases by each organization to the others.

Interorganizational division of labor can also be geographical. One example is the NAACP's 1970s concentration on northern school desegregation cases while LDF focused its school efforts primarily in the Southeast. Voting rights lawyers had what amounted to a geographical division of labor, with one law firm, on retainer to the LDF, focusing on Georgia and Alabama; another, connected to the ACLU, focusing on Georgia and South Carolina; another lawyer handling cases mainly in Louisiana; and MALDEF operating in Texas and the Southwest along with the Southwest Voter Education Project. There can also be local division of labor, as occurred at the county level in Mississippi in voting rights work after the breakup of the Council of Federated Organizations (COFO). There were "NAACP" counties, which the Lawyers Committee represented in court, and Mississippi Freedom Democratic Party counties, where the Lawyers Constitutional Defense Committee undertook legal representation.

Education.   Education litigation shows interorganizational division of labor. In higher education, LDF was the "prime mover," as it was in the *Adams* litigation to get the federal government to desegregate higher education by enforcing national laws. However, there was little NAACP action on the subject, perhaps as a result of considerable resistance from black administrators, professors, and alumni of predominantly black or historically black institutions, an important part of the NAACP's constituency, to desegregation plans that would eliminate those institutions.

In elementary and secondary education, by contrast, both the NAACP and the LDF made major efforts, and other groups were involved. Interorganizational division of labor developed in the late 1960s. LDF litigated on schools almost exclusively in the South, while the NAACP focused on the North. LDF had only brief involvement in the North. After litigating the Indianapolis and Detroit cases, it participated in the Denver case, linking its southern busing cases to northern issues and making a successful argument about burdens of proof, but the case was an "accident" for LDF, although if it were to take a case in the North, Denver was appropriate because of the "quality of legal and factual preparation." Although after Denver, LDF did continue to bring cases to develop legal principles, it was not "geared up for major enforcement of northern school desegregation" and "had no enforcement strategy"[9] and thus "appeared to withdraw effort," leaving northern cases to the NAACP, and to a lesser extent the ACLU and the Justice Department.

The North-South division of labor resulted in part from the NAACP's and LDF's opposing litigation theories. The NAACP, at least when Robert Carter was general counsel, had pursued a theory of de facto segregation, a "pure" theory that separate is unequal. However, according to one NAACP attorney, the theory had "proved a disaster in a number of cases," in particular, Cincinnati and Gary, Indiana, which "knocked out" the de facto argument.[10] However "alluring" such a theory may have been because it avoided problems of proving state action, the LDF was "never committed" to it but instead pursued a theory that school districts should be required to dismantle the vestiges of de jure segregation.

When the NAACP was left without its earlier theory, it "had to develop a whole new litigation thrust." However, it stayed in the North, where it had gone because it saw "many groups shying away" from northern school cases because of the remedies necessary there. The NAACP began to win in the North on the theory that northern school districts were maintaining de jure segregation, and LDF began to win in the South on its theory that vestiges of segregation had to be dismantled, in so doing accelerating enforcement of school desegregation and drawing LDF into greater activity ("hundreds of cases") there and reinforcing the division of labor. After successfully concluding its southern cases, LDF "didn't go to start up cases in the North and West."

A related explanation is that LDF, making a "tactical choice as to where to get mileage," felt it could do so in southern and border states rather than in northern cases, which others, particularly the NAACP, were litigating. Likewise, when the NAACP invested new effort in school desegregation litigation in the late 1970s, it brought its cases where the LDF "was not." However, an LDF attorney says that if LDF didn't bring cases, it was not because the NAACP was there, but because "it was not the right time to bring them." Indeed, LDF "brought many cases where the NAACP was present" because of its legal representation of NAACP members and branches, resulting from a "community organizational history" of proceeding through LDF. The result was a "nice synergy" as the efforts of the two organizations fitted together.

The NAACP's Choices

Among factors affecting the NAACP's choice of areas of law has been the "significant input" of the organization's branches, which feeds into and interacts with "overarching policy"—determined in broad outline by resolutions passed at the annual convention—and the general counsel's and staff lawyers' interests. Between conventions, the board of directors provides policy direction. However, such direction is often general, and, because of the interplay between board votes and general counsel's views, board votes do not translate directly into litigation campaigns. The general counsel has had considerable autonomy to pursue his own interests, for example, Thomas Atkins and criminal justice matters or Nathaniel Jones and northern school desegregation, particularly in his home state of Ohio. General counsel's views predominated in part because his litigation decisions "don't get reviewed" and because he had authority to decide how his budget would be divided. However, requests for more money for litigation could be used to review and limit general counsel; some outside the organization say that, as a result of the executive director's asserting his authority within the organization, general counsel "doesn't have authority over the budget," even over specific foundation money for school desegregation.

A "primary consideration" in NAACP's choice of areas of law is availability of resources. Where resources were not available "in-house," NAACP would try to refer types of cases to other agencies where possible. Greater resources for schools and employment came from foundation grants and from other gifts with restrictions limiting their use to those areas, establishing a constraint in adjusting the litigation agenda and reinforcing the NAACP's emphasis on school desegregation. However, a Ford Foundation report made no specific mention of earmarking while noting that Ford provided over $4.3 million to NAACP's Special Contribution Fund from 1967 through 1975 "for both general and project support," with a "significant portion . . . applied by the NAACP leadership to defray the litigation and related expenses of its Legal Department."[11]

Injustices to blacks caught in the snares of the criminal justice system have led to attention to aspects of that area of law. One of the organization's earliest campaigns was the effort to outlaw lynching, although it was directed at legislation rather than at the courts. In addition, the most complex early NAACP litigation dealt with criminal procedure, particularly due process and fair trial issues,[12] which helps explain the organization's involvement in *Moore v. Dempsey* and in the still more famous Scottsboro Boys cases, where NAACP involvement was also affected by the element of competition with Communists to represent the defendants.

In something of a revival rather than an innovation, in recent years the NAACP has showed "willingness to give assistance to impoverished defendants enmeshed in the criminal justice system, to guarantee due process." Although litigation in this area has generally been reactive, as when the NAACP came to the aid of a retarded young

man found guilty of rape in Alabama, it did slate the criminal justice area for particular concern in the late 1980s and early 1990s. The
significant "racial subjectivity" in such matters as prosecutorial discretion, jury selection, police use of deadly force, hiring and promotion
in police departments, and military justice provide the organization
the opportunity to "raise the costs of police mistreating minorities."

School Desegregation

For quite some time, school desegregation has been the NAACP's
consuming interest, something that has "always been done and [thus]
had to be continued," indicating the importance of inertia as a limit on
organizational choice. It has been general counsel's "virtual concern"
and is said to take up "90 percent of the conscious effort" in the organization's litigation efforts. Indeed, the NAACP's extended attention
to desegregation, particularly as *Brown* failed to produce desegregation and desegregation did not seem to produce improved quality
of education, ultimately prompted criticism for being an "excessive
commitment of resources." School desegregation efforts, which the
organization seemed "hell bent to continue," were, said critics, "lost
on the masses of people" and did not "deal with dollars in the person's
pocket in the short run"; proper emphasis would have put school desegregation "into parity with other concerns," particularly economic
issues "critical to the masses," such as Title VII litigation.

The NAACP's involvement in school desegregation litigation now
seems natural and may appear to have been foreordained, with school
cases "more programmatically developed" than litigation in other
areas. However, this focus has been problematic. The NAACP "was
never committed to destroying school segregation because it was central to the system of racial subordination," but chose school segregation for attack, as "just one of many targets" along with lynching and
Jim Crow laws, because it fitted with the organization's needs at a
given time, and because it "became an increasingly attractive [target]
as precedents dealing with schools accumulated precisely because the
NAACP had been litigating school cases for nonstrategic reasons."[13]

The NAACP's earlier involvement in education litigation shows
that its activities were dictated in part by organizational concerns. In
particular, just as the litigation to open graduate and professional education to blacks had an advantage of providing a multiplier effect by

"increasing the size of groups likely to provide leadership for the black community," [14] the litigation to equalize teachers' salaries, which preceded the attempt to eliminate "separate but equal" from elementary and secondary education, was seen as a means of increasing the organization's membership by providing incentives to join the NAACP. Although the salary equalization effort was initially seen as providing greater benefits to the organization than its costs, by the late 1940s it no longer met the "cost-benefit" test because cases became more complex as school boards shifted to using merit rating systems; teachers did not maintain enthusiasm; and, perhaps more important, "each suit threatened serious ruptures among the segments of the black community interested in eliminating segregation," [15] thus doing damage to the community the NAACP wished to attract.

The decision on whether to seek equalization in elementary and secondary schools or to mount a root-and-branch attack on segregation there also posed the possibility of disrupting the NAACP's constituency. This led to postponing cases for several years while Thurgood Marshall tried to demonstrate to potential supporters the attractiveness of the direct attack option; thus the timing of the direct attack on "separate but equal" in education was "most significantly affected by organizational politics." [16] In the end, NAACP branches—by and large, black middle-class people with an interest in broad issues, the organization's articulate members and its contributors, not fully representative of the organization's total membership—provided support for desegregation, and court victories in graduate and professional education cases and changes in the political environment also helped overcome resistance.

Where direct attack cases were brought—the geographic component of the choice of area—was also affected by organizational factors. Particularly important was the proximity of the upper South to NAACP headquarters and the lack further south of lawyers who would help with the cases. Although the conventional wisdom has been that the NAACP chose the upper South for strategic reasons including the greater possibility of success, "The various planning documents do not show the NAACP strategists deliberately selecting the upper South as a site for litigation on the ground that success would be more likely, or opposition less heated, there." [17]

Employment

Not as well known as its school desegregation work is the NAACP's litigation on employment discrimination, particularly under the 1964 Civil Rights Act. The several NAACP general counsel differed considerably in the extent of their interest in employment discrimination activity, at times providing input into development of litigation theories and strategies, but at other times paying little attention to Title VII work because their preoccupation with school cases became total. In the latter situation, the NAACP exhibited only a "willingness to take employment cases where local branches brought attention to them," but the result was "no programmatic orientation" to cases brought to the NAACP by lawyers in the field; "given the nature of the organization," the NAACP did "have to have some ad hoc cases."

The NAACP did have a labor law program. However, it was an "idiosyncratic" campaign run from outside the NAACP's Legal Department by the NAACP Labor Director, Herbert Hill. Operating with a high degree of autonomy, he functioned as an "independent operator" as a result of organizational confidence in his skills. The result of this arrangement was that the NAACP gave more attention than otherwise to Title VII, but another result of absence of Legal Department control of the employment cases was absence of organizational coordination of the NAACP's total civil rights docket.

Hill began developing employment discrimination cases even before the effective date of Title VII, resulting in "literally hundreds of cases" so that he "needed lawyers desperately." The NAACP made some resources available by providing one lawyer, "bureaucratically in the Legal Department" but working full-time with the labor director, and two other attorneys who worked on some cases, but this allocation was insufficient. NAACP house counsel were used "as much as possible" but they did less than did cooperating attorneys, and less still than the LDF. (That some NAACP officials considered the organization to be making a major effort in an area of law such as Title VII when one lawyer was working full-time in that area says something about the NAACP legal staff's size.)

Hill, although frustrated by lack of resources, was "not going to be stopped" by that situation: "He had the cases and he was going to bring them," whether it took private attorneys, staff attorneys, NAACP-retained counsel, or even the LDF's attorneys to do so. Thus he went to Executive Director Roy Wilkins with the unprecedented request that the NAACP work with LDF "because LDF had the resources." Although Wilkins was a stickler for protocol and despite friction between the NAACP and LDF, he approved the request. The outcome was that the NAACP funneled many of the employment discrimination cases it initiated to LDF, with "the strategy [being] LDF strategy" and LDF doing the "biggest piece" of the NAACP cases. Yet despite LDF's prominence in the NAACP's work in this area of the law, there were "things the NAACP did that the LDF did not do"; in particular, the NAACP handled virtually all the cases involving the building trades, because of its previous specialization in that area, although this "was not so much discussed as it just happened." Hill was able to avoid "bureaucratic control" within the NAACP as to which cases got litigated and thus saved "time and procrastination built into the process."

The NAACP's lesser litigation emphasis on Title VII than on schools was part of a continuing debate within the organization as to the emphasis to be given to economic issues. It took the form of the questions: Should the focus be on education or on matters of more immediate economic relevance to large numbers of the minority community, such as employment discrimination? and Should litigation be used to aid individuals or to seek larger goals such as desegregating a school system, changing a company's employment practices, or seeking precedent for other cases? Earlier, the NAACP had given considerable attention to economic issues, for example, showing concern about the poverty of southern blacks during the Depression and the low pay of railroad firemen and black schoolteachers (the basis for its many equalization suits), and it had pressed for fair employment practices and for antidiscrimination measures with respect to government employees.[18] The outcome of historical debates within the organization, however, was that the NAACP "has never given the economic problems of blacks sustained attention comparable to its attention to the question of segregation per se." Like the LDF, the NAACP was "most confident and most energetic in economic matters only if they would choose antidiscrimination grounds on which to stand."[19]

In the contemporary period, giving less attention to employment discrimination has meant that a principal avenue of success was not used to focus on a major matter of direct concern to many African-Americans, while, in a reflection of differences in outlook between the

NAACP leadership and the larger black population, it continued to emphasize an issue of larger symbolic importance for blacks' inclusion in the polity (school desegregation). If the solution to the situation of the "underclass" is economic, then the law orientation—the fixation on "rights"—of leaders of traditional organizations like the NAACP and the NAACP Legal Defense Fund, while important overall and very important to those who have left the ghetto, may at best have been tangential to those concerns. However, that economic issues might come to play a larger role in civil rights activity can be seen in the different agenda espoused by Rev. Benjamin F. Chavis, Jr., when he was the NAACP's executive director. He promptly moved to add to the NAACP's agenda efforts to improve economic opportunities for African-Americans and other minorities.

The LDF's Process of Choice

Both staff attorneys and observers generally agree that LDF litigation was focused in particular areas of the law. Decisions as to these foci were made in a fairly simply policymaking structure. Jack Greenberg has said that the seventy-member board of directors "makes general policy decisions on what I call rather large issues," such as whether to establish a poverty law program, but "staff really operates the organization,"[20] and others confirm that view. According to a Ford Foundation report, "The board as a whole mainly ratifies staff proposals," but the Board's executive committee of sixteen members "is active in policy formulation, and individual members of the board play a role in determining policy [and] developing litigation strategy."[21]

Funding, particularly foundation funding, has been important but not determinative in LDF's choice of areas in which to litigate. As one participant observed, in any civil rights organization there was the question, "Do you undertake work in an area because the money is available or because you want to do it anyhow?" LDF has been thought quite persuasive in getting foundations to support what LDF wanted to do, although it may have been more a matter of LDF "soliciting for specific issues" and making choices among available sources "to help bring about a balanced program."

Passage of the Civil Rights and Voting Rights Acts in 1964 and 1965 shifted LDF's attention and provided a "natural dividing line" marking changes in its emphasis on areas of law in which to concentrate litigation. Considerable effort was devoted to defense of civil rights demonstrators in the early 1960s, although at least initially most of this activity was responsive. The extent of the activity was so great that LDF's school desegregation "work was complicated and its litigation timetable delayed by a redeployment of Fund resources."[22] After passage of the 1964 Civil Rights Act and its public accommodations provisions vindicated the demonstrators and "closed that chapter in our work," LDF continued work on voting rights demonstrators' cases for several years but on a decreasing basis.

LDF then turned its attention to enforcing the provisions of the 1964 Act, particularly Title VII. The result was that, within the idea that LDF gave attention to "racial discrimination wherever found" and pursued "any opportunity to change the law as it affected discrimination, attention would be given to voting one day and courtroom discrimination another," there were "quite conspicuous" shifts in the areas in which LDF litigated. In 1975, Jack Greenberg noted that "[c]apital punishment, employment, and education each generally accounts for 200 to 300 cases on our docket," with housing and prisoners' rights accounting for roughly seventy-five each, plus roughly 100 miscellaneous.[23]

Another shift involved voting rights, in which LDF had always been engaged to some extent. In an instance of the LDF's internal "free-market" approach, in which a lawyer can come in and develop an area as long as it is within the organization's guidelines, one estimate held that probably one-fifth of LDF's time was devoted to voting rights by the mid-1970s, with those cases taking up some portion of two staff persons' time by the end of the decade. There was also "substantially greater voting rights activity" in the 1980s, as a function of the 1982 battle over renewal of the Voting Rights Act and redistricting activity after the decennial census. The increased activity entailed a change in emphasis. Efforts to eliminate barriers to minorities' participation were replaced with attacks on vote dilution, such as suits to enforce pre-clearance under Section 5 of the Act and challenges to at-large local elections.[24] More recently, there has been a shift from attacks on maintaining at-large elections to challenges to the way in which single-member legislative districts are drawn.

Housing

Of the traditional major areas of civil rights litigation activity, housing was the one in which the LDF was least involved. "Generally," claimed

LDF, "we select significant numbers of cases that are responsive to local needs and that will open up decent housing to substantial numbers of blacks." While it "encourage[d] others to bring fair housing suits,"[25] its housing cases were primarily ones in which there was discrimination against blacks in public housing, part of its poverty concern. Although comparative advantage would be a sufficient reason for low LDF involvement in housing, Jack Greenberg in 1975 talked about the difficulty of achieving results from housing litigation: "If there isn't new construction, there's not much you can do about integrating housing. The falling off of housing starts and of large-scale housing programs slows down implementation." Moreover, "you can't force communities to put up housing. All you do, perhaps, is require them to stop excluding those who want to do so." He did, however, say "there's still a hell of a lot of law to be made up there."[26]

These comments help explain not only LDF's relatively minimal attention to housing but also the larger pattern in civil rights litigation which it reflected. Just as housing was the last area to receive congressional attention, housing litigation lagged far behind schools and jobs as a major area of civil rights litigation, and may have moved down to fourth place among areas of litigation focus behind capital punishment litigation. Housing is the area in which least progress has been made, perhaps because it is the area where whites' views of not wanting to be in contact with large numbers of blacks comes most into play.[27] Despite the suggestion that economics, not racial discrimination, leads to residential separation because minorities are less able to afford housing that more whites can afford, "blacks of every economic level are highly segregated from whites of similar economic status,"[28] in part because of discrimination in financing for home purchases, even though it is covered by the 1968 Fair Housing Act.

No major general purpose civil rights organization has made housing a premier matter in recent years. Among the reasons for this lesser attention, in addition to Greenberg's just-noted suggestion, are that unlike jobs, "housing is not perceived as bread-and-butter," and that, although "you can see you are getting results for people, the effects of change are not as dramatic as school or lunch counter desegregation." Moreover, many blacks, particularly working-class or low-income blacks living in central cities, could see little "relationship between suburban zoning and housing, employment, and educational opportunities."[29] Other reasons are resistance from the real estate business and the difficulty of bringing cases, in part because of rules on standing to sue, and the presence of few lawyers who will stay with housing litigation. Moreover, according to a housing attorney, with housing cases, civil rights lawyers are often suing individuals, particularly small owners, making the cases more bitter than in employment, where one is suing a company.

Welfare

Welfare litigation is an area to which LDF devoted significant attention in the late 1960s and early 1970s but substantially less in the 1980s. Questions of poverty law were a focus in the earlier period because, while "they were not as obviously race-oriented" as job discrimination and school segregation, they had "great impact." Included were *Thorpe v. Durham Housing Authority* (1969), limiting evictions from public housing, and *Sniadach v. Family Finance Corp.* (1969), providing protection from garnishment. In this area of law as in others, most of LDF's clients were blacks because cases came through cooperating attorneys, but welfare was an area of concentration in which more whites were represented than in others.

There were several reasons for LDF's reduction in emphasis on welfare-related issues after only six years, in addition to the conclusion of the second three-year Ford grant through which the National Office for the Rights of the Indigent (NORI) had been established. One was that courts, after establishing procedural rights, "weren't going to deal with substantive matters or reallocate resources." Another was a difference from welfare organizations in approach. LDF did provide legal advice to the National Welfare Rights Organization (NWRO) but "never really believed in the theory of overloading the system" to make it collapse. Yet another was that the Office of Economic Opportunity and the Legal Services Back-Up Centers had come into existence. With their presence and the fact that "no one was doing as much with the Fund's traditional areas," it made sense for LDF to shift emphasis.

The Title VII Campaign

LDF had not been significantly involved in employment discrimination cases before passage of Title VII, which finally provided the basis for a coherent body of law in that area. LDF highlighted employment discrimination "for major expansion" and it became one of LDF's two

major post-*Brown* focused litigation campaigns outside its school desegregation work. Indeed, the Title VII campaign probably was larger
in scope than the *Brown* campaign, but it received less attention because it had to compete for attention with many other litigation efforts
and did not lead to a single Supreme Court ruling of Brown's stature,
although *Griggs v. Duke Power Co.* was very important.

Once LDF began to work on employment discrimination, it remained one of its major areas of litigation, in 1980 "continu[ing] to
occupy the greatest portion of LDF staff-time."[30] One LDF attorney
estimated a couple of years later that Title VII cases accounted for 30
to 35 percent of the organization's total caseload, although types of
Title VII cases had changed because of affirmative action's increasing prominence and the 1972 amendments to Title VII, which allowed
suits by government employees. In 1985 "nearly half" of the organization's current cases involved employment matters, if one combined
private, public, and federal matters.

Job discrimination was a "natural" for LDF, combining economic
and racial concerns—an issue with substantial, immediate, and visible
economic ramifications for minorities. With jobs, "people saw the law
and asked what it meant for them," something far more concrete than
fund cutoff cases under Title VI of the 1964 Civil Rights Act. Title VII
cases also meant more to the individual than did public accommodations cases: "Would you rather eat in Hatchet Man's restaurant or
have a job?" Yet the new emphasis on employment was not related to
the state of the economy, but stemmed from finding Title VII to be "a
very powerful weapon in attacking racial discrimination"[31] and from
the government's not doing very much, "despite the liberal bent of
the LBJ administration."

LDF's "new focus on the economic status of blacks and other minorities" stemmed from a 1965 Chicago conference of academics and
civil rights activists convened to decide what directions to take. Looking "at what parts would lend themselves to litigation," participants
thought that with the use of Title VII, employment discrimination
would lend itself to "a broad approach" best used in a "new area"
of litigation. According to someone involved in the campaign's initial planning, the Title VII campaign was "very deliberate" strategy
that "came from academics, not clients—from New York City, not the
mills and factories," "a response to constituent need not so much from
demand" as from an "elitist" decision as to "what people need," al-

though this was done without the organization or its staff "getting off on their own 'trips.'" It was "the best of the elitist targeting system" because it was "done by sensitive, committed, knowledgeable persons." In short, the campaign came from staff, not from black workers whom the campaign was undertaken to help.

LDF's employment discrimination litigation campaign was "the most expansive and programmatic" of private efforts to enforce Title VII, with "a large volume of cases in the federal courts, and a monitoring system to identify cases, issues, and industries." Like the NAACP staff working on employment discrimination, LDF anticipated a "several-stage campaign" in which the lawyers would have to deal with prerequisites for suit and "procedural technicalities" "before substantive interpretations could be reached"[32] in part because there was no body of employment discrimination law when Title VII of the 1964 Civil Rights Act was enacted. Indeed, there were "three generations of issues" in the law's development: procedural issues, such as when a filing was timely, which had to be resolved first although rulings on them were handed down over an extended period; on the substantive law of Title VII; and on remedy.[33] In fact, the early years were "consumed" with procedural questions; later, in cases against the government, LDF had to go through the "same progression as with private litigation." By the early 1970s, much of the "procedural underbrush" was removed, and it was "clear that it was possible cases could be maintained successfully." Cases dealing with definitions and proof of discrimination followed, to be followed in turn by a "third generation" involving questions of "appropriate affirmative relief and implementation." Questions concerning attorneys' fees, "not all that important in the original cases," also became important later.

When it wished to initiate this campaign, LDF did not have the staff with which to proceed so "resources had to be collected and a staff developed." In the summer of 1965, before the Act's effective date, LDF set up the Division of Legal Information and Community Service and a project in which people were "sent out . . . to talk to black workers' groups, to acquaint them with Title VII and to get them to file complaints with EEOC, and to coordinate with local lawyers." Columbia Law School faculty provided substantial assistance; law professors and recent law school graduates were recruited to prepare model papers (pleadings, discovery documents) to facilitate Title VII complainants' use of private counsel.

Industries in the South were targeted for litigation. These included expanding ones—among them trucking, pulp and paper, textiles, and tobacco—"to have a broad impact where there would be employment," and industries where there had not previously been litigation. The targeted industries were also ones with high-paying positions and "lots of blacks in crummy jobs," because it was "easier to move blacks within companies than to bring them into companies." The result was geographic targeting coupled with industry targeting: North Carolina (trucking, tobacco, textiles) and Birmingham, Alabama (steel), with targeted areas adjacent to rural poverty areas. These were also places—in the Fourth and Fifth Circuits—where the LDF had lawyers and there were some liberal judges.

At least once the campaign had been initiated, there was another target. In the late 1960s, "when it became clear cases would be getting to trial," feedback from conferences and from talking to people in the field led to a "very conscious decision to go after written tests" and "paper requirements" (a high school diploma or an aptitude test for a position in the labor pool) and seniority. Later, in conjunction with LDF, the Lawyers' Committee also acted upon employment tests when it initiated an Employment Testing program growing out of its successful earlier employment discrimination cases, with the new project intertwined with its Employment Discrimination Project.

The campaign was not without problems. Government involvement in enforcement, along with activity of other civil rights organizations, such as the Lawyers Constitutional Defense Committee, the Lawyers' Committee, and Columbia University's own Employment Rights Project, meant that neither LDF nor other organizations had full organizational control, although LDF did have considerable control because it carried its own cases plus those from the NAACP. Moreover, the presence of a governmental administrative mechanism, requiring exhaustion of administrative remedies before a complainant could go to court, increased the likelihood that cases which were seen as appropriate vehicles for establishing legal precedent would be settled in a way unsatisfactory to development of precedent.

Criminal Justice and Capital Punishment

Criminal procedure and due process cases were always "part of the program," even before LDF was established as a separate entity. However, "it was not LDF's job to get reversals of wrongly-decided criminal cases" because that "would swallow up LDF resources," but instead to focus on "rules that had particular effects on minorities." That criterion led to LDF's spearheading litigation against capital punishment.

LDF's attention to criminal matters increased when LDF set up NORI, producing a "broad-ranging criminal law program," but most concern about criminal procedure under NORI was "very ad hoc"; although "the sensitivity was there," there was no "reaching out." Attention was given to police misconduct, with efforts made "to develop standards through the federal courts" concerning police department operations, but they suffered a "death blow" from the Supreme Court's decision in *Rizzo v. Goode* (1975), not an LDF case. Another area of law which received attention, but in which LDF had "no success *at all*" in developing litigation, was bail for those without money. When NORI terminated, not all concerns in which LDF had become involved during its existence came to an end. Significant criminal justice involvement continued, including a prison reform program developed by adding a staff attorney with experience in the area and undertaken because "blacks found themselves in prisons in disproportionate numbers."

Work also continued on capital punishment, which had started with an infusion of NORI funds, use of which was thought justified because "many thought discrimination against the poor in the application of capital punishment more blatant than discrimination against blacks." These funds were used because, despite LDF's relatively large resources, the organization was not well prepared for systematically challenging the states' death penalty procedures; its headquarters staff "was still small, spread dangerously thin, and plagued by almost daily civil rights movement crises that required immediate action." [34]

An LDF attorney has said that LDF did little about other aspects of the criminal justice system because so much effort was put into the death penalty campaign. One cooperating attorney not altogether pleased with LDF's operative priorities also commented that LDF took death penalty cases "like that [snapping fingers]" but not a high proportion of police brutality cases. That, however, was not accidental. By comparison with its other criminal justice work, attention to capital punishment was not ad hoc but was very carefully planned.

The capital punishment campaign, like that on Title VII, did not reach full growth instantly. LDF lawyers initially looked at cases of blacks sentenced to death for crimes against whites. They decided to focus only on rape and spent their time developing a national strategy to abolish the death penalty for those rape cases.[35] A law student-conducted survey throughout the South, under the direction of law professor Anthony Amsterdam and criminologist Marvin Wolfgang, provided information that led to plans for an effort to block executions in rape cases on equal treatment grounds. Such an effort would, however, require a "complicated factual inquiry" and would be "a grueling, expensive, and tedious enterprise."[36]

Efforts to prove discrimination on the basis of statistics did not prove effective, leaving the possibility that some convicted men whose cases might have been won on other grounds would be left worse off if judges not convinced by the statistics were scared off by the cases.[37] In part for this reason, "we quickly realized we couldn't restrict ourselves to rape: the issue had to be raised in all cases, not just blacks'." So, in a planning shift "not easy to trace" that "came about only after a number of complex, interrelated, tactical and moral considerations coalesced,"[38] LDF moved beyond the rape cases to all capital cases and sought to obtain a moratorium on executions until constitutional issues could be litigated. That shift required major involvement because, for a death penalty moratorium to be successful, for example, there was a need "to intervene directly in hundreds of cases in over thirty of the forty-two jurisdictions whose law still provided the death penalty."[39]

Several factors in combination were central to LDF's efforts. Among reasons for LDF's involvement was the availability of a legal remedy—the greater ease of using federal habeas corpus, after the Supreme Court's 1963 decision in *Fay v. Noia*—and the apparent inevitability of execution of a number of black men with the election of governors in California and Florida (Reagan and Kirk) who succeeded governors who had imposed moratoria on executions. Especially important was the "almost unique" involvement of one person, Anthony Amsterdam, who had what one colleague called a "personal, passionate commitment" to eradicating capital punishment and who thought a project to that end by the LDF was feasible. Significant, and perhaps the crucial element in LDF's involvement in death penalty litigation, according to Michael Meltsner, an LDF staff attorney at the time, were lawyers' values and professional pride, their need to use "tools [that] had been developed which now threatened to collect dust" as civil rights activity "shifted from the courtroom to the streets" in the early

1960s. The seed of the death penalty litigation, immediately nour-ished by the organization's previous litigation successes, is said to have been planted with the comment made one day that if LDF was receiving cases of blacks sentenced to death—cases that couldn't be turned away—the organization ought to focus on capital punishment itself.[40]

The availability of resources was also very important. Indeed, LDF, in considering whether to proceed to attack capital punishment, "felt it was the only organization that could sustain such a campaign" be-cause of its resources or those available to it, and one participant says a "principal impetus" for the death penalty effort was that "we had resources to bring to bear to save people's lives. Otherwise, those people would have been dead." Yet only ten percent of LDF's budget was committed to capital punishment and only two staff attorneys (of twenty-four) were assigned to full-time work on death penalty cases, an indication of the pull of the organization's other commitments on its total resources.[41]

LDF activity in death penalty litigation has remained strong, with the number of lawyer hours devoted to it "comparable" to that before the NORI phaseout—a result of so many people being on death row, with more "at the end of the line" after appeals—and several attor-neys spend most of their time on death row matters. The organization continues to advise attorneys directly involved in capital cases; for ex-ample, providing a manual on how to bring habeas corpus actions in such cases. Through foundation grants to academics, new empirical research is also under way on the arbitrary and discriminatory applica-tion of the death penalty. LDF has increased its activity principally in its role "as the coordinator of capital defense litigation efforts through-out the nation"[42]—the organization's way of extending resources by involving other lawyers and assisting them.

Because LDF had already made the decision to oppose capital pun-ishment and had begun to organize its litigation campaign by the time the ACLU came to oppose the death penalty, the ACLU, because of its involvement in other issues and its activity in the legislative arena, was content to leave LDF as the primary litigator and ACLU lawyers "looked to the LDF for support."[43] Although LDF has been the lead organization in the campaign against the death penalty, the large and growing number of inmates awaiting execution and the problem of obtaining lawyers to bring appeals on behalf of these inmates led to a proliferation of offices, some receiving state funding, to obtain lawyers to handle these cases. Examples are the Office of the Capital Collateral Representative in Florida; the Death Penalty Resource Center in the Office of the Appellate Defender in North Carolina; and the California Appellate Project. In 1986 this led to the establishment by the American Bar Association of a Postconviction Death Penalty Representation Project, to represent death row inmates in post-conviction proceedings.

9

Choice Of Cases

Having selected areas of law in which to participate, litigating interest groups must then decide on cases in which to participate. That participation takes two major forms: direct involvement in a case as a party or, more likely, as the organization providing resources (money and lawyers) to one of the parties, or participation as *amicus curiae* (friend of the court). Amicus participation is important, but for organizations regularly involved in litigation, more direct participation in litigation is crucial; as a result, there has been an increase in the intensity of participation: direct participation has increased more than amicus participation. In recent years, fewer than ten percent of interest groups that engaged in litigation limited their litigation activity to filing amicus briefs.[1] In death penalty litigation, for example, "LDF attorneys represented parties before the Supreme Court in twenty cases and filed amicus briefs in fourteen additional cases."[2]

In this chapter, case selection is examined, with amicus activity the subject of the next chapter. Here attention is given to the sources of cases for litigating groups, which has implications for later dynamics of litigation, and the processes by which the NAACP and the NAACP Legal Defense Fund make their decisions about cases, including the criteria which are used in case selection. Particular attention is given to the timing of an organization's involvement, related to ability to control a case.

Interest groups' choices of specific cases and their choices of areas of law in which to litigate are closely related. If the latter are adequately communicated to lawyers in the field, certain types of cases and not others will be channeled to organizational litigators. In this regard it was important, as one NAACP attorney observed, to "pick a subject with broad interest and appeal through which branches and attorneys could get a feel for what they could do to implement law on the books," not to "use a shotgun and spray pellets." Working in a new area of law, an organization can "cast its net broadly and bring lots of cases," a certain proportion of which will "turn out not to go very far" but from which appropriate issues can be identified. Thus cases not chosen as part of a plan may assist with that plan. "By starting with a significant number of cases, we don't put all our eggs in one basket and find the basket has holes." Thus as issues develop, the organization can "send out the word," indicating what cases it is looking for.

Seeing litigation for social change as planned leads one to believe that the choice of cases is *deductive*. That groups try to build the law incrementally requires that they be engaged in the effort for some time, have cases from which to choose, and do so carefully on the basis of clearly delineated criteria, instead of acting *inductively*, making decisions in response to pressure, circumstances, and available cases. Organizations' choice of areas of law on which to focus, although hardly a matter of neat blueprints, might partially reinforce the deductive view. So does the role of organizational planning, which demonstrates that civil rights lawyers are not completely free to select their cases. For example, those engaged in the school desegregation litigation campaign "were not independent, free-floating, foundation-supported lawyers that could pick and choose their cases," but instead "grew out of and were intimately tied to the social reform groups." Yet case selection, like much else about "planned" litigation, is problematic, and "cases sometimes present themselves in such a way that interest groups have little chance but to involve themselves. Sometimes a case can choose an interest group, rather than vice versa. A degree of chance, and even disorder, is also clearly present."[3] Moreover, group decisions to litigate are less subject to at least an implicit cost-benefit analysis than are an individual's decisions,[4] and such cost-benefit analysis, even in rough form, may be less likely in civil rights litigation because it often involves principle or constituency (member or contributor) pressure to persist despite effects on resources. Not only plaintiffs but also defendants can be affected by such pressure; for school boards, pressures from a hostile community became the paramount consideration in lawyers' decisions.[5]

The picture of litigators' choices of cases is considerably less tidy than that for choices of areas of law; it thus reinforces the picture of selection as inductive. The stream of cases to an organization will help it decide areas of law on which to concentrate. One NAACP Legal Defense Fund lawyer said that while "some issues are discrete enough that there is little problem in getting cases" and that his organization usually gets a "reasonably good match" between case and the issue LDF wishes to pursue, in some areas of the law it is "difficult to get clients" so that bringing cases is not easy, and the ability to choose is therefore limited. Although there is talk of evaluating individual cases in terms of previously identified criteria, in fact evaluations are often made, at least implicitly, in terms of the set of cases the lawyers have or in terms of caseload,[6] so that one lawyer's "important" case may not seem important to another because each has a different set of cases.[7]

There are several aspects to the choice of cases. Because we think planned litigation entails an interest group being able to choose cases "at their creation," one aspect is which cases will receive resources from the beginning of the case. Because not all cases are entered at their initiation, and may indeed occur as late as when a case is at the Supreme Court, quite important is the decision as to the cases in which to intervene or in which to assume responsibility after others have initiated them. When a case turns out to be more than it first seemed because litigators did not anticipate its importance or complexity, a group's assistance may be the only way *not* to discontinue the case. For example, in the Wilmington, Delaware, school case, involving inter-district remedies, "as dimensions of the task became known, it was clear that outside help was necessary." There are also situations in which a lawyer would realize after class action certification "how big" the case is. A case on appeal, class action or not, may "overwhelm the lawyer with its importance" and thus make the lawyer more willing to involve others. This occurred in one Title VII case, where the plaintiff's lawyer son, who had taken the case for the experience, only later realized how important the case was; LDF's involvement was suggested when he went to a member of the LDF board. At times local lawyers, caught up in the ongoing dynamics of local activity, did not think of having national organizations participate. For example, one Denver lawyer had been in contact with LDF staff in New York about the Denver school desegregation controversy, but two of the attorneys had been paying heed to electoral strategies, not thinking of litigation.[8] And it is also not uncommon for litigants to be so focused on proving defendants' liability that they may not understand remedy formation, often a case's most complex element. This happens often in school cases, where despite the close relation between violation and remedy, defining "segregation" and proving constitutional violations means less attention to remedies.[9]

Then there is the decision to proceed with the case, which can be separate from deciding to become involved in a case, particularly when later elements in a case are not seen when it was initiated. Circumstances may prompt a decision not to proceed even after expenditure of considerable resources in a case. If the record was not well developed, or meant the case would be presented in less than optimal light, proceeding further might not be wise. When a case seems, in midlitigation, to have become unlikely to be productive, a group may withdraw. Thus the LDF withdrew from the Atlanta school case, not only because of the NAACP branch's position but also "because we just couldn't get any rulings out of the district court or the court of appeals, [so] the case bounced back and forth inconclusively," leading to the decision "that there were a lot of other places where we could make some headway for integration."[10]

Some of the lawyers involved with *Griggs v. Duke Power Co.*, where there was "nothing during the pretrial discovery or the trial indicating its potential as a landmark case," thought it less than the ideal Title VII test case to take to the Supreme Court, and did not anticipate the result obtained or its effects.[11] As this suggests, whether a case is suitable for developing precedent may not be clear until litigators see the fact pattern developed at trial—or even later. In the Legal Services Program, whose units began few cases intending to take them to the Supreme Court, "the decision on whether or not to use a case as a vehicle for policy reform was almost always made after the case had been through the trial courts."[12] Having taken a case for an individual client to resolve narrow issues, a lawyer may realize that the judge is interested in having broader issues raised. In the litigation resulting in the challenge to the Alabama prison system's constitutionality, a federal judge's former law clerk, appointed by the judge to take a prisoner complaint case, realized that the judge was "interested in additional prisoner litigation" and "persuaded his client to enlarge the case into a class action in behalf of all inmates." When a companion case, assigned to a university law professor, underwent the same sort of transformation, the lawyers obtained the assistance of the Southern Poverty Law Center, and the American Civil Liberties Union, respectively.[13] The South Carolina component of the *Brown* case illustrates a favorable judge pushing an organization further than it had originally intended to go: Federal Judge J. Waties Waring "began to lobby NAACP officials to file an immediate and uncompromising appeal," and through his contacts on the NAACP board "to push the association's counsel into a more aggressive posture than he thought they had been pursuing."[14]

Factors affecting initial choice of a case and affecting the decision to continue with it, including whether to appeal and how far, may be different. However, where a litigating interest group initially takes cases seen as having potential for appeal to the Supreme Court for precedent, the initial decision to undertake a case is often related to the choice of cases to appeal after the trial stage, "the central and most crucial strategic step for all constitutional litigators."[15] If cases are brought only for short-term goals, such as school cases initiated to obtain a trial court order, for example, "to apply clearly defined principles to recalcitrant school boards" or to bring district judges into line,[16] considerations affecting possible appeal will be different. Litigators did agree there was a distinction between cases in which precedent was sought, with education cases a prime example, and those where relief for the individual was emphasized, with Title VII cases in that category, although precedent and individual effect may occur in the same case.[17] Yet "non-landmark" cases, taken even though it was felt they would not be precedent-setting, have received "some of the most difficult, creative work" in order "to get something for someone and to keep them from becoming bad precedent."

Lawyers' professional training provides them with some criteria for choosing cases to undertake and to appeal; their values and ideologies also come into play. Appellate attorneys, we are told, tend to appeal "only when they agree with their side of the case," with that agreement resulting from their immersion in the case and the matching of clients' and attorneys' views.[18] However, factors affecting decisions to appeal from trial court to the first appellate level are not necessarily weighted the same as those affecting appeals to the Supreme Court.[19] Attorneys arguing in federal appellate court generally agree on the weight given many factors, with "strategic coordination to achieve preferred organizational policy outcomes" rather of relatively low importance.[20] However, those who hold a social welfarist orientation, including many civil rights attorneys, rate timing and strategy somewhat more heavily than do those with an entrepreneurial orientation. For Legal Services Program lawyers, "motivations peculiar to the local attorney involved in the case," whether the importance of appellate advocacy or "commitment to their client, irrespective of the suitability of the case for policy making or the case's place in a larger litigation design," in part influenced decisions to appeal.[21] An individual lawyer's concerns may be particularly important when the attorney has an "almost unfettered choice" among cases, as is true of lawyers at Legal Services Program backup centers, as this creates the possibility that some cases would be ignored if they "don't fit with the ego-trip at the backup center." This made it important, said an attorney for a major backup center, to "de-emphasize one's own agenda."

Litigating interest groups' case choices have parallels in government lawyers' decisions. For example, after passage of the Voting Rights Acts of 1957 and 1960, Justice Department lawyers, on the basis of "makeshift guidelines," identified a county in each federal judicial district in which injunctions against discriminatory voting practices would be obtained. Somewhat earlier, faced with southern resistance to enforcement of the 1957 statute, a Justice Department lawyer "had decided to pursue only the three test cases doggedly to victory—no matter how long it took—in order to establish a legally tested avenue toward binding court orders," and had not filed other suits in the meantime, "as redundant suits only risked adverse precedents in weaker cases."[22]

Litigating challenges to economic regulation in the 1930s, government lawyers faced a "complex process of planting and weeding a litigation docket of hundreds or even thousands of cases, in search of the sturdiest test cases."[23] They paid close attention to the sequence in which cases were brought or taken up on appeal, keeping particularly in mind the need to have available other cases with which to follow up some already underway. And in choosing cases, their criteria were both legal, as when NLRB lawyers in the agency's early years selected cases "which would most easily fit into the certainty of existing law," and psychological, such as "which cases would involve the most 'flagrant' violators and the most compelling victims; [and] which would most appeal to the sense of fairness of the judges."[24] And, like interest group lawyers, government lawyers did not always follow their own plans, not being able to fit cases to a preferred sequence, or always apply criteria they had developed; their involvement or immersion in some cases at times also led them not to plan adequately for later activity.

Sources of Litigation

Sources of cases need to be distinguished from a case's *precipitants*, the event or occurrence that leads a prospective plaintiff to an interest group, or its *origin*, in community action or in group activity creating fertile soil for litigation when the right precipitant occurs. The precipitating event in the Prince Edward County, Virginia, school case was students walking out of school; the source of the case was the individual who contacted the NAACP about the case. Precipitants include parties' conflicting interests, specific irritants that activate latent conflicts, and crucial disruptive events that prompt people to seek assistance;[25] cases themselves provide precipitants of later cases, particularly as new precedents are implemented.

In some organizations, there is a system for facilitating the movement of cases and sources are part of relatively structured processes for obtaining cases. For example, the National Committee Against Discrimination in Housing learned about cases through some sixty fair housing centers, mostly east of the Mississippi and in California, and had frequent contact with Legal Services lawyers, many of whom called for technical help, help in drafting complaints, or more direct NCDH involvement in litigation. Cases arrive at other groups in a more diffuse fashion, "from individuals, branches, helter-skelter," as one NAACP-affiliated lawyer observed—even "walk-in" or "call-in" cases from headquarters' or regional offices' immediate vicinity. Test cases can result from individuals coming to an organization or from their lawyer seeking help, as a result of which the organization decides to test the statute affecting the client. A lawyer may come to the organization with a case, hoping that the organization will help cover expenses and perhaps lend the prestige of its name. In one lawsuit to obtain access to transportation for the disabled, lawyers read in a legal services publication about such a lawsuit elsewhere and then contacted the Center for Independent Living, whose work for disabled persons they knew, and found that the Center knew of the local situation and was interested in participating in litigation about it.[26] In a different scenario, individuals go to a lawyer affiliated with an organization, perhaps a cooperating attorney, so that the organization's source is the lawyer. If individuals contact a community group that does not engage in litigation, the group may call in a knowledgeable attorney, who if associated with a litigating organization will contact it for help or refer the case to it.

Alternatively, the organization may determine to test the statute and even develop a case or at least its core ideas, seeking out a plaintiff appropriate for challenging the law instead of waiting for a case to walk in the door or "come over the transom." In what may be standard practice in litigation to assert principle, a former LDF lawyer observed that the organization's lawyers "did not always wait for clients to appear at their door" but instead "often they planned a case and then sought out those wishing to sue."[27] In one variation, lawyers decide to bring a suit and contact a nonlitigating organization, which then uses its own members or other individuals as plaintiffs in the lawyer-proposed suit. At other times, an organization selects a plaintiff for a putative law suit and then contacts a lawyer. Or a nonlitigating interest group contacts a litigating organization before a plaintiff is in hand; once client-organization and organization-as-lawyer have come together, plaintiffs are then found.

The ability to solicit, at least through announcements of general availability to affected groupings of people, is crucial in civil rights litigation. It is not a recent phenomenon or one limited to race discrimination cases. In what became the Scopes case, challenging statutes barring the teaching of evolution, the ACLU placed an advertisement in a Chattanooga, Tennessee, newspaper after that state's antievolution statute was enacted: "We are looking for a Tennessee teacher who is willing to accept our services in testing this law in the courts. Our lawyers think a friendly test can be arranged without costing a teacher his or her job. Distinguished counsel have volunteered their services. All we need now is a willing client."[28]

Organizations may have to use intermediaries to arrange suitable plaintiffs for cases. In some areas of litigation such as mental health, "case finding" seems particularly important, as laypersons who are mentally ill or who have been institutionalized have played a very active role as "case finders" in the initiation of such litigation. However, even with "case finders" available, it could still be "difficult to get a group of vulnerable, isolated, and often difficult people to become part of a lawsuit."[29]

Even though solicitation occurs, many clients in civil rights cases are "self-selected" individuals who initiate contact with lawyers; they are likely to play an important part in the case as it proceeds. Some efforts to obtain disabled people access to transportation were "quite pure examples of 'lonely crusades'" where "[i]ndividuals took the initiative themselves to find a lawyer to help them with the problem";[30] these initiating clients were the only individuals active in the litigation once groups became involved. In another instance, activist seminarians became aware of the availability of land that could be used for open housing, and came to the Leadership Council on Metropolitan Open Housing because they knew that if the building were built, it would be integrated. The Council had a subsidiary to develop housing in the suburbs, and its chief counsel saw "a chance to build a zoning case like one that had never been built before." However, the NAACP Legal Defense Fund seldom receives cases directly from prospective plaintiffs because "people don't know how to contact them." In New York City, individuals do call from time to time, but they are often referred elsewhere. When a prospective plaintiff makes initial contact with the organization, a lawyer will likely receive the case from it, so that, although a prospective plaintiff has been the organization's source, the lawyer's source is the organization. Some lawyers were asked to participate by NAACP General Counsel, and some served as NAACP's "hired gun" rather than taking cases directly from clients.

There is a wide range of sources from which cases come to organizations. An organization may receive cases directly: someone knows about the organization and contacts one of its offices. This is likely with the NAACP, with its network of branches. Field staff may also be an organization's source of cases. The NAACP Legal Defense Fund's involvement in James Meredith's efforts to enter the University of Mississippi came from NAACP field representative Medgar Evers. At its national convention, the NAACP also has an office staffed by the general counsel, to which individuals can bring complaints, and someone who has assisted with that operation says that eight of ten cases brought to the "convention booth" are "viable." The NAACP receives some cases via a letter from branch presidents, who also contact the NAACP Legal Defense Fund directly. In some of those situations—indeed, in most cases coming from a branch—the case may already be associated with an attorney. The legal problem resulting from arrests in the Montgomery, Alabama, sit-ins "was brought to Johnnie Jones who in turn brought the problem to us at the Inc. Fund just as Montgomery's leading black attorney, Fred Gray, had brought the problem posed" in a major case on university discipline.[31] There can be an interorganizational element to such contact. In a highly visible criminal case, after initial NAACP representation seemed inadequate, the defendant's father was reported to have gone to an Alabama LDF attorney, who came to a national LDF staff attorney. "Given their request," LDF "had to participate," he said. (Another said that SCLC contacted the family and got them to change from the NAACP to LDF.)

There may be multiple sources for the same case. In one aspect of the Boston school case, black parents upset by the Boston School Committee's failure to desegregate a new school "came to Boston's Lawyers' Committee for Civil Rights,"[32] which then contacted a private law firm doing significant pro bono work. The parents also contacted the local NAACP branch and the national NAACP, which then contacted the Harvard Center for Law and Education. (The law firm and the Harvard Center knew of each other's involvement and engaged in a "joint venture.")

When a lawyer or law firm in a community is identified as *the* civil rights firm, direct contacts by individuals with complaints ("walk-ins") are likely, and more generally, a local attorney is "typically the person of initial contact for local blacks complaining of racial discrimination."[33] One lawyer active in public accommodations-related cases was contacted about discrimination in access to community swimming pools by people who "lived in the next subdivision." In Charlotte, North Carolina, people regularly went directly to the firm of Julius Chambers, later LDF director-counsel. A firm not well known in the minority community but well known to others will receive referrals from other lawyers, ministers in the black community, and officers and active members in NAACP branches. An attorney with more civil rights cases than his firm could manage asked other lawyers, most of whom knew him from earlier activities or through professional contacts, for help; thus he was their source. The credibility of such a source is important. High credibility leads some litigators to take some cases simply because the source asked them to do so, or to support the cases for the same reason. As one cooperating attorney noted, "If I call up and say I have a good case, they'll generally fund it unless they are short of funds."

One lawyer became involved in a major school desegregation case when younger lawyers in the community, some of whom were also in the same law firm with him, needed a trial counsel after deciding to initiate litigation against a school board that had backed off from voluntary desegregation plans. Illustrative of the sometimes accidental way in which lawyers and cases became connected, he had just settled a major commercial case and was available and "ready for something new and different." In another instance of this "accident" phenomenon, an individual teaching the Civil Liberties Practicum at Ohio State University Law School, in order to learn the ropes about the school's clinical program, asked a criminal attorney who supervised some students in that program to have lunch. The lawyer, handling a state penitentiary inmate's prison conditions case said, "I've got a case you'd be interested in" (for the practicum).[34]

One organization may serve as another organization's source of cases. When LDF declined to take a case, Jack Greenberg suggested people on the staff of the National Center for Policy Review, which became involved. An organization may get calls from client groups or other organizations working in the same field. The NAACP and the ACLU were among those sending housing cases to the Metropolitan Leadership Council on Civil Rights, which had "developed a good reputation with those organizations," so that "the people felt they'd been adequately represented." And the NAACP Legal Defense Fund learned of cases from PUSH, the Voter Education Project, and local black voter registration groups, among others.

For some cases, the government may also be the source although usually not openly, as when cases were "sent by EEOC or [another] government agency on the sly." Superintendents of education and school boards have called in civil rights lawyers to discuss desegregation, particularly when central-city school districts were plaintiffs against suburban school districts. Or a judge may invite an organization into a case. LDF lawyers report that the organization was asked by a federal district judge to enter a case involving zoning and publicly subsidized housing "because he believed that our participation would enable plaintiffs' claims to be better presented before the court." [35]

Process of Case Choice

Particularly significant in organizations' choice of cases to pursue are several questions: Is clearance from the national organization necessary before a group may proceed with a case or do local units have autonomy vis-à-vis the national organization? Within national organizations, do lawyers operate as colleagues in a relatively "flat" organizational structure, having some individual autonomy in choice of cases, or in a tightly structured, hierarchical fashion under the direction of a general counsel? To what extent do multiple factors, including caseload and client demand, constrain attorneys' decisions? Although in neither NAACP nor LDF is there a single point of intake or fixed locus at which decisions are made on which cases to pursue, observers' overall impression is that LDF, retaining flexibility, has kept matters under control, while the NAACP failed to hold its decision-making process together and thus lost effectiveness.

NAACP

The NAACP's cases came from individuals, lawyers with whom NAACP staff lawyers had worked, members of Congress to whom armed service personnel wrote with complaints about military justice, and, most particularly, from NAACP branches. "Any major litigation," and all major 1970s NAACP school desegregation cases, came through the branches after they had tried to work things out locally. *Adams v. Richardson*, also an example of special situations in which the organization initiated litigation with other organizations (here, LDF and the Center for National Policy Review), is said to have grown "from the cooperative effort of several hundred branches in the North and West."

The organization's view is "that general counsel and the New York staff will control litigation in which the organization is involved." The director's views may outweigh those of other staff, but in general staff lawyers have played an important role in decisions to litigate. They "orchestrated," certainly in tactical matters, and their views often dominated the branches' views, particularly when the latter did not have lawyers as officers. However, staff attorneys' leverage was reduced when branches contained lawyers and particularly when the branch president was a lawyer.

Before branch initiation of a case under the NAACP name, cases "from the hinterland" were supposed to flow up to the general counsel's office for prior approval. Generally, a case from a branch would come to national NAACP headquarters either as a letter from the branch president or the chairman of the branch's legal redress committee, asking permission to bring a case or to get involved in one. Sometimes a call might come from national, state, or local board members. When people in New York City (then the NAACP's headquarters) directly contacted NAACP headquarters, branch involvement came later. When individuals sought help directly from general counsel, as many did, contact was made with the local branch (if one existed) before further decisions were made. The presence of a branch was not imperative: indeed, there were times when NAACP litigation helped produce a local unit.

The national office wanted to assure that there was "an opportunity for consultation or an opportunity for someone to raise hell about the inadequate amount of consultation." Consultation "helps debug the process" and is aimed at providing supervision by the national office of NAACP-related litigation. Thus, "if a branch went off with inconsistent litigation, or hadn't precleared the case, there would be hell to pay." Moreover, to avoid development of situations like the *Claiborne Hardware* judgment, general counsel had to devise a method to keep branches from getting involved in coalitions where, as at times the only non-temporary coalition member, it would be "fair game" for those unhappy with its actions and would be held liable in a civil suit.

Before the NAACP would accept a case, the national legal staff also "insisted that the branch demonstrates it's done its homework." Indeed, the executive director would ask, "How the hell is the case going to be financed?" Because the NAACP always had to shepherd its resources carefully, including using its small number of staff attorneys efficiently, general counsel didn't want branches "using the staff as a Legal Redress Committee," as had happened in earlier days when branches wanted the services of Charles Houston or Thurgood Marshall because they were prestigious and their services were free.[36] Because it was "infeasible for the New York City staff to handle cases directly," the local branch would be expected to get lawyers to serve as a legal committee for the branch or, in the situations in which lawyers were not already attached to cases, to arrange for a local attorney with whom the national office could talk. Here the group wanted potential clients to have an attorney, but if the client already has one, a group may hesitate to commit its limited resources, because of the need to allocate what little the organization has to those who most need it, that is, those without counsel.

"The book" also required branches to make contact with the NAACP's state and regional levels and to seek help from the state conference's legal committee. Copies of requests from a branch for legal assistance were to go to the state conference and regional director, with whom national staff "must touch base." One way of determining branch and/or conference commitment to a case was to require that the branch and conference provide a stated measure of their involvement, particularly in cases that appeared to be complex and thus likely to run a long time and be expensive. That NAACP support was conditioned on branch and conference contribution of a certain percentage of the finances prompted "significant branch involvement." This process, which "allows resources to be stretched further" and gave the branch and conference a "direct stake" in the case—or, put differently, "permits the branches to be less lazy"—was national headquarters' way of "finding out how important a case is to them" and also served as headquarters' way of "rearranging their agenda." Yet whatever the book said, some critics claim the process by which cases came to NAACP was "helter-skelter" and that preferred organizational processes were often not followed. For example, the requirement that support be obtained from the state or regional conference is said to have been "frequently bypassed" in practice.

However, critics have commented on the "need for structure that was lacking," with disorganization in the Legal Department limiting the organization's effectiveness. Decisions were said to be made by the general counsel without consultation with staff attorneys; the basis for general counsel's choices did not seem to follow priorities or a clear pattern and was unclear to at least some of the staff. Even when priorities had been discussed at meetings of lawyers and there had been some indication of "which cases should be accelerated and which slowed down," there was "no follow-up." Moreover, the NAACP was "relatively flexible internally as to [staff] lawyers' choices," so that at times it was up to individual attorneys to decide whether NAACP should take a case, an arrangement that was "sometimes good, sometimes bad." An individual staff attorney might "benefit from the lack of direction" and exercise his or her own preferences. The "supervision" talked about at national headquarters was also said to be not a reality in the field, frustrating lawyers there. Some in the field found the national legal staff unavailable or unresponsive, and encountered logistical problems in receiving adequate secretarial assistance or financial support for litigation to which the organization had commited itself. Thus, in general, "Whatever gets done, gets done, rather than by design."

LDF

Cases came to LDF in a variety of ways, including referrals from other organizations, contact with NAACP branches and community organizations, and some direct client contact. In the South, contacts between lawyers and the civil rights movement were the "principal source of clients" in several communities for the Lawyers Constitutional Defense Committee, of which LDF was a part. When there were LDF regional offices, "cases just came in off the street," but LDF has not had many field offices. This helps explain why cooperating attorneys or "lawyers who ask" were the "largest single source" of cases for LDF, accounting for "many" or "most" cases, perhaps over 90 percent. Likewise, having many cooperating attorneys was necessary to provide the large number of cases if the organization was to have a choice of those to pursue.

Case searching by LDF, whose lawyers at times "would see the need for intervention and would stimulate forces" leading to initiation of a case, indicates active organizational planning. It also suggests that a nonmembership organization like LDF, particularly if its cooperating attorneys are effectively socialized to organizational priorities, is in a better position to attempt to engage in planned litigation than one with local units, like the NAACP's branches, which affect the basic pattern by which cases come to the organization.

LDF's process for choosing cases was not highly structured. Instead of having "lots of bureaucracy for doing such things," the process was "not organized, it's organic." Indeed, LDF was criticized for not having done more to institutionalize decisions on which cases to take and for not developing criteria for the purpose. There was "not a formal procedure" in the office. Instead, "Operational decisions on policies and priorities are made by the legal staff in response to the nature and importance of the problems and cases that face both the central office and the cooperating attorney network, and on the basis of available resources." "Greater organizational sophistication," a result of experience and organizational growth, meant "an ability to deal with the brushfires" with which the organization had to contend.

Characterizing the process at LDF, one lawyer said that "policy pretty much came out of [Jack] Greenberg's office," although Greenberg himself has said there were instances in which LDF's board "will . . . consider whether or not we should file and pursue particular cases." [37] The weight of Greenberg's views when he disagreed with the staff was considerable. In the Angela Davis case, in which LDF did not participate, members of the staff "disagreed with [him] almost unanimously," but Greenberg conceded it was "sort of" a "Lincoln's Cabinet situation then—your decision carried more weight than all the others combined." (He pointed out that "the Inc. Fund board unanimously supported me.") [38]

The amount of discretion Greenberg had was also possessed by well-respected project directors in other organizations. For example, the decision on whether the Lawyers' Committee Voting Rights Project should take particular cases was "still pretty much discretionary with [the project's] director." The Lawyers' Committee's executive director, who "theoretically has a veto," had never used it as of the mid-1980s. Instead the director was the "conduit for dealing with the organization's board." Although "there was no case" which board members prevented Lawyers' Committee staff lawyers from filing, board members from time to time did "complain after the fact" about the choice of certain cases—a "problem of relations between the Board members and government agencies with whom the board members (partners in major law firms) as lawyers had close working relations."

Criteria for Choosing Cases

Once cases are channeled to an organization, decisions must be made as to which ones to pursue. Criteria for choosing cases are also related to an organization's choice of areas of law in which to litigate. Although attempts to apply criteria in case selection are affected by a number of constraints, criteria for case choices do exist. This is true even when, as in one organization, there were "no written criteria for taking cases" or when they are ambiguous (cases with "high impact," cases with novel legal principles, or those which "interested us"). Many criteria identified as affecting NAACP and LDF choices are the same as, or similar to, those used by other civil rights organizations. One reason is that some LDF staff members have moved on to other organizations, such as the Lawyers' Committee or MALDEF; another is that in the relatively small civil rights bar, there is considerable communication about how to pursue cases. However, lawyers associated with civil rights groups do not share a clear consensus on the criteria used for case selection; they identify a variety of criteria used to select cases either at their initial stages or at later stages at which the group might intervene, although much of the latter is defensive, as lawyers try to avoid conflicting with overall strategy and to minimize "bad" precedent.

Under most circumstances, no single factor determines the choice of any case, but a set of factors influences the choice. Not only may each be given varying weight in different situations, but different organizations vary in the weights they assign to them. This helps explain why one organization's declining to take a case does not mean others will refuse, as when the NAACP became involved in the Wilmington, Delaware, interdistrict remedy school case after LDF declined to do so. At times, as in the Atlanta school case, one level of an organization takes a case another level would rather not be taken or takes the case to achieve a goal the other level does not share.

A lawyer associated with two major civil rights organizations has, without ranking the major criteria, stated some of them:

- Issues and defendants—"the legal questions and who you want to sue," so that one targets one's cases. This includes where a case fits on the organization's agenda and how it relates to priorities.
- Quality of the case or its feasibility—the "quality of the named plaintiff," the facts and proof. This is applicable "even when one wanted a legal ruling, not one on the facts," because "it is better to have a good set of facts to win even an abstract legal issue." Some cases are chosen by civil rights litigators "so long as they offer some possibility of advancing the law in a significant way or can bring about reform," perhaps with "spillover effects" to other cases, making precedent a key criterion in case selection. More

generally, a case's impact is crucial, and . . . "the potential impact at the trial or settlement level" is said to be "the most common criterion for selection" for public interest law firms.[39]

• Geographic location—because there are "certain places one wanted to do things or could do things." If the site of litigation was some distance from headquarters, an "absolute criterion was competent, committed local counsel" because one "needs to be tied in locally" because "all civil rights cases are political ones."

• Resources available—"what there's money for," including an organization's own funds and the availability of attorneys' fees. A case might not be pursued if the task is "overwhelming"; and if considerable resources are tied up in big cases, an organization would be forced to limit acceptance of new cases. If a public interest litigator wishes to use attorneys' fees awards to support its budget, "taking the 'good' case will tend to restrict its freedom of choice and mode of operation."[40] The role of attorney's fees can be seen in the comments of an LDF lawyer commenting on LDF's aid to U.S. Civil Rights Commission member Mary Frances Berry when she was fending off being fired by President Reagan. Even though "there's no way one could get attorneys' fees representing Mary Berry," he said, "We'll take that sort of case," explicitly distinguishing his organization from public interest law firms, which "would look at attorney's fees a case will bring in." However, his raising the issue suggests that in fact attorneys' fees are a desideratum in case selection.

• Commitment to the case—a lawyer (both staff and cooperating attorneys), a client, and an organization all are "needed to keep cases going in the tough times that any cases has," or "the case may fall over halfway through" the litigation process. There can also be commitment to community, seen as a lawyer speaking of his group's concern for its "obligation to a particular group" such as those in a particular Mississippi community with whom the organization had a continuing relationship.

In case selection, choosing plaintiffs may be the single decision receiving the most attention.[41] This includes the numbers of plaintiffs to use, the personal influence or prestige of named plaintiffs, and the composition of a plaintiff class (to stress diversity and representativeness).[42] Litigation over access by the handicapped to transportation illustrates that it may be desirable to have multiple plaintiffs, with a broad range of characteristics (such as different disabilities), and other cases show that in addition to any organizational plaintiffs, at least one named individual plaintiff should be included to avoid problems of standing.

At least some civil rights litigators prefer class actions over cases brought on behalf of only one or a few named plaintiffs. Breadth of remedy (impact) is one reason; resource concerns provide another, as larger attorneys' fees from class actions assist in defraying costs of other complex cases; and facilitating introduction of evidence in "disparate impact" discrimination cases is another. A Title VII class action directed at a large industry is likely to be brought not only to obtain financial remedies for the plaintiffs but also to change basic industry practices and to create precedents favorable to other potential Title VII plaintiffs.[43] By contrast, "You don't win one-on-one cases and don't accomplish anything with them," as one LDF attorney observed, making the class action "absolutely crucial." More generally, class action suits may be used by civil rights organizations because they are consonant with "the classic outside strategies of mobilizing interests through protest and the manipulation of mass media."[44] This suggests an additional criterion for case selection: a case's possible "publicity effect." A housing litigator noted that a case won against the private housing and home finance industry has such an effect because it causes "embarrassment and bad image" as word travels in the industry.

As to desirable plaintiffs, civil rights organizations may encounter two opposite problems: available, willing potential plaintiffs are inappropriate and sometimes must be fended off, or clients who would allow their names to used in a case may be difficult to find. Both could be seen when blacks wished to challenge the segregated bus system in Montgomery, Alabama, where some possible plaintiffs had backgrounds that would be damaging at a trial, and local attorney Fred Gray found an absence of single black males "willing and able to be a suitable plaintiff."[45] School desegregation cases were also affected by lack of willing plaintiffs. Because lower-class blacks did not place the same priority on desegregation as did the black middle class central to the NAACP, the organization had difficulty convincing parents to initiate cases, a difficulty that recurred when desegregation fell out of favor in parts of the black community.[46]

Organizational jealousy can, however, affect this element. In a version of "we'll deal only with those who seek to deal with us," organizations may not wish to take a case if the local attorney is not associated with the group. For example, staff recommended the ACLU not take one of the Japanese-American exclusion cases because the potential client already had a local lawyer "who had not himself approached the ACLU with a request for assistance."[47] However, involvement in a case might be forced if a local lawyer mishandled it. For example, the NAACP undertook a major school case because of concern—conveyed initially to the national office by a branch president—that the local attorney was not competent and that the case was formulated in too narrow a fashion. Because the case was thought too important to be allowed to proceed on that basis, national NAACP officials turned to outside counsel to pursue the case. National organizations often have more concern with a case's national ramification than with effects on the local community in which the case arises, and action from a central (national) point would affect more people than would a case focused on a small community. For this reason, one housing litigation unit doesn't pursue "one-on-one cases, discrimination in the rental of an individual apartment," because "that doesn't help on a broader front" in the same way as a case that could lead the Department of Housing and Urban Development (HUD) to make a national change.

NAACP Case Selection

The NAACP applied varied criteria in case selection. One criterion that hardly needs stating is protection against threats to "organizational integrity." Thus the organization had little choice but to respond to Alabama's (successful) efforts to prevent it from operating there and to other attempts to obtain NAACP membership lists and to prevent it from pursuing litigation. More recently, the NAACP joined litigation against city police department "Red squads" which had conducted improper surveillance of the NAACP and other organizations.

The NAACP also took cases when state and local governments engaged in "affronts [that] had to be challenged," even if the cases did not fit with litigation strategy and even when the organization was "not sure where the resources will come from." The NAACP had "no choice" but to get involved when the Michigan legislature stepped into the Detroit school situation to throw out a limited voluntary desegregation plan. Likewise, when the Boston School Committee built a school with state aid given on the promise of "racial balance" under state law, opened the school with the balance plan, received the money, and "then reneged," this was the "spark that set things off" for the Boston school case by reinforcing the black community's sense of frustration in its dealings with the committee.

In general, the "guiding star" in the NAACP's case selection was the group's charter, particularly the theme that discrimination was to be eliminated in all areas of American life. Even if there were branch and conference involvement and support for a case, the NAACP was unlikely to take it on unless the case was "consistent with organizational policy." If accommodation rather than the elimination of discrimination was sought, the NAACP "would not enter unless we could assert NAACP policy"—or would enter *to* assert such policy, as it did in the Atlanta school litigation to offset the local branch's willingness to compromise over school desegregation in the interest of short-term local goals (more black school administrators).[48]

Another major criterion was a case's potential significance. To "husband resources," the NAACP was less likely to take "strictly an individual matter, without implications beyond the single person," and "would give more serious attention" to cases with "potential impact on a broad group or a broad number of individuals." Neither the NAACP nor the LDF liked employment discrimination cases involving individual workers. Cases appearing "to be in isolation or an aberration" were, if possible, referred, and it did not like "ad hoc" cases, those not fitting properly into the lawyers' proposed progression or not from industries targeted for litigation. Although critics have said the NAACP had "no sense of direction" and tended to "jump into cases without an idea of the factors or what the costs will be," "given the nature of the organization," that is, its membership basis, the NAACP did "have to have some ad hoc cases." One could see this earlier, when the NAACP entered a case in which an African-American, Hocutt, sought admission to the University of North Carolina's School of Pharmacy and assignment to a dormitory room. Although Charles Houston "would rather have had another time, place, and team" to bring one of the first direct challenges to *Plessy*, with the case to be handled by inexperienced lawyers whom Charles Houston could not assist because of his other responsibilities, the case was seen as not the worst possible one to bring in the worst possible place, and so Houston assigned a leading lawyer to assist.[49]

Although responding to important local units meant expending considerable resources on cases "low on anyone's priorities," sometimes NAACP took cases because "a branch might get mad if ignored." With the Detroit NAACP branch the NAACP's "largest in numbers and dollar commitment," the local chapter's pressure was one reason the national NAACP entered the Detroit school case. Although the NAACP had honored the school superintendent and school board president for working toward desegregation, litigating there over school desegregation was ad hoc, "forced upon the NAACP by an unlikely series of events."[50] This was like the situation facing the Southern Christian Leadership Conference (SCLC), which had strong ties to particular communities through the ministers who constituted its core. When Rev. Martin Luther King, Jr., turned his attention to the North, his decision to focus on Chicago "was more a case of Chicago choosing SCLC than SCLC choosing Chicago" because Chicago was the only city of major importance whose civil rights groups "gave SCLC a warm and unambiguous invitation."[51]

The NAACP's attorneys said there were also many other factors extraneous to policy which helped "determine whether a case was brought in one place rather than another, in one state rather than another." Several were related to organizational politics, such as whether a president of a state conference was loyal to the national office or a maverick and whether he would meddle in the lawsuit, and whether local organizations were internally cohesive or were split by ideological or personality disputes.

Case Selection at LDF

The "received tradition" about LDF's planned litigation might lead one to expect its case selection to be governed by a highly developed and regularly applied set of criteria. And LDF's staff was well socialized to organizational criteria, with continuity of leadership reinforcing attention to those criteria, and experience and organizational growth producing "greater organizational sophistication." This provided "an ability to deal with brushfires," and, without local units, "the LDF found it easier to resist litigation which did not fit into some larger strategy."[52]

Yet, as stated by one senior LDF attorney, "LDF didn't make policy in the abstract," "it made it through cases," deriving legal theory inductively; there was no "unified legal theory" from which LDF operated.

The situation was "not the National Security Council with a weekly sitting-down"; instead, "by sitting in the doctor's office, you get a view of the world." Cases, assessed "as they come to you," are evaluated to determine their "strength." "On a day-to-day basis, you pick the best cases," with particular attention to those which have the "best factual basis" and with a focus on " 'how to get the job done' in the case."

Among LDF attorneys' desiderata of "strength" of a case were its cost, the quality of the cooperating attorney ("legal firepower" attached to a case), "other cases doing the same thing," the state of the law, and the likelihood of winning. Perhaps most important, for LDF to take a case, there had to be "a person or an issue of significance to the black community," although white clients or issues that did not overtly touch on race were included.[53] Attention to "significance" meant LDF watched for the broader implications of action in key ongoing situations, for example, the Norfolk school case in the mid-1980s, about which Julius Chambers noted, "If Norfolk prevails, it will be an open invitation to school districts all over the country, particularly in the South, to go back to neighborhood school zones and resegregate the schools."[54] A related desideratum was "whether the interests of the plaintiffs were compatible with the interests of all others who would benefit from a successful resolution of the issue" where a ruling, like the *Griggs* employment discrimination case, would affect "millions of other blacks." The interests of those affected also "had to be weighed against [LDF's] concern for an institutional programmatic development" of the law.[55]

LDF might take some cases "not because of important legal issues" but because the organization "felt an obligation"—true of cases of black teachers, principals, and coaches who had lost their jobs in desegregated school districts. It took these because of a "responsibility for those in desegregation." Another instance was the Meredith case, where LDF, although it did not think the timing good and even though the Justice Department "repeatedly called the Inc. Fund and asked that they postpone Meredith's application," "had little choice" when he sought its assistance.[56] LDF staff also said it was "not afraid to take a case merely to implement an existing right, as opposed to creating a new one"; and "LDF litigation," we are told, "consists in large part of such implementation cases."

The choice of cases to pursue implies, of course, that cases are not taken, and situations in which participation is declined provided a view of why cases are chosen. Most declined cases, many of which are smaller, low visibility cases, simply do not meet enough of the organization's criteria. Others, however, appear to have entailed unacceptably radical politics—at least from Greenberg's perspective. The fear of being associated with radicalism may well explain why LDF did not defend Julian Bond when he was excluded from his seat in the Georgia House of Representatives for statements critical of America's involvement in Vietnam—in *Bond v. Floyd* (1965), the Supreme Court later declared the legislature's action unconstitutional—or Angela Davis when she was accused of aiding in a courtroom breakout.

The latter instance badly split the LDF staff, pitting most younger members against Greenberg and his chief aide, James Nabrit III. Greenberg did not accept a young black woman staff member's argument that "a black woman who had become the symbol of resistance to white oppression" should be defended. Greenberg's reasoning was that Davis "was able to get good legal advice elsewhere" and that LDF was "not really asked to represent her, make litigation decisions, and so forth" but was "asked essentially for money and our endorsement," or, as he said elsewhere, "I just didn't think it was a civil rights matter."[57] It was, however, not only radical individuals LDF declined to defend; the organization also did not assist radical *tactics*. Thus, although LDF later helped defend those involved in sit-ins and demonstrations, it "refrained from defending the first students arrested" in part because the sit-ins were "not controlled or approved by the adult civil rights organizations."

Timing of Involvement

The important criteria of whether to enter after the beginning of a case and the amount of control one will have over a case, are related, as entering a case late may reduce the extent of a lawyer's dominance. There are two different aspects to the very important notion that "timing is everything." One is when to become involved in a case, with organizations showing an increasing preference for participation *ab initio;* the other is ability to take advantage of situations as they develop. Staff attorneys at LDF were divided as to whether their organization's willingness to become involved in a case was affected by its ability to control litigation and whether LDF avoided cases in which it was not involved from the beginning, so it was "hard to make a general rule." Because "cases come to LDF in all shapes," in some instances

"the complaint is drafted at 10 Columbus Circle [then the organization's headquarters], while in other cases it is drafted elsewhere and
LDF gets involved later."

LDF made an "enormous commitment to initiating cases," said staff
attorneys, and "we prefer to be in from the beginning" because there
are "obvious problems if you'd not had a part in planning and developing a case." "If discovery is closed and the trial is next week," it
would be an "extraordinary situation" for LDF to get involved. Many
cases are, however, taken at advanced stages, and LDF is even said to
go looking for some already initiated cases. It was particularly likely
to enter a case if a case was seen to have a potentially significant
precedential effect or if a cooperating attorney had handled it because
cooperating attorneys were "good at developing the record in cases."
LDF would look at such cases "without any prejudice" and might
actually view them favorably because the developments in the case
provided more information than might otherwise be available. LDF
might take a case for appeal after completion of a trial, particularly if
it could play no other role, because it would have a clear picture of
what it might be facing, with "the issues pretty well sorted out" at the
appellate stage. In some situations, LDF "stepped in after trial work
when the trial lawyers may have lacked appellate skills" or couldn't
devote more time to the nonremunerative case because they "needed
to eat."

Like LDF, the NAACP preferred to be in cases from the beginning,
but it too entered cases after their initiation. It did so at the appellate
level, for example, in employment cases when the plaintiff had prevailed at trial, the defendant appealed, and the lawyer realized he did
not have the resources to continue the case. When such cases "had
been undertaken in accord with NAACP principles," the NAACP was
"trying to vindicate" its position by agreeing to undertake the appeal.
The NAACP was, however, likely to enter a case only if it could "exercise significant direction" over the case. The Columbus school case,
for example, was "started on theories which would have provided a
setback" to NAACP desegregation efforts, but after NAACP General
Counsel was contacted by the branch president, who was concerned
about the narrowness with which the case was being presented, the
NAACP "agreed to get into the case only with an amended complaint"
and with the ability to "reshape the case" in order to obtain appropriate relief. Although this situation in which the case is taken away from

local counsel poses "a delicate and not always soluble problem" because local attorneys may not wish to follow a national organization's suggestions, a national organization may actually suggest directly that local clients change attorneys and engage the organization as their attorney.

10

Amicus Participation

The amicus brief, "the traditional vehicle for presenting unrep-resented views to the court in an advisory capacity,"[1] has long been seen as interest groups' way of lobbying the courts, although as "a much more restricted kind of policy advocacy, by representatives act-ing in behalf of clients" than is activity directed at the legislature.[2] Amicus curiae briefs perform several functions. Some, endorsement briefs, "either repeat the party's position or offer a variation," while technical briefs provide nonlegalistic specialized information. Less frequently, amicus briefs present unconventional legal arguments or make emotional appeals.[3]

Participation in a case as amicus curiae can be an important element of planned litigation, in lieu of sponsorship of litigation or as a default position when others have initiated cases. In earlier times, while some organizations participated in cases primarily as amicus curiae at the appellate level, others, although quite active at the Supreme Court, seldom took the amicus role, and still others regularly filed amicus briefs in addition to their other litigation activity in the Supreme Court. For example, in thirty-one employment discrimination cases between 1970 and 1981, the NAACP Legal Defense Fund directly sponsored ten cases in the Supreme Court and filed amicus briefs in thirteen.[4] Over time, at least among interest groups that participate in litigation regularly, there has been a shift away from participation in litigation only as amicus. Yet even the limited device of an amicus brief remains "an extraordinary occasion" for many organizations who file them, but they are not likely to participate regularly in litigation to state their views on policy.[5] In this chapter, after a brief look at the location and frequency of amicus briefs, we look at why organizations become amici, then at the process by which that decision is made, with particular attention to the effect on the process of interorganizational relations.

Location and Frequency

Amicus briefs appear almost exclusively in appellate courts, where they have "greatest utility" as a way of "marshaling legal arguments or in presenting sociological data designed to expand the general informational basis for decision-making."[6] At the trial level, where factual proof is more central to the case, status as a party intervenor may be more appropriate than being an amicus because a party can better insure that issues and supporting evidence are consonant with the party's viewpoint than can an amicus.

An increase in amicus filings in the U.S. courts of appeals in the 1970s included an increase in amicus briefs in civil rights cases, with more such cases in those courts,[7] but most amicus briefs are filed in the Supreme Court. A civil rights lawyer observed that we "have so many of our own cases going, with our resources focused at the Supreme Court level we tend not to get involved with amicus at the court of appeals level." In employment discrimination cases, "nonfederal amici" on behalf of both plaintiffs and defendants appeared in slightly over 10 percent of the cases in the courts of appeals but participated in *83.5 percent* of the Supreme Court's decided cases.[8] Indeed, in the Supreme Court, organizations' amicus activity is now standard practice, with key cases attracting one hundred organizations or more. Despite a decline from 1941–1952 to 1953–1966 in the overall proportion of cases with amicus participation, such activity remained high in specific subareas—in six of thirteen voting rights cases, nine of thirty-six cases involving associational activity, and eleven of thirty-four on racial discrimination and segregation (in 1941–1952, there were amici in twelve of nineteen racial discrimination and segregation cases).[9] The number of race relations cases with amicus participation in the Supreme Court has increased, rising significantly after World War II and accelerating considerably in the late 1960s and 1970s, leading to amicus filings in over two-thirds of noncommercial cases the Supreme Court decided in 1979.[10] (More recently, there has been still more amicus activity, with well over 80 percent of the Supreme Court's 1986–1991 full opinion cases having at least one amicus brief, and with more than four such briefs on average in a case in which there was at least one.[11])

Most amicus participation comes after the Supreme Court has granted review, but over one-fourth of amicus participation takes place when review is sought.[12] Because the Supreme Court less often allows amicus participation without the parties' consent at the review-granting stage than after the Court has accepted a case, a party has "the ability to exercise considerable control over the presence of amici during this initial presentation to the Court."[13] Defensive action may lead an organization to urge the Court not to grant certiorari in cases that might create negative precedent. For example, the Mexican-American Legal Defense Fund (MALDEF) joined another fifteen organizations in an effort to have the justices not grant review in the *Bakke* affirmative action case.[14] Such action may, however, simply make the Court more aware of a case's importance and more likely to grant review; indeed, the Court is more likely to grant review when there is a brief in opposition to the grant.[15] Thus those opposing review might be better off if they "held their fire," because the very act of opposition calls the justices' attention to the fact that many people consider the case important—one of the principal factors considered in granting review.[16] Indeed, in one instance, counsel for an organization whose racial discrimination was challenged effectively blocked Supreme Court amicus participation by the NAACP Legal Defense Fund by threatening to call to the Chief Justice's attention the presence of federal judges on LDF's board of directors.[17]

When the Court, having granted review, considers a case on the merits at the plenary stage, the Court generally places no limits on amicus participation. Having failed to block the Court's granting of review in a case a group would rather not have the Court decide, the group might argue as amicus that the Court "get rid" of that case. An example is the *DeFunis* affirmative action case, where LDF urged a "dismissed as improvidently granted" (DIG) disposition in that case and suggested mootness as a basis for the Court's disposition because the record was "bad" and important issues had not been raised until the appellate level. It did so although it "made enemies" among those "gung-ho to have the affirmative action question decided." Likewise, when the Court accepted the *Witherspoon* case on "death-qualified" juries, LDF, which was interested in the question of whether such juries were "prosecution-prone" (that is, more likely to convict), asked in its amicus brief that the Court avoid ruling on that issue "because it had yet to be factually developed in published, systematic research." [18] Likewise, amicus arguments on the merits may be basically defensive, aimed to soften potentially negative precedents and limit defeats in cases others have brought. For example, the Women's Rights Project (WRP) often was forced into amicus activity, through which it provided the justices with fallback positions so that a direct sponsor's loss might be diminished. The increasingly conservative civil rights position of the Reagan administration's Justice Department, along with LDF's inability to rely on the federal government to defend its own cases or to file amicus briefs, also led to an increase in the number of LDF Supreme Court amicus briefs to answer the administration's position and to protect the interests of LDF clients. [19]

Why Become Amicus?

Increased amicus participation in civil rights cases indicates that, given their resources and other options, litigating organizations view such activity as at least minimally worthwhile. Many recurring elements play a part in an organization's decisions to become amicus. As cited by an LDF lawyer, they include "the importance of cases to minorities; the importance of the issue; the possibility of adverse precedent; the ability to limit negative precedent; [and] workload." Resource considerations are quite important. As women's organizations found, "Those organizations that limit themselves to amicus curiae activity find substantial savings while retaining a voice in Supreme Court litigation." [20] The view that groups should proceed hesitantly in filing amicus briefs stemmed in part from resource constraints, as when Citizens for Decency through Law found amicus activity "the least expensive way to affect the Court," and also allowed it to work with law enforcement officials, one of its goals. On the other hand, lack of resources may have placed direct sponsorship outside the group's means and may have left an organization with no choice but to file an amicus brief.

Generally "[t]he amicus process itself helps minimize costs and risks while emphasizing the potential rewards and benefits of participation."[21] For any litigating organizations, and particularly those with few resources, the amicus role allows one to be heard across a spectrum of cases rather than to be limited to financing of only a few; the National Chamber Litigation Center, for example, relied heavily on amicus participation "to decrease litigation expenses and to become involved in a broader range of business cases."[22] Even when finances are not scarce—true in recent decades of conservative PILFs like the National Chamber Litigation Center—goals of publicizing one's position may be better advanced through amicus participation than by full sponsorship, or at least by combining the two rather than by investing solely in sponsorship.

In general, the "time of staff and their workload" were important considerations; it was a "question of whether such participation was an appropriate allocation of scarce resources." As an amicus, an organization may be able to conserve resources—or not tie up its own attorneys—because it "might be able to get a law professor to write a brief." Outside lawyers may be quite willing to help staff attorneys in big cases; at times, an organization found enough such offers "that it could divide up exploration of topics." Expenses were further diffused if an organization joined others in a coalition brief.

Cited over and over again as a factor in deciding to become an amicus is the "importance of the issues to the litigating organization or to its clients." Sometimes this is stated in terms of whether the issues are "compatible with the [organization's] fundamental mandate." One civil rights lawyer said that his organization's basis for amicus participation was "the judgment that it's an important case." This "sounds totally subjective," he said but argued it isn't: "a person looking at a case has to form ideas as to *why* it is important, has to write that down," and has to indicate the legal issues in the case that are important to the organization's work.

"Importance" can have other meanings. One is that a case is "critical to another bunch of cases you're litigating." Thus an organization might submit a brief in one case because of involvement in a number of other cases on the same issue. The relationship between cases may not, however, be obvious. One lawyer noted, as a hypothetical, the need to file an amicus brief in a "run-of-the-mill criminal case" that had an issue, perhaps a procedural point, that "could affect other civil cases." Another instance was a class action securities case with implications for civil rights cases: an amicus brief would be filed "where the parties don't have the interest we have," to show the effect on civil rights cases of another portion of the class action rules. Another aspect of importance is a perceived need to offset the stated positions of other participants in cases. In recent times, conservative public interest law firms have entered litigation as amicus in part because they did not wish to have "the public interest" defined solely by liberal litigating interest groups. For example, the Washington Legal Foundation often filed amicus briefs "to counter-balance the claims of liberal groups when it cannot sponsor a case directly."[23]

Attorneys' fee cases provide still another, perhaps more obvious, example: civil rights groups will file amicus briefs in environmental cases in which attorneys' fees are at issue, because the relevant statutory language is like that in the Civil Rights Attorneys Fees Act. This is part of filing an amicus brief where important "interests are not being brought to the Court's attention," perhaps "to alert potentially friendly judges" to an organization's interest and the case's importance; however, one lawyer observed that it was "hard to measure the 'atmospheric effect' on judges" of a particular organization's amicus participation. Even when "whole chunks" from an amicus brief were used verbatim in an opinion, for example, in *Miranda* or the privacy theory in *Griswold v. Connecticut*, "It is hard to tell whether the Warren Court led the ACLU or vice versa"; one could not be sure the amicus brief *persuaded* the Court or whether the justices, already predisposed to adopt the amicus's position, simply found the language useful.

"Estimates of the quality of representation" connected with a case thus play a part in decisions about amicus participation. At times amicus participation comes when organizations "are dissatisfied with the quality or type of argument filed by the primary parties in the pending action."[24] Likewise, "if the cause is worthwhile, but the advocate is inept," an organization might be more likely to file an amicus brief "to avoid bad law because the case would be decided," a type of defensive participation in which one files an amicus brief to "supplement a weak presentation by lawyers who don't have your expertise." And when an organization has "an area of litigation we're trying to protect," and a case is brought by lawyers who aren't specialists in that area of law, an amicus brief can "signal the court to be narrow in its ruling." This is an aspect of "too much of an imbalance in a case"— lawyering imbalance, for example, when a solo attorney faces a major firm. Here an amicus brief may be necessary to put a case "in context," to provide a "look at more than the individual facts" stressed by the party's lawyer. The organization, familiar with the issues, could do this better than could a solo practitioner lacking experience before the Supreme Court. Not only the quality of parties' presentations but also the quality of other amicus briefs affects whether to file an amicus brief: "Where some amicus briefs are in but we didn't trust the quality, we put our own in," said a lawyer for a public interest organization whose lawyers felt it was likely "to be listened to for its expertise."

An amicus brief may be necessary to supply missing points or when the parties do not address an issue exactly as dictated by an organization's litigation strategy. There are "cases which raise significant questions with efforts for our clients," but which are "without a record"—a poorly constructed one or one deficient because the case had been decided on summary judgment instead of after development of facts at trial. Such "supplementing" amicus participation occurs "when there are points that need to be made that are not made, perhaps for strategic reasons." LDF thus has participated as amicus in cases not handled "as LDF would have handled them." At times, an organization which is a party may need to have another entity say something that cannot be blended with its own argument. This might even lead it to arrange for an amicus brief containing an argument the organization did not wish to have appear in its principal brief. In the Japanese-American cases, the ACLU national staff wished not to make one argument— that General DeWitt, the officer who had issued the report justifying relocation of the Japanese-Americans, was racist—so a separate brief, prepared by allies, made the point.[25]

An organization might also file amicus briefs when it could make a "special contribution that no one else will offer," such as a particular perspective that came from representing interests different from others in the litigation. An example is MALDEF's *Bakke* amicus brief, which "insisted on the unique character of Chicano problems in California and the country generally," and was intended to alter the commonly held view that all "minorities" were the same and had identical problems.[26] The "special contribution" might also be expert knowledge. In the *Bakke* case, the NAACP Legal Defense Fund contributed "a long, careful analysis of the 'clear and unequivocal' history of the Fourteenth Amendment," material not replicated in other groups' briefs. Earlier LDF had not intended to participate, out of the feeling that " 'we had nothing to contribute,' " as briefs filed by others " 'were quite competent to deal with the issues.' " Then a staff member, remembering an 1866 veto message by President Andrew Johnson, looked at the underlying legislative history, which "shed new light on the original intent of the Fourteenth Amendment." [27] Thus LDF's *Bakke* brief was said to be important, because it was "informative" and "made a unique contribution about the history of the Fourteenth Amendment vis-à-vis affirmative action and about the Freedman's Bureau."

Amicus participation may, however, be undertaken more for one's constituency than to affect policy, or to demonstrate to its members and clientele that it is effective, a matter of organizational maintenance. Some amicus participation results from this need to "show the flag," to participate to remind others—including judges, opposing parties, and one's allies, as well as one's constituents—that the organization is there. At times, a group may file an amicus brief because it realizes that its absence (its failure to file the brief) would be noticeable, and would give rise to the Court's suspicion as to why it was not a participant. Thus, suggests an LDF attorney, his organization would on occasion file briefs in cases simply to be "there" because its absence might be more noticeable than its presence. For example, some of the "redundant" amicus briefs in the *Bakke* case "reflected an organizational desire to be on the public record." This can be done both by veterans of the litigation process and by relative novices, particularly in "big" decisions. Thus, in *Bakke,* the Puerto Rican Legal Defense and Education Fund saw the case "as an opportunity to introduce itself to the Supreme Court as a major civil rights legal program." This consideration added to the group's belief that "the symbolic value of being associated with the 'right' side of the controversy"—another aspect of "showing the flag"—overcame expending resources to participate.[28]

There are problems associated with amicus activity, just as there are with other elements of litigation. Most serious is that amicus participation indicates an organization's lack of control over litigation. If others will not cooperate to allow an organization to participate in a case more directly, being an amicus may be the only option if it wishes to participate at all. For example, because Americans for Effective Law

Enforcement needed prosecutors' permission to sponsor cases, it had to resort to amicus activity.[29] However, lacking litigation control, an organization finds that amicus participation allows at least some participation in line with group strategy: "Even when we lose, we protect the law." This is particularly important when the other side may have sought certiorari in cases in which civil rights plaintiffs prevailed in the lower courts.

The "basic problem" with amicus participation is that it "divorces the group's legal (constitutional) argument from the conduct of the case," the details of building a case in the trial court and in that way shaping the legal argument. This is related to the complaint, by a veteran civil liberties litigator, that amicus participation is "detached, distant, uninvolved, and abstract," with amicus briefs reading "like law review articles." "No one," he added sourly, "reads them but one's secretary and the printer (maybe)." There is also the very pragmatic difficulty that "one doesn't get money (attorney fees) for amicus participation." Another pragmatic aspect is that, for all the claims made by organizations that their amicus briefs made a difference, comparison of cases with one or more amicus briefs on one side and none on the other with cases involving the same issue where there was no amicus supporting the litigant showed no difference in success rates— although there was a minor advantage for amicus-supported parties in civil rights and liberties cases.[30]

Despite these problems, when an organization engaging in planned litigation considers its strategic interests, the choice not to participate may be illusory. For example, when the *McGautha* and *Crampton* death penalty cases were before the Supreme Court, the extent of what was at stake prevented LDF from staying on the sidelines, and it filed an amicus brief.[31] Likewise, the Council on Legal Education Opportunity (CLEO), which saw both *Bakke* and the previous *DeFunis* case as threats to its central objectives, filed an amicus brief in *Bakke*, because it feared that if the lower court ruling invalidating the university's affirmative action plan were sustained, its own special admissions program would be challenged.[32] When an organization is a confederation of other entities, like the National Chamber Litigation Center, the litigator may have to file amicus briefs because the members asked that it be done. An organization may also have little choice about amicus participation if important cases do not come to its attention until they are well along in the appellate process, as an amicus brief may then be the only way the organization can make its views known. Such a case for LDF was *City of Kenosha v. Bruno*,[33] an obscenity case—and thus hardly grist for the LDF mill—but "important for remedies under §1983." When such a case surfaces only when certiorari is granted, LDF lawyers "would run around and file briefs." An organization thus might be "derelict in its duty" if it did not state its position, and if it "didn't get involved," would "get what it deserved" in potential precedents not achieved or negative precedents received, as well as in lost opportunities to improve its position vis-à-vis other organizations.

The Process of Decision

The process of deciding to participate as amicus, including the amount of discussion before a decision is reached, varies. An amicus brief may appear to be a seamless web but the process leading to it is not always smooth, even in older organizations like the ACLU and the NAACP. It may reveal, or produce, internal division, particularly when a case poses new or unusual questions so that organizations lack a reportory of standard responses, and can also strain relations with normally friendly groups.[34]

At times discussion about filing an amicus brief is extended, occurring over several meetings; at other times, it is brief. A key element of the decision process is the range of people consulted. Is the decision made by staff or by the board of directors, or is effort made to obtain input from the organization's membership? Staff lawyers are quite likely to take part and people beyond legal staff and the board may become involved, but the membership is not likely to be involved. The need to proceed expeditiously affects the process by which decisions to file an amicus brief would usually be made. For some organizations, with respect to the *Bakke* case "[t]he imminence of the peril outweighed concerns about consulting the members."[35]

Legal staff may initiate action and may even dominate the decision process through their view of the course of future litigation, or, while insisting that the organization intervene, they may adopt "a position of studied neutrality on the case's merit." If debates had taken place earlier so that the broad outlines of the organization's position have already been hammered out in debates, the lawyers have parameters within which to operate. Fear of "the potential divisiveness of an internal debate" or fatigue at extended debates may lead other organization

officials to "leave it to the lawyers," and the lawyers may make decisions on their own, as can be seen from the claim by one lawyer that
because the decision "was not a policy decision in the normal sense
of the word," "We did not contact the board because we are paid to
make the decisions on the law." [36]

LDF and Lawyers' Committee

The NAACP Legal Defense Fund did not readily undertake amicus
participation, either on its own initiative or when asked by others.
However, being an amicus was recognized as necessary activity and
amicus briefs were thought "useful in discrete cases," particularly
when LDF had "something important to say," with participation
coming in important cases where "we think our participation will
highlight its importance." Yet, with "any case going to the Supreme
Court, presumptively LDF had something to say." This was not ar-
rogance, but stemmed from LDF's frequent Supreme Court amicus
appearances, which showed that being a "repeat player" in the legal
system was advantageous. LDF's "good relations with a spectacu-
lar group of academics" (including Charles Black, Louis Pollak, and
Anthony Amsterdam) meant the group had available lawyers "who
might bring out issues in a special way." This would be particularly
important when the courts wanted advice and turned to LDF briefs
because of the organization's credibility, which had been acquired
through the high quality of its earlier briefs and oral arguments. The
weight given to a case by LDF's amicus participation imposes on it
a particular obligation to choose such participation with exceptional
care.

LDF's prestige and active participation as a direct sponsor of cases
allowed it to be chary about its amicus participations, not using them,
as other groups were said to do, "to justify to their constituency the
work being done." Because "We have no need to puff up what we're
doing," amicus briefs were not necessary for purposes of publicity,
and LDF staff attorneys felt it was not a good idea to file redundant
amicus briefs that might merely reflect that purpose. Indeed, LDF
had a predisposition against joining in amicus participation, dislik-
ing "signing on" to others' briefs, often declining requests to submit them, and rarely stimulating them from others, although when
they were submitted, they "did try to make the most of them." The
staff certainly wanted to avoid "people filing ecumenical amicus briefs

with the thought of persuading the Court," a situation characterized as "typically a pain." They quoted former federal judge—and LDF board member—Marvin Frankel, "If you want to file a petition, go to Congress," and added that the organization did itself no service by "loading up judges with them," because "As judicial workload grows, judges pay less attention to those briefs without a unique perspective to bring to bear." LDF also worked to avoid the recognized risk of irritating the parties' lawyers by what was said in the amicus briefs.

As in so much else, LDF appears to have been quite well organized to handle amicus participation. Initiation of LDF amicus participation would come from the staff lawyer working on a particular case, who would talk with LDF's senior staff (for example, Jack Greenberg, James Nabrit III, Stephen Ralston) and then write the first draft. In general, the "interest of a staff attorney in the area of law" would provide the impetus for amicus participation; if an attorney was really "hot," he would go to Greenberg, who had authority from the board of directors to decide whether LDF participated in any case, authority delegated further to some of the senior attorneys. As a staff lawyer observed, you "couldn't have one person [making those decisions] with hundreds of cases," but the lead counsel in the case did consult with the senior attorneys. Ultimately, of course, the decision was the director's: a brief was never filed in LDF's name without his approval, "with more or less input from staff attorneys." For Supreme Court amicus participation, Greenberg and Nabrit handled matters. By comparison, NAACP, which "programmatically didn't write as many amicus brief as LDF" although it participated as amicus in major cases like *Bakke* and *Weber*, suffered from "confusion in the whole structure," with a state of affairs "midway between helter-skelter and organization."

The Lawyers' Committee's decision process for submitting an amicus brief is of particular note because of the role of its committees. Until the early 1970s, most Lawyers' Committee Supreme Court amicus briefs were prepared by cooperating firms in New York City and Washington. This carried with it the disadvantage that the lawyers were not "following civil rights in the Supreme Court on a day-to-day basis." The executive director then began to have some amicus briefs prepared in-house, while staff worked with outside firms on others. The staff, which had "continuous discussions about what cases to file amicus briefs in," proposed amicus participation to an amicus committee of the Executive Committee. That "handful of people do more than vote: they lay out their views in a letter." Even those who oppose amicus participation in a particular case, when the vote goes against them, are likely to contribute ideas to be brought up in a brief. The Lawyers' Committee has been said to believe that "only four–five cases per term are important for amicus participation; there is no rigid rule but we try to limit it to that number." In part this stems from an earlier concern on the part of some members of the group's executive committee, who were said to have a "paternalistic view of the Supreme Court" and not to "want the Supreme Court to get tired" of the organization's amicus participation.

Relations with Other Organizations

Other organizations filing or which asked your organization to file—a group's interorganizational relations—provide an important element in the decision to file an amicus brief. An organization might be able to forgo filing if others do so because its point of view will be presented to the court, but it might also have to file a brief to avoid appearing uninterested in the issues the case poses. The choice of whether to participate may likewise be limited when other amicus filers or the case's sponsor request an amicus brief or the signing of their brief because of the need to reinforce or supplement others' positions, although an organization can allow others to proceed with their cases and can plead scarcity of resources—"the constraints of a small staff and limited resources"—to retain its freedom of action in responding to requests for amicus participation.

Joint briefs are an increasing fact of litigation life, as can be seen in the 78 briefs involving over 400 groups in the 1989 *Webster* abortion rights case, with briefs supporting abortion rights having an average of ten signers per brief.[37] However, some groups do not wish to join others. The American Civil Liberties Union, for example, has had a policy "to refuse to join with other organizations in sponsoring briefs *amicus.*"[38] Such disinclination may even lead to transforming a request for amicus participation into more active involvement, as when a request for an amicus brief in the *Zauderer* lawyer advertising case came to Public Citizen, and its chief attorney suggested that Public Citizen handle the Supreme Court appeal.[39]

A predisposition almost the reverse may contribute to the increase in joint amicus filings. One general counsel, who made amicus participation decisions, said his response was "generally 'Yes'," and the chief attorney for another organization said that he "would want to have a very good reason to turn down a request" for amicus participation, particularly as there was a staff person with the appropriate experience who "could put together a brief without difficulty." Even here, however, the decision to participate was not automatic, with effects on staff workload taken into account. This is, of course, a resource-related reason, also mentioned by a number of other civil rights litigators. As one litigator said, other organizations' requests were approached "within the constraints of small staff and limited resources," at times used as an excuse for not responding affirmatively: "In saying No when asked, we tell them of resource problems." Workload could be a reason for larger organizations as well, although one of them made exceptions for cases identified by "scholarly and academic consultants," because having them prepare a brief "would support [the organization's] program with an educational program."

Joint amicus activity occurs despite the feeling of many lawyers that "just to have a listing of organizations supporting the plaintiff or defendant is not worthwhile." Indeed, some organizations decline to file amicus briefs of the "me, too" variety, particularly when doing so deprives the organization of the opportunity to show its special qualities. Yet even this basic preference against joining has been overcome: "When everyone else did it, we went along, to satisfy constituent expectations." And at times there were positive attractions to joint amicus participation. "It's to one's advantage to work with" some groups, observed an LDF attorney, because "there are first-rate lawyers" working for those groups.

Organizations by and large apply the same criteria to requests by other organizations to submit an amicus brief as are used in deciding on amicus filings without such a request: whether the group can make a special contribution, the importance of the case to its own clients, and the quality of the parties' presentation. Multiple factors often operate on any decision, as can be seen in the considerations entering into the National Legal Aid and Defender Association's *Bakke* amicus participation, which came about because "time pressures foreclosed the writing of a distinctive NLADA-oriented brief; the principal backers of the National Council of Churches' brief were well known to the NLADA and the latter had great confidence in their abilities; the brief had already been endorsed by key allies; and the NLADA expected to increase the impact of its actions in *Bakke* by joining a solidly written brief backed by several powerful and respected private organizations." [40]

Who asks is important. At times this means the requesting individual more than the organization for whom that individual works. Thus an organization "would figure out a way to do it" because of personal ties and respect, often deriving from "membership" in the civil rights bar or from participation in overlapping organizations. At other times it means the organization making the request as a result of its institutional ties with other organizations. In some situations, when a request is from an organization "with whom you have been cooperating, you would feel like an S.O.B." not to file the brief. Thus meeting allies' expectations could become quite important, perhaps leading to coalition filing a brief. There are also cases in which "all join" because it is "important for the civil rights bar to show it feels strongly about the importance of an issue." Likewise, it is important that the Supreme Court know the broad range of community concern in cases like those on capital punishment, where the moral issue or public sentiment infuses legal concepts in the brief. Showing increased numbers in these situations could be done through the filing of many briefs or by adding signatories to existing briefs. Indeed, in the capital punishment cases, "a number of nongovernmental coalitions did materialize," and many repeat players also joined amicus coalitions. [41]

In general, groups do not want to be associated with others in amicus participation—and particularly not to be part of the same amicus brief—unless the posture of the parties requesting participation is compatible with the organization's fundamental mandate, which is an overriding value. Indeed, an organization may risk "an occasional break with its friends over an especially important issue . . . in order to defend its concept of the values at stake" in a case, and may go its separate way if another group "could not adequately represent [its] viewpoints," as when MALDEF was concerned that interests of non-African-American minorities would be submerged in LDF's *Bakke* brief. [42] Nor did they want to participate without input into the brief; the effort to "try to have substantive input" was fairly general. The principal lawyer for one litigating unit was willing to have his group's name on a brief he'd commented on and approved "where the advice is of more than cursory nature." Similarly, LDF didn't want to be associated with other organizations' briefs "without greater LDF involvement"; at any level, "LDF was less likely to sign on to briefs we've not had a major part in writing" because LDF "has its reputation to be concerned with."

Another organization's request to file an amicus brief may entail co-ordination with that organization. Instances of groups linked together can be found. In the restrictive covenant cases, coordination was made difficult because each organization had its own constituency and wanted to make certain points.[43] In the contemporary period, women's groups regularly supported each other, with the National Organization for Women regularly supporting the ACLU, and in em-ployment discrimination litigation in the 1970s, the Lawyers' Com-mittee frequently filed briefs after consulting with LDF or at LDF's request.[44] We must nonetheless be careful not to overestimate either the frequency of coordinated amicus participation or to underestimate the difficulties in carrying it out. In the *Bakke* case, it was difficult for large coalitions to maintain consensus, especially if a particularly powerful "lead" organization was behind a brief.[45] There was also "little confirmation" for "the myth about the careful orchestration of amici arguments" in church-state litigation. Instances of "careful use of amici to supplement or complement the arguments of the principal parties, to float constitutional trial balloons, or to provide alternative rationales for reaching the desired results" were "rare," in large mea-sure because "amici take the positions of their organizations, and not necessarily the position the plaintiff would prefer."[46]

Contemporary civil rights litigators talk less of "active coordina-tion" than of "informal" and "detached" cooperation. For example, an ACLU lawyer talked of "some meetings with other church-state attorneys," but he said that otherwise there was "not close coordina-tion" and the meetings were not helpful. More likely than meetings were occasional conversations or calls to see if his organization's par-ticipation was welcome; often the conversations occurred as part of the process of preparing a brief. This process also took place among conservative public interest law firms; although others did not, some attended luncheons sponsored by the Heritage Foundation, and there was informal contact among lawyers for some of the groups.[47]

Some civil rights groups were, nonetheless, engaged in "active co-ordination," and civil rights lawyers on the whole felt—perhaps be-cause of their frequent interaction—that coordination was not par-ticularly difficult and that they were successful in achieving it. An attorney for a group contemplating filing an amicus brief in another group's case might meet with the sponsoring group and might "feed arguments to the attorney writing the brief" because "the judge will pay more attention to them than to amicus." Indeed, potential amici may "help them develop their principal arguments." One lawyer involved in school desegregation cases said that the NAACP Legal Defense Fund and the Lawyers' Committee "have both been diligent in coordinating amicus input with other groups," such as the ACLU in the Columbus and Dayton, Ohio, cases. Efforts to coordinate the large number of potential amici in *Webster* led to attempts "to discourage duplication among the briefs and to encourage coalition building among amici with similar interests," with grouping of organizations into coalitions "so that each argued points most appropriate to their interests and expertise."[48] Communication was often undertaken as part of an effort to reduce duplication, although that could not be eliminated; moreover, it "may at times be good to have three groups saying the same thing," with "independent assessment leading to the same conclusion."

Likewise, when an attorney for the principal litigator in a case was contacted by another group wishing to file an amicus brief in the former's case, he "would indicate the general direction of his brief," because he would be "concerned that their briefs contributed to the case." This would not, however, be a matter of "orchestrating" the other organization's amicus participation; he simply "would try to make them assist his case" by making suggestions to another lawyer after reading proposed briefs, at times this as substitute for filing one. Only rarely did this lawyer stimulate briefs from other groups, but he "did try to make the most of them." For another attorney, coordination took the form of "trying to help," but "within limits of what we thought appropriate." However, "it was not always liked" when the group tried to coordinate, and there was a "problem of having to send a brief around" to everyone: "they all have their comments." As one organization generally found, "writing briefs by committee doesn't work very well," so that the organization took the posture that "if we have something to say, we'll say it; if others want to join, OK."

11

Litigation Dynamics

Litigators' plans are subject to the vagaries of the course of particular cases or the interaction of sets of cases—the internal dynamics of litigation. Even when a litigating organization has control at the beginning of a case—not always true, as we have seen—it may lose that control during the litigation. The length and lack of resolution of civil rights cases, with the emotional nature of their underlying controversies, makes it quite likely that during the course of litigation there will be not only events affecting that case but other changes—in political environment, in personnel, and in legal issues. In these "continuing controversies . . . the meanings of the operant terms . . . are constantly changing, [and] the demands constantly expanding."[1] As litigation lengthens, the likelihood increases that events not subject to control will impinge on a case. Here judges' rulings are particularly important, as is the participation of additional players who, although not initially in the case, have become intervenors.

Among the changes external to litigation may be alterations in the political environment, which can shift drastically between initiation of a litigation campaign and judges' decisions on the major cases in the campaign. This can be seen in the efforts to change the welfare system through litigation, where the election of President Nixon and changes in the composition of the Supreme Court intervened between the relatively successful beginning of the campaign and its unsuccessful conclusion. Changes in political environment can occur locally as well as nationally. Changes may be affected by, perhaps even caused by, the litigation, particularly at the local level, but this can also occur nationally. For example, the course of abortion litigation was affected by the development of groups whose activity was stimulated by *Roe v. Wade* itself. While political environment may set initial conditions for a litigation campaign, a campaign once started develops its own dynamics. These dynamics can themselves cause difficulties by decreasing flexibility, but they make external conditions less important because "the external elements were loose enough to allow the small number of people involved in the litigation effort to draw whatever conclusions they desired."[2]

Aspects of Litigation Dynamics

The importance of litigation dynamics for the effectiveness of planned litigation can be seen in many situations. The time-pressure under which civil rights lawyers must work is a principal element of litigation dynamics. Such pressure means that deliberation is not likely to be the order of the day. In one case, Arthur Kinoy had "a little less than a month to complete an appeals brief, have [William] Kuntsler read it before rushing off to another of his pressing Mississippi court dates, and get it in the mail to Holt for his signature as the Virginia lawyer responsible for the case, so that it could be filed in Richmond where the Virginia Supreme Court sat."[3] As a school desegregation litigator observed, "Lawyers are caught up in proving a violation, framing relief within the short period allowed by precedent, and dealing with emergencies," with those assisting in developing desegregation plans "busy people with a nationwide clientele, who often do not reach the scene until there is little time left."[4]

Some cases initiated only to obtain a trial court disposition but not an appellate ruling are nevertheless taken to the Supreme Court, just as cases thought likely candidates for appellate precedent fall out of the process with many employment discrimination cases, particularly those involving only individual plaintiffs, being settled. As to the former, in a case on blacks' access to community swimming pools, there was "no original intent to go to the Supreme Court" but only to get the particular neighborhood association that operated the pool to comply with the law. The "irresistible force" that propelled the case to the Supreme Court was a ruling in which it was "patently clear that the Fourth Circuit was dead wrong in not following precedent," with the appeals court distinguishing the Supreme Court's *Sullivan v. Little Hunting Park* ruling on "minute factual grounds" and several judges dissenting from the appeals court's refusal to grant an en banc re-hearing. Cases likewise can expand from initial narrow goals. When parties to a case wish to settle, bargaining may dissolve when either party appeals a trial court order either to limit the remedy or to obtain one "more ambitious" than the initial one adopted.[5] New Jersey litigation that became a major effort at mental health law reform had started with a narrow scope but the scope increased as the case became a federal court class action, one that would be "comprehensive enough to apply to all the relevant members of the class and that raised all the important issues that made it a worthwhile attempt at law reform." Massachusetts mental health litigation likewise expanded from the initial plaintiffs to a class action and also expanded in scope.[6]

Griggs v. Duke Power Co., the Supreme Court's first pronouncement on the substantive issues in Title VII, provides an example of the effect of dynamics which strengthened a case and made it more important as it proceeded. The district judge, in addition to ruling that plaintiffs had failed to show that company transfer requirements led to disproportionate rejection of blacks, defined "professionally developed" (employment tests or requirements) in an unacceptable fashion and rejected the important theory that one must deal with "present effects of past discrimination." Only after this ruling was the decision made to proceed to the first appellate level. When plaintiffs did not fully succeed in the Fourth Circuit, their lawyers did not see *Griggs* "an ideal 'test case' for review by the Supreme Court."[7] Yet the "powerful" partial dissent supporting the plaintiff's position by Fourth Circuit Judge Simon Sobeloff, "one of the most respected federal judges in civil rights litigation," was thought to give the dissent particular weight, particularly in the Supreme Court's eyes. This gave support to a decision to seek certiorari, a decision which had to be weighed against the potential of developing other cases "to present more appealing records to raise the testing issues."

The Denver school case provides an instance of a tactical choice's effects on the course of litigation. When a newly elected school board majority rescinded desegregation plans, plaintiffs had to challenge that action and sought an injunction restricted to that part of the city covered by the rescinded desegregation plans. As plaintiffs had intended to bring a full-scale desegregation case, their action "required bifurcating what was, in embryo, a comprehensive and all-out attack on the entire school system," and that "arguably added four years to the lawsuit." More important, however, was the school board's rescission which precipitated the bifurcation; it contributed to the plaintiffs' ultimate success because their evidence in the injunctive portion of the case became the basis of the Supreme Court's *Keyes* ruling.[8] Another occurred in the Mt. Vernon, New York, case, where the state's education commissioner had initiated charges against the school board. Black and white parents, who had earlier initiated a state administrative proceeding with the commissioner, became concerned about possible delay by the school board, which the commissioner had ordered to carry out desegregation; they therefore intervened in a state court case and won a summary judgment against the board. However, that had the unanticipated consequence that the school board's power to levy additional taxes remained concealed. If the commissioner had told the intervenors he could order the tax levied, several years of delay would have been avoided.[9]

Not only a single case's internal dynamics but also the dynamics of developments in several related cases may limit litigation planning. Rulings in other cases in the same judicial district or the same circuit affect a case. Thus the Winston-Salem, North Carolina, school case was affected by the *Swann* school litigation in Charlotte-Mecklenburg County.[10] Lawyers bringing other cases seeking the same goal may at times pose more of an obstacle to implementation of strategy by getting their cases to the appellate courts, including the Supreme Court, ahead of those engaged in planned litigation and before the latter can do much about it. Those attempting planned welfare litigation could not get their preferred case challenging maximum welfare grants to the Supreme Court when they wanted to. Lawyers who "appeared to want nothing to do" with those planning litigation brought a case and won, leaving the decision to go to the Supreme Court in the defendant state's hands.[11] In another example, national organizations were interested in the Indianapolis school case, but the local lawyers did not want to give up the case although they did not do much with it, so that the case went to the appellate court without assistance from experienced school desegregation lawyers. The result was that "national experts had no opportunity to develop the record, the briefs, and the proposed remedies in ways likely to produce extensions of important principles of case law."[12] (Interrelations between cases can affect defendants as well as civil rights plaintiffs, as can be seen in Boston, where the School Committee's response to one case was affected its being absorbed in another.[13])

Unanticipated rulings within a case are a key part of dynamics. When lawyers seeking to produce school desegregation in Richmond, California, found a state judge's court order "far less encompassing than anticipated" and the judge unwilling to adopt a proposed remedy which the defendant school board was willing to adopt, they found themselves unable to proceed because they would have had to assert that they "had somehow lost an uncontested case."[14] The Japanese-American Exclusion Cases provided further examples. Lawyers who thought the *Endo* case would proceed first were surprised by the Ninth Circuit's *Korematsu* decision after the Supreme Court had returned that case to the appeals court. (Lawyers for *both* sides were surprised and thus were put in the same situation.) Then, Ninth Circuit Judge William Denman's hurried certification of *Endo* just before the end of the Supreme Court's term in Spring 1944, at first scrambled lawyers' strategy of having *Korematsu* and *Endo* argued together, although the two cases were argued together in the next term.[15]

The major Denver and Detroit school cases provide a clear picture of the effects on litigation dynamics of Supreme Court rulings. The Denver decision affected much litigation that was in progress. The Boston school case was one, as the Court's ruling in *Keyes* came after the trial although before Judge Garrity's ruling. Plaintiffs had dealt with both effect and intent, by "saying we don't need to prove intent but we will," because the question of whether intent or effect was the proper standard for proof had not been resolved when the suit was brought, and it "looked as if a pure effects test wouldn't survive," as it had not in the already decided Tenth Circuit's Denver ruling. Apparently wanting to be sure his decision on liability would withstand appeals, the judge reopened the case for argument on *Keyes*' implications and then made the findings it required.[16] *Keyes* also affected Hispanics' place in the Boston school system. Judge Garrity handled the linkage between desegregation and bilingual education program procedurally by granting Hispanics intervention at the remedy stage, and then working through the linkage.

The Detroit ruling was seen as significantly limiting desegregation remedies. In the Indianapolis case, on appeal when the Detroit ruling was handed down, the result was a considerably limited interdistrict remedy. When, after a remand from the Seventh Circuit, the trial judge renewed the remedy and the Seventh Circuit affirmed, the Supreme Court remanded for reconsideration in light of the *Washington v. Davis* and *Arlington Heights* cases requiring a showing of intent.[17] A "prayer for possible metropolitanization, as appropriate or necessary, was included" when the Boston suit was started, said a lawyer in the case, but by the time it was decided, "we knew we wouldn't get that relief" because of the Supreme Court's ruling. When, at a later stage of the proceedings, the Mayor of Boston did propose metropolitanization, plaintiffs opposed it: "It was an ingenious theory but it was not plausible so it would fail; it was a waste of resources; and blacks viewed it as diversionary, and it would alienate the suburbs."

One of the NAACP's lawyers noted that the Detroit decision "forced us to concentrate on single districts, except for the Indianapolis case," and made the Cleveland, Dayton, and Boston cases "all the harder." Had the ruling gone the other way, he said, "city districts would have aligned with blacks against suburban school districts"—true in Detroit itself, in Wilmington, and later in St. Louis. Yet not all civil rights advocates were prepared to give up on interdistrict remedies after the Detroit ruling. One lawyer said he and his colleagues "felt the Court had not closed the door on metropolitan remedies, but one would have to go carefully to avoid another major loss," and a housing litigator suggested that metro-area remedies including "only one or two suburban jurisdictions" would be possible, as well as easier to prove in housing. However, he counseled against "confront[ing] the Supreme Court immediately with another case involving a desegregation plan applying to a large number of suburban jurisdictions—certainly without solid evidence that each of them, individually and collectively, constituted a causal factor in the segregation."[18]

Changes in Personnel

Litigation dynamics are affected by changes in personnel, including shifts in judges and in counsel. Three district judges were involved in the Detroit school case—Stephen Roth, who died after the trial;

Robert DeMascio, who decided the 1977 *Milliken* case and whose departure came in part from plaintiffs' request that he withdraw; and Avern Cohn. Litigation challenging selection of school principals in New York City also saw three judges: Walter Mansfield, elevated to the Second Circuit but who continued as the trial judge until the circuit council agreed to designate a specific judge to continue with the case; that judge, Harold Tyler, Jr., who became deputy attorney general in the Ford administration; and Milton Pollack, who took the case to its conclusion.[19] The cases on access by the handicapped to transit facilities also illustrate that elections, deaths, and elevations to higher courts can affect who sits from one part of a case to another.

In the Richmond, Virginia, school case, both judge and plaintiffs' chief counsel changed. When Judge John Butzner joined the Court of Appeals for the Fourth Circuit, Judge Robert R. Mehrige, Jr., took over the case, and plaintiffs' lawyer Henry Marsh III, on the case since 1961, was elected to the Richmond city council (he was to become mayor) and so had to turn over the case to others, but veteran civil rights lawyers in his firm were available and the support of the LDF continued.[20]

In an instance of a shift not stemming from anything specific to the case, the departure from the NAACP of its legal staff, including General Counsel Robert L. Carter, as a result of the firing of Lewis Steel, led eventually to the NAACP Legal Defense Fund's taking over the Mt. Vernon school case after Steel had remained counsel in some state court proceedings for a brief time.[21] Lawyers changing jobs lead to their departure. In the Ohio prison conditions cases, a lawyer who had become plaintiff's counsel against the Columbus Correctional Facility (the former Ohio penitentiary) when she joined the ACLU office continued with the case when she moved to Legal Services, but when she left the area, another lawyer at ACLU inherited the case.[22] The departure of a major figure in the LDF's bail campaign to take a teaching position was one of the factors leading to the demise of that campaign.[23]

Even when personnel do not change, relationships among them may change during litigation, affecting its dynamics. Acrimony is not unknown. Indeed, "organizational and personal disagreement . . . seem to appear with more than ordinary frequency in cases seeking to advance principles"[24] like much civil rights litigation, and those trying to advance a position may find that they are fighting each other rather than their purported opponents. Conflict within the ACLU about the Japanese-American relocation cases, which "stemmed from conflicts both of personality and policy" and was of "unusual depth and endurance," provides an illustration. This visible conflict continued through the filing of briefs by both the national office and the local affiliate in the *Hirabayashi* case; and it led the organization to approach argument in the Supreme Court "both divided and dispirited." Conflict also occurred within the defense, as lawyers for the Justice Department and for the War Department were in particular disagreement, although they managed to conceal it from plaintiffs and the courts, so that conflict "split the shaky legal teams on both sides."[25]

Intervenors

Forcing responsive action in the midst of planned litigation, and thus affecting its dynamics, is one or more groups' intervention in a case. This intervention, which makes patterns of relationships among the parties more complex, is more likely in longer cases as groups realize, at times slowly, that their interests are involved. The Chinese Six Companies which dominated Chinatown realized only midway through the San Francisco school case "that what they had viewed as a squabble between blacks and whites might well disrupt their community-based public schools," and thus sought to intervene.[26] Among intervenors in school desegregation cases are disgruntled antibusing whites; minorities other than blacks, such as Hispanics or Asians; suburbanites in districts which would be affected by metropolitan school desegregation remedies; and groups of blacks who seek education programs or an end to busing, not plaintiffs' desegregation remedy.

The Detroit school litigation shows that intervenors can have a substantial effect on a case. There intervenor white homeowners (Concerned Citizens for Better Education), seeing that the NAACP would prove the schools were segregated, began to look toward a metropolitan remedy, particularly after the Supreme Court ruled in the *Swann* busing case: if they couldn't have segregation, they would at least try to retain a white majority by bringing suburbs into the remedy. Their intervention meant that the NAACP, which had preferred the Wilmington, Delaware, case as a vehicle for metropolitan desegregation, "got on the train as it was leaving the station." Part of the NAACP's reluctance may have come from the belief that pursuing this mechanism "would deny plaintiffs the speedy remedy they sought," a concern that "proved well-founded" as several additional years of delay ensued.[27] The Chinese intervenors also had great effect in the San Francisco school case, as they were able to get a Ninth Circuit panel to stay the trial judge's order until an appeal was heard; the appeals court panel questioned why Chinese (and Irish and Italians) were caught up in a black-white problem and caused the black plaintiffs' lawyer much anxiety and much extra work before the stay order was vacated.[28]

Principal civil rights litigation groups can themselves be intervenors in others' cases, particularly where the government has initiated charges but there is concern it will not press sufficiently or demand the most appropriate remedy. They may also intervene in other groups' cases. In the *Adams* case, this produced significant expansion of the litigation and led to its unraveling. Instead of being limited to forcing the government to proceed with desegregation of higher education, the case came to cover demands that the government process discrimination complaints promptly. The expansion began in 1976 when MAL-DEF, on behalf of parents of Mexican-American students in southern states, sought intervenor standing for them based on their charge that the Office of Civil Rights had been refusing to accept their discrimination complaints because of efforts required by the earlier *Adams* decree. The Women's Equity Action League (WEAL) had also brought a separate case in 1974 over government inaction in enforcement of sex discrimination laws, including inadequacies in Office of Civil Rights' enforcement of Title IX, barring sex discrimination in education. Because of the connection to education, WEAL also sought intervenor status in the *Adams* case on behalf of women.

When Judge Pratt ruled in favor of the Mexican-Americans' intervention but against WEAL, the District of Columbia Circuit reversed him as to the latter.[29] Judge Pratt's ruling forced WEAL to return to its own case to pursue its Title IX concerns, but WEAL then found that the judge there had ruled its preliminary injunction motion moot because of its motion to intervene in *Adams*,[30] illustrating that if intervention can cause difficulties, so can the inability to intervene. Additional interventions brought the Department of Education's enforcement of several other statutes into the case with detrimental effects. With not only Title VI (now for linguistic as well as racial minorities) and Title IX, but also Sec. 504 of the Rehabilitation Act of 1973 (for the handicapped) in the case, the agency used its increasing court-compelled responsibilities, coupled with the absence of funds to carry out the additional duties, to avoid taking action to deal with the very complaints that had first prompted the lawsuit.

Intervention usually means action by those who have sought formal status as parties intervenor under court rules, but other people can "intervene" in a case. Sometimes, of course, a political figure—a mayor (Kevin White of Boston), a president (Gerald Ford, also in the Boston case)—brings overt public pressure. At other times, behind-the-scenes activity becomes part of litigation dynamics. In the Atlanta school case, Judge Griffin Bell, who had earlier written a Fifth Circuit opinion limiting Atlanta integration but was not hearing the case in the 1970s, "helped engineer a negotiated compromise solution," in which blacks received more administrative positions in the school system in return for less desegregation. This in turn angered the national NAACP, which removed local NAACP officials.[31]

Shifts in Legal Position

Another aspect of litigation dynamics is shifts in legal arguments in a case. Parties' positions may shift significantly during litigation. As with other aspects of litigation dynamics, the length of civil rights litigation makes more likely shifts in issues and the introduction of new legal arguments over the course of a case's history. However, momentum operates as a brake against major changes in the legal theory a party advocates, so that lawyers' adoption of initial positions may well later bar them from asserting new arguments. Thus NAACP lawyers seeking to desegregate Cincinnati's schools in the 1980s found themselves bound by the organization's earlier unsuccessful efforts in the *Deal* litigation to have the courts invalidate segregation per se, that is, even if there were no acts of intentional discrimination, as the later judges held the earlier Sixth Circuit ruling *res judicata* when the NAACP sought to show intentional acts.

Yet not infrequently, "issues ultimately litigated—and on which substantial resources are spent—may depart significantly from the questions that stimulated the suit,"[32] with the introduction of new arguments affecting the speed at which a case moves, perhaps slowing it down.[33] At times, there is a shift from a substantive claim to a procedural issue. In the *Parham* litigation concerning retarded children, the substantive issue of provision of a "less restrictive setting" for the children changed to procedures for admission to facilities. In a shift from one substantive claim to another, plaintiffs seeking to improve Hispanics' school situations in a Colorado community initially wished the hiring of more Chicano teachers, but the primary claim became entitlement to a comprehensive bilingual-bicultural program; at the end, however, the employment issue was the only one remaining.[34]

Transformation of cases can occur between the trial court and the appellate court stages of the litigation. At times civil rights issues surface only at the appellate stage, perhaps because of filing of amicus curiae briefs so that cases which are appealed are often quite different at their second hearing than when they were first tried, with the case's substance often shifting on appeal. In the Third, Fifth, and Eighth Circuits from 1956 through 1961, such issue transformation occurred in civil liberties cases, particularly in race relations cases, although in the Second, Fifth, and District of Columbia Circuits in 1965–1967, there was very little issue transformation as the trial and appellate courts defined issues in specific cases differently in only a small percentage of cases.[35]

Some issues do not reach full growth until the Supreme Court, perhaps not even until after briefing and argument when the justices deliberate. *Mapp v. Ohio* provides an instance of justices' responsibility for changing issues, known as *issue fluidity*, which includes addition, deletion, expansion and narrowing of issues.[36] *Mapp*, known for the Supreme Court's enunciation of the exclusionary rule (prohibiting use at trial of improperly seized material), started with the focus on whether someone not intending to distribute obscene materials could be convicted for possessing them. At trial the defense attorney had asked to have the material excluded because of an illegal search, but it was admitted because Ohio had no exclusionary rule. The Ohio Supreme Court, where Ms. Mapp's attorneys pressed both the obscenity question and the search issue but pursued the latter in terms of the "shocking" nature of the search instead of asking for adoption of the exclusionary rule, focused primarily on the obscenity issue and upheld the admission of the evidence. In the U.S. Supreme Court, both the ACLU and the Ohio Civil Liberties Union did raise the exclusionary rule issue, but certainly did not make it central, raising it only in the concluding paragraph of their brief. Yet the Court focused on the exclusionary rule, not even deciding the obscenity question.[37]

Lawyers for the parties most often decide to shift their claims on

their own initiative, although they may be in responding to others' actions, external events, or other court rulings. At times they take their
lead from other actors in the litigation, such as other players on one's
own side of the case. Examples of a national organization's adopting a posture different from a local affiliate's stance are the conflict
between national and local NAACP in the Atlanta school case and
between the national ACLU and its Northern California affiliate over
the Japanese-American relocation cases.

Judges may, however, affect the scope of a case by their suggestions.
In the South Carolina component of the *Brown* litigation, *Briggs v.
Elliott*, Judge J. Waties Waring noted that the NAACP had not directly
challenged segregation and suggested dismissing the case without
prejudice so that it could be refiled with a direct allegation that segregation was unconstitutional. The NAACP acted promptly on the
suggestion.[38] Likewise, Judge Frank Johnson's interests changed the
scope of two major Alabama institutional reform cases. The challenge
to prison system conditions was initially brought by an individual
but was transformed into a class action in part because the lawyer,
a former clerk to the judge, began to understand the judge's interest
in the broader litigation.[39] In a case brought by personnel laid off at
one of the state's facilities and some patients who claimed that denial
of treatment would result from the layoffs, Judge Johnson's interest
in the rights of mental patients transformed the suit into a challenge
to institutional conditions, with employees' claims becoming secondary. Once Judge Johnson had decided the state's liability, the case also
took on a new cast, as the parties had to decide how the judge could
regulate mental health institution. This led many organizations—the
American Psychological Association, the American Association on
Mental Deficiency, the National Legal Aid and Defenders Association,
the Center for Law and Social Policy, the American Orthopsychiatric
Association, and the ACLU—to become involved in the case.[40]

Flip-Flops: Shifts in Administration
Litigation Posture

Another important aspect of litigation dynamics are changes in the administration's litigation posture, or flip-flops. These can occur within
a single administration, for example, when the Bush administration,
after filing a brief challenging spending more money on historically
black institutions of higher education in the attempt to bring about

desegregation, supported a new brief explicitly recognizing the positive role of such colleges and universities.[41] However, flip-flops are more likely between administrations, and are particularly likely from an administration of one party to one of the other party. Although changes in *policy* from one administration to another may take place with some frequency, changes in litigation position in continuing cases are thought to be far less frequent. It is more likely that a new administration will not pursue on appeal cases initiated by its predecessor or that the former will abandon an area of litigation. For example, after a district judge had not required further desegregation action by the Houston school district, the new administration's Justice Department did not appeal, and the Kansas City, Missouri, school desegregation case, where the Carter administration Justice Department considered participating but the Reagan administration decided not to do so. Flip-flops do occur nonetheless, and they were particularly visible in the first years of the Reagan administration.

A flip-flop can be favorable to civil rights organizations, for example, in the transition from the Ford to Carter administrations, when there was greater government willingness to settle cases in which the organization and the government were opposed. In another, within-administration, instance, the *City of Port Arthur* voting rights case, the Reagan administration Justice Department had agreed to settle the case on terms less desirable than what civil rights groups wished; when intervenors were able to persuade a federal court to turn down the settlement and the case was appealed, the Justice Department, reversing its position, supported the district judge's order.[42] Another instance in which civil rights groups fended off a flip-flop—or flipped the flip-flop—came in the challenge to the PACE exam for entry-level workers for many federal civil service positions. Those attacking the exam had shown its discriminatory effect on minorities and the failure to scrutinize it under EEOC guidelines, and that showing had led to a consent decree to abolish the exam. Then the Reagan administration tried to change the settlement, but meetings between Justice Department officials and civil rights groups lawyers prevented reversing the agreement.

More significant for civil rights litigators have been shifts from executive branch support of their position, with government and organization perhaps even being on the same side of the case, to government and interest group divergence or even strong opposition to each other.

The extent of that divergence in litigation position from one administration to the next has varied, from a modest alteration in emphasis,
as in the shift from Truman to Eisenhower or (with the benefit of hindsight) Johnson to Nixon, to a distinct reversal of position, as in the
change from Carter to Reagan. That ideological shift led the Leadership Conference on Civil Rights to assert that the new Reagan Justice
Department, instead of waiting for new cases, had "abruptly switched
sides in cases pending before the Supreme Court and announced that
it would seek the overturning of Supreme Court decisions of very recent vintage, in disregard of the importance of certainty and continuity
in the law."[43]

One instance involved the controversy over whether religion-based
private schools that discriminated on the basis of race should be deprived of their tax exemption because of that discrimination. The government had won a lower court challenge to the revocation of Bob
Jones University's tax exemption, and the acting solicitor general felt
the government had properly won the case. A group of high-level Justice Department officials then persuaded Attorney General William
French Smith to adopt the changed position that the IRS lacked authority for revoking the exemption. The Court, left with no party to
argue the position the government initially had advocated when the
administration argued in its brief that the case was moot, appointed
an amicus curiae to do so—and chose William Coleman, former Cabinet member *and* chairman of the NAACP Legal Defense Fund.[44] (The
Court then ruled against the Reagan administration.)

Another flip-flop came in the Seattle school desegregation case. The
Carter Justice Department had supported a major busing plan, but
the Reagan administration changed sides. Here the Supreme Court
noted in *Washington v. Seattle School District No. 1* (1982) that the government "has changed its position during the course of this litigation,
and now supports the State" (which opposed the busing plan), and
upheld the initial, not subsequent, government position. In the 1993
City of Lockhart voting rights case, in the lower courts the Carter Justice
Department had supported minority voters challenging certain election changes, but the Reagan administration argued that the changes
did not leave the voters worse off. (Here the Supreme Court accepted
the new administration's position on nonretrogression.)

Flip-flops, which often occur as a case moves up the appellate ladder, have also occurred in the lower courts. One involved the efforts

to desegregate higher education. The Carter administration had been unwilling to agree that settlement of its Title VI action against North Carolina be submitted to the U.S. district court in North Carolina as a consent decree. However, just six months into the new administration, the Reagan administration agreed to such a submission, thus insulating the settlement from attack by those challenging inadequate Title VI enforcement.

Another switch in the lower courts involved elementary and secondary education. After earlier Department of Justice intervention to seek busing in the East Baton Rouge Parish, Louisiana, school case, in August 1982 the Reagan Justice Department sought to reopen the busing order before the Fifth Circuit and reassigned lawyers who were reluctant to argue the changed position. When senior Civil Rights Division lawyers wouldn't take the case, Assistant Attorney General for Civil Rights W. Bradford Reynolds assigned lawyers to argue the administration's new position. After the Reagan administration decided to use only an intent theory of discrimination instead of the earlier-used effects test, lawyers from the Civil Rights Division were told not to use the effects test in new cases and to abandon it in pending litigation, which forced the argument to be abandoned in the Parma, Ohio, housing case.[45] Such flip-flops clearly limit what government lawyers can do and place them in a difficult position.[46]

A significant change in litigation position involving abandonment of enforcement efforts which have served to assist litigating interest groups can produce a substantial caseload increase for such groups. Their workload will also be very much heavier if the new administration seeks to reopen litigation once thought to have been resolved on terms favorable to the group. This resulted from the Reagan administration's reopening of consent decrees obtained in the Carter administration and earlier. For example, in the Cincinnati police case, an initial consent decree with percentage hiring goals had been approved by the Justice Department, which followed through by taking the city to court when it followed seniority in layoffs and winning a preliminary injunction against reduction in the minority percentage below the pre-layoff percentage. Then, the Justice Department, in a 1983 volte-face, appealed. In another instance, in 1975 the Ford administration Justice Department had sued to end employment discrimination in the Birmingham, Alabama, police department, and in 1981, before the attorney general attacked numerical goals in hiring, a consent decree had been approved. However, in 1984 when white men claimed they had been denied promotions because of the plan, the Reagan Justice Department intervened on their behalf—but the decree was upheld.

Ethical issues are said to arise when the government changes position and are more severe if, prior to the flip-flop, the government was a co-party on one side of a case and worked with other parties in the litigation. The actual shift itself has been called behavior that "violates the spirit of the Code [of Professional Responsibility] and presents the kind of behavior that undermines public confidence in the justice system." [47] This is true even if the government is thought to have been in a lawyer-client relationship with the co-parties on its (original) side of the case. The "appearance of impropriety" standard is clearly violated "when the government switches sides in the middle of a lawsuit, deserting its co-party and zealously advocating in one court exactly the opposite of what it advocated in another." [48] A major part of the problem is that government may obtain some of its information from its co-parties, as it did in the Seattle school desegregation case, remains in possession of that information when it changes position, and uses the information against the school district for whose benefit it was obtained. This "breach of confidence" could lead to decreased future openness between civil rights parties and their government co-party.[49] A counter position is that, because democratic accountability of elected administrations may require changes in the government's litigation position, there is no ethical violation in the government's switching positions, with any difficulties cured if the government's original lawyers do not work for the government after its position has changed.[50] Regardless of the ethical issues, there is no question that flip-flops are a part of litigation dynamics that makes litigation planning difficult and litigation very complex.

12

Staff Attorneys and

Cooperating Attorneys

Cooperating attorneys—local lawyers involved in the organization's cases—and an organization's own lawyer staff are crucial resources for any litigating organization. In this chapter, after some introductory observations, types of cooperating attorneys are examined, including the use of African-American and white lawyers in civil rights cases. Considerable attention is given to the working relationships between staff attorneys and cooperating attorneys, including the assistance the former provide the latter, with a particular focus on working relations and on "Who decides?" in the NAACP Legal Defense Fund and in the NAACP.

A key element in interest group litigation is the relationship between national lawyer staff and cooperating attorneys. According to an active voting rights litigator, "Cooperating attorneys are at the intersection of horizontal and vertical relations" in civil rights litigation. In the vertical relations between organizations' national level and their local affiliates, local units' officials work with national officers, who in turn may deal with national legal staff, or national legal staff may work directly with lawyers at the local level. LDF, with the "ability to connect . . . isolated attorneys to the lawyers and institutions which serviced the New York and Washington liberal leadership,"[1] was like a "parent legal firm with law offices all over the country," and the appropriate national LDF staff lawyer was the "common focal point."

Use of staff attorneys and cooperating attorneys is related to an organization's relative centralization or decentralization. Increasing the number of staff attorneys has facilitated centralization but also leads to greater use of cooperating attorneys, with concomitant decentralization. That an organization's local elements have their own staff also fosters decentralization, which is also affected by whether and to what extent local units and cooperating attorneys are guided by the national organization's goals. Guidance or control from the national level, the transmission of national litigation priorities to cooperating attorneys, and the translation and incorporation of those priorities into the attorneys' priorities is necessary if decentralization is not to cut against a group's national strategy and if local membership pressures are not to dominate determination of the cases to which cooperating attorneys give greatest attention.[2] NAACP staff have suggested, for example, that the resolutions passed by the NAACP's annual convention are "known" by the NAACP's branches, which "act within the ambit of those statements."

Pressures toward decentralization, which reduces the organization's control over a case, derive from lawyers' ability to act independently, which is likely if they have reputations in their own right, and which may create problems for a national organization. Even without a "cult of personality," a cooperating attorney may have independence stemming from closer association with other organizations than the one for whom he or she is officially the cooperating attorney. For example, the law professor handling the Buffalo, New York, school case received funding from the New York Civil Liberties Union (NYCLU) but had closer contact with the NAACP Legal Defense Fund's school desegregation attorney because of the latter's expertise. Decentralization is reinforced when an organization's local units can initiate litigation without national approval, even if the national organization is supposed to approve taking cases to the Supreme Court. That ACLU cooperating attorneys are often active in the organization's state affiliates, perhaps serving on the lawyers' committee which screens cases for the affiliate, reinforces the local nature of their ties and loyalty, and decreases the national level's leverage over the local units. Local attorney autonomy can also be reinforced by the rules of client-lawyer relations, which prevent an outsider's interference in a lawyer-client relationship.

Both staff attorneys and cooperating attorneys are also involved in horizontal relations—cooperating attorneys with local branches with which they may be affiliated and the community networks in which they are located, and staff attorneys and with other national-level personnel of their own organizations and with other organizations. Internal horizontal relations may be complicated when a lawyer leads an organization, because the lawyer-leader may be less likely than a layperson to defer to the lawyers. However, some nonlawyer leaders like the NAACP's Walter White also had little hesitation to become involved in legal strategy. Because "litigation figured so centrally in the NAACP's actions," White "took a great deal of interest in what the lawyers did" and believed "that as a result of his position he ought to participate in the litigation decisions being made by the lawyers," although his interventions, which often stemmed from the concerns NAACP branches expressed to him, were "occasional, and occasionally erratic."[3] This sort of intervention, added to the White-Thurgood Marshall rivalry, stemming from growth of the legal program while White "attempted to preserve a sphere for his special talents" and to "protect his position within the NAACP and the black community," led staff counsel to have cases sent directly to them.[4] This illustrates that while the chief attorney (general counsel) serves at the pleasure of the organization's executive, who thus is formally in charge, the executive's authority may be constrained if the lawyer has support in the organization's board of directors or among the membership.

Use of cooperating attorneys is frequently associated with civil rights and civil liberties litigation, perhaps because of the ACLU's use of several thousand of them. However, not all litigating organizations have networks of such attorneys, and some litigating entities, such as Public Citizen Litigation Group, limit themselves to being public interest law firms with staff attorneys. In the extreme, not having any attorneys means relying totally on others to supply them, that is, becoming a client oneself; when an organization must enlist other organizations' assistance, its control of the litigation is limited. Having an inadequate number of staff attorneys forces greater reliance on cooperating attorneys, particularly those who will absorb both otherwise billable hours and expenses as they pursue cases.

Use of cooperating attorneys is essential for an organization to handle a large volume of cases, whether or not as part of a strategic campaign. At the same time litigating organizations, including conservative public interest law firms, built strong staff attorney components, they were quite likely to have created cooperating attorney networks as soon as possible, "to draw on the talent of sympathetic attorneys throughout the United States" and thus "to keep abreast of pending litigation throughout the nation."[5]

Because not many cooperating attorneys can "commit their time to or absorb costs" in large cases, attracting lawyers is easier when cases are less complex. That the ACLU's civil liberties cases have, on the whole, been less complex than LDF's cases has made it easier for the ACLU to attract cooperating attorneys, because "it would be an unusual case where the local ACLU lawyers required the kind of access to specialized experts and technical information that the national office of the LDF provides to its local affiliates and cooperating attorneys."[6] If the "controlled, limited constitutional litigation of the *Brown* case could be managed by a handful of lawyers," the situation posed by employment discrimination litigation was quite different, requiring many more attorneys, both in the field and at headquarters, and LDF could handle its large volume of employment discrimination cases only because it could call on cooperating attorneys. Indeed, LDF's expansion of its use of cooperating attorneys made it "a very different organization . . . from that which had planned and successfully brought the *Brown* case," turning it into "a partnership—a mix of staff and cooperating attorneys managing a nationwide, heavy-volume caseload through a pooling of professional resources."[7] With cases becoming more complex, local attorneys are more likely to need a national organization's assistance to serve as cooperating attorneys and this binds them more closely to the national organization. Effective aid to attorneys who wish to be affiliated with an organization in their *pro bono* litigation work will also make them wish to continue associating with that organization.

Obtaining cooperating attorneys is not always easy, despite the frequency with which newsletters publicize their participation, and may require continuous and extensive searching. When an organization contacts a lawyer handling a case to offer organizational participation, the latter becomes a cooperating attorney. This happened when someone associated with the national ACLU saw a notice of the Idaho court ruling in *Reed v. Reed* (on automatic preference for men to adminis-

ter estates) and suggested that the ACLU participate.[8] According to
a recent Lawyers Committee survey, "the lack of a lawyer was the
most frequently encountered difficulty in placement" of cases.[9] The
difficulty can be seen in the San Francisco school case, when a black
attorney "volunteered to 'coordinate' the effort, but . . . lacked the
time to undertake the needed legal and factual research," so a "young
solo practitioner . . . took on the case" although he was not an NAACP
member "and had no previous involvement in San Francisco's civil
rights dispute."[10] Even the ACLU was said by a former national staff
member to be "desperate for local lawyers with expertise," as well
as to be lacking in mechanisms for transmitting information to them.
Lawyers not associated with law reform organizations stayed away
from race relations cases not only because of "costs, expenses, and
protracted litigation," but also because "the unpopular status of civil
rights litigation made these cases unattractive to the private bar."[11]
Starting in the 1960s, however, lawyers' increased interest in public
interest work offset this reluctance and translated into greater participation in employment discrimination cases than in school desegregation or voting rights cases.

Retaining cooperating attorneys once they are obtained is also a
problem. MALDEF, for example, found high turnover among Legal
Services attorneys on whom it relied for many of its cases. Although
those lawyers were "not as concerned about attorney fees," a difficulty
was that "there were political pressures" from the local community
"and cases they couldn't bring." By contrast, although the unpopu-
larity of causes LDF advanced affected obtaining cooperating attorneys, private attorneys handling cases for LDF were said not to be
subject to political pressure but instead to financial pressure—they
had to get enough paying cases to survive—although for some, "their
business was enhanced by being rebels" in the community.

Types of Cooperating Attorneys

The term *cooperating attorney* requires qualification. For one thing, the
distinction between a staff attorney supervising a case from headquarters and a cooperating attorney in the field may at times be blurred.
Some of the NAACP's early school cases were within easy traveling distance of headquarters to facilitate staff attorneys' appearance

in court, which was particularly important in the absence of local counsel. Staff attorneys were *the* attorneys, as is true today when, even if cooperating attorneys are available, a headquarters staff lawyer handles a case that arises nearby. For example, NAACP staff attorney James Meyerson handled the Coney Island (Mark Twain) school de-segregation case in Brooklyn, and headquarters staff also handled a Mt. Vernon, New York case. If a staff lawyer handling a case leaves the organization but continues to serve as counsel, as when Thomas Atkins continued as lead counsel in some NAACP school cases even after he no longer was the NAACP's general counsel, staff attorney has become cooperating attorney.

There are different types of cooperating attorneys. The most fre-quent type is an attorney who has a regular fee-generating practice to gain a livelihood—or who, less frequently, works for another associa-tion or the government[12]—who handles cases for an organization on a pro bono basis and who may receive expenses and perhaps even a fee or honorarium well below usual rates. Another type of cooperating at-torney is usually the furthest thing from our minds when we think of civil rights lawyers: the large, big-city law firm that obtain civil rights cases from either the national or local Lawyers' Committee, which per-forms a "matching service" for case and law firm. The firm can assume responsibility for pro bono work and thus absorb its own expenses and also is less likely to need technical assistance from the national organization than would small law firms or solo attorneys. It is like a cooperating attorney in one regard, in being affiliated with a national litigating organization for one or more cases, and although the law firm has agreed to take the case, it obviously assigns one (or several) lawyer(s) to that case, making them more like cooperating attorneys in the usual sense. Many such firms now handle civil rights cases because they found them "more respectable," because their younger associates have pressured them, and because attorneys' fees provide an incentive to do so. Major law firms handle some ACLU cases, al-though individual lawyers with direct contacts with the ACLU and its affiliates constitute the majority of ACLU cooperating attorneys. Large prestigious firms, particularly in Washington, D.C., have also taken Title VII and fair housing cases for the NAACP Legal Defense Fund, in "sort of a recent development."

Regulars and Superregulars

Some cooperating attorneys work frequently with a particular organization and can be considered *regulars,* while other cooperating attorneys have only isolated or infrequent contacts with the organization they assist. There are also firms of two or three lawyers in cities like Little Rock, Arkansas, and Tuscaloosa, Alabama, who handle some civil rights cases and whose costs are reduced by help from the law schools in those communities. In addition, other lawyers, for example, solo practitioners who handle Title VII employment cases with a single client, simply use materials ("canned" briefs and other technical assistance) developed by an organization. Thus a case they handle is not "an LDF case" in the sense that a case handled by an ACLU cooperating attorney can be called "an ACLU case," and they are not usually considered cooperating attorneys even if their undertaking such cases was encouraged by and resulted from LDF's development of employment discrimination law.

Regulars are well connected to the national organizations, which may seek out their services for their special skills. Some, who are not affiliated solely with any single national organization and who may handle cases for several groups and perhaps for both NAACP and LDF, may have a primary but nonexclusive attachment. They are likely to consider the organization's perspective even when handling a case independently, making important attorneys' previous association when there is a legal campaign; thus "lawyers in seven of the eleven non-NAACP [equalization] lawsuits [who] had significant past contact with the NAACP legal campaign" were more successful than the lawyers without such prior involvement.[13]

An organization beginning to litigate in a new area of law may come in contact with lawyers different in style or outlook from its previous regulars. A former LDF staff attorney has commented that when LDF undertook a set of cases in poverty law, it "found itself in relations with lots of attorneys it had not previously been involved with—poverty attorneys, public defenders, legal services lawyers." "Less prominent" than its earlier cooperating attorneys, they altered the "relatively small and ethnically homogeneous group" of lawyers with whom the organization had worked. This affected working relations, as the national office "would relate to a Northern ghetto attorney on a consumer problem differently from a Southern NAACP lawyer," who was often a product of Howard University Law School and a segregated environment whereas San Francisco or Denver poverty lawyers were "white and liberal." Attorneys willing to undertake litigation when an area of law is new may also differ from those who come to it when the basic law has been developed, as "altruistic pioneers, strongly identified with their clients' 'cause,'" are replaced by "profit-seekers who can afford to finance the case." For example, the type of lawyer in the early "soul cases" in employment discrimination law was "displaced by those who could make the investments necessary to finance computer analysis of hiring patterns." [14]

Some private attorneys are *superregulars*. An example is a set of attorneys who handled a long set of complicated school desegregation cases and which included a lawyer for a major private firm with a substantial focus on civil rights litigation whose reputation for effectiveness led to his receiving calls for help from all over the country. Working primarily for the NAACP, this set of lawyers became closer to being staff attorneys than typical cooperating attorneys. NAACP branches contacted them directly, for example, when the chairman of a branch's legal redress committee had people who wanted to bring cases, but they also were associated with other groups which engaged them directly as they came to know of their work. For example, one of the superregulars was contacted by local attorneys after their major school case was turned down by LDF because of an overload of cases and because no foundation assistance for the case was available; he suggested another superregular, who was retained by the school board, which had become a party plaintiff. That the "cadre of five or six" superregulars is no longer available, as most have gone on to other projects, deprives present NAACP general counsel of the "luxury" of their presence in school desegregation cases, and general counsel has to do more himself.

Another set of superregulars are those who started their civil rights lawyering as interns for the NAACP Legal Defense Fund. Because there was not an adequate pool of black attorneys or cooperating attorneys in the South, because few white southern lawyers would undertake civil rights cases, and because the southern state and local bench and bar was not exactly congenial to northern civil rights lawyers, there was a need in the 1960s and later for a program to train lawyers in civil rights. LDF developed an intern program, through which over ninety people passed. Lawyers, many black and from the South, spent a year at LDF headquarters and then set up private law practices in the South, in areas where the need was acute and where young lawyers would not likely have gone without the type of support LDF provided—a three-year declining subsidy for equipment and books. That these interns—the Earl Warren Fellows—were expected to make their civil rights cases LDF cases made LDF "the single largest 'client' of many of its cooperating attorneys." By the early 1980s, more than two-fifths had caseloads in which civil rights accounted for at least 25 percent of the work.[15]

The NAACP did not develop an internship program like LDF's because, with the two organizations operating very much in tandem until the early 1970s, the NAACP did not need such a duplicative program. As observers have suggested, the problem for the NAACP has been that many of the increasing number of black law school graduates of the 1970s were "lost" to the NAACP as a result of the LDF's recruitment mechanism when the NAACP lacked a comparable program. As long as the NAACP and the LDF, although formally separate, had relatively effective working relations, the NAACP had had less need to set up its own network of cooperating attorneys. Moreover, to the extent that NAACP branches sent cases to the LDF, the NAACP lost opportunities to develop effective working relations with cooperating attorneys.

Julius Levonne Chambers, later LDF's President and then Greenberg's successor as director-counsel, was one of the first two LDF interns; Marian Wright Edelman, subsequently head of the Children's Legal Defense Fund, was the other. Other products of the LDF program included, in Alabama, U.W. Clemon, appointed to a federal judgeship by President Carter, and Oscar Adams, elected to the Alabama Supreme Court. Also built from the program were Chambers's Charlotte, North Carolina, practice and the Richmond law firm of Henry Marsh, later the city's mayor, who was in practice with veteran civil rights lawyers Oliver Hill and Samuel Tucker. Both firms had extremely close ties to LDF, making them extensions of national headquarters and something like regional offices, and, before he became LDF's director-counsel, Chambers was close to being a "hybrid" between cooperating attorney and staff counsel.

The interns' existence was one reason that among LDF regulars, distinctions are essentially generational, and cooperating attorneys whose relationship with LDF is relatively recent are said to have a "different reaction" and would show more deference to Jack Greenberg than would those "who remember Jack Greenberg carrying Thurgood Marshall's briefcase." There was a set of older cooperating attorneys—men now in their eighties if still alive—who were among the few black lawyers in the South, and compared to whom staff attorneys—often "young, idealistic" lawyers with "little of the way of the world"—often were less senior. Then there was a "newer wave," both black and white, including the products of the intern program, not trained at Howard like most of the older attorneys but at other law schools, often in the North.

Skill

In deciding whether and how to work with a prospective cooperating attorney, staff make judgments about competence. Although organizations usually do not develop formal standards for judging that competence, efforts are made to exclude participation by those without the necessary experience, knowledge (derived in part from experience), or skill. (LDF did consider a project to develop standards but it "was assigned a low priority because of the need first to develop the legal concepts of employment discrimination." [16])

Because cooperating attorneys cover the "whole gamut of skill and efficiency," relationships with them must be adjusted to take into account their backgrounds and the issues being litigated, and division of labor depends to some extent on a combination of skills and personal preferences. At times some participation is allowed but the lawyer's role is limited, for example, to that of liaison between staff attorneys and community members. Staff attorneys say some cooperating attorneys are "uncomfortable with trial work," such as preparing exhibits and interviewing witnesses; others like to try cases but not to do appellate work, so they send case records to staff attorneys, who handle the appeals. With a new attorney, LDF "would have to put in more LDF resources than with an experienced lawyer, given the same set of facts" and would provide "civil rights input," making the organization "equivalent [in] status to tax or patent counsel to a law firm." Should the organization not do this, the lawyers' lack of experience might lead them to restrict the scope of the case to the particular clients and not to pursue some larger issues. Cooperating attorneys who recognize their own deficiencies are more likely to seek organizational assistance, as they did in the Wilmington school case. [17]

Attorneys' inexperience certainly can damage a case, as in the Richmond, California, school case, undertaken by lawyers for the local legal services office who "had little experience in civil litigation. None had ever worked on, let alone put together, a major case." As a result, they made decisions "that, although plausible at the time, proved ultimately fatal," including going to state rather than federal court and failing to challenge segregation on a districtwide basis. Their inexperience also "marred the [trial] proceedings," and their appeal briefs "were disorganized, poorly documented, and weakly argued."[18]

Lawyers Black and White

Roger Baldwin, overseeing disbursement of the remainder of the Garland Fund grant to the NAACP, objected to lawyers the NAACP had proposed "at least in part because he was unpersuaded that the NAACP's black candidates were as qualified as the white ones he proposed."[19] And in its early litigation, the NAACP was hesitant to grant control of cases to local attorneys in part because of their perceived inadequacy in civil rights and constitutional law. Interacting with perceptions of lack of training was concern that local lawyers might take initiatives counter to the national organization's preferences. The preference against use of black lawyers was reinforced when major local black attorneys brought a "white primary" test case and adopted a position that the national NAACP disliked, leading to the Supreme Court's decision against black plaintiffs in *Grovey v. Townsend.* It certainly did not please the NAACP that "the lawyers in Houston responsible for bringing the case were as militant afterward as they had been aggressive and independent in initiating this test case."[20]

More generally, "experience showed that delegating the campaign to local attorneys led to victory only by luck, caused at least one disaster, and created serious problems in the relations among the national legal staff, the national office of the NAACP, the local attorneys and the local NAACP branches."[21] Thus to handle its cases, the NAACP instead relied on a set of nationally prominent white lawyers who were well known to the organization. Indeed, for some time the preference of both national and local NAACP was for white lawyers, even in the North. Despite resentment from older black lawyers, prestigious white lawyers handled cases brought by southern NAACP branches, particularly in communities with less repressive racial atmospheres like New Orleans, Richmond, Louisville, and El Paso, and white lawyers generally carried "the principal burden of the national office's legal activity."[22] However, local NAACP branches used black attorneys and blacks and whites worked together in some situations, such as *Moore v. Dempsey*, where the NAACP "retain[ed] as counsel in Arkansas a white attorney who was an ex-Confederate officer and a black attorney who was an ex-slave," and other instances when a local black attorney urged the use of white attorneys at least as co-counsel in a case.[23]

The NAACP's preference for use of white lawyers as local counsel in the South can be explained partly by the small number of black lawyers. In the mid-1920s, however, the growing number of blacks trained at Ivy League law schools, unhappy over the NAACP's reliance on white lawyers, brought pressure for change. This was reinforced by the National Bar Association, whose 1931 convention criticized the lack of use of black lawyers by civil rights organizations without mentioning the NAACP by name. This activity led to black lawyers' greater involvement in NAACP work, as Executive Director Walter White oversaw a shift from use of Nathan Margold, James Marshall, Louis Marshall, Arthur Spingarn, and Moorfield Storey to increasing reliance on Charles Houston, Thurgood Marshall, and James Nabrit.[24] The 1935 Supreme Court *Hollins* case involving an Oklahoma black man sentenced to death for rape, which came hard on the heels of the Scottsboro Boys decisions, was the first one where only black lawyers appeared before the U.S. Supreme Court for the NAACP.[25]

An adequate pool of black attorneys, or of cooperating attorneys in the South, was not found even when lawyers like Charles Houston and William Hastie were brought into NAACP cases. Questions of the adequacy of black counsel continued into the 1960s in the South, where they remained a scarce commodity—for example, only three in Georgia outside of Atlanta[26]—and civil rights leaders did not believe that the few black lawyers were able to cope with the cases that would have to be brought: "There were few available and fewer still who were able to manage significant civil rights litigation by themselves."[27] The black attorneys also often had very conservative views of what law could accomplish, so civil rights activists saw them as unable or unwilling to help their cause.

As a black LDF attorney observed, black lawyers were also seen as having "elevated their own professional and social standing and economic interest above the interest of their black brothers and sisters and [as] more interested in the fees they would receive rather than in the results achieved for their clients." This was evident when leaders of the Birmingham movement called LDF directly to report that "the black lawyers who had been approached in Birmingham were reluctant to act without assurance of the payment of their fees."[28] This is a new version of the earlier problem of white counsel retained by the NAACP demanding payment. Albion W. Tourgee was willing to direct what became the *Plessy* case without fee, but two local attorneys asked, respectively, $3,000 and $2,500,[29] and there were repeated problems in obtaining local counsel, some of them financial, in the case that became *Moore v. Dempsey*. When the first counsel died, the NAACP was hesitant to name his partner "because of his aggressive requests for money." Use of the firm was continued and additional sums paid, in part because to shift firms would have further drained resources, but NAACP refused to pay the funds the firm sought for handling a retrial, with NAACP's executive director "charging that McHaney and his firm 'remained in the cases until they felt that they had gotten all of the money out of us that they could and then they dropped the cases.' "[30]

Despite an increase in the number of black attorneys and in those willing to take civil rights cases resulting from LDF's intern program and the graduation of black attorneys from desegregated Southern law schools, questions of scarcity remained, both outside and within urban areas in the South, and it was also difficult in the North to obtain black lawyers to work on major civil rights cases. When several black Alabama attorneys became federal and state judges in the late 1970s, replacing them was not easy. Continued use of white lawyers also meant that the tension between white and black attorneys, which does not facilitate planning or implementation of coordinated litigation strategy, did not fully abate, as in Topeka in the mid-1970s, when concern that a white civil rights attorney involved in the continuing school litigation there had upstaged Charles S. Scott, the Browns' long-time local black attorney, led Scott to take action that trumped a lawsuit the white attorney had filed.

Working Relations

Working relations between staff attorneys and cooperating attorneys take a variety of forms, with a high level of variation among cases in any single organization and from one organization to the next. The ways in which cases come to national organizations help serve to define cooperating attorneys' varying roles, as does "power factor" between the staff attorney and cooperating attorney, although involvement by both in the civil rights bar tends to level superior-subordinate relations.

Relations extend from the directive, with very frequent calls and contacts between staff and cooperating attorneys, to the supportive and nondirective, with the cooperating attorney proceeding autonomously. Throughout, staff attorneys provide an "overall perspective concerning development of the law [and] special expertise"; serve as sounding boards for cooperating attorneys' ideas; and respond to a request for information, write a brief, or edit one the cooperating attorney has drafted. That cooperating attorneys know that advice comes from the national organization that controls locally needed funds "insures that the local lawyers will keep in touch with the national office and be amenable to its suggestions."[31]

There are both short-term and longer-run constraints on a national organization's acting in too directive a fashion, although LDF is said to have tried to control attorneys even when they are not affiliated with the organization. An organization wishing to engage in extensive litigation must use cooperating attorneys and thus is dependent on them. Only in the unlikely event that it had a surplus of cooperating attorneys and was willing to accept "bad P.R." by overruling, or even discharging, them could it have total control. The national organization may nonetheless use its money to exert control. LDF had offered to pay legal expenses during civil rights activity in Danville, Virginia. Local leaders then "asked whether the Danville movement would have to consult with NAACP lawyers before engaging in demonstrations," and were told, " 'Since the NAACP will be footing the bill, we will want to be able to caution against anything unwise.' " The NAACP's representative also made clear that " 'NAACP money can go only to NAACP lawyers'," not the lawyer the local movement preferred to use. (Those in the local movement rejected the conditions and filed a document in court as NAACP lawyers even though the document contained legal positions LDF had rejected.)[32]

Cooperating attorneys often handle the initial stages of cases, at trial where they are likely to serve as "lead counsel" if they have generated the cases themselves, and at the first appellate level. As one moved into the 1970s, local attorneys, gaining expertise, "handled every aspect of a case both at the district court level and on appeal."[33] Because of their greater familiarity with state court rules, they may be used for state cases, with staff attorneys handling federal litigation. At times, however, they only apply new theories of litigation developed by staff lawyers.

Some cooperating attorneys do little more than "carry water" or act as a "sort of errand boy" and "medium of exchange" for national staff attorneys, serving only as required local counsel to file papers while staff attorneys handle all the trial work. Such limited roles may be undertaken without complaint. In a major school desegregation case, a young attorney was engaged by the (plaintiff) school board because defendant suburban school boards, retaining the "cream of the city's legal talent," "pretty much wiped out the private bar." By his own evaluation "not very active" in the case and doing "what a home base tender does," he served primarily as liaison between the litigators and his nominal client, being contacted when documents had to be sent to lead counsel or when the school board "would need to know the status of a case." Both plaintiffs' outside counsel, who was a recognized school desegregation expert, and the school board could "call up and ask for an explanation," or, if certain statistics were needed, he would work with the school board statistician to develop them.

In general, the more important the case and the higher the level of court, the greater the involvement of staff attorneys.[34] In the Jackson, Tennessee, school case, the local attorney handled the district court work and LDF, which appears to have provided much guidance at trial, handled matters that went further. The national organization's involvement is shown in the claim, made by the defendant school board lawyer in arguing against an attorneys' fee award, that attorney Avon Williams was on an NAACP retainer and that "all communications and telephone calls are directed to 10 Columbus Circle in New York City."[35]

Efforts by the national organization to shape local attorneys' arguments and how they construct the record are frequent, to facilitate successful appeal of the case. Thus in the Denver school case, for which LDF provided legal research litigation strategy suggestions, a staff attorney was in Denver for part of the preliminary injunction hearing and another came to assist with the trial itself. If a national organization is not able to persuade a cooperating attorney to include or emphasize certain arguments at trial, those arguments may be altered on appeal. In one of the Tennessee school desegregation cases, the appellate brief, largely the product of an LDF staff lawyer, "relegated to a consulting role" the local lawyers and "largely ignored the arguments made by [one of them] in the district court hearings." [36] Earlier, when the national ACLU managed to gain control of the *Hirabyashi* case, one of the national organizations' counsel "immediately began legal surgery on [the local attorney's] draft brief, cutting out arguments" made to the federal appeals court. [37]

Even if cooperating attorneys have handled a case at trial or at the first appellate level, national staff attorneys are likely to take charge when a decision must be made on taking the case to the Supreme Court. Groups like LDF can provide considerable overall experience and resources when a case is being prepared for the Supreme Court. Thus in one case, LDF senior staff attorneys and several law professors who regularly helped LDF were able to "spend several days off-and-on discussing what they wanted the Supreme Court to do." National organizations also are quite likely to handle cases *in* the Supreme Court. One local lawyer, aware that his Supreme Court appearance in an LDF case was unusual, did divide with LDF staff counsel, but, he said jokingly, he was "given the losing part of the argument." External counsel may, however, be used to argue appeals in particularly important cases. For example, after an NAACP staff attorney tried the *Claiborne Hardware* boycott damages case in federal district court, Lloyd Cutler argued in both the Fifth Circuit and the Supreme Court. [38]

Different types of cooperating attorney involvement may occur in a single case. For example, in one case, outside counsel (a superregular) "handled the bulk of the case" and "made the trial decisions." A local attorney, who had been present at meetings during initiation of a more recent stage of this extended case and had sought outside counsel to handle it, did some briefing, particularly about a recent state education statute, while his partner worked on the remedy stage of the case. A veteran civil rights lawyer (earlier a regular LDF cooperating attorney) who had been quite active in the case at an earlier stage, joined in filing the complaint but later played a limited role thought appropriate because his age precluded major involvement; but he attended court every day, something important for his black clients. None of these local attorneys felt they could carry the case: "We had local law practices we couldn't abandon." There was obviously a good working relationship between these lawyers and lead counsel, whose expertise, capability and "enormous energy" they recognized. When faced with short deadlines before the start of a school year, that attorney and his associates were extremely effective—"like expert mechanics tuning a Porsche for LeMans."

Providing Assistance

A national organization can and does provide cooperating attorneys with "core expertise," including model remedies. The national organization is likely to have better contacts from which to obtain the information and to have expertise in the form of its staff to assimilate and prepare it for others' use, making it economical for it to gather and then provide information. As with litigating organizations' choice of cases, the amount of assistance varies depending on "a number of factors, such as the complexity of the issues, the expertise and availability of the cooperating attorney, and the import of the case."[39] Here the comment of a lawyer for a backup center is instructive: a request for assistance is "not a situation of putting in one's quarter and getting a canned brief."

LDF's widely acknowledged expertise, which allows it to give focused help quickly even if not in large quantities, can be seen in a number of stories. A public defender trying a capital punishment case was given some limited help by LDF and then was referred to Anthony Amsterdam, who called back "within hours, from a phone booth" to tell him of an "odd case directly on point." (The lawyer's sense of amazement as well as appreciation obviously continues to the present.) In a major school desegregation case, one of the two LDF attorneys working with local counsel came to the litigation site "to counsel on the sequence of witnesses." Counter to the local lawyers' initial preference to put on a national school experts first, LDF counsel suggested putting on the fact case first so as to avoid "getting tied up in sociological mumbo-jumbo." Said local counsel, the LDF staff attorney "was totally right." Later, when a stay of an appellate ruling shortly before the beginning of the school year was needed, LDF "knew in-chambers procedures, what the standards were for stay and vacation of stay." Obtaining a Supreme Court stay (it was obtained) could not have been done "on a timely basis without their opinion." This sort of help makes others say that LDF's "competent legal staff" provides "substantive as well as financial backup" for the cooperating attorney;

one can call to "get substantive responses," making LDF "like a backup center only more so," a "parent legal firm with law offices all over the country."

National organizations frequently provide technical assistance to community groups and lawyers; at times, this is done at conferences. In addition, the Lawyers' Committee "established a comprehensive pleadings and brief 'bank' of materials and provided training and/ or technical assistance to nearly one thousand attorneys representing plaintiffs in employment discrimination cases." After it sent an initial legal memorandum on attorneys' fees to 150 civil rights and poverty lawyers, many letters and phone calls made it "clear that a more organized and broadscale approach to informing lawyers was necessary." This prompted preparation and circulation of a guide on attorneys' fees. That in turn led to an Attorneys' Fees Project "to serve both as an information clearinghouse, collecting cases and disseminating information, and as a backup center, providing legal advice and filing *amicus* briefs in important attorneys' fees cases."[40] In similar activity, the Native American Rights Fund, realizing the absence of centralized knowledge of cases concerning native Americans, worked to develop a clearinghouse for materials about those cases. Established with Legal Services Corporation help, the clearinghouse provides legal information when requested and holds training sessions through the Indian Law Support Center.

Financial assistance is also important, for without it, some lawyers could not serve as cooperating attorneys. An organization's policy concerning reimbursement for expenses affects its relations with cooperating attorneys. Difficulties arise if an organization, particularly after paying cooperating attorneys some fees or an "honorarium" and expenses, attempts to capture attorney's fees the lawyers have won in the cases they brought for the organization. When the Civil Rights Attorneys Fees Act was adopted, the ACLU's position that fees had to be turned over to the ACLU, said to derive from the notion that "ACLU attorneys had to be pure as driven snow," "made an attorney thinking of a pro bono case think of bringing it under some other organization." Perhaps because of cooperating attorneys' reaction, the ACLU revised its policy to continue the ethical obligation to turn back the fees while granting affiliates authority to adopt other options, such as allowing lawyers to keep fees but strongly recommending that the fees be donated to ACLU or a comparable organization. (The Lawyers'

Committee allowed lawyers to keep fees, but its policy was not to pay cooperating attorneys' expenses, which their law firms generally can absorb.)

A particularly severe conflict over fees erupted in 1987 when the NAACP filed a suit against former general counsel Nathaniel Jones and Thomas Atkins and former staff attorneys Teresa Demchak and William Wells for over $2 million in fees. The NAACP, claiming an implied contractual employer-employee relationship that would have made the attorneys' earnings the organization's, said they had improperly retained the fees. Atkins, from whom $680,000 was sought, said the fees derived from suits preceding his tenure as general counsel and, moreover, that he had repaid the NAACP's honoraria. He claimed that the NAACP's actions resulted from his criticism of Executive Director Benjamin Hooks's handling of NAACP funds,[41] but Hooks said that the suit, in which he had not been involved, was handled directly by the board so it would not look like a "personal vendetta" against Atkins. Criticism of the suit from within the NAACP was immediate. Before it was filed, a committee of the NAACP's Ohio organization had asked that efforts to recover the fees from the lawyers be dropped, and others joined in their position that the effort hurt rather than assisted the organization.[42] The NAACP did persist with the suit but was unsuccessful against any of those it had sued.[43] However, the NAACP successfully sought a portion of the attorneys' fees originally awarded to Atkins in a Florida case he continued to handle after leaving the NAACP.[44]

Apart from policy, if national organizations are slow in providing promised financial assistance to cooperating attorneys, some lawyers will have to terminate their relationship. The NAACP's difficulties in disbursing funds were the subject of frequent comments, with the problem of nonpayment, or underpayment, perhaps exacerbated to the extent that the NAACP became involved in particular cases "without any ideas of what the costs will be." Its serious delays in reimbursing lawyers drove away lawyers "who would have gotten in to the elbows if their bills could have been paid," but because they need to support themselves and had "cash flow problems," they "can't be tied up for a month in a class action." This was particularly true of new attorneys, who, "struggling to make a living, . . . may suffer from the slowness of payment from the national office."

Geographic Separation

Cooperating attorneys' distance from national headquarters is a principal problem in a national groups' use of local attorneys rather than their own staff. Certainly distance was a problem in days before jet travel. In the *Plessy* case, "consultation at a distance was unavoidably time-consuming," so that the lead attorney in the case, Albion Tourgee, "did not go to New Orleans to participate personally in any stage of the Louisiana proceedings," but the local attorney did clear each step with lead counsel. However, a serious problem later developed when the Supreme Court Clerk's office informed only local counsel, and not Tourgee, of a step in the proceedings.[45] Even with travel easier, maintaining a complicated civil lawsuit from New York City or Washington remained "very difficult," as organizations learned when they became directly involved in a case because local lawyering resources were lacking. There can also be serious problems in trying to tie attorneys from the national organization to local communities.

Problems are not eliminated by having staff attorneys in the field. For one thing, the staff attorney's task of coordination—and of being several places at once—may be extraordinary. Former LDF attorney Norman Amaker writes on the "sheer volume of lawsuits that we seemed to be filing on almost a daily basis to try to cope with the repressive conduct" in Selma, Alabama, in the early 1960s. Not all activities took place in one community, as had been the case in Birmingham, where he had also been in the field; activities in and around Selma "required an enormous expenditure of physical effort in coordinating the movement of lawyers by automobile among Selma and the other communities in the black belt where the events were occurring and where the state courts were located; Mobile, approximately 100 miles to the south where the federal court was located; Birmingham, where the local attorneys were, and New York, from which I and my associates were traveling incessantly by plane to all these places then driving at all hours to observe events, interview witnesses, consult with the clients, file papers and make court appearances."[46] Longer-term supervision also poses problems. For example, the Lawyers' Committee's Mississippi office, not able to obtain the services of white Mississippi lawyers, had to rely on "short-term visits by attorneys from major law firms on its board of directors," but coordination of those visits was difficult, with the result that the office "operate[d] without sufficient backup benefit from experienced civil rights attorneys."[47]

National counsel often lack familiarity with the communities which are the sites of cases, although staff attorneys might be sent to try cases to give them a better feel for lawyering in the community.[48] The lack of familiarity can, however, lead to less-than-optimal decisions. In San Francisco, for example, NAACP general counsel Robert Carter, "whose acquaintanceship with San Francisco was limited, thought that desegregation could be accomplished simply through re-zoning neighborhoods," a method that had been successful in the East where most NAACP school cases had taken place. Here the "more knowledgeable local committee realized the limited utility of such an approach," and sought another remedy. They even wished to use the lawsuit "to force a host of policy changes," that is, to use litigation in a manner different from the NAACP's usual use.[49]

Who Decides?

In the relation between staff and cooperating attorneys, "Who decides?" is often answered, "the national organization and its staff attorneys." Staff attorneys, particularly if part of a "large and well-trained legal staff," often supervise cooperating attorneys.[50] Where the cooperating attorney regularly consults the national organization or seeks advice from it, such supervision is easy to accomplish without friction. For example, despite the Northern California ACLU affiliate's resistance to national direction, the Southern California affiliate "looked to Baldwin for guidance and rarely disputed broad policy."[51] And cooperation does characterize most working relations between national staff and cooperating attorneys. However, in part because of cooperating attorneys' autonomy, friction at times reflecting national organization-local affiliate disagreement over policy is perhaps inherent in the situation, and at times it leads to conflict, almost to the point of open warfare. A particularly glaring example came in the Japanese-American Exclusion Cases when both the Northern California affiliate and the national organization filed briefs in the Supreme Court, and a local lawyer—no longer participating as an ACLU attorney at this stage of the case because of the organization's displeasure with him—also filed an amicus brief for which neither lawyer arguing the case in the Supreme Court had responsibility.[52]

This perhaps extreme instance raises the questions, Can the national organization control staff attorneys? and When the two are not in agreement, who decides? At times, simply by taking action, the local attorney preempts the national organization's ability to decide even when not intending to do so, but the local attorney may also purposely hold off involving a national organization out of fear of losing control of locally initiated efforts to produce change. Cooperating attorneys at times feel "overcontrol" by staff attorneys, who do not allow them to do very much, and there were "some instances when a cooperating attorney feels the staff is just coming down and telling them what to do." Some lawyers who initiated mental health cases were ambivalent about bringing into their cases lawyers associated with the Mental Health Law Project. The local lawyers knew that MHLP, as "the leading source of information and litigation assistance regarding mental health law," had important resources to offer, but "worried that they and their clients would lose control to attorneys who were too concerned with establishing broad principles and too little concerned with solving the problems of the individual."[53]

LDF

There have been changes in staff-cooperating attorney relations at the NAACP Legal Defense Fund over the years, although these have meant "not so much that use of cooperating attorneys has changed but the use of staff attorneys has changed." Some changes resulted from LDF's own actions, such as its internship program, as former interns became active civil rights attorneys in the South. Some, deriving from environmental changes such as increased case complexity, paralleled developments in other litigating organizations. The need to spread resources has also meant changed financial relations. There is a "more formal" relationship deriving from "budgets for cases and agreements for attorneys to sign" and less ability to provide interim fees to cooperating attorneys.

Staff attorneys see little change in the way LDF used cooperating attorneys. " 'Cooperating attorney' is an informal status" at LDF; there is no "secret handshake." Almost anyone who wants to work with LDF can do so: we "don't anoint." (However, a staff lawyer said, LDF could do better "at keeping up the list" so as to include in its annual Airlie House conferences lawyers who want to work with the organization.) Because a lot of staff attorney-cooperating attorney work is "one-on-one," working relations depend heavily upon the people involved, and are adjusted for skills and background. Greater weight is given to the work of "someone who has built up a track record": if such a person "tells us something, we know we can rely on it." Staff might be able to help an experienced cooperating attorney simply by providing briefs developed for other cases, and by answering a question from time to time, but LDF might take a "smaller case" from new attorneys because of their lack of experience. However, among the occasional problems that arose from having cases come to the organization through cooperating attorneys were "cases brought by lawyers without staying power" such as "itinerant civil rights lawyers," cases LDF wished to avoid.

Staff attorneys, perhaps because they wish to leave their own mark on a case in at least some way, prefer to work with those who do much work but "need support and help." Staff attorneys also like to work with new attorneys, particularly young black ones or white attorneys in integrated law firms, "to give them training in civil rights and skills," although "we would have to put in more LDF resources than with an experienced lawyer, given the same set of facts." However, in trying to "keep to a minimum" the cases handled solely by staff, staff attorneys don't appreciate a cooperating attorney who "tries to dump all the work on the staff": the organization "can handle as many cases as we do because we don't have primary responsibility" for many. When LDF could not find competent attorneys in the field able to devote time to extended cases, it "ate up a large amount of resources." However, staff attorneys do "virtually all the work" in some Title VII cases, particularly in new areas of the law, a "subspecialty in a subspecialty"; even then, however, LDF tries to "develop trial techniques others can use."

Relations between LDF staff attorneys and cooperating attorneys vary, but overall the relationship is said to be "remarkably cooperative and supportive," with "remarkably little competition" between the two sets of lawyers, and with most problems thought to be the sort that occur "whenever people/lawyers work together," such as working out a co-counsel relationship. Problems in use of cooperating attorneys are relatively small "given that the LDF staff attorney is young, white, and not from the community, while the cooperating attorney is older, has many trials, is black, is from the community, and those are *his* clients," with "physical separation" of cooperating attorney from headquarters potentially creating "conflict between local and national perspectives." "People don't usually work as well as these do," one LDF staffer said, but a "recognized common enemy" and a common purpose facilitates cooperation. One reason for the positive relationship may be the benefits cooperating attorneys receive by having a connection with an organization like LDF. These include association with the skilled lawyers on national staff, even if some are younger than the cooperating attorney, and a halo effect bringing respect to the cooperating attorney from the national civil rights community and in state and local circles as well.

Cooperating attorneys provide advantages for the parent organization. Contact with the cooperating attorney provides the client with someone local associated with the organization. This person, because closer to the client, is more accessible, someone nearby who can be called: "It is the visibility of the local cooperating attorney that serves as the crucial link between the organization and its clientele,"[54] so having good local counsel "avoids additional travel expenses and the difficulty of communicating with clients" that occurs if a staff attorney at headquarters has to communicate with them directly. The organization can also use the cooperating attorney as a buffer, to limit or prevent direct contact with the client. Cooperating attorneys work with people to whom a case means a great deal; a class action employment discrimination case may be the most important part of plaintiffs' lives. "Clients don't understand that when they talk to a lawyer, it takes time and takes them away from their cases and income." Thus, said a staff attorney, cooperating attorneys "insulate us from having to deal with clients," who "can be a real nuisance."

The cooperating attorney also provides LDF staff lawyers a contact knowledgeable about the local community, a "very important connection of LDF to the community" through whom it "establishes and maintains lines of communication to its constituency that give it a sustained link to the concerns and aspirations of the clientele."[55] Cooperating attorneys, often local leaders who understand the judges and the local courthouse, "tend to know local people and problems better, and are not regarded as outsiders." Because even judges not favorably disposed to the organization may respect local attorneys, having the cooperating attorney "helps you gain the judges' respect" so the judges don't make it hard for the lawyer to put on his case. Local attorneys also have "the way of the world" that LDF's "young, idealistic" staff lawyers often lack. Moreover, a white northern attorney would have difficulty "getting trust from a room of 400 steelworkers" without the cooperating attorney "introducing you and saying good things."

NAACP

NAACP staff lawyers, like their LDF colleagues, saw cooperating attorneys as important to their work: there is "always a desire to have such involvement"—and found them a crucial bridge to the community, with "better sense of community and court politics."[56] Use of cooperating attorneys has been essential for the NAACP because, as a matter of resources, the organization "couldn't afford to retain full-time or part-time attorneys." The NAACP had had regional counsel, as many as five at one time, and such a system was said to have "worked very well where we had it," but the resources didn't exist to retain them on either a full-time or part-time basis, and it put an "awful load on someone to coordinate" them. Despite having local affiliates, the NAACP was less able than LDF to obtain cooperating attorneys, did not always have cooperating attorneys available when it needed them, and faced difficulties in providing cooperating attorneys the kinds of services they needed with the "great demands" made on them. That may help explain why many of the growing number of black law school graduates of the 1970s were "lost" to the organization as potential cooperating attorneys, perhaps a result of the LDF's recruitment mechanism at a time when the NAACP continued to rely on contacts between NAACP branches and local attorneys.

One NAACP staff attorney characterized the relationship between staff attorneys and cooperating attorneys as one in which "generally" there were "good relationships," with local counsel "anxious to have assistance from national staff." Conversely, cooperating attorneys could be "very stimulating" and an important source of ideas, which staff at times would "exploit . . . outrageously," making the relationship between staff attorneys and cooperating attorneys "a very fruitful arrangement." This was particularly the case where a national staff person would develop a particular working relationship with a special set of cooperating attorneys who worked on one type of case. An important instance was the special cadre of cooperating attorneys assembled to work on employment discrimination law by the NAACP's long-time labor secretary, Herbert Hill. He developed a working relationship with a small group of lawyers who had been at EEOC but for a variety of reasons wanted to leave, and was able to guarantee them a minimum amount of work in employment discrimination law to help them survive their early years in private practice, and the arrangement was successful despite the NAACP's delay in paying them. However, such a special group of lawyers will disperse as career patterns take them in different directions unless the organization systematically develops their attachment to it as LDF did.

The NAACP, like LDF, has dealt with cooperating attorneys who "represent a wide range of experience. There are some on whom it "can rely greatly." Others have the financial ability to handle a case but are inexperienced with civil rights litigation, thus requiring "substantial supervision and a greater dollar commitment"; because they are "struggling trying to make a living, they may suffer from the slowness of payment from the national office." Young lawyers with "inexperience and shallow pockets" require more supervision from the staff "so the lawyer won't go off half-cocked."

A free hand was given to some experienced lawyers. One in the Boston school case said that although NAACP General Counsel Nathaniel Jones was "overall lead counsel," with his name on the pleadings, and came to Boston for meetings, much of the work was handled by local lawyers, some of them associated with the Harvard Center for Law and Education or with Foley Hoag and Eliot, who consulted with the local NAACP "when decisions had to be made" and with the national NAACP. The "regulars" among the NAACP's cooperating attorneys, who had been retained, as one of them put it, because the NAACP felt the lawyers "shared world views" and a "view of what ought to be happening" with the NAACP, also had a relatively free hand in the way they pursued cases. They were able to "fine-tune or even make major changes in litigation," in part because NAACP general counsel didn't think he knew everything, which the lawyers felt was a different situation from that involved in working with LDF. Once NAACP general counsel "felt your legal strategy fell within the NAACP's substantive goal, he let you run the case" and gave "no 'marching orders'." The lawyers kept general counsel informed as to what they would do, and general counsel "would make suggestions but never overruled" them. This was one way in which he "retained support of his 'legal troops' over the years" even when NAACP did not pay its bills.

Relative involvement of NAACP staff and cooperating attorneys varies with the stage of the case, but distribution of responsibility differs somewhat from that at LDF. NAACP national office involvement occurs earlier, in part because of its review of cases that branches seek to bring. It also increases as the case moves closer to trial, because "when there is a screw-up in the trial, it is irretrievable; New York City [headquarters] involvement increases with the degree of irretrievability of the process." Although there were said to be "very few instances with friction or policy differences"—indeed, said a staff attorney, there was "no policy difference" because the cooperating attorneys "are bound by the policy of the association"—the NAACP adopts a posture toward local attorneys that is more directive than LDF's general stance toward its cooperating attorneys. Indeed, local counsel's involvement in the community is thought to make them inappropriate for cases of much "divisive potential," in which NAACP may "assign" lead counsel from outside the community, action justified as being done to "protect local lawyers from pressure."

NAACP lawyers talk of intervening rather directly in cases. "Policy matters may be so important they can't be left unresolved," said one NAACP attorney, who indicated that staff attorneys showed no reluctance to insert themselves into cases "to be available to assist or redirect" the case, and even to disapprove a local lawyer's settlement of a Title VII case. When a judge had questioned such a disapproval, general counsel suggested that the relationship between local counsel and general counsel was not unlike that between a judge's law clerks and the judge, who clearly had the responsibility and authority.

Intervention may include removing local counsel because of disagreement with their positions in a case. It may occur more frequently than at LDF because of cooperating attorneys' ties to a local NAACP branch, whose views may pull them away from national NAACP policy; LDF's internship program and conferences have provided better socialization to organizational values. Criticism of NAACP's willingness to engage in such "strongarm" tactics—which continue in part because the organization has "weathered the storms" in the past—should be no surprise, and attention has been called to the risk that the organization "becomes what it fights; it responds to power by becoming powerful." Yet NAACP staff attorneys shrug off "negative publicity" from local intervention, saying that the organization "doesn't care how those outside see how the problems are handled inside" the organization.

Comparison.   Lawyers who served as cooperating attorneys for both NAACP and LDF, primarily in school cases, saw both similarities and some distinctions between the two organizations' relations with cooperating attorneys. One similarity is that the national organizations, because they do not pay cooperating attorneys—at least not at the lawyers' regular rates—are all polite: "Everyone says 'May I?' very nicely." Echoing staff attorneys' views, cooperating attorneys see relationships as in part a function of the two sets of lawyers' relative experience and expertise, with the staff attorney not always the senior. Nathaniel Jones wasn't an expert in school cases when he became NAACP general counsel and thus played less of a role vis-à-vis expert cooperating attorneys than he did later "as he became comfortable." By comparison, the school lawyers at LDF (Greenberg, James Nabrit III, and Norman Chachkin), who "had a stronger background" and "could discuss cases in detail," were so knowledgeable about the law that a cooperating attorney sitting in on strategy conferences in a case with them might "wonder whether they thought he was necessary."

Those who worked with LDF, an "organization with a long history of experience in litigation," thought it to be a "reasonably well organized, competent, effective litigating organization," as well as one "more adept at affiliating local lawyers and involving them in litigation" and "far more organized" as an "organization to service lawyers." The NAACP, by contrast, "consistently fails" to have local attorneys "become a presence" in litigation, particularly crucial at the remedy stage, where "clients are short-changed" if monitoring—difficult to do without such local presence—is not carried out.

Lawyers' frustration can also be seen in frequent comments about NAACP's difficulties in raising and disbursing funds. The difficulties may have resulted from the executive director's authority over the budget and general counsel's concomitant lack of authority but nevertheless drove out lawyers "who would have gotten in to the elbows if their bills could have been paid." LDF "had some significant delays in paying bills in the 1970s," but paid them in six months, and then, quite aware of new attorneys' "cashflow problem" as well as their need for assistance on legal issues, became "far more organized in its payments" to lawyers. On the other hand, in the 1980s, the NAACP was still four to five *years* behind, a chronically bad situation not dependent on who was general counsel, although it was apparently worse under some than others—a recurrent, systematic situation "so bad as to be malfeasance."[57] "They can't get the system organized, or blame the system." Indeed, the matter was so bad that "lots of people" were "in a position where all they can do is sue the NAACP for fees," which they don't do because "they don't want to hurt the NAACP." These people even called the LDF seeking the name of a lawyer who would handle the fee cases for them, with one LDF staffer telling them "to swallow the fees and costs" that would be involved.

These negative views of NAACP come from people highly committed to civil rights litigation who, some despite adverse working conditions, continued a relationship with the NAACP in one capacity or another for a considerable period of time; they appear not to result from personal vindictiveness. However, one must keep in mind that battlefield lawyers, like company-grade infantry officers, will always be hostile and critical in their speech about commanders and general staff who do not give them their head, give them full logistical and political support, and get out of the way to let them fight.[58] General disaffection by cooperating attorneys is, however, not the sole explanation as one does not hear the same criticisms of LDF. There is genuine frustration directed at the NAACP on the part of the lawyers committed to working long hours for a cause.

Even some national staff agreed that there were problems—not of recent vintage—created for cooperating attorneys when the NAACP was late in paying its bills. "Roy Wilkins was always dilatory in paying bills," so cooperating attorneys were always "screaming about nonpayment." The nonpayment occurred because NAACP was "in a financial bind," and the officers had to "juggle things," with a constant cash flow problem leading the treasurer to draw checks and "sit on them." The NAACP "behaved outrageously," even lying about checks coming the next month, although the behavior was "forced upon us" by the organization's financial plight. Part of the problem may stem from the structural element that NAACP's general counsel must "double in brass" in having to provide "organizational services to the Board, to branches, and to attorneys" plus running the Special Contribution Fund's litigation work.

13

Client and Counsel

Closely tied to relations between staff attorney and cooperating attorney are those between attorneys and their clients—not only the parties to a case, both named plaintiffs and unnamed class members, but also others like members of an NAACP branch or the broader minority community. Not only does the attorney-client relationship affect the ability to undertake litigation, but the type of litigation undertaken, particularly when a case is intended to be part of a litigation campaign, can also affect attorney-client relations. After an initial look at traditional and alternative lawyer-client relations and at complications when organizations attempt planned litigation, we look at the NAACP's relations with its school desegregation clients, including organizational solicitation of clients, as seen through the *Button* case. In the core of the chapter, we examine "Who decides—lawyer or client?" There we give attention to lack of contact between attorney and client, attorney-client conflict, and particular problems of attorney-client relations in class actions. A systematic empirical inquiry of client-attorney relations in civil rights litigation, although necessary, is beyond the scope of the present enterprise.

Lawyer-Client Relations

In the traditional, idealized lawyer-client relationship, the client sought out and selected an attorney, who did not seek out (or solicit) the client. In the "professional model," supposed to characterize most cases, particularly routine ones, the attorney, although expected to advise the client on the law (in a version of "informed consent"), is expected generally to follow the client's instructions. As stated by one former LDF staff attorney, "The decision . . . was theirs alone to make and I did not try, nor would I have succeeded had I tried, to make it for them. I could only advise as to what the state of the law was and predict what the results of defiance could be."[1] Because clients' wishes and interests are supposed to dominate lawyers' goals, the case is the *client's*, not the lawyer's.

But who is to define the client's interest? We expect the lawyer to exercise judgment based on knowledge and experience. That, along with the difficulty of learning the client's perceived interest, may well lead to substitution of the lawyer's view of the client's interest for the client's own view, particularly when clients are deferential and passive, as they often are, being "all too willing to turn everything over to the lawyers,"[2] particularly those who have been successful. Yet even well-educated and informed individuals serving on organizations' boards defer to lawyers and do not question the basis or wisdom of their decisions, even when there had been disputes within the organization over the position to be adopted. Even a group active in litigation like the ACLU was "willing to leave the final decision with the legal staff," perhaps assuming that the lawyers would operate within a set of expectations identified in previous discussion within the board.[3]

At least to clients, legal issues often seem clear or "closed" rather than "open" or unclear, so "professional problems have a best technical solution inaccessible to lay understanding." If that is the case, "client welfare and the public interest are best served by the professional's exercise of predominant control over and responsibility for . . . problem-solving."[4] Lawyer dominance is thought less likely with "ideologically motivated public interest clients," or "with highly organized groups with knowledgeable and articulate leaders who know how to deal with lawyers and carefully assess the litigation in terms of their organizations' goals and needs." However, the view that professionals should control has carried over into "open" and unclear issues like many in civil rights litigation, in part because "activist lawyers," who anticipate and shape constituencies' needs, "are not so much guided by a concern with the public interest as by a sense of personal responsibility to act in furtherance of goals and values in which they believe."[5] As one observer put it, "One suspects that, at bottom, the lawyers who decided to challenge the death penalty acted as much for themselves and for the order of things they wished to call into being as for the condemned."[6]

The civil rights bar has long recognized that lawyers' goals could diverge from client goals. Lawyer—or group—and client may share interests,[7] but when they do not do so, elevation of the lawyer's goals or those of the lawyer's organization over the client's becomes a serious possibility, if not a likelihood. As one lawyer put it, "The public interest attorney has divided loyalties: a duty to client and to organization and its limited resources and to avoid bad appellate decisions, which impede the work of other lawyers." The Legal Services Program, committed both to provide service to individual clients and to seek legal reform for the poor collectively, also faced the tension "between the attorney's desire to help his client and the Program's desire to help its clientele."[8] That poor clients had a "recurring and institutionalized" relationship with Legal Services Program lawyers served to resolve the tension in the attorney's favor.[9]

A client may be disadvantaged by being associated with major test-case litigation.[10] When, in a case that might create a new precedent, a client is offered a settlement, the lawyer might be tempted to recommend against accepting it, as that would sacrifice the group's investment in seeking new legal principle. One lawyer said it was "drummed into my head" that he was a lawyer "for a class (of clients), not for issues," so that if there was a good settlement, one had to settle. "We resolved the ethical tension between developing the law and looking out for the client," said another lawyer, "by placing the client's interest first." However, he noted, in addition to recommending taking the settlement, "we might also point out that we took the case to develop the law," a statement to which clients might give disproportionate weight because it came from a lawyer.

In answering the question posed to lawyers contemplating a test case, "Are the goals of the individual client different from the goals of those who will benefit from a successful resolution of the test issue?"[11]

lawyers can solve the problem of potentially divergent goals in various ways. One is to limit their representation to interest groups with a cause which recruit volunteers for specific cases, or to clients willing to be parties to test-case litigation, while referring other potential clients elsewhere. Another is to frame a case first, only locating an ideal plaintiff through personal contacts; rather different is not to make a case into a test case "unless there is no better way to promote the interests of the *individual* client."[12] How these options are used in lawyer-client relations has, however, received little attention, but a twenty-year-old study of client participation in tort litigation decision making showed that active participants had significantly better results than for clients who, in the traditional relationship, delegated matters to the lawyer. Because clients' lawyers from large law firms (high-status lawyers) *and* active clients *each* got better results, effects of client participation and of lawyer status are confounded, preventing isolation of client participation as the key variable.[13]

The changing politics of the 1960s, with growing rights consciousness and attention to empowerment, placed greater emphasis on client control. This change stemmed in part from recognition that lawyers could not contribute in traditional ways when, perhaps because of negative prior experience, potential clients were hesitant to accept assistance from lawyers—indeed, the contribution of any professionals —because once an organization hires the lawyer, "the clients become consumers of the professional service rather than employers of the professionals."[14] This reluctance occurred even in the black community, where willingness to turn to lawyers to deal with civil rights had been assumed. One reason was that clients upset about discrimination felt that attorneys were inadequate because they obtained an inadequate remedy.

Even southern black ministers who were at the heart of the leadership of the civil rights movement were distrustful of the few black lawyers who were willing to take civil rights cases because they doubted their ability to deal with the legal system and felt they had "elevated their own professional and social standing and economic interest above the interest of their black brothers and sisters" and wished to prosper financially through their cases; thus the ministers were uncomfortable about using the legal system.[15] More recently, in affirmative action litigation, leaders of some groups, suggesting that lawyers were encroaching on their domain, were uneasy about having their organization participate in litigation. Indeed, 43 percent of those questioned "expressed apprehension about the growing influence of lawyers in the nonlegal decisions made by the organization." In a finding that was perhaps surprising but which illustrated the pull of traditional views of lawyers' place vis-à-vis clients, almost a third (31%) of the lawyers gave the same response.[16]

Disabled persons seeking access to transportation were also hesitant to become involved with lawyers, and the disability rights movement was "ideologically antiprofessional" because the disabled "have the dubious distinction of having a large number of professionals who specialize in *their* problems."[17] The mental health liberation movement also had "an antiprofessional ideology," but it was directed mostly at doctors, not lawyers, who were seen as being able to provide former mental patients the proper mix of autonomy and support.[18]

The lawyer's role as expert, indeed attorneys' traditional monopoly over certain issues, was reduced when litigation was seen as like other types of politics, and more attention was given to having an autonomous *client* than having an autonomous lawyer. Such a *participatory approach* "assumes that client welfare and public interest are best served where clients participate actively in dealing with their problems and share control and decision responsibility with the professional."[19] However, this model is "costly" in the "energy, intelligence, and judgment" demanded of the client, as well as the "patience and tolerance" required of the lawyer,"[20] unless lawyer and client have negotiated an agreement as to how the lawsuit is to be pursued, letting the clients refrain from active involvement *during* the suit.

Because of the involvement of interest groups in civil rights litigation and the groups' efforts to engage in planned litigation, questions about the relationship between client and lawyer arise there with particular force. Indeed, lawyers "engaged in litigation as a form of political expression and association" adopt a "more active role," perhaps contributing to client passivity, and lawyers' involvement with an organization engaged in bringing a set of cases will create the basis for lawyer dominance of clients.[21] When litigating organizations, particularly those with a national scope, enter a case, plaintiffs—even those active in early stages of the litigation—become more passive.[22] Because litigating organizations sought to create precedent through much of their litigation, they have not generally followed the participatory approach. The NAACP's activity in the *Brown* school desegregation litigation, showing lawyers' ability "to supervise and control desegregation litigation to an extent unmatched since by any other group litigating on any other issue, is a classic example of lawyer independence of clients."[23] Lawyers undertaking large employment discrimination cases also had much freedom to act and independence from clients because they were not dependent on the clients for financing and dealt with organizations "which either have no membership to speak of or do not exert significant control over the leaders." Named parties and other class members thus often seemed to be submerged, perhaps being "simply necessary instruments to be dealt with at the tactical level."[24]

Because a litigation campaign is based on some long-term plans and a series of cases, lawyers may be tempted to persuade clients to follow the lawyers' plans instead of setting and pursuing the clients' own. Making separate cases into a linked series takes away the idea that each case is *that person's case,* and thus can be said to be a misuse of the lawyer's position. (In these terms, only with a single client, perhaps, for example, the Justice Department, could one engage properly in planned litigation.) With a "tension between the pace of mobilization and the degree of lay participation," law is mobilized most quickly when lay participation is lowest, and if planned litigation is to proceed without plaintiff-caused delays, active clients are not a boon.

NAACP v. Button

In 1963, the Supreme Court created a constitutional charter for public interest litigation in *NAACP v. Button* by giving it a First Amendment foundation and saying that the NAACP, for which "litigation may be the most effective form of political association," could not be charged with barratry for seeking to bring cases challenging discrimination and segregation.[25] Both Justice Brennan, writing for the Court, and Justice Harlan, in dissent, spoke about client-attorney relations. Brennan described NAACP practices, implicitly dismissing challenges to them as he did so, perhaps glossing over them out of concern that criticism of organizations for not following the canons of legal ethics would be seen as an attack on their cause. Brennan noted, first, that the NAACP's state conference, when it encouraged its branches to get parents of school children to file petitions with school boards, "advised branch officials to obtain, as petitioners, persons willing to 'go all the way' in any possible litigation that may ensue"; second, that the NAACP Virginia state conference's staff lawyers, who "must agree to abide by the policies of the NAACP," made the choice of which potential clients (who need not be NAACP members) to assist; and, third, that the conference "ordinarily will finance only cases in which the assisted litigant retains an NAACP staff lawyer to represent him." These served to "limit the kinds of litigation which the NAACP will assist."[26]

Justice Brennan also reported that NAACP lawyers would explain at a meeting what had to be done to bring about desegregation and would distribute forms on which individuals could authorize the NAACP to represent them in school desegregation cases. "On occasion, blank forms have been signed by litigants, upon the understanding that a member or members of the legal staff, with or without assistance from other NAACP lawyers, or from the Defense Fund, would handle the case. It is usual, after obtaining authorizations, for the staff lawyer to bring into the case the other staff members in the area where suit is to be brought, and sometimes to bring in lawyers from the national organization or the Defense Fund." From this, he concluded simply that "the prospective litigant retains not so much a particular attorney as the 'firm' of NAACP and Defense Fund lawyers." Plaintiffs, stated Brennan, "make their own decisions to become such" and were "free at any time to withdraw from an action."[27]

Brennan did acknowledge, but only in a footnote, that several named plaintiffs in school desegregation cases "did testify that they were unaware of their status as plaintiffs and ignorant of the nature and purpose of the suits to which they were parties." However, he said that while these individuals may have attended meetings, the NAACP did not appear to have been the cause of their involvement in the cases. Indeed, the record was "devoid of any evidence of interference by the NAACP in the actual conduct of litigation, or neglect or harassment of clients."[28] Nor had there been a "showing of a serious danger . . . of professionally reprehensible conflicts of interest." An NAACP lawyer's "personal satisfaction" from the "neither very profitable nor very popular" cases would not create "the kind of interest or motive" leading to the proscribed unethical behavior. Without monetary stakes, Brennan asserted, there was "no danger that the attorney will desert or subvert the paramount interests of his client to enrich himself or an outside sponsor."[29]

Justice Harlan looked at the NAACP's practices more closely, from the perspective of a model of lawyer-client relations in which "avoidance of improper pecuniary gain is not the only relevant factor in determining standards of professional conduct," and client chose lawyer, client fully controlled the case, and there was no "interference with the uniquely personal relationship between lawyer and client and to maintain untrammeled by outside influences the responsibility which the lawyer owes to the courts he serves." [30] That led him to view the practices negatively.

Harlan first believed the NAACP did much to "advocate litigation and . . . wait for prospective litigants to come forward" or "provid[e] . . . competent counsel for the prosecution or defense of individual claims." It chose its plaintiffs, not the reverse, and its staff lawyers, compensated for their work in the desegregation cases, were "necessarily subject" to the NAACP's direction, with "the form of pleading, the type of relief to be requested, and the proper timing of suits . . . to a considerable extent, if not entirely, . . . determined by the Conference in coordination with the national office." [31] He also found "substantial evidence indicating that the normal incidents of the attorney-client relationship were often absent in litigation handled by staff lawyers and financed by petitioner." For support, Harlan pointed to instances of "specific directions . . . as to the types of prospective plaintiffs to be sought" and selection of locations where suit was to be brought; use of blank forms to obtain signatures authorizing bringing of lawsuit; addition of counsel after forms had been signed; and evidence of clients' lack of knowledge that their names had been used in filing lawsuits and their lack of "personal dealings with the lawyers handling their cases." [32]

For Harlan, interests of clients and of lawyers for organizations might differ. The NAACP's interests such as a frontal attack on segregation "may well often deviate from the immediate, or even long-range, desires of those who choose to accept its offers of legal representation," with individual plaintiffs, facing schools closed as the result of litigation, perhaps prefering negotiation to litigation or more time for the local school board to act rather than prompt desegregation. [33] Under that circumstance, and regardless of "whether or not the association is organized for profit and no matter how unimpeachable its motives," it would not be possible for the lawyer "to advise the client with that undivided allegiance that is the hallmark of the attorney-client relation." One problem was that an entity "not itself a litigant" controlled the lawyer; another was that "the lawyer necessarily finds himself with a divided allegiance—to his employer and to his client."

Particulars of how NAACP-associated lawyers dealt with clients during the pre-*Brown* desegregation cases provide the basis for a response to Justice Harlan. By making it known that "lawyers were available to assist people who wanted to challenge segregation," the NAACP, which was closely tied to the community, did look for clients not only by coming to communities but also through *The Crisis* (the NAACP magazine) and "general publicity," but this was done far more for community education than for soliciting of clients. Indeed, although NAACP lawyers "occasionally discouraged potential litigants who wanted to assert claims other than those favored by the staff," in no instance did they approach a potential individual client uninvited. Clients "usually initiated the contact with the lawyers," and "every case had a real client with whom the NAACP lawyers had personal contact."[34]

Lawyers were not able to dominate clients. One reason was that clients, with ideological, not material, incentives prompting their actions, came forward "because they saw the congruence between their views and those publicized by the NAACP lawyers." Those who disagreed with the NAACP's preferred position would either not come forward or if, after a client had entered a case, "disparities in views became apparent," the client was likely to abandon the case. Another reason was that the cases were brought "on behalf of well-educated blacks, who could be expected to, and usually did, take greater interest in their lawsuits." In that situation, lawyers could easily present and explain options to their clients, that is, educate them about the lawyers' preferences, thus eliminating the "need to impose decisions on their clients." In addition, those with varying views in the black community could find different outlets for those views; if they did not agree with the NAACP's emphasis on litigation, they could turn to different organizations for other means of dealing with segregation— for example, the National Negro Congress or the Urban League for direct political action or help in finding jobs.

This line of argument held up best when almost all saw equalization as the appropriate path; in that circumstance, NAACP lawyers' "uncontroversial" actions could be said to have "exhausted the community demand for litigation." However, when the direct attack on *Plessy* became a likely option, the possibility of divergence in views between NAACP lawyers and potential clients increased; however, the lawyers avoided the problem by choosing communities on the basis of the extent of communities' support for the direct attack; they "did not go into communities where they have faced substantial internal dissent." Individuals who did not prefer the direct attack strategy, it is said, could go to other lawyers in the community. That, however, is a far from satisfactory answer because, while "the national NAACP staff and the lawyers on the NAACP's Legal Committee were not the only lawyers available to the black community, . . . they probably were the best ones"; and other lawyers were either unwilling to engage in even conservative approaches to the segregation issue or were not well trained in civil rights law. As more time passed, the argument fitted even more awkwardly, particularly with a growing divergence in views in the black community.[35]

Who Decides?

The most important question in clients' relations with lawyers is who makes decisions—about whether to file lawsuits, to settle or to proceed, to appeal. In litigation for social change, the dichotomous answers "lawyer" and "client" are insufficient as other decision makers are also present. One is the organization with which the lawyer is affiliated. With a foundation-funded organization, there is greater divergence from client control and "toward fitting client needs to law reformer needs," while client control is greater if the litigating entity is an "affiliated law reformer" attached to a parent group. Also involved in decision making is the constituency or clientele, that is, the contributors to litigating organizations, its "conscience constituency" in civil rights work, liberals who contribute money.[36] Division between client and clientele is accentuated by differences in characteristics. In school desegregation, lower-class parents of black children are client while middle-class blacks along with some whites are the clientele. Even when a lawyer is independent of the client, the clientele/constituency may fully dominate, although such constituent constraints dissolve if a litigating organization has access to a broad range of resources.

A host of factors can affect the lawyer-client relationship. These include the lawyer's age, race, gender, and status in the legal community; the relative status of lawyer and client; their resources and sources of those resources; and payment relations between lawyer and client. Whether the relationship between client and lawyer is direct, as when staff attorneys venture into the field and meet the organization's client, or, as is more likely, indirect, with a cooperating attorney usually the client's contact with the organization, also has an effect, as the latter creates psychological as well as physical distance.

When lawyer and client are of roughly the same age, gender, and race, their compatibility, and client participation, may be increased. Well-educated clients may even dominate attorneys. When the LDF provided legal representation for the SCLC, the latter's minister leaders presented strong views about key legal decisions, views reinforced by their own experiences in dealing with southern officials. For example, they "understandably looked with a measure of scorn on a lawyer's decision to deal with [state] courts" because of how those state courts had dealt with blacks.[37] A "repeat player" client is in a good position to influence a lawyer's actions, particularly if the lawyer is not a regular. While repeat-player clients are likely to have repeat-player lawyers and to share their views, lawyers are more likely to be the "repeat players" than are the clients, and when a client comes to a lawyer who is already attacking the client's target, the client is likely to be subordinate. The likelihood of clients being active participants in litigation is increased if they are organized, because group members can help gather evidence and can maintain contact with the lawyer, making the tasks less onerous for any one individual. Clients are more likely to be passive consumers if they are subsidized as Legal Services Program clients are, but organization of those clients may counter their dependence,[38] although because of the effort involved to remain an active client, organization per se is not enough to make clients active participants.

Attorney-Client Conflict

Client and lawyer may quickly reach an agreement that one or the other will make the key decisions. Even with such an initial agreement, attorney-client conflict is not difficult to find and tensions can be substantial. For example, in the Chicago Contract Buyers League case, the plaintiffs' leaders became "impatient with the initial inability of their own lawyers to appreciate" the symbolic importance of their payment strike, and even sought advice from another lawyer; and in Milwaukee, disagreements about strategy between a lawyer and the local NAACP membership in a school desegregation case led to "a split that caused the departure of the NAACP's attorneys and the termination of the group's direct support of the case."[39]

Friction is quite likely when clients are activists trying to achieve goals with a minimum of assistance, because lawyers are not accustomed to dealing with such active and assertive clients. However, some lawyers handling civil rights cases, particularly if with large firms and their civil rights activity is pro bono work, are accustomed to active clients and even assume clients will be involved in cases. They may even encourage such client activity, indicating "that such behavior is acceptable and even expected."[40] More likely, however, assertive clients will create disagreement over the pace of litigation and, generally, over lay persons' roles in litigation planning and strategy, as happened in mental health litigation. At times a lawyer "would not take a stand in support of an issue that the mental patient groups saw as directly relevant . . . but that the lawyer saw as threatening the legal precedent he wanted to set."[41] In those situations and in others, lawyers would want a victory but the activists would be far more interested in advancing movement goals, even if a case were lost; they would also be willing to accept settlements less than litigation would have produced and also might reject settlements better than they could have won.[42] Conversely, clients "may call the tune" in the decision to take a case to the Supreme Court, wishing to go ahead when lawyers would prefer not to do so because of the organization's strategic plans or because their experience tells them more about the justices' case-selection criteria.[43] A client who need not pay may wish the lawyer to go further than if the client were paying; on the other hand, particularly if a settlement offer appears favorable to the client but the lawyers entered the case to make favorable precedent, the litigator may wish to proceed further than the client—and further than either client or lawyer would have done with a fee-for-service arrangement.

The LDF's death penalty litigation provides examples of conflict between attorney goal and client interest. In a late stage of the *Maxwell* case, the first direct challenge to the death penalty to reach the Supreme Court, the attorneys for the state conceded a violation of the *Witherspoon v. Illinois* rule on selection of death-penalty jurors. For the NAACP Legal Defense Fund to win on the basis of that concession would not have added to the law "in helping to save the lives of other prisoners on death row," because LDF wanted the death penalty itself declared unconstitutional. Thus Anthony Amsterdam, arguing the case, "was faced with a classic example of a conflict that periodically confronts litigators for causes: a conflict between his responsibility to his immediate client, Maxwell, and the interests of his other clients in the nationwide campaign against the death penalty."[44] (In the *Gilmore* case, when the ACLU attempted to block Gilmore's execution although he wished it to proceed, "Gilmore's plainly expressed interests were subordinated to those of the ACLU even though it purported to act in his interests."[45])

Conflict over remedies between clients and lawyers associated with national organizations is common, as when clients desired improved education in the ghetto but lawyers sought desegregation, because the lawyers, most interested in establishing precedents to use in later efforts, do not "suffer from the immediate, day-to-day problem as much as the clients do."[46] However, local attorneys who are closer to and involved in the community know that refusal to compromise may be detrimental to their clients, particularly in post-lawsuit continuing relations with defendants.[47] Economic differences between lawyer and client add to friction over remedies, particularly settlement of class actions, because, unless the case is a test case, plaintiffs may wish to proceed while the lawyer would accept a "modest settlement" providing a better fee in relation to work performed than would further action.[48] Conversely, where a defendant offers much to the client but only token attorney's fees, which is said to take place in a significant portion of civil rights cases, the lawyer is also in a conflict, because refusing the settlement will be to the clients' detriment.[49]

Lawyer or Client

We cannot determine the proportion of instances in which clients either take an active role, lead lawyers, are at least equal in authority to them or even dominate them in civil rights litigation sponsored by organizations. At times, with multiple plaintiffs or a class action, a single active client is enough to prevent dominance by lawyers or their organizations.[50] In the Detroit school case, after the Supreme Court had turned aside a metropolitan-area-wide remedy, a number of groups and individuals, including leading black political figures, made efforts to get the NAACP to drop the case, but "One strong-willed physician on the [local NAACP] board has been credited with single-handedly preventing the local and national NAACP from even talking with the mayor about a compromise."[51] And we can without difficulty find instances when lawyers seriously consider the wishes of those to be affected by a case. When some people wanted to initiate what became the Boston school desegregation case, the lawyer to whom they had come, who did not want to proceed in the absence of community interest, made efforts to find out whether the black community wanted desegregation. When remedies were proposed, there were further contacts with parents through open meetings and through black leaders, as well as through a black lawyer "brought in as someone in whom people had confidence."

More frequently, lawyers are said to dominate and the complaint is made that "Some civil rights lawyers . . . are making decisions, setting priorities, and undertaking responsibilities that should be determined by their clients and shaped by the community." Such lawyer dominance is reinforced by the complexity of litigation; by the code of ethics, under which lawyers are not to allow laypersons to direct their decisions, and which affects situations when a lawyer is working with an interest group; by organization financing of litigation, which leads the organization's lawyers to point out that the financial support requires that they control the case,[52] as well as by lay client deference to professionals, which we can see in the comment by clients in access-to-transit litigation, " 'We let the attorneys advise us on the legal stuff,' " or that they were satisfied when "the lawyers generally prepared the proposals and 'run them by us.' "[53] Also relevant, and visible when lawyers impose a policy on the organization with which they are affiliated, is delegation of cases to them, time pressures, the heat of battle, or battle fatigue deriving from weariness of disputes over the issue.[54]

A major basis of lawyer dominance of clients is lawyers' "informational monopolies, their legal knowledge." This can encompass knowledge of relevant facts and interpretation of legal doctrine, as well as the "mysterious procedure and trade language" in which they deal; other elements of lawyers' power over clients are "better access to levels of effective power such as judge and court officials," "skill in negotiating with clients through threats, dire forecasts of probable alternative outcomes, and similar psychological pressures."[55] The lawyers' psychological advantage is reinforced when they act like "busy professionals"; being inaccessible to often hesitant clients is part of how "lawyers' techniques of 'impression management' can readily reshape client sentiment."[56]

Interpretation of leading precedents is a part of the knowledge differential. For example, in the Boston school case, although the NAACP's lawyers "listened respectfully to the views of the black community group, they made clear that a long line of court decisions would limit the degree to which [the clients'] educational priorities could be incorporated into the desegregation plan the lawyers were preparing to file."[57] As one civil rights lawyer put it, "once our abstract analysis was explained to our clients, who didn't know what 'legal avenues' to take, they agreed." Making such suggestions to one's civil rights clients was civil rights organizations' responsibility: "We were house counsel to the black community." A lawyer's taking the "primary initiative" is like what happens all the time in the corporate world when "house counsel suggests to a CEO that a case be filed."

Differences in background between staff attorneys for national organizations and the group's membership make working relations between lawyers and clients in a case difficult to maintain, and this has long been so. Black parents in the District of Columbia were reluctant to take their complaints about school conditions to the NAACP's Charles Houston "because to their minds he was part and parcel of the upper class of blacks who had shown no understanding of, interest in, or sympathy for blacks less fortunate" and was "one of the 'big people' who as a class, in general, had 'hurt' the 'little people.' "[58] Such status differentials are reinforced by incentives to which lawyers respond as they seek to engage in interesting work and maintain status among their peers. This leads them to take cues not from clients but from colleagues in the civil rights bar, who give great weight to major cases challenging public institutions.[59] Not all lawyer divergence from client concerns to improve personal reputation is conscious or the result of attempting "personal aggrandizement"; it may come from "selfless idealism" in attempting to attain that which is best or in the public interest. Yet disentangling "selfless idealism" from ego is difficult and certainly lawyers' actions are affected by "the inner drive to obtain ego satisfaction, to dominate the scene."[60]

Because clients must "have access to [the lawyer] before or during the legal process" to be able to have some say about the case, lawyer dominance is also assisted by lawyer separation from client.[61] At times that separation means that the lawyer has never met the client, or at least the named plaintiff. Even once there has been contact, there may be extended periods—even years when school desegregation cases were on appeal—in which there is no further contact.[62] The significant geographical distance between the headquarters of national organizations, usually New York City or Washington, D.C., and the communities in which an organization's members or clients live and litigation takes place, where the principal lawyer may spend little time, reinforces lawyer-client separation. When the client is an organization, the question is whether the lawyer will consult the organization's policymakers, most often its board; when the board does not consult the perhaps widely scattered membership, lawyer-client separation is even further reinforced.

Class actions.   Class actions strongly reinforce separation of client from lawyer, even where there is no divergence of views between them. Although the organization sponsoring class action litigation may have assumed that a commonality exists between it and other class members, consensus is not likely to exist within the class as to all elements of the suit, serving to compound differences between lawyer and at least significant segments of the client class. Even if, at the time when the class was constructed, there was agreement on general goals to be obtained, disagreement within the class occurs as one moves from abstract consideration of rights to be protected to specifics of application. It appears at virtually every stage and over every element of a lawsuit, from whether it should have been brought, where some may fear the consequences of a successful suit (such as the closing of a favorite school) or even retaliation, to the lawsuit's scope, such as whom to sue, and remedies to be sought.

Disagreements over how to proceed, including whether to negotiate or to press on, including how hard to push for certain remedies, result from class members' varying levels of commitment to the suit or to the sponsoring organization.[63] When there is such disagreement, lawyers may learn little, in part because of class action procedures themselves, which "make see-no-evil-hear-no-evil postures far more likely," with each actor assigning responsibility for learning of intra-class conflicts to someone else. Lawyers also have strong disincentives to learn very much, as inquiry would make them aware of differences—and might even produce, rather than simply reveal, division.[64] Both opponents (by attempting to decertify the class) and possible allies (by seeking to join the case as intervenors) would seek to exploit that division, posing serious problems in maintaining control over litigation and adding to the length and expense of a case.

Even without such dissensus, lawyer-client separation is endemic in class actions, in large measure because each class member becomes submerged within a larger group. At an extreme, if named plaintiffs drop out of a class action after a judge has certified the class, the suit remains alive, with no named class representatives to give the lawyers direction. More generally, however, in any class of significant size, "the profession's customary mechanism for coping with counsel's self-interest—disclosure and informed client consent—is simply not a workable approach in class adjudication" because "obtaining informed consent from all members is simply infeasible."[65] Even if some lawyers try conscientiously to stay in contact with representatives of a class and "make considerable efforts to appreciate and accommodate the broadest possible spectrum of class sentiment,"[66] many do not. When they do not, named plaintiffs, often figureheads, are not likely to be "well situated to monitor the congruence between counsel's conduct and class preferences,"[67] nor are paying class members likely to be motivated to look beyond their own interests to protect possible divergent interests within the class. Because few if any class members are paying, it is less likely the lawyer will attend to the nonpayers.

The Federal Rules require court approval of pretrial settlements in class actions, thus providing dissident class members an opportunity to come forward with objections to proposed remedies. However, although some judges insist on determining carefully if all class members have been dealt with properly to "be certain that the settlement does not compromise the legal rights of class members without their consent,"[68] judges, perhaps to avoid lengthy trials, tend to defer to lawyers' settlement arrangements. Thus those who disagree with positions taken by lawyers for the class, particularly those favoring alternative remedies, usually lack effective ways of being heard in court.[69] Along with the separation of lawyer from client noted above, this might suggest that civil rights plaintiffs may be ill-served by initial approval of class action status for a lawsuit. However, if a class is not certified, the result is likely to be multiple, largely duplicative, lawsuits. Even if individual clients received closer attention from lawyers, resources would be diffused rather than focused. Moreover, when any individual lawsuits reached the remedy stage, the effect of any one of them would likely be class-wide, presenting the same issues of division and how to cope with it.[70]

14

Interorganizational

Relations

The set of interest groups litigating in the field of civil rights can easily be denominated a *policy community*—"a network of interest groups active in a particular policy domain."[1] Not only is the proliferation of litigating organizations important, with other organizations' presence an important part of any organization's environment and affecting its actions, but so, as we have already seen, are their interrelationships. Interorganizational relations are closely related to resource questions. Competition for limited resources such as foundation grants is one element, with the larger number of organizations turning to the foundations meaning "increasing both competition for funds and rivalry detrimental to coalition building."[2] Another is resource-related cooperation, for example, when LDF joined several other public interest law firms to form the Public Interest Law Center and to reduce rental expenses by moving together into new offices with shared facilities and services and shared use of photocopying and LDF's larger library.

Interorganizational relations with respect to litigation are crucial in litigation strategy, because "no one group has the money, the administrative structure, or even the desire to coordinate all the . . . cases"[3] in any one area of the law, and the activities of any one organization attempting to carry out a litigation campaign can be disrupted by other groups acting without consultation. With a grand plan or overall strategy unlikely, cooperation and coordination become particularly important so that each group will not get in the way of those with parallel or relevant litigation. Thus although ACLU chapters could "mobilize resources available to the national civil rights litigations in some cases," ACLU activity in school desegregation cases was "not always seen as an unmixed blessing by the civil rights groups" because the actions of those local ACLU groups "may occasionally run against the grain of whatever fragmentary litigation strategy has been evolving by consensus among the small group of civil rights professionals."[4]

A factor to be considered by an organization deciding whether to litigate in a particular area of the law is whether other organizations are already engaged in such litigation, with other litigators' presence allowing an organization to leave an area of the law because it knows its previous clients' interests will still be protected.[5] Other organizations' presence also affects involvement in a particular case, as when those bringing the *Chapman* challenge to Ohio prison conditions tried "to avoid interfering with other institutional litigation in progress at the time," specifically that involving a challenge to operation of a state mental hospital.[6] Decisions to file an amicus brief also have an interorganizational component.

Interorganizational relations with respect to litigation are not independent of interorganizational relations generally. There are parallels between relations among litigating organizations and the relations among organizations which do not litigate.[7] Some interorganizational relations occur because an organization focusing on litigation provides litigation assistance to groups which emphasize different modes of political action; at other times, interaction over litigation is strongly affected by other aspects of the groups' interorganizational relations that have nothing to do with litigation. There is also a linkage between intra- and inter-organizational aspects of group activity. This can be seen in the fallout from the NAACP's intraorganizational dispute over Lewis Steel's *New York Times* article criticizing the Supreme Court, as the firing of Steel and the resultant departure of most of the legal staff allowed LDF to increase its predominance as the prime civil rights litigator.

In this chapter, greater attention and more specific focus is given to types of interorganizational relations. Both dispersion and competition, and convergence and cooperation, characterize intergroup relations affecting litigation. Relations "mix trust and suspicion, competition and cooperation, informal ties and formal organizations."[8] No single organization engaged in litigation is able to operate with total autonomy or complete independence, although there is order and stability rather than fragmentation in race relations litigation because of LDF's litigating predominance, NAACP's major involvement, the regular presence of the Lawyers' Committee and specialized litigating entities, and the existence of the civil rights bar.

The relations among organizations involved in civil rights litigation could be arranged along a continuum, from cooperation to conflict. This range of interorganizational relations can be found within particular areas of civil rights litigation. School desegregation provides examples. There one could find joint action by groups, division of labor, and lack of cooperation. In some instances, there were meetings to plan strategy. This was done to consider a case against New York City; participants included the NAACP, the NAACP Legal Defense Fund, the Puerto Rican Legal Defense Fund, and the New York Civil Liberties Union.[9] Joint action can be seen in several cities. In the Indianapolis case, for example, the Harvard Center for Law and Education helped the NAACP intervene in a case brought by the federal government.[10] At one stage of the Boston school case, parties formed the Joint Plaintiffs to prevent a school closing; the coalition, not a usual one, included black parents, the Hispanic group El Comite, the Boston Teachers Union, the Boston Association of School Administrators, and the Citywide Parents Advisory Committee created by the court itself earlier in the case.[11] Division of labor, which does not leave a neatly and completely divided litigation pie, could be seen in school districts with both Hispanic and black populations. For example, in Denver, Latinos, represented by MALDEF, "devoted . . . resources to the effort to make bilingual programs an integral part of desegregation," and general desegregation issues were left in LDF's hands; a similar, if less cooperative, division of labor could be seen in Boston.[12]

The Wilmington, Delaware, case illustrates an aspect of lack of cooperation. The NAACP branch, which "feared that blacks would bear the brunt of desegregation and would lose newly won power . . . in the city school district," did not initially support the lawsuit by some black parents and thus failed to help the ACLU.[13] Friction between the ACLU and NAACP, along with conflict between local NAACP officials and the national organization, also occurred in Atlanta. After the Atlanta NAACP branch was displaced by the national NAACP, the ACLU, at the request of black parents and "overriding the advice of national civil rights groups," took over the case.[14] The Indianapolis case also illustrates conflict between local organizations as "local NAACP lawyers reportedly refused to tell their local allies what they were doing."[15]

Most interorganizational relations, and certainly most cooperative ones, have been among groups "on the same side of the fence." Yet there have been times when an organization would "cross over" and engage in an alliance, even if only tactical and short-term, with an organization of divergent ideology. In the 1980s, the ACLU seemed to do this increasingly, prompting serious internal criticism from those who felt this compromised the organization's principled position. Among the allies with whom the ACLU unexpectedly affiliated itself were tobacco and alcohol companies (to fight a ban on advertising of those substances), bankers (to protect customers' privacy rights), the National Rifle Association (to prevent unverified data being entered into a computer network), the National Conservative Political Action Committee (NCPAC) (to oppose Clean Campaign Act provisions that would require broadcasters to give free response time for "negative advertising"), and conservatives and moderate Republicans (to oppose the ban on lobbying by former White House staff).

Cooperation

Cooperation among civil rights groups, which can take a variety of forms, is seen not only in litigation but also in legislative lobbying, where one sees "precisely the same cooperative strategies as in other types of political participation."[16] In the efforts to change provisions of the Voting Rights Act at the time of its 1982 renewal, LDF, NAACP, MALDEF, Lawyers' Committee, the Center for National Policy Review, and ACLU all were involved, at times through their principal voting rights attorneys. Particularly important is the Leadership Conference on Civil Rights, an umbrella lobbying organization of roughly 160 groups (blacks, Hispanics, women, senior citizens, the handicapped, religious groups, and labor unions).

Litigation activity involves a wide range of interorganizational cooperative relations, and is important because an organization "(1) . . . may rely on others for amicus assistance in its conduct of an outcome-oriented litigation strategy, and (2) if among organizations with the same constituency, disagreement on goals is present and widely reported, the Court may prefer not to become involved in the fray,"[17] group cooperation thus is necessary to get to the Supreme Court and to be effective there. Some cooperation is direct joint participation in cases or meetings to plan strategy. In addition, one organization may provide services to another, and indeed may assist in the creation of another organization. Communication and the sharing of information is another form of cooperation. At another point along the continuum, groups engage in a division of labor, perhaps staying out of each other's way, but by engaging in different activities, particularly with respect to litigation, cooperating in the larger endeavor of seeking a common goal. However, some cooperation is uneasy or tenuous, so it is not far to active noncooperation and even to outright conflict.

Even one organization dominant in a particular area of the law will work with other organizations, as LDF did with the NAACP, Lawyers' Committee, the Lawyers Constitutional Defense Committee, and Columbia Law School's Employment Rights Project in employment discrimination litigation. There is more than enough work to go around, and if dominant organization tries to do everything by itself, not only is the workload not diffused but other organizations' actions may interfere with the primary litigator's plans, so organizational self-interest leads to cooperation. (If more than one organization is dominant, as in church-state litigation, together they will not necessarily "act as a monolith," but instead will demonstrate a wide range of interactions—a "combination of cooperation, competition, and division of labor."[18])

Joint Participation

Perhaps the most obvious type of interorganizational activity is mutual involvement by teams of attorneys in a single case. There are numerous instances of such joint involvement. In one variation, different organizations may take responsibility for different parts of the case simultaneously or may be involved in a case at different times, as in the Los Angeles school case, which was filed by the ACLU but on which NAACP-sponsored attorneys worked later, challenging the state constitutional provision limiting busing.

Efforts to enlist other groups as fellow plaintiffs have produced multiple organizational plaintiffs,[19] just as some efforts to present a combined—if not "united"—front result in co-signed amicus briefs. Joint participation could be seen in school desegregation cases. In the federal suit to desegregate Texas elementary and secondary schools, intervenors included the Texas State conference of the NAACP, the League of United Latin American Citizens (LULAC), and the GI Forum, with the Texas Civil Liberties Union playing an amicus role.[20] Lawyers' Committee lawyers worked with NAACP lawyers in representing black parents and students in their efforts to intervene in the Chicago school desegregation case, which like the Texas case had been filed by the federal government, and the Lawyers' Committee joined lawyers from the NAACP and other attorneys in Los Angeles and Prince Georges County, Maryland, school cases. Because of extensive resources necessary to litigate the issues, the Lawyers' Committee also joined with MALDEF and other civil rights groups to challenge federal civil service examinations and related training programs.[21] There was also joint participation in voting rights cases, where, for example, Voting Rights Project attorneys worked with the Alaska NAACP, the ACLU, the Native American Rights Fund and Alaska Legal Services on a case involving Anchorage, Alaska.

Groups may also assist each other in defensive litigation, as when LDF, the Center for Constitutional Rights, and the Southern Poverty Law Center joined to provide a defense when the Justice Department charged Alabama blacks with vote fraud in the mid-1980s, and the NAACP Legal Defense Fund was joined in contesting the Reagan administration's exclusion of legal defense funds from the federal employees' fund-raising drive not only by the Lawyers' Committee and the Puerto Rican Legal Defense Fund, but also by the Sierra Club Legal Defense Fund, the Indian Law Resources Center, the Natural Resources Defense Council, and the Federally Employed Women Legal and Education Fund.

The amazing thing is that joint participation takes place at all in view of the potential and actual problems that serve to interfere, which remind us of the old saw, "With friends like that, who needs enemies?" One faces "organizational jealousy, different priorities, protection of one's reputation against being tainted by disreputable groups, and disagreements over strategy," to which one should add disagreements over strategies on nonlitigation activity, all of which occurred in the transit litigation by the disabled.[22]

Facilitating intergroup interaction is that some lawyers work first for one organization and then for another, making them effective conduits for interorganizational communication. For example, one of the premier school desegregation attorneys, Norman Chachkin, worked first for the Lawyers' Committee and then for NAACP Legal Defense Fund. Other individuals are simultaneously members of multiple organizations engaged in civil rights activity, as in the considerable overlap between the leadership of the Southern Christian Leadership Conference (SCLC), Rev. King's group, and local NAACP leadership, because "a large proportion of the NAACP's southern branch presidents were ministers," and "it was common for a community leader to function as president of both the local NAACP branch and the local SCLC affiliate."[23]

Earlier interest-group theorists felt this cross-cutting and "overlapping membership" might place the individuals under cross-pressures,[24] as in the situation where if ministers exerted their fund-raising efforts for SCLC, they might engage in less such activity for the NAACP. However, to the extent that the organizations have the same goal, multiple memberships are more likely to reinforce commitment rather than reduce it. Here we see that the SCLC's presence allowed civil rights activity to continue when the state's attack effectively put the Alabama NAACP out of business, and there was joint fund-raising and sharing of receipts, as well as use of comparative advantage, with the NAACP restricting itself more to the legal role, "leaving the SCLC to specialize in direct action at the community level."[25]

Planning and Coordination

Organizations may actually get together to plan litigation activity, either through infrequent meetings or more frequent formal contacts. For example, in the "very cordial" working relations between LDF and the Lawyers' Committee, the two groups "regularly confer about cases and assist each other whenever possible."[26] In church-state litigation, the principal organizations—the ACLU, American Jewish Congress, and Americans United—formed a "litigation consortium," and other groups were also represented at their meetings. "Informational ties" and frequent communication also existed between pairs of the three

principal litigators, with the American Jewish Congress and its premier litigator, Leo Pfeffer, at the core of the network. They also held
several formal meetings, which produced formal agreements, including "a set of 'guiding principles'." [27] There were similar meetings leading up to *Brown* and in connection with the restrictive covenant cases
of the 1940s, and, more recently, there were planning sessions in connection with the LDF's capital punishment litigation campaign [28] and
with the joint efforts of the LDF and the Lawyers' Committee to support affirmative action consent decrees in response to Justice Department efforts to overturn them. Discussions between groups, however,
most frequently have *not* been about allocating litigation between the
groups. Thus when people from the Harvard Center, MALDEF, and
other organizations sat down to discuss bilingual education, the discussion was about policy issues, a "general discussion about what you
can do with particular issues" with some "of what you can emphasize," but, it was emphasized, "nothing like 'You'll do cases on this,
we'll do cases on that.' "

Conservative public interest law firms have not as actively engaged
in coordination, in part because the National Legal Center for the Public Interest did not perform the coordinating function intended when
it established its network of conservative PILFs in 1975. However, they
have maintained contact in part through a series of luncheons, including representatives not only from conservative PILFs but also from
other conservative interest groups that engage in litigation like the
National Right to Work Legal Defense Foundation and the National
Chamber Litigation Center, [29] at the Heritage Foundation, which has
tried to provide some coordination.

When an organization does develop a coordinating role, this can
stem from its recognized predominance in an area of law. We see
this with the LDF and capital punishment litigation and in prisoners'
rights, where the National Prison Project connected with the ACLU
"reached out to other organizations to establish a coordinated network
of prisoners' rights litigators." [30] There are, however, several reasons
why not much formal coordination occurs, leaving efforts dispersed
among a large number of groups, apart from the fact that at least some
participants think planning sessions are ineffective and others are
ideologically opposed to national coordination. One is that to engage
in coordinated activity is to some extent to give up one's own identity,
created through earlier commitments to particular means of operat-

ing, and important for the organizations' leaders and for obtaining resources. Another is the large number of groups, for example, "scores of organizations across the nation . . . involved in open-housing litigation, ranging from local groups pursuing very specific objectives in a single court action to national civil rights groups seeking sweeping changes in a variety of cases."[31] Still another reason is the pressure of pending cases, which leaves little time for sitting in meetings to plan.

Providing Services

One form of interorganizational cooperation is providing services to other organizations. At one extreme, this can result in the formation of new organizations to carry out certain tasks more effectively, with established groups generally having "assisted in the creation of new groups in their fields, especially if these new organizations promised to perform services or reach constituencies that had not yet been exploited by existing organizations."[32] In the civil rights litigation arena, this was perhaps clearest in the LDF's role in creating the Mexican American Legal Defense Fund (MALDEF) and the Puerto Rican Legal Defense Fund, which were established to operate in the same way and with the same organizational structure as LDF itself but to deal with different constituencies that LDF leaders realized needed help in pursuing civil rights litigation. After LDF had set up MALDEF, staff at LDF "understood we'd not directly represent Hispanics," but would cooperate as amicus. During the 1960s, LDF also helped found the Lawyers Constitutional Defense Committee "to respond to the civil rights movement's needs which LDF could not effectively handle."[33]

More frequently provided to other organizations are legal services, particularly representation, although at times this is done reluctantly —when dominant national organizations look askance at small local entities that are not affiliated with the national group. This could be seen in the NAACP's earlier years, with the NAACP showing "condescension toward, and arm's length treatment of, less well-educated blacks and those who were not members of the Association," for example, during *Moore v. Dempsey*.[34]

LDF performed the at-times auxiliary function of providing representation during the civil rights movement when it provided counsel not only to NAACP branches but also to SCLC, particularly after the SCLC-affiliated Gandhi Society ceased to exist; CORE; and SNCC, although SNCC may have been less dependent on LDF because of its acceptance of the National Lawyers' Guild's assistance despite others' avoidance of the Guild "for fear of being linked to a Communist front organization."[35] In its role as lawyer for other groups, LDF also provided legal services to *members* of other organizations.[36] In the area of women's rights, both liberal (Women's Legal Defense Fund) and conservative (Americans United for Life Legal Defense Fund) litigating groups also represented other organizations.[37] When the Lawyers' Committee was engaged in the effort to head off the Reagan administration's attack on consent decrees, it sent materials to defense attorneys in more than fifty cases and to lawyers for private plaintiffs in those cases, and, working through the national ACLU, provided similar information to local ACLU offices where the cases were located, and informed them of lawyers and law firms who would provide representation or file amicus briefs.[38]

Even if they did not handle litigation or supply lawyers, an organization might help pay for legal defense, as when the NAACP assisted civil rights figures who encountered trouble, for example, paying some of Rev. Martin Luther King, Jr.'s legal expenses despite the friction between King and the NAACP's Roy Wilkins.[39] In a service important for control of cases as well as for more efficient resource allocation, an organization may also help others find lawyers, as the LDF has done in recent efforts against the death penalty, where it assisted state and regional units working to oppose capital punishment, including the Southern Poverty Law Center and the Florida Clearinghouse on Criminal Justice. Or because of its legal expertise, an organization may function like a backup center for other organizations in particular areas of litigation, as the Lawyers' Committee did in the mid-1980s for the Virginia ACLU, the Center for Constitutional Rights, and the Native American Rights Fund.[40]

Division of Labor

Division of labor is another method of cooperation. When groups have similar views, instead of participating in conjoint activity each may decide to go its separate way as long as another of their number is advocating the groups' basic position, as seen in the comment, "If ACLU was involved, NAACP need not be." Dispersion, even with competition, at times produces greater effort toward common goals and thus is not antithetical to cooperation. In public interest law generally, one also finds groups "often try[ing] to stay out of each other's cases, believing that the issue already is being handled in the best possible way." For example, conservative groups certainly are able to coordinate their efforts, but operate differently so that each group can best focus its efforts on particular cases.[41] This is, of course, not merely a matter of courtesy but of economic efficiency, what economists call "comparative advantage," with each organization doing what it does best and with the central thrust each organization develops leading to maintenance of differentiation as some groups concentrate on certain subjects or activities while others focus their efforts elsewhere— because of the former's efforts. As a result, more effective litigation occurs across a broader range of topics.

Division of labor also helps prevent turf-raiding, which may have been avoided, as when a lawyer for LDF said it was "not out to get into other organizations' turf"—perhaps one reason "relations with other organizations are pretty good." However, turf-protection did occur, with an "extremely insecure" LDF having protected its territory in the early 1960s, when "Jack Greenberg didn't want anyone treading on his turf" because he had "a greater concern than appropriate for the Inc. Fund's standing, as if it were an entity and creation in its own right, beyond the good it does.[42]

An organization with primacy, or at least the reputation for primacy, in its area of endeavor will work hard to protect that position. That the NAACP had been the predominant, even the sole, organization speaking for African-Americans' interests is undoubtedly one reason for friction between it and other organizations, whose activity the NAACP saw as a threat even when there was more than enough civil rights work for all to do. Trying to retain primacy by heading off other organizations from establishing themselves or from pressing different methods, the NAACP, believing that litigation was the most appropriate means toward racial equality, was unwilling to support more direct action. To have done so would have been an implicit concession of the accuracy of criticism that litigation had not met its expectations, such as that from an SCLC's spokesman that the NAACP was "too conservative" and preoccupied with fundraising and lawsuits.[43]

Division of labor is more likely to be informal and implicit than the result of explicit agreement, to be more a matter of "we saw what they were doing" and of groups "trying to stay out of each other's way" than of explicitly "carving up the territory," as one LDF lawyer put it.

Yet the observation by an ACLU lawyer that it was "not a matter of 'others are doing this so we don't have to' but of 'How can we help?' " and the further comment that, notwithstanding other groups' involvement, the NAACP needed to cover some of the same issues suggests that division of labor is not complete.

One type of division of labor relates to the arenas in which activity is carried out and the types of activity carried out in those arenas, with each of several groups developing and emphasizing its own methods for making demands. Thus the NAACP and the LDF have focused on litigation, while CORE and SNCC engaged in more direct action such as demonstrations and sit-ins, with the NAACP-CORE rivalry showing conflictual rather than cooperative division of labor.[44] Mississippi civil rights activity provides empirical evidence of division of labor, as there was less Lawyers' Committee litigation in counties where SNCC was active.[45] Division of labor concerning different activities can also be seen with respect to efforts to overturn the death penalty, where the NAACP Legal Defense Fund took the lead in litigation and the ACLU, particularly at the state level, focused more on legislative endeavors.[46] Yet the ACLU also litigated against capital punishment.

When division of labor takes place within litigation, it may look like noncooperation because of the result that organizations do not work together in the same areas of law or same cases. Yet "a strategy of noncooperation" requires that groups know which ones will participate in what cases, as in the informal division of labor among conservative public interest law firms when the National Legal Center for the Public Interest established regional legal foundations: water and land rights cases were handled in Denver, education in Philadelphia, farming in Kansas City, unions in Atlanta, and regulatory agencies in Washington, D.C.[47]

Division of labor has led organizations to defer to each other in several areas of litigation. Thus, LDF did not initially direct its resources to the campaign against exclusionary zoning because other national groups already were investing their efforts in that cause, and in women's rights litigation, "By the mid-1970s, . . . most groups were willing to defer to the expertise of the ACLU," while WEAL became the "leader in academic discrimination litigation" because most women's organizations had avoided that area of law.[48] Although initially challenging the death penalty only when it resulted from unfair trials, the ACLU, by the time it decided to attack the constitutionality of capital punishment per se, found that LDF had already begun to organize its campaign against capital punishment. As a result, ACLU lawyers sought support from LDF. The ACLU's willingness to play a secondary role stemmed in part from its involvement in, and commitment of resources to, Vietnam-related clients (conscientious objectors and antiwar demonstrators) and from the argument that application of the death penalty was racially discriminatory, which "helped to make it seem proper that the LDF should lead the fight against it."[49] Yet the ACLU did continue to litigate, establishing a Capital Punishment Project, which conducted studies (for example, on wrongful convictions and executions) and assisted in litigation. For instance, it worked on a death penalty case before the U.S. Court of Military Appeals, in which the courts had invited the ACLU to file an amicus brief, and in which a lawyer for a committee of the Association of the Bar of the City of New York joined.

When an organization has doctrinal primacy, retaining it is important. When an organization is trying to orchestrate a litigation campaign, where control of a multiplicity of cases and of their sequencing is crucial, the need to "stay ahead of the troops," particularly other troops, is quite important. When groups seeking ground-breaking precedent are not well equipped to do follow-up work, it becomes necessary for other groups to undertake that sort of litigation. One litigator may, however, focus on precedent-setting cases in order to open up litigation opportunities for smaller or more localized groups or for individualized lawyers; this was certainly an effect of LDF's ground-breaking Title VII litigation and apparently part of its participation in litigation on housing discrimination.

Subject matter division of labor can also lead to interorganizational referral of cases. For example, freedom of speech cases that came to LDF were generally referred to the ACLU unless blacks were involved, as in the *Caldwell* case involving media coverage of black militants' activities and in which LDF had been contacted by "black media folk." In intergroup interaction at the field level during civil rights activities in Mississippi in the 1960s, explicit division of labor included cross-referrals of cases. The Lawyers Constitutional Defense Committee (formed by civil rights and liberties organizations to protect people during the 1964 "Freedom Summer") "took the lead" in cases involving brutality by police or guards, "LCCRUL generally referred school desegregation cases to LDF, and the LDF generally referred its criminal and various other types of cases to LCCRUL," particularly those "they didn't have time to handle." Thus LDF "specialized in cases most directly related to the goals of [the] national organization," while "the bulk of the defensive litigation" was handled by LCCRUL and LCDC attorneys, but dividing lines, although clear, were not hard-and-fast as "LDF shouldered its share of 'routine' cases (e.g., demonstrations, marches, boycotts, public accommodations)."

Closely related is division of labor as to the courts in which organizations focus their efforts, as LDF operated primarily in federal court, while the organizations defending civil rights workers were primarily in state court. This distinction was also tied to the various organizations' litigation goals, with the LDF "more inclined to argue cases on Bill of Rights grounds in an effort to establish broad principles," while other litigators "might be expected to be more concerned with freeing jailed demonstrators to allow them to continue their work."[50] Division of labor can also be geographical, as in school cases, with the NAACP's Special Contribution Fund (SCF) to be "the moving party in northern and western school cases, LDF in the South." Some say this was decided after "both formal and informal discussions" between lawyers for the two organizations, with "constant contact and dialogue," but others suggest that the division of labor developed not as a result of open discussion but implicitly. Geographical division of labor also occurred in church-state litigation, where it was based on geography and types of cases in which three principal organizations "work in different cases in different parts of the country, a division that reflects differences in their clienteles, their separationist commitments, their skills and capacities, and even their styles of managing litigation."[51]

Noncooperation

One should not assume that smooth relations between civil rights organizations always predominate. Allies, real and potential, in addition to exhibiting cooperation and division of labor, may also demonstrate noncooperation and even open friction. Within any set of potentially cooperating organizations, there are "persistent centrifugal forces" which "make it extremely difficult to organize those groups into a relatively cohesive whole."[52] A major reason for noncooperation is that each entity has its own, different maintenance needs. Some difficulty comes from the different thrusts of individual organizations' past efforts, leading to vested interests, some from any individual organization's internal divisions. Efforts to bring the handicapped together into a disability rights movement faced the further difficulties of "the real difference in the concrete problems and experiences of persons with different kinds of disabilities" and organizations which had developed for each disability, a division of labor which had made consulting other groups unnecessary.[53]

Interorganization friction can be "horizontal," between two or more groups at the same level, national or state. Or it can be "vertical," between a national organization and one at the state or local level, such as its own affiliates or independent organizations which form to pursue specific litigation. The latter can be seen in action leading to *Moore v. Dempsey*. Both the national NAACP and an Arkansas-based Citizens Defense Fund Commission had raised legal defense funds for those charged in Arkansas riots. The NAACP mentioned its own contribution in *Crisis* magazine without mentioning the Arkansas group's contribution, adding to "old suspicions and resentments between the Association and the Arkansas black leaders."[54] Such friction is certainly present within litigation. Even when, as in church-state litigation, "an impressive degree of order and stability" was imposed by three principal litigators, "the potential for legal chaos" and "fragmentation" exists, and any cooperation may be tenuous at best. Distance between the ACLU and American Jewish Congress, on the one hand, and Americans United—a compound of perceptions of lesser quality in legal work and of the latter's conservatism which led them to devalue Americans United—affected the contacts among these three principal litigators, although it did not prevent all interaction.[55]

At times, lack of cooperation is inadvertent, for example, when litigators duplicate each other's work without knowing it. In the early stages of the Boston school case, both a private law firm doing pro bono work and the Harvard Center for Law and Education assigned lawyers to develop a federal court case after different groups of parents had approached them; when they joined forces they realized that both were working on a case. In Philadelphia duplicative efforts to deal with police brutality proceeded further before the lawyers learned of each other's case.[56] In other situations, noncooperation is intentional. Organizations may wish not to work together or may be leery of doing so. In litigation against exclusionary zoning, where there was ideological opposition to coordination, those seeking open housing were hesitant to join forces with developers wishing to build low- or moderate-income housing because of the latter's self-interest,[57] but the Supreme Court's rules on standing at times made the developers the only ones who could get into court.

Perhaps because of its predominance, LDF, Jack Greenberg said, was "not much for what you might call ecumenical litigation." In one situation, the ACLU wanted LDF to join it in a case when the state education officials "issued a statement watering down the preexisting school integration policy" in New York. According to Greenberg, LDF felt "that we ought to wait until there was an effort to implement the new policy and then we'd have a concrete situation to deal with in the courts," adding "In any event, there was no reason to have both of us there." Moreover, he said, having many organizations put their names on a brief "seems a waste of energy, and it creates an association with issues and their development over which you have no control."[58]

Generally litigation undertaken to achieve ideological or organizational (including publicity) goals does not produce alliances with groups whose ideology differs. To join with others may mean the loss of publicity for one's own organization, just as is true in legislative lobbying, where "groups are reluctant to share credit, particularly with rival (as distinct from opponent) organizations, with whom they compete for members" and who can also "pose a threat to a group's reputation."[59] Tension between organizations resulting from organizational jealousies even produces a reluctance to "farm out" cases to other organizations' attorneys even when they have necessary expertise, although "some work was done that way" nonetheless. And refusal to share credit, an aspect of noncooperation, adds to friction, as it did when the Suburban Action Institute (SAI), a prime mover in the battle against exclusionary zoning, had "turbulent" relations with other housing litigators as a result of SAI's rarely giving credit to other groups in its publicity.[60]

Noncooperation has also been a direct result of ideological differences. The NAACP Legal Defense Fund, like other liberal avowedly staunchly "anti-Communist" groups, was very careful not to become involved with the National Lawyers' Guild and its lawyers, out of fear that LDF would be criticized for being associated with "subversives." This disinclination was clear in Freedom Summer (1964), when some board members of the Lawyers Constitutional Defense Committee (LCDC), established by LDF, ACLU, and others, "tried to disassociate themselves from to the Guild and William Kunstler," to which LCDC was hospitable, because they were "fearful of being tainted by too much of a leftish blemish."[61] Jack Greenberg also "threatened to cancel plans to provide legal assistance to the [civil rights] volunteers if he had to work with the Lawyers' Guild lawyers." Although criticism led to a compromise in which the volunteers could choose lawyers from either organization, LDF's initial unwillingness to provide legal assistance except on its own terms created resentment and led some to believe that Greenberg was trying to direct, instead of to assist, the movement in the South.[62] Establishment lawyers appear to have taken even stronger action to exclude Guild influence. "People's lawyer" Arthur Kinoy reported that pressure was brought on the Council of Federated Organizations (COFO) and the Mississippi Freedom Democratic Party (MFDP) "to shift away from work with Kunstler, Smith, myself, and the recently established Lawyers' Guild office in Jackson," with "foundation funding and substantial material resources . . . openly tied to eliminating the influence of the 'Guild lawyers.' "[63]

Thus ideology led some lawyers to maintain control to avoid having the "enemy" take over, even when the "enemy" was seeking the same short-run goal. This indicates that there are times when the relationship between litigating entities supposedly on the "same side of the fence" becomes one of conflict and there can be considerable conflict within what is supposedly "one side" in litigation. That had happened earlier in race relations litigation, starting with the Scottsboro Boys case. Thus in addition to difficulties turning on developments within the case and divisions within the set of lawyers representing the black defendants, other problems stemmed from the very basic differences in the approaches of the NAACP and the Communist Party to political change. The International Labor Defense, which had been effective in wresting the case from the NAACP, had ties to the Communist Party and saw "legislatures and courts [as] simply the faulty mechanisms of a corrupt, capitalist system, . . . to be used as forums to discredit that system."[64] The NAACP did not help itself when its officials made patronizing and condescending statements about the black defendants' poor, ignorant parents who had been duped by the Communists.[65] Such conflict over a single case may lead supposed allies, starting from different assumptions, to feel that each needs a separate presence, perhaps as intervenors, in a case. In other situations, their different perspectives and the elevated tensions between groups stemming from them may even lead to efforts to initiate separate, competing cases.

The NAACP and the NAACP Legal Defense Fund: Observations on Conflict between Allies

The difficulties that can develop between allies, including bitterness much greater than that characterizing relations with one's usual enemies, are best illustrated by the conflict between NAACP and the NAACP Legal Defense Fund.[66] In May 1982, those who paid heed to civil rights were startled, even shocked, to learn that the NAACP was suing the NAACP Legal Defense Fund to prevent the latter from using "NAACP" in its name. Supporters of the civil rights movement much decried the fight because it used resources that could have been expended to achieve the two allies' civil rights goals and was a patent embarrassment that should never have occurred. It also would have been better for the civil rights community if the unfolding situation had not mandated the lawsuit. The lawsuit was particularly troublesome because it came when the political atmosphere and legal environment were considerably less favorable to the active pursuit of racial equality and when it appeared that the nation had reached, if not already passed, the furthest point of white society's willingness to deal with racial questions.[67]

The NAACP prevailed at trial but lost on appeal on the ground it had waited too long to assert its rights. The litigation, which had a variety of causes, is noteworthy as a serious dispute between allies because of its sometime intensity and because of the groups' joint origin, which may help explain the intensity. Some of the claims, for all the legal language in which they were cast, did not seem to carry their own weight, but the dispute itself certainly was not petty and the lawsuit was treated as serious business by the parties, both of whom mobilized high-powered legal talent. Although Vernon Jordan provided LDF's defense pro bono, the NAACP paid $15,000 to Samuel Pierce to draft a complaint and $25,000 to Edward Brooke when Pierce became Reagan's Secretary of Housing and Urban Development. That the NAACP had to pay lawyers to work on the case may also say something about the quality of the suit, an observer commented, and it has also been suggested that after the NAACP had laid out funds to draft the complaint and the LDF would not respond to entreaties and rejoin the NAACP, the latter's "bluff had been called and they felt they had to proceed with the suit." The case did not distract defendant LDF from its work and did not rupture working relations between staff lawyers (staff or cooperating) for the two organizations, but it was a "working" issue for plaintiff NAACP, with considerable reputational and financial costs. If someone had wanted to immobilize the NAACP by expending its resources on non-goal-related activities, they could have done no better than to have placed a mole in the NAACP suggesting that suing the LDF would be a good strategy.[68]

The Case

The NAACP filed its case in late May 1982, as a trademark case, claiming that, under the Lanham Act, LDF was using the name "NAACP" improperly, that such use had never been permanent but only contingent, and that the LDF had failed to cease such use after demands that it do so, for example, by the NAACP's 1979 annual convention. One claim, common to trademark actions, was of "public confusion"—that people making contributions did not understand that the two organizations were in fact separate and thus donated to the "Inc. Fund" when they intended to give to the NAACP. Arguing the case in the federal district court in Washington, D.C., Brooke also attacked the "Inc. Fund" for taking credit for *Brown v. Board of Education.* Jay Topkis, a leading intellectual property lawyer, argued for the LDF that the organization "need[ed] our name in dealing with our clients" because the public had come to "associate these initials with help" and that the organization had long used the "NAACP" initials—without complaint.[69]

In March 1983, Judge Thomas P. Jackson, ruling for the NAACP, ordered the LDF to stop using the NAACP initials within six months; for two more years it could indicate that it was "formerly NAACP-LDF," but beyond that, such references could take place only in the text of statements. Judge Jackson devoted most of his opinion to the history of the two organizations, and thus put much of the dispute's history on the public record. The "tensions between the two had begun to emerge" by 1960, he said; efforts made to reconcile the two groups were unsuccessful and conflict increased. By mid-1965, the NAACP's board had called upon the LDF "to curb its autonomic impulses and revert to 'special contribution fund status' or reincorporate under a

name which would not include the initials 'NAACP.'" Subsequent
efforts, also unsuccessful, came apart over which entity should have
greater credit for civil rights advances, but money was still fundamental, with the NAACP "growing even more concerned about its
ability to compete for funds with its aggressive *and* tax-exempt cohort
now concurrently approaching many of the same sources." Judge Jackson then noted that "the NAACP remained reluctant to provoke the
final break with the LDF and endured the situation in silence except
for sporadic internal expressions of discontent"—a fact that was to
be determinative in the appeal. In late 1978, the NAACP had again
raised with LDF its concern over use of the initials, but LDF would
do no more than discuss the two groups' relations. An NAACP ulti-
matum was rejected by LDF "ironically, on October 9, 1979, the 40th
Anniversary of the fateful original authorization." [70]

The judge ruled that the LDF, not the NAACP, had the burden to
show that it would be "injustice" to stop LDF's use of the initials and
that delay in bringing the suit was "inexcusable." The LDF, he found,
had not shown that "the NAACP, aside from forbearance, said or did
anything to mislead the LDF as to its willingness to let the *status quo*
remain undisturbed forever" and had regularly called on LDF to cease
using the initials; the LDF's refusals had led the NAACP to give up its
effort. That the NAACP had not acted previously through a lawsuit
"is less consistent with acquiescence freely accorded than with a reluctance to antagonize a onetime ally or to abort hopes of an eventual
reconciliation by anything so divisive." The passage of time, moreover, had not prevented the LDF from "recast[ing] its public identity
in a form *sans* the initials." [71]

On the merits, the judge sided with the NAACP. He noted that
"even sophisticated contributors who might have been expected to
know better" at times mistook the two groups and found many instances of confusion by the press and others. (Some *judges* appear to
confuse the two organizations, particularly when an attorney appears
on some occasions for the NAACP and at other times for the LDF.)
As to the future, which under the law was crucial, the judge did find
"potential for confusion," which would be particularly serious were
the LDF not to use the initials "worthily" as it had in the past, for that
would leave the NAACP "without . . . the ability to affect the vicarious
image it will thus acquire." Moreover, the NAACP had intended "to
confer upon the LDF less than a right to use the initial in perpetuity,"

with "the 1939 resolution . . . intended as a revocable license to use, and not an irrevocable assignment of, the disputed initials."[72]

Judge Jackson's ruling for the NAACP was not, however, to be the final word. In February 1975, a unanimous panel of the U.S. Court of Appeals for the District of Columbia—Senior Judge David L. Bazelon and Judges Robert Bork and Abner Mikva—reversed, ruling that the NAACP had delayed too long to assert its rights, and that under the doctrine of laches, the suit had to be dismissed. Judge Bazelon found that the NAACP, although threatening to sue as early as 1965, had not tried either to negotiate or to make good on its threat of legal action. "Laches," he said, "is founded on the motion that equity aids the vigilant and not those who slumber on their rights." When the NAACP took the case to the Supreme Court, review was denied.[73]

Causes of Conflict

The conditions for the NAACP-LDF conflict were laid long ago and developed over the years from the Fund's "complete divorcement" from the NAACP that Thurgood Marshall brought about; and no one cause of friction can be said to be independent of the others. Among them are *organizational history* and *internal friction* within the NAACP, including officials' authority. Some plausible NAACP grievances may have been adduced largely as cover for internal difficulties, and one observer has even suggested that the NAACP, exhibiting much ritual and little accomplishment, "has to have an enemy" to explain its difficulties: That enemy "has to be the LDF."

The factors to be given particular attention in this section are, first, the matter of personality, perhaps the least compelling of hypothesized causes of the dispute although at times it sets the tone for it, and competition for racial recognition and racial credit, which is central to resource mobilization because organizations need to demonstrate their effectiveness to foundations and other contributors. Next is the relation between staff attorneys and cooperating attorneys, where differences between the NAACP and the LDF cast some light on the perceived relative litigation effectiveness of the two organizations. Among other interrelated hypothesized causes bearing most directly on resource mobilization is competition for financial resources, seen in the NAACP's concern that funds it should receive are going to the LDF. Another is competition for cases, important because, to demonstrate effectiveness, litigating organizations must maintain a flow of potential cases; to which is added a further look at competition for racial credit, centering on the question of whether black lawyers or white lawyers have received appropriate credit for the litigation strategy leading to *Brown v. Board of Education.*

Personality and racial recognition.   At times the attribution of dispute to particular personalities disguises more consequential relationships. For example, while a look at the exercise of authority within the NAACP at first seems to reveal that leaders' personalities are crucial, closer examination reveals that such authority is exercised even by new leaders, thus indicating that organizational history and internal structural matters are perhaps more appropriate explanatory factors. Nonetheless, in this particular dispute, it is difficult to escape the view that LDF's director-counsel, Jack Greenberg, was himself highly controversial. Some NAACP people have always resented Thurgood Marshall's choice of Greenberg as his successor without consulting the NAACP board. This tied subsequent unhappiness with Greenberg to the manner of his selection. However, opposition to Greenberg went beyond that, with "dominance" seen as "part of the empire he has built, part and parcel of his personality." His qualifications as a brilliant lawyer have never been faulted, but he was seen as "stubborn and aloof," as having "perhaps more of an intellectual than emotional commitment to his task," and as unwilling to compromise; he was "not at all warm" and "not very cordial or charming, except when he's trying to raise money for the Inc. Fund."[74] (Greenberg's success as a fundraiser indicates the relationship between personality and other sources of interorganizational friction, such as competition for financial resources.)

Race was another obvious, related part of the equation. Robert Carter's reaction to not having been selected to succeed Marshall was that "if he didn't get it, another black lawyer should." This position was taken by others, including *The Amsterdam News,* a major black newspaper, and unhappiness over the selection crossed NAACP-LDF boundaries: "At a conference of New York chapters of the NAACP, delegates tried to pass a resolution opposing Greenberg's appointment. They were stymied when told that the Legal Defense Fund was legally separate from the NAACP even though they shared the same initials—and that it would be wrong for one civil rights organization to criticize another."[75]

Yet instead of race, Carter's litigation approach, which differed from Marshall's, may help explain why he was not chosen; this view is reflected in the comment that "Marshall played it safe picking Greenberg" as his successor[76]—in choosing a highly skilled technocrat, as Greenberg has been described, over someone more adventurous. In the words of a former colleague, Greenberg, who prided himself on "being a technician," "seemed very mechanical, obsessive in how he functions." Disputing this view, someone else who worked with him said he was "very active in program development," with "expansive and far-reaching" ideas. Carter was said to be was more "adventurous" and "innovative" in his approach to the use of the law and more "ideologically and programmatically centered" than was Marshall, who, several observers have said, was, like his mentor, Charles Houston, more cautious and pragmatic, even conservative, in his approach.[77] (Such a difference was perhaps rooted in their backgrounds, Marshall having come from "the conservative mulatto aristocracy of Baltimore" while Carter "was a dark-skinned product of Newark's Central Avenue ghetto."[78])

Greenberg's continuing as head of an organization dedicated to the civil rights of blacks for almost twenty-five years and not being replaced by a black attorney until 1984 was a related source of resentment. A (white) cooperating attorney put the matter thus: "Greenberg kept his job, a sinecure, for the whole time—at least twenty years, when [James M.] Nabrit [III], a competent black lawyer, was there as number 2." After Greenberg's appointment, the views identified by the slogans "Black Power" and "Black is Beautiful" catalyzed the strong feeling that, just as blacks had succeeded whites as president of the NAACP, they should do so in directing LDF's work. That William T. Coleman, Jr., was Chairman of LDF's Board, followed by Julius Chambers, who ultimately succeeded Greenberg, was not enough.[79] This problem was reinforced by the substantial portion of white attorneys on LDF's staff, posing the long-standing question of the use of white counsel rather than black counsel in cases brought by the NAACP or LDF. As an outspoken observer of both organizations stated, those at LDF "don't have any respect for black lawyers!" However, this view was disputed by a white LDF staff member who said that in the 1970s the staff was roughly fifty-fifty white-black and that the charge also ignored black cooperating attorneys, including the many African-American graduates of LDF's intern program.

Objection to Greenberg's continued tenure also made him a target for other complaints about white dominance of blacks, with his status as arguably the nation's most knowledgeable civil rights attorney almost irrelevant. This was illustrated by a controversy at Harvard Law School in 1982 and 1983. When Chambers was asked to teach a three-week intersession course on civil rights law but, citing the demands of his own law practice, asked Greenberg to share teaching of the course, the result was a widely reported boycott of the course by blacks and other ethnic minority students. Its initial principal point was the lack of tenured black faculty at Harvard Law School, but the focus shifted to whether Greenberg, as a white lawyer, should teach a course on civil rights law, particularly when capable black attorneys could also do so.

Conflict over Greenberg, his selection, and his continuing tenure became intermixed with tension between the African-American and Jewish communities. Even if Jews, Judaism, and Israel are never mentioned, the temperature of a disagreement pitting blacks against whites is not lowered—and is likely to be increased—when a major white participant is obviously Jewish. This can be seen in the question by one black attorney, who shall go unnamed. After telling Richard Kluger that Greenberg was an excellent fund-raiser, he immediately volunteered the question whether that was because Greenberg was Jewish. Greenberg's presence played into the increasing black disaffection with Jews that resulted in large measure from Jewish resistance to affirmative action because of quotas' negative connotations for Jews. That affected LDF's consideration of filing amicus briefs in the *DeFunis* affirmative action case, where there was fear that endorsing quotas, disliked by the organization's Jewish constituents, would be a retreat from the organization's "color-blind" position. Greenberg later said his leaving LDF had nothing to do with the split between blacks and Jews, "a schism he views as serious and as largely the fault of Jewish groups" like the Anti-Defamation League.[80]

Legal staffs and cooperating attorneys.   NAACP-LDF conflict may have been reinforced by the widely held perception that LDF was the more effective litigator. As the two organizations increasingly went their separate ways, LDF had trained lawyer resources and NAACP did not. Lawyers who had contact with both organizations draw distinctions between the two. To them, the LDF, with "competent legal staff" local lawyers could call to "get substantive responses" was "more adept at affiliating local lawyers and involving them in litigation." The NAACP, by contrast, not only was thought to have done less well than the LDF in obtaining cooperating attorneys but, despite having formed the Special Contribution Fund "has not had a credible legal department since the Steel/Carter matter," with the situation so bad in the mid-1980s that "the NAACP can't function in the legal community." LDF benefited from continuity of leadership while lack of such continuity, particularly in the NAACP general counsel's position, both hindered the NAACP and impeded relations between the two organizations. Robert Carter and Jack Greenberg are said to have carried on an "undeclared war" concerning the extent to which the two legal arms would cooperate.[81] According to Carter, the LDF later adopted rules for the processing of litigation in which LDF "would no longer accept requests for legal assistance directly from NAACP units" but only "from lawyers or individuals themselves." This produced the result, at least in Carter's view, of "plac[ing] the lawyer and the litigation outside the NAACP orbit, once the Legal Defense Fund enters the picture."[82]

Nathaniel Jones, less headstrong than Carter and without Carter's personal investment in the situation, is said to have buried the hatchet with Greenberg , and each had high respect for the other. This new atmosphere even led to some joint NAACP-LDF participation in litigation, as in the Detroit school case. Some suggest that Thomas Atkins, like Jones, had "cordial, cooperating relations" with the LDF, with no "policy differences over civil rights." Others, however, feel he was not as inclined to encourage cooperative working relations as Jones had been, but this may have been because when Atkins became General Counsel, the friction over the LDF's continuing use of the NAACP name was heating up, particularly among his superiors.

Despite friction at top organizational levels, the lawsuit, while "affecting the larger picture," operationally was of "no concern" to the two organizations' staff attorneys working on cases, and the LDF even argued an NAACP case in the Supreme Court, although one relating to an issue also of concern to LDF.[83] During this time, relations between the two organizations "were never impaired at all at the staff level." The conflict "would get much 'air time' but didn't affect my work," noted a senior LDF staff attorney during the 1970s. Boundary matters are "very important" because "they define what the organization is," he added, and "organizational jealousies" may at times have limited "farming out" a case to an attorney who had worked with the other organization, but such matters were of "extraordinarily little importance" from the perspective of the staff person. LDF staff attorneys' belief "that no one on NAACP legal staff is working on the case," which was handled by outside counsel, or that, if they were, were "only doing what they have to do," helped keep working relations between the two organizations' legal staffs from atrophying.

Competition over finances. Foremost among the NAACP's specific complaints against the LDF was the issue most explicitly related to resource mobilization—that contributors actually gave money to the LDF when they intended to give it to the NAACP, so that the LDF had drawn off funds that otherwise would have gone to the NAACP. Evidence that money may really be at the heart of the NAACP-LDF interorganizational friction, at least as an accompaniment to jealousy, was the centrality of money to earlier friction between the NAACP and other entities. But were contributors actually confused? It is highly unlikely that, whatever the general public's ignorance, major contributors were so unsophisticated as not to know the difference between the two organizations, or, if concerned about tax deductibility, not to know of the existence of the NAACP's Special Contribution Fund. Yet some confusion by contributors of small amounts is not unlikely. Although NAACP branches could have made the difference clear to any of their own members who did not already know, dealings between NAACP branches and the LDF on litigation matters, including help they have received on local matters from the LDF, raise questions as to whether and how forcefully local officials would make the distinction.

The confusion claim, while not frivolous, would not likely have been pressed so hard but for the NAACP's long-standing tenuous financial situation, including its much smaller litigation budget. The increase in funds for civil rights litigation during the late 1960s and early 1970s may have reduced LDF-NAACP financial rivalry but certainly did not eliminate it. More NAACP funds might not have meant parity with LDF but would have brought at least an increase in the number of the NAACP's staff attorneys. Moreover, the NAACP's financial difficulties may have been an independent reason for LDF's keeping its distance from the NAACP, as, matters of tax-deductibility aside, LDF avoided use of its funds to alleviate the NAACP's financial situation and to fund NAACP's nonlitigation programs.

Especially significant in this regard was the severe financial threat from the million dollar-plus damage judgment in the Port Gibson boycott case. Until the Supreme Court removed that threat, LDF might have wanted to avoid reestablishing ties with the NAACP for fear of having its much fuller coffers opened to satisfy the judgment. However, as LDF expected the judgment against the NAACP to be overturned on appeal, LDF leaders' reasons for not rejoining the NAACP were likely not dependent on the presence of that case. And after the Supreme Court ruling, when NAACP Executive Director Benjamin Hooks called for the LDF to return to the fold, there was still no detectable movement of the organizations toward each other; indeed, this was the period in which the NAACP's lawsuit against the LDF was filed.

The concern instead was broader than the financial threat. If LDF had rejoined NAACP, said one LDF staff lawyer, "we would be swallowed up by their problems; it would be five years when LDF would not have its own existence" and LDF would have been seriously damaged. Ironically, in 1994, when the NAACP's financial difficulties and other internal controversies became public knowledge, the LDF was reported to have given some thought to deleting "NAACP" from its name in order to avoid confusion with the NAACP; LDF staff claimed that the NAACP's association with some radical individuals had led to a decline in contributions to LDF. Of course, the issue of confusion was the very one that had been at the core of the NAACP's earlier lawsuit, but the shoe was now on the other foot.

Competition for cases: racial credit revisited.   Competition over cases, closely related to racial credit, occurred just as it did over funds, and was heightened when NAACP branches dealt directly with the LDF instead of bringing cases to the NAACP's legal staff. (The lawsuit against LDF dissuaded people in the NAACP's branches from coming to LDF with cases and the national NAACP discouraged the branches from doing so, although some continued the practice.) Friction between the NAACP and the LDF over litigation not suprisingly developed soon after the formal separation of the two groups, as Marshall's designated successor, Greenberg, and the NAACP's Carter were without bonds of close communion, friendship, values, or a sense of needing each other. Carter, after being sent to work at the NAACP, "with one secretary and no mandate,"[84] found himself, as general counsel, with functions "limited to that of a house counsel, concerned solely with organizational issues and problems."[85] Had Carter been willing to resign himself to being solely NAACP's in-house counsel, leaving litigation solely in LDF hands, one source of friction would have been removed, but he was not a person to sit still and "decided to build up his own office." In developing the NAACP's own litigation capacity, he produced NAACP-LDF competition over litigation itself.

Carter's handling of the fundamental challenges to the organization itself were, in the words of a long-time LDF attorney, "instrumental in putting Carter back in business" as he "built up a new power base and office to rival the Inc. Fund."[86] By winning the legal fight in *NAACP v. Alabama*, with its threat to the entire NAACP organization, Carter "thereby gained a new lease on life as a leading civil rights advocate"; indeed, he "was able to set up a comparatively autonomous office, not unlike what Marshall did earlier with the Inc. Fund."[87] Carter also pursued some cases he had brought with him from LDF, notably the racial redistricting case of *Gomillion v. Lightfoot*. As Carter reestablished litigating capacity at the NAACP, Greenberg perceived that Carter was making efforts to get NAACP branches to funnel cases to himself rather than to the LDF, that is, to change the situation described by an LDF attorney who suggested that the LDF provided greater representation to the NAACP branches than did the NAACP itself. Although Carter was, according to Greenberg, unable to "undercut our sources of money," he "did try to dry up our sources of litigation."[88]

Carter's and Greenberg's divergent approaches also to litigation helped limit the extent to which the Inc. Fund and NAACP legal arms would cooperate. "The militants and insurgents swung somewhat to Carter" as he hired "younger militants, to fight cases that the Inc. Fund office didn't want to argue partly because the Inc. Fund's board was pretty conservative, too." For example, Carter undertook cases with the Congress of Racial Equality (CORE)'s Norwalk, Connecticut, chapter and became involved in the Ocean Hill-Brownsville dispute over community control of education. Because this litigation "looked awfully risky to NAACP fund managers and white sources of income," it also caused problems for Carter within the NAACP: Roy Wilkins's "monolithic structures and dominance of the [civil rights] Movement" are said to have been "threatened" by Carter's less traditional view of litigation.[89]

Conflict between the LDF and NAACP over particular cases, although not frequent, also provided evidence of bases of interorganizational friction. One type of conflict occurred when LDF pursued litigation that the NAACP did not feel was in the interest of at least some of its constituents or was "contrary to the Association's position or wishes."[90] The presence in the NAACP's constituency of graduates of historically black institutions required less than a mechanical position on desegregation in higher education, so when the *Adams* case was "filed without notice or consultation with the NAACP or its Board of Directors," NAACP leaders felt that the organization had been put in "the untenable position of appearing to foster the elimination of black colleges."[91]

Another type of conflict came when NAACP officials, particularly at the state level, and LDF officials disagreed as to who would represent someone and what specific actions would be taken in cases, as in the defense of Tommy Lee Hines, a mentally retarded black defendant. After NAACP had provided the initial defense, LDF took over the case on a claim of inadequate assistance of counsel and on some of the grounds earlier argued by NAACP. Of particular irritation to the NAACP is that, in one observer's words, "Despite Greenberg's disclaimer, LDF knew NAACP had provided assistance" and "didn't follow the amenities in such situations in changing counsel." LDF's involvement "had nothing to do with the NAACP," said a staff person, although the person contacted "anguished" over the case's NAACP angle, and the NAACP "overreacted" because when someone is trying to set aside a criminal conviction, "everyone has been charged with incompetence of counsel."

Competition for recognition is related to this conflict. It rankled NAACP officials when reporters referred to NAACP cases, such as the Supreme Court's Dayton and Columbus school desegregation decisions, as "NAACP Legal Defense Fund cases" and interviewed Jack Greenberg about them; Greenberg didn't explicitly claim NAACP cases as his own but didn't correct others' inaccurate attributions. More serious, and closely tied to competition for racial credit, was the LDF's handling of the twentieth and twenty-fifth anniversaries of *Brown v. Board of Education.* This created more nearly permanent rancor. The LDF's 1974 celebration of the twentieth anniversary of that landmark ruling particularly struck sparks at NAACP because Greenberg and other whites, not black lawyers, were "center stage." Nor did they turn away from the spotlight with respect to major cases in which the LDF, when it had been much more completely a part of NAACP, played a part; to make matters worse, the NAACP asserted, LDF downplayed the role of black lawyers in the process that led to *Brown*. Here one sees the symbolic aspect of organizational maintenance, apart from any perceived or real effects on financial income: an organization has a "sense of self" and LDF's taking credit for what the NAACP believed was rightly its own activity was disconcerting at least, and depressing as well.

The 1974 events prompted Robert Carter, by then a federal judge in New York City, to depart from keeping "in-house" his unhappiness with Greenberg to whom he sent a blazing letter, with copies directed to a variety of high-ranking NAACP and LDF officials of both races. In it he raised two principal issues. One concerned the LDF's celebration of the anniversary: "What was . . . unforgivable about the Fund's celebration was that it afforded no black personage, lawyer or non-lawyer, a featured role in the commemoration of an historical happening 20 years ago, which . . . had been conceived, planned and executed by blacks."[92] In Carter's view, the exclusion of blacks, coupled with the inclusion of whites like former Attorney General Elliot Richardson, who had expressed views on busing "which I had presumed were directly antithetical to the Fund's position," illustrated both "the Fund's confusion since Thurgood Marshall's departure as to what the real priorities must be in the ongoing struggle of blacks for equal rights" and "the Fund's insensitivity on critical occasions to the sensibilities of the black community—the constituency it seeks to serve."

Carter also deplored what he believed was Greenberg's depiction of a major role for white lawyers and a diminished role for black lawyers in the school desegregation litigation. He protested the impression created by articles commemorating the May 17 anniversary and LDF's celebration "that the strategy, planning, and preparation that went into *Brown* and all that occurred since have been culled from the brains of white lawyers." On a more personal note, he charged LDF with attempting to "rewrite the history of the legal activity culminating in *Brown* by studiously omitting my own participation." Although white lawyers had contributed to planning and preparation for *Brown*,

Carter said, "they, you included, played a peripheral and at best a secondary role." Indeed, Carter asserted, "Black brain power was the predominant force that fathered and nurtured *Brown* to fruition in 1954." Whatever Carter's personal pique at Greenberg's succeeding Marshall at the LDF, Carter's comment that "it is critically important for blacks of present and future generations to know that it was blacks who spearheaded the social engineering that resulted in the *Brown* decision" reflects far more—the issue of racial credit, which is whether African-Americans are to be understood, or are to understand themselves, as dependent beneficiaries of other people's skill and purpose, or whether they are to be credited with some active role in creating the terms of their own existence in the polity and society.

15

The Complexity of Civil
Rights Litigation

Some Concluding Thoughts

In the picture of litigation by interest groups some hold, those organizations not only were successful most of the time but also had little difficulty in moving from their initial plans to their ultimate goals. In this view, a litigating interest group chose a major goal, then chose the cases that moved it, inexorably, to that goal, and proceeded apace—perhaps incrementally, as called for by its plan, but uninterruptedly nonetheless. Certainly that picture was widely held with respect to civil rights litigation, thought to be the quintessential "planned litigation for social change." Not only did the activities of the NAACP Legal Defense Fund resulting in *Brown v. Board of Education* provide the model of "planned litigation" adopted by other groups, but portrayals of the LDF's path to *Brown* were the principal basis for, or reinforcement of, the view that planned litigation followed a linear path.

Evidence existed to contradict the picture of relatively unhindered straight-line development. However, it was either overlooked or was not the focus of those interested in telling the story that needed to be told of how interest groups operated in the judicial arena. In looking back at that and other heroic cases, where one knew the (positive) outcome, it was easy to overlook and diminish difficulties along the road. Statements of leading actors in the drama, such as Charles Houston, made it still easier, for those actors talked of strategy involving straight-line activity. This talk of strategy, coupled with hindsight, made it easy to miss the fact that if these actors and their organizations were following a line, it was serpentine, and that statements about strategy had been made for reasons of organizational maintenance— to keep members believing in the cause and contributors donating resources so that movement toward the goal could occur; one could say there were strategic reasons behind the statements of having a strategy.

The picture presented here should make clear that the earlier picture is certainly neither accurate nor complete. How did we come upon a changed picture? *Brown* was a landmark decision and was crucial as a symbol of racial equality and of inclusiveness in the polity. However, perhaps the fact that it was not successfully implemented— at least not by the judiciary from which it came—was one reason for the change of focus. Another reason, part of the argument in these pages, was that many other groups adopted the "*Brown* model," a fact which itself changed the environment in which litigating interest groups operated—and made it more difficult for any of them. When we stress the complexity of litigating interest groups' situation and their difficulty of achieving their goals except a bit at a time, we should also keep in mind that this change in perspective may be a result not of the external events we believe we are (correctly) interpreting but of the deficiencies of the analytical perspectives that social science can bring to bear on such observation. As a political scientist has recently observed about efforts to make sense of the presidency, in words applicable to the study of litigating interest groups: "As a profession, we are more rich in data than in theory, and the weight of our information, because we lack system transformation rules, leads us to emphasize the ideas of incremental change, of complexity, and of environmental constraint. We tend to be less a dismal science than a myopic one."[1]

That interest group litigation is complex has certainly been true for the period beginning in the mid-1960s and extending to the present. But—and it is an important "but"—it was also certainly true for the period before, and leading up to, *Brown*. The NAACP's activities from 1925 through the immediately pre-*Brown* law school cases so indicate, as do the many examples that can be adduced from earlier periods to illustrate, or match with, current phenomena. That one can engage in such matching should indicate that planned litigation encountered the same difficulties in the first part of the twentieth century (and earlier) as in the second half.

The crucial point, however, and the basic argument of this book, is that civil rights litigation undertaken by, or with the assistance of, interest groups beginning in the mid-1960s should be seen as complex—indeed, extremely complex, problematic, and contingent both on external events and intraorganizational developments. Such litigation is particularly contingent on obtaining the greater resources which are needed, making mobilization of law particularly contingent on mobilization of resources. For example, being able to finance cases and thus control them, rather than being limited to amicus participation in a case, is highly dependent on availability of resources. And control is crucial to implementing strategy effectively.

Much interest group-related litigation has not been part of an overall plan. Even where such a plan has existed, and there are instances of such planned litigation campaigns—organizations find themselves having to pursue certain cases even when the cases don't optimally fit the plan, perhaps to satisfy important clienteles. Or they find themselves without sufficient cases to provide the proper sequence of legal issues or to provide the Supreme Court with a choice of "good" cases to which to grant review. Organizations at times must rely on lawyers whom it would rather not use, because there are not sufficient numbers of cooperating attorneys socialized to the organizations' values. In addition, lawyers not affiliated with the organization, and even some who have been privy to the organization's strategy, will not stay in harness and act on their own, so that some cases arrive at appellate courts before the organization wishes them to, "out of sequence."

The success of an overall strategy, and of the particular cases that compose it, are, moreover, highly dependent on the dynamics both of the individual cases and of the set of cases in a targeted area of law. Making the dynamics more complex yet are the rulings of the Supreme Court; because much complex litigation is lengthy, the Supreme Court's doctrine does not remain stable during that extended time. Lawyers thus face changes in the law—even significant changes in direction. This helps explain why much interest group-related civil rights litigation is responsive; lawyers find they must respond to external events, instead of planning and then proceeding on a clear track. Responsive litigation, or a reactive posture, is also necessary when the executive branch poses obstacles to the civil rights organizations' goals.

Without further multiplying the types of difficulties which can occur, there is little question that many difficulties do occur. This leads us to speak of the problematic nature of "planned" litigation; indeed, it may be more accurate to assume that planned litigation cannot happen—that the bumblebee cannot fly—than to assume it can. At times it does fly, without crash-landing, but it flies with great difficulty: getting the awkward creature off the ground almost requires JATO (jet-assisted takeoff) and, once it is airborne, its tribulations are far from over. Some argue that those who used litigation and believed it could work believed, inappropriately, in the myth of rights; they also argue that litigation should have been used in ways that would more directly assist political mobilization. Those arguments are important, but, for most of the litigators discussed here, the arguments in a way were beside the point: they had chosen a path and they were going to stick to it, even if one wants to speak negatively of the inertia involved and of the difficulty of changing their perspectives and habits. Such a situation forces us to attempt to understand the difficulties— the atmospheric complexity—that civil rights litigators were able to overcome.

There are a variety of dimensions to the complexity that characterizes civil rights litigation. Some dimensions are aspects of the environment in which the litigation takes place, including the political environment; some are internal to the litigation itself; and some deal with organizational elements—intraorganizational matters and the multiplicity of organizations noted above. Ironically, the greater complexity of civil rights litigation begins at the point of the greatest legislative civil rights victories (the 1964 Civil Rights Act and the 1965 Voting Rights Act)—legislative actions that were necessary because implementation of judicial victories, including *Brown,* had produced little concrete action. The new statutes themselves contributed to the complexity by forcing civil rights organizations to expand their attention from constitutional issues to statutory and administrative elements of the law. The judicial elaboration of statutory elements and the increasing complexity of the constitutional questions facing the judiciary— with the "simple" question of the invalidity of segregation by statute now decided—were major elements in the increased complexity civil rights litigators faced as they attempted to deal with lengthy, evidence-heavy northern urban school desegregation cases containing major remedy components, or with class action employment discrimination suits.

Such litigation—indeed, all the work of the civil rights litigating organizations—required greater resources. Resource mobilization, a way of translating support from the environment into the wherewithal to carry out litigation campaigns, would have become more difficult even if civil rights were still focused only on African-Americans, but now others, following their lead, had joined the arena. Associations seeking to litigate on behalf of elements of the Latino community, women, the handicapped, and, later, gays and lesbians, found that while the resource pie did expand somewhat as more actors entered the arena, competition increased for resources available from key sources like the Ford Foundation. Thus resource mobilization, which had always plagued those seeking to assert the rights of minorities, continued to be a severe problem.

Although the Ford Foundation was a sturdy source of support, the larger political environment was not stable nor did it remain favorable. From high levels of legislative support and of supportive public opinion in the mid-1960s, matters turned down, not up. Political leaders distanced themselves from civil rights concerns. They provide less rhetorical support—and even rhetorical opposition, for example, to "forced busing" and the "reverse discrimination" of affirmative action "quotas," even when, for the time being, they continued quiet implementation of basic civil rights laws. However, after increased cooperation between government and civil rights groups during the Carter administration, the political environment abruptly turned not benignly neutral but distinctly hostile, including government efforts to undo earlier victories, for example, by upsetting consent decrees reached only with considerable difficulty. Here, illustrating the importance of a responsive posture in civil rights litigation, the only "planned" litigation campaign civil rights groups could carry out was one of responding to the administration's efforts, hardly the sort of litigation for social change in which they wished to engage.

Part of the increasing conservatism of the political environment was the change in direction in the Supreme Court once considered to be more liberal than the public. This shift began slowly under President

Nixon's appointments but accelerated when the nominees of Presidents Reagan and Bush made the Court more conservative than the public opinion.[2] At first the Nixon Court was more liberal than had been expected and the Court issued important pro-civil rights rulings such as *Swann* in school desegregation, and *Griggs* in employment discrimination. However, by the mid-1970s the Court, requiring proof of intentional discrimination, reflected the more conservative public opinion that had earlier been reflected in its criminal procedure rulings. While civil rights litigators' work was made more complicated by having to deal with the new Court rather than the Court of the late 1960s (and even of the early 1970s), some state courts began to provide some relief from the Supreme Court's conservatism, as they used their own state constitutions to provide greater protection for civil rights than the Supreme Court provided under the U.S. Constitution. At the same time, however, this made the litigators' choices more complex still. Here we can see the drag of inertia, as lawyers quite accustomed to turning almost reflexively to the federal courts had to weigh the possibility of obtaining better outcomes—even if local or regional in scope rather than the preferred national precedent—from state courts. In some instances, where the Supreme Court had cut off federal causes of action, most obviously in the case of attacks on inadequate funding for public education, the lawyers had no choice, but even then some time elapsed before they adjusted to the need to pursue their goals in state rather than federal courts.

An important aspect of the changed and changing environment for civil rights litigators was the proliferation in the numbers of groups dealing with any single interest—like that of African-Americans— and a like interest in the number of interests represented, as "civil rights" now meant the rights not only of African-Americans but also of Latinos, women, the handicapped, and gays and lesbians. Moreover, "Latino" was not a monolithic grouping, and one saw ideological division within the African-American community about goals to be sought and about the usefulness of litigation itself, as well as internecine warfare between the NAACP and the NAACP Legal Defense Fund. And this was only the proliferation on the "liberal" side; one saw as well a resurgence of conservative litigating groups—the conservative public interest law firms. This proliferation would have affected any single group's litigating activity even if there had been no direct group-to-group interaction, because of competition for scarce resources. However, the groups did interact, but explicitly, as when they joined in submitting amicus briefs, and implicitly, as when a group, in its decision-making process, would look at what the others were doing, so that each could benefit from comparative advantage.

This picture of the many facets of complexity of civil rights litigators' environment, of difficulties and contingencies, is important to keep in mind when we read or hear about "a case brought by the NAACP Legal Defense Fund" (or ACLU). It is necessary not to forget the nonlinear course the litigation has likely taken prior to that point of public recognition. Having said that, it is also important to realize that far from all is random or serendipitous; the problematic and contingent are aspects of what is at times attempted as purposive activity—indeed, activity into which people put much directed effort. That is, they are problematic and contingent *in relation to* a plan. Much litigation in the area of civil rights and civil rights is single-case, "we'll take what comes in the door" litigation, responsive to immediate concerns. However, planned litigation does exist. Sets of cases *are* undertaken as part of an overall plan; even if not all the details are plotted in advance, litigators have certain goals in mind, a rough plan exists and efforts are made to follow it. Those involved in a litigation campaign choose the area of law on which they will concentrate; the LDF's efforts in employment discrimination (Title VII) and capital punishment litigation are illustrative. Furthermore, the litigators select particular targets within the subject area, and then bring cases many—indeed, most—of which are chosen according to understood criteria. That there are cases "extraneous" to the plan or which do not fit the criteria well should not distract us from the underlying core of planned activity.

Thus, there is planned litigation for social change; there are litigation campaigns which are not only recognizable after the fact as people speak of strategy, but which exist ex ante in the minds of those who carry them out after having sat around a table or communicated by other means about how the litigation should go forward. Less civil rights litigation is carried out according to grand, or large, strategy than the story of *Brown v. Board of Education* would lead us to believe. But, although there is ex post facto talk of strategy when strategy did not precede action, planned litigation is carried out—perhaps more significant because of the greater complexity of the environment in which it takes place and of the environment itself.

One might ask how far the pictures presented here reaches. In social science terms, what is its generalizability? Although the focus has been on civil rights—primarily for African-Americans—the picture seems directly generalizable to litigation on behalf of other racial and ethnic minorities, not least because they adopted the "*Brown* model," both organizationally and as a strategic plan. It also is generalizable to civil liberties litigation; indeed, the American Civil Liberties Union, the preeminent litigator on behalf of civil liberties, figures prominently in these pages; and other groups—some working with the ACLU—seeking religious freedom also have been a source of examples. The picture's "umbrella" would also seem to fit interest groups litigating on behalf of conservative ideological causes as well as those litigating for "liberal" ones. This is particularly so as contemporary conservative public interest law firms drew on the NAACP Legal Defense Fund model for their operations; however, as noted earlier, conservative groups are likely to participate in litigation on an amicus basis than are liberal groups, which are more likely to use amicus participation as a means of spreading resources.

This is a study of litigating interest groups, but it has broader applicability to other interest group activity. Organizations other than those that litigate have had to make the same sorts of choices litigators made. For example, organizations engaging in direct action had to decide on the areas on which to concentrate—public accommodations, bus boycotts, or voter registration—and, in the equivalent of the choice of cases to pursue in the courts, on communities in which to carry out those activities. Likewise, such organizations needed to acquire resources—a continuing difficulty, and an increased one if they were in competition with litigators seeking resources. Like litigators, advocates of direct action also had to be concerned about relations with the government. And they certainly had to be concerned about interorganizational relations—with other direct action organizations and with those focusing on litigation.

NOTES

TABLE OF CASES

INDEX

Preface: Can the Bumblebee Fly?

1. The principal recounting is Richard Kluger, *Simple Justice: The History of Brown v. Board of Education and Black America's Struggle for Equality* (New York, 1976).

2. Mark V. Tushnet, *The NAACP's Legal Strategy Against Segregated Education, 1925–1950* (Chapel Hill, N.C., 1987), p. 144.

3. Ibid., p. 197.

4. See Stephen L. Wasby, Anthony A. D'Amato, and Rosemary Metrailer, chap. 8, "The Civil Rights Movement: Public Accommodations and Protest," *Desegregation From Brown to Alexander: An Exploration of Supreme Court Strategies* (Carbondale, Ill., 1977), pp. 265–375.

5. Frank J. Sorauf, *The Wall of Separation: The Constitutional Politics of Church and State* (Princeton, N.J., 1978); Karen O'Connor, *Women's Organizations' Use of the Courts* (Lexington, Mass., 1980); Robert H. Mnookin, *In the Interest of Children: Advocacy, Law Reform, and Public Policy* (New York, 1985); Susan M. Olson, *Clients and Lawyers: Securing the Rights of Disabled Persons* (Westport, Conn., 1984); and Neal Milner, "The Right to Refuse Treatment: Four Case Studies of Legal Mobilization," *Law & Society Review* 21 (1987): 447–85.

6. Susan M. Olson, "Interest-Group Litigation in Federal District Court: Beyond the Political Disadvantage Theory," *Journal of Politics* 52 (1990): 855, 877.

7. See David Truman, *The Governmental Process* (New York, 1951), which, with sixteen chapters, has only one chapter on interest groups and the judiciary; and Jack L. Walker, Jr., *Mobilizing Interest Groups in America: Patrons, Professions, and Social Movements* (Ann Arbor, Mich., 1971). For texts, see, for example, Jeffrey Berry, *Lobbying for the People* (Boston, 1989), and Kay Schlozman and John Tierney, *Organized Interests and American Democracy* (New York, 1985).

8. O'Connor, *Women's Organizations' Use of the Courts*, p. 16.

9. On mobilization of law, see, inter alia, Donald J. Black, "The Mobilization of Law," *Journal of Legal Studies* 2 (1973): 125–50; Neal Milner, "The Dilemmas of Legal Mobilization: Ideologies and Strategies of Mental Patient Litigation Groups," *Law & Policy* 8 (1986): 105–29.

10. The effectiveness of judicial rulings is discussed at length in Gerald N. Rosenberg, *The Hollow Hope: Can Courts Bring About Social Change* (Chicago, 1991).

11. For powerful allegorical statements on the present state of race relations, see Derrick Bell, *Faces at the Bottom of the Well: The Permanence of Racism* (New York, 1992), as well as Bell's earlier *And We Are Not Saved: The Elusive Quest for Racial Justice* (New York, 1987).

12. Gerald David Jaynes and Robin M. Williams, Jr., *A Common Destiny: Blacks and American Society* (Washington, 1989), pp. 3, 4 (emphasis in original).

13. See Peter Clark and James Q. Wilson, "Incentive Systems: A Theory of Organization," *Administrative Science Quarterly* 6 (1961): 129–166; Robert S. Salisbury, "An Exchange Theory of Interest Groups," *Midwest Journal of Political Science* 13 (1969): 1–32; Mancur Olson, *The Logic of Collective Action*, rev. ed. (New York, 1971); and Terry Moe, *The Organization of Interests: Incentives and Internal Dynamics of Political Interest Groups* (Chicago, 1980).

14. Kobylka reported that ACLU Legal Director Melvin Wulf "could not remember any specific obscenity litigation with which he was involved during his time as Legal Director, despite the fact that he argued two such cases before the Supreme Court and signed onto nine amicus briefs presented there." Joseph F. Kobylka, "Organizational Response to a Changing Litigation Environment: The Effect of *Miller v. California* (1983) on the Litigation Patterns of Libertarian Organizations," paper presented to Midwest Political Science Association, 1984, p. 32 n.

15. B. Fischoff and R. Beyth-Maron, "Failure Has Many Fathers," *Policy Sciences* 7 (1976): 391.

16. Stuart A. Scheingold, *The Politics of Rights: Lawyers, Public Policy, and Political Change* (New Haven, Conn., 1974), p. 109.

17. Casper has shown that from 1957 through 1966 interest groups played a major role in civil rights litigation (more so in earlier school desegregation litigation than in public accommodations cases), and in some loyalty-security cases, but a far smaller role in criminal justice topics, the loyalty-security area generally, and reapportionment. Jonathan D. Casper, *Lawyers Before the Warren Court: Civil Liberties and Civil Rights, 1956–66* (Urbana, Ill., 1972), p. 6.

1. The Political Environment of Civil Rights Litigation

1. For the most recent thorough examination of such matters and more, see Jaynes and Williams, *A Common Destiny*.

2. Tushnet, *The NAACP's Legal Strategy*, p. 158.

3. See Mary L. Dudziak, "Desegregation as a Cold War Imperative," *Stanford Law Review* 41 (1988): 61–120.

4. Quoted in Esther B. Fein, "Liberals Accused of Lagging on Civil Rights," *New York Times*, Aug. 18, 1987, p. 47.

5. Johnson, "Blacks and Whites Are Found 'Worlds Apart'," *New York Times*, Jan. 12, 1989, p. A18.

6. Jaynes and Williams, *A Common Destiny*, p. 151.

7. Adam Fairclough, *To Redeem the Soul of America: The Southern Christian Leadership Conference and Martin Luther King, Jr.* (Athens, Ga., 1987), p. 287.

8. Ibid.

9. Ibid., p. 322.

10. Jaynes and Williams, *A Common Destiny,* p. 117.

11. Ibid., p. 11.

12. An earlier study had shown little change in the attitudes toward busing of individuals who were directly affected by it. See Douglas S. Gatlin, Micheal S. Giles, and Everett F. Cataldo, "Policy Support Within a Target Group: The Case of School Desegregation," *American Political Science Review* 72 (1978): 985–95.

13. Paul Burstein, *Discrimination, Jobs, and Politics: The Struggle for Equal Employment Opportunity in the United States Since the New Deal* (Chicago, 1985), pp. 52, 58, 62, 66, 83, 86, 90. For a discussion of the findings of this study in relation to other studies of the relationship between public opinion and congressional action, see Anne N. Costain and Steven Majstorovic, "Congress, Social Movements and Public Opinion: Multiple Origins of Women's Rights Legislation," *Political Research Quarterly* 47 (1994): 111–35. This article reported that the relationship between public opinion and legislative action is bilateral; public opinion serves to initiate policy change at some times, while at other times the social movement or Congress itself initiates policy, and public opinion responds.

14. Mary Alice Nye, "Changing Support for Civil Rights: House and Senate Voting, 1963–1988," *Political Research Quarterly* 46 (1993): 820.

15. For an explanation of types of quotas, advocating proportional ones, but not disproportional quotas even as a remedial measure, see Ronald J. Fiscus, *The Constitutional Logic of Affirmative Action,* ed. Stephen L. Wasby (Durham, N.C., 1991).

16. Stephen L. Carter, "The Candidate," *The New Republic,* Feb. 22, 1993: 33.

17. Abigail Thernstrom, "'Voting Rights' Trap," *The New Republic,* Sept. 2, 1985: 22.

18. David L. Kirp, "Multitudes in the Valley of Indecision: The Desegregation of San Francisco's Schools," *Limits of Justice: The Courts' Role in School Desegregation,* eds. Howard Kalodner and James Fishman (Cambridge, Mass., 1978), p. 424.

19. Derrick Bell, Letter to *Civil Liberties Review* 3 (no. 1, April/May 1976), p. 7. Also see Bell, "Serving Two Masters," and response to it, in *Limits of Justice,* pp. 569–620.

20. For a recent excellent discussion of whether blacks' interests can be represented in Congress only by blacks or also by whites, see Carol M. Swain, *Black Faces, Black Interests: The Representation of African Americans in Congress* (Cambridge, Mass., 1993). An earlier example of the dispute is a reapportionment case, *Wright v. Rockefeller,* 376 U.S. 52 (1969), in which blacks were found on both sides of the case.

21. See Kenneth L. Karst, *Belonging to America: Equal Citizenship and the Constitution* (New Haven, Conn., 1989), for an exposition of the inclusion argument.

22. See, for example, B. Dan Wood and Richard W. Waterman, "The Dynamics of Political Control of the Bureaucracy," *American Political Science Review* 85 (1991): 801–28, particularly 806–7; and Wood, "Does Politics Make a Difference at

the EEOC?" *American Journal of Political Science* 34 (1990): 503–30. For some recent studies of the presidency and civil rights, see "Symposium on the American Presidency and Civil Rights Policy," *Policy Studies Journal* 21 (1993): 508–98, with articles on, inter alia, the president's role in the public's civil rights agenda, presidential communications in the making of civil rights policy, presidential leadership, and implementation of housing policy.

23. Walter F. Murphy and Joseph Tanenhaus, "Publicity, Public Opinion, and the Court," *Northwestern University Law Review* 84 (1990): 1018.

24. Matthew Holden, Jr., "President, Congress, and Racial Stratification," Ernest T. Patterson Memorial Lecture, University of Colorado, Oct. 11, 1984, p. 52.

25. Gary Orfield, *The Reconstruction of Southern Education: The Schools and the 1964 Civil Rights Act* (New York, 1969), and Beryl A. Radin, *Implementation, Change, and the Federal Bureaucracy: School Desegregation Policy in HEW, 1964–1968* (New York, 1977).

26. Holden, "President, Congress, and Racial Stratification," pp. 47–48.

27. For a more complete examination of Little Rock, see Tony Freyer, *The Little Rock Crisis: A Constitutional Interpretation* (Westport, Conn., 1984).

28. Holden, "President, Congress, and Racial Stratification," pp. 34, 35. The reference is to Fred Greenstein, *The Hidden Hand Presidency: Eisenhower as Leader* (New York, 1982).

29. Michal R. Belknap, *Federal Law and Southern Order: Racial Violence and Constitutional Conflict in the Post-Brown South* (Athens, Ga., 1987), pp. 27, 32.

30. See Bruce Miroff, *Pragmatic Illusion: The Presidential Politics of John F. Kennedy* (New York, 1976).

31. Norman C. Amaker, *Civil Rights and the Reagan Administration* (Washington, 1988), p. 21.

32. The suggestion that the Nixon administration would be called "benign" with respect to anything, and civil rights in particular, once would have led me and many others to scoff, but the Reagan administration prompted a different perspective. There is a substantial difference between moderate or lukewarm support and outright hostility—the difference between Assistant Attorneys General for Civil Rights Jerris Leonard and William Bradford Reynolds.

33. Rosemary Salomone, "Judicial Oversight of Agency Enforcement: The *Adams* and *WEAL* Litigation," *Justice and School Systems: The Role of the Courts in Education Litigation*, ed. Barbara Flicker (Philadelphia, 1990), p. 139.

34. Drew S. Days III, "Turning Back the Clock: The Reagan Administration and Civil Rights," *Harvard Civil Rights/Civil Liberties Law Review* 19 (1984): 313.

35. See Howard Ball and Kathanne Greene, "The Reagan Justice Department," *The Reagan Administration and Civil Rights*, ed. Tinsley E. Yarbrough (New York, 1985), p. 10.

36. Amaker, *Civil Rights*, p. 110; Charles S. Bullock III and Katharine Inglis

Butler, "Voting Rights," *The Reagan Administration and Human Rights*, ed. Tinsley E. Yarbrough, p. 34; and Charles Lamb, "Education and Housing," Ibid., pp. 82–105.

37. See Allen E. Schoenberger, "Desegregation in Chicago: Settlement Without a Trial," *Justice and School Systems*, ed. Barbara Flicker, pp. 307–62. And see Gary Orfield, *Turning Back the Clock: The Reagan-Bush Retreat from Civil Rights in Higher Education* (Lanham, Md., 1992).

38. NAACP Legal Defense Fund Director-Counsel Julius Chambers, after arguing *Thornburg v. Gingles* (1986) in the Supreme Court against the administration, said it was the first case in which he had ever been in court with the Solicitor General as "the enemy." Quoted in Lincoln Caplan, *The Tenth Justice: The Solicitor General and the Rule of Law* (New York, 1988), p. 242.

39. Lewis M. Steel, "Nine Men in Black Who Think White," *New York Times Magazine*, Oct. 13, 1968, pp. 56, 117.

40. Leroy D. Clark, "The Lawyer in the Civil Rights Movement—Catalytic Agent or Counter-Revolutionary?" *University of Kansas Law Review* 19 (1971): 464.

41. *Heart of Atlanta Motel v. United States*, 371 U.S. 241 (1964), and *Katzenbach v. McClung*, 379 U.S. 294 (1964) (Civil Rights Act); *Cox v. Louisiana*, 379 U.S. 536 and 379 U.S. 559 (1965), and *Adderly v. Florida*, 385 U.S. 39 (1966) (picketing at jails and courthouses).

42. *United States v. Jefferson County Board of Education*, 372 F.2d 386 (5th Cir. 1966) and 380 F.2d 385 (5th Cir. 1967).

43. *Wright v. City of Emporia*, 407 U.S. 451 (1972), and *United States v. Scotland Neck Board of Education*, 407 U.S. 484 (1972) (separation of city from countywide school district); *Norwood v. Harrison*, 413 U.S. 455 (1973) (loan of textbooks to private schools that discriminated); *Gilmore v. City of Montgomery*, 417 U.S. 556 (1974) (private school's exclusive use of public park).

44. *Dayton Board of Education v. Brinkman*, 433 U.S. 406 (1977); *Columbus Board of Education v. Penick*, 443 U.S. 449 (1979); *Dayton Board of Education*, 443 U.S. 526 (1979).

45. *Crawford v. Board of Education of City of Los Angeles*, 458 U.S. 527 (1982); *Washington v. Seattle School District No. 1*, 458 U.S. 457 (1982).

46. *Albemarle Paper v. Moody*, 422 U.S. 405 (1975); *Franks v. Bowman Transportation Co.*, 424 U.S. 747 (1976).

47. *United Steelworkers v. Weber*, 443 U.S. 193 (1979); *Fullilove v. Klutznick*, 448 U.S. 448 (1980). For a thorough discussion of legislative failure to identify adequately the justifications for minority set-aside programs and an argument that courts, in upholding such programs, have done not much better, see Drew S. Days III, "Fullilove," *Yale Law Journal* 96 (1987): 453–85. Later rulings on set-asides pointed in somewhat different directions. In *City of Richmond v. J.A. Croson Co.*, 488 U.S. 469 (1989), the Court indicated that government units (like city councils) other than Congress wishing to adopt MBE set-asides would have to show

discrimination in their past practices. However, *Metro Broadcasting v. Federal Communication Commission*, 110 S.Ct. 2997 (1990), sustained congressional and FCC policies designed to increase the number of radio and television stations owned by minorities by facilitating their acquiring stations, because the government had a valid interest in diversity in broadcasting and had not placed impermissible burdens on nonminorities.

48. *Firefighters v. Stotts*, 467 U.S. 561 (1984); *Wygant v. Jackson Board of Education*, 476 U.S. 267 (1986); *United States v. Paradise*, 480 U.S. 149 (1980).

49. *Local 28, Sheet Metal Workers v. E.E.O.C.*, 478 U.S. 421 (1986); *Local 93, International Association of Firefighters v. City of Cleveland*, 478 U.S. 501 (1986).

50. This period was one of two in the twentieth century during which our nation experienced such agreement in the domestic policy sphere. The other was from 1937, when Franklin D. Roosevelt won the war with the Supreme Court, to the time of our involvement in World War II. Others have suggested that the period from the 1964 presidential election through the Supreme Court's Detroit school desegregation ruling in 1974 is one of two periods in our nation's history when there was a will to deal with the racial issue.

51. For a listing of instances where Congress has reversed the Court on civil rights, see *Patterson v. McLean Credit Union*, 491 U.S. 164, 200 n.9 (1989) (Justice Brennan).

52. In addition to reversing *Wards Cove v. Atonio*, 490 U.S. 642 (1989), the Civil Rights Act of 1991 also reversed *Lorance v. AT&T Technologies*, 490 U.S. 900 (1989) (holding that the statute of limitations for complaints about new seniority systems ran from the adoption of the system, not from when an employee recognized that he or she was adversely affected); *Patterson v. McLean Credit Union*, 491 U.S. 164 (1989) (racial harassment); *Price Waterhouse v. Hopkins*, 490 U.S. 228 (1989) (standard to be used in gender discrimination cases); *Martin v. Wilks*, 490 U.S. 755 (1989) (consent decrees); *West Virginia Hospitals v. Casey*, 111 S.Ct. 1138 (1991) (fees for expert witnesses); and *E.E.O.C. v. Arabian American Oil*, 111 S.Ct. 1277 (1989) (limiting extraterritorial effect of Title VII).

53. Drawn from Philip Cooper, interview with Louis Jacobs, The Ohio State University School of Law, April 4, 1985.

54. Karen O'Connor, "The Amicus Curiae Role of the U.S. Solicitor General in Supreme Court Litigation," *Judicature* 66 (1983): 260.

55. Joel F. Handler, with George Edgar and Russell F. Settle, "Public Interest Law and Employment Discrimination," *Public Interest Law: An Economic and Institutional Analysis*, ed. Burton A. Weisbrod, with Joel F. Handler and Neil K. Komesar (Berkeley, Calif., 1976), p. 273; Joel F. Handler, *Social Movements and the Legal System* (New York, 1978), p. 197.

56. Paul D. Kamenar of the Washington Legal Foundation, quoted in John A. Jenkins, "Mr. Power," *New York Times*, Oct. 12, 1986, pp. 18–19, 89 ff., at p. 96.

57. Comments made by W. Bradford Reynolds at the conference on Legal History of the South, Feb. 5, 1983 (author's notes).

58. Lee Epstein and Joseph F. Kobylka, *The Supreme Court & Legal Change: Abortion & The Death Penalty* (Chapel Hill, N.C., 1992), p. 98.

59. Gregory A. Caldeira, "Litigation, Lobbying, and the Voting Rights Bar," *Controversies in Minority Voting: The Voting Rights Act in Perspective* (Washington, 1992), p. 236.

60. Stephen C. Halpern, "Title VI and Racial Discrimination in Educational Institutions: The Unenforced and Unenforceable Civil Rights Provision," paper presented to American Political Science Association, 1980, p. 10.

61. Handler, *Social Movements and the Legal System*, p. 23 n.20.

62. Timothy J. O'Neill, *Bakke & The Politics of Equality: Friends & Foes in the Classroom of Litigation* (Middletown, Conn., 1985), pp. 182, 186.

63. Handler, *Social Movements and the Legal System*, p. 147.

64. Robert Belton, "Employment Discrimination Litigation," *Public Interest Practice and Fee Awards* (1980), pp. 235, 292–93.

65. A 4–3 Supreme Court majority, finding no violation of First Amendment rights of association, upheld the administration. *Cornelius v. NAACP Legal Defense and Educational Fund*, 473 U.S. 788 (1985). Also excluded from the fund drive were the Lawyers' Committee for Civil Rights Under Law, Puerto Rican Legal Defense Fund, Sierra Club Legal Defense Fund, Federally Employed Women Legal Defense and Education Fund, Indian Law Resource Center, and Natural Resources Defense Council.

66. See Taylor Branch, *Parting the Waters: America in the King Years, 1954–63* (New York, 1988), particularly pp. 850–51.

67. "Eighty-four trustees of the Lawyers' Committee [for Civil Rights Under Law] said they were 'compelled for the first time ever' to oppose a nominee for federal office." Lawyers' Committee, Annual Report 1985–1986, p. 7.

68. However, the situation is not one in which the activity stemmed from growth of government bureaucracy; the interest groups developed and acted largely without government stimulus. See Walker, *Mobilizing Interest Groups in America*, pp. ix-x.

2. The Supreme Count's Impact on Litigation

1. Aryeh Neier, *Only Judgment: The Limits of Litigation in Social Change* (Middletown, Conn., 1982), pp. 181–82.

2. Michael Combs, "The Federal Judiciary and Northern School Desegregation: Law, Politics, and Judicial Management," paper presented to American Political Science Association, 1984, p. 28. See also Combs, "The Policy-Making Role of

the Courts of Appeals in Northern School Desegregation: Ambiguity and Judicial Policy-Making," *Western Political Quarterly* 35 (1982): 362.

3. Paul Gewirtz, "Remedies and Resistance," *Yale Law Journal* 92 (1983): 664; Combs, "The Federal Judiciary," 362.

4. See Epstein and Kobylka, *The Supreme Court & Legal Change*, p. 132, on LDF attorneys treating the *Furman v. Georgia* (1972) majority as more unified than it was.

5. *Rudolph v. Alabama*, 375 U.S. 889 (1963); *Snider v. Cunningham*, 375 U.S. 889 (1963).

6. Epstein and Kobylka, *The Supreme Court & Legal Change*, p. 43.

7. Michael Meltsner, *Cruel and Unusual: The Supreme Court and Capital Punishment* (New York, 1973), pp. 28–29. Justice Thomas recently called attention to this account in suggesting that the Court itself has effects on interest group litigation campaigns. *Graham v. Collins*, 113 S.Ct. 892, 905 (1993).

8. Gerhard Casper and Richard A. Posner, *The Workload of the Supreme Court* (Chicago, 1976), p. 31.

9. Wasby et al, *Desegregation from Brown to Alexander*, pp. 230–35.

10. Clement E. Vose, *Caucasians Only: The Supreme Court, The NAACP, and the Restrictive Covenant Cases* (Berkeley, Calif., 1959), pp. 156–57.

11. Milner, "The Right to Refuse Treatment," p. 469. See *Rogers v. Okin*, 478 F.Supp. 1342 (D.Mass. 1979), vacated sub nom. *Mills v. Rogers*, 457 U.S. 291 (1982).

12. Jack Greenberg, "Litigation for Social Change: Methods, Limits and Role in Democracy" (New York, 1973), pp. 12–13. See also Neier, pp. 39–45, and Charles A. Lofgren, *The Plessy Case: A Legal–Historical Interpretation* (New York, 1987), p. 149.

13. Richard C. Cortner, *A Mob Intent on Death: The NAACP and the Arkansas Riot Cases* (Middletown, Conn., 1988), pp. 143–45.

14. C. Michael Abbott and Donald C. Peters, "*Fuentes v. Shevin*: A Narrative of Federal Test Litigation in the Legal Services Program," *Iowa Law Review* 57 (1972): 994–95; Susan E. Lawrence, *The Poor in Court: The Legal Services Program and Supreme Court Decision Making* (Princeton, N.J., 1990), p. 53.

15. Greenberg, "Litigation for Social Change," p. 38.

16. Dennis Mihelich and Ashton Wesley Welch, "Omaha, Nebraska: Positive Planning for Peaceful Integration," *Community Politics and Educational Change: Ten School Systems Under Court Order*, eds. Charles V. Willie and Susan L. Greenblatt (New York, 1981), p. 273.

17. "ACLU Chief Won't Battle With Court," *Chicago Tribune*, Jan. 23, 1978.

18. Bruce J. Ennis, "In the Courts," *Civil Liberties*, no. 335 (Nov. 1980), pp. 1, 6; "New Appointments Would Strengthen Court's Hostility to Civil Liberties" (Interview with Burt Neuborne), *Civil Liberties*, no. 352 (Winter 1985): 4.

19. Joseph F. Kobylka, *The Politics of Obscenity: Group Litigation in a Time of Legal Change* (Westport, Conn., 1981), p. 128.

20. Peter Irons, *The New Deal Lawyers* (Princeton, N.J., 1982), p. 186.

21. "The *Brown* ruling itself was more symbolic than substantive." Derrick Bell, "The Dialectics of School Desegregation," *Alabama Law Review* 32 (1981): 293.

22. Robert L. Carter, "The Warren Court and Desegregation," *Michigan Law Review* 67 (1968): 247.

23. Joseph Kobylka, "A Court-Created Context for Group Litigation: Libertarian Groups and Obscenity," *Journal of Politics* 49 (1987): 1065.

24. The case was *Gonzalez v. Warden*, 21 N.Y.2d 18, 286 N.Y.S.2d 240, 233 N.E.2d 269 (1967), cert. denied, 390 U.S. 973 (1969). Greenberg, "Litigation for Social Change," p. 34.

25. Robert Cover, *Justice Accused: Antislavery and the Judicial Process* (New Haven, Conn., 1975), p. 166; Neier, *Only Judgment*, p. 45.

26. Michael Danielson, *The Politics of Exclusion* (New York, 1976), p. 180.

27. Ibid., p. 183.

28. Clement E. Vose, *Constitutional Change: Amendment Politics and Supreme Court Litigation Since 1900* (Lexington, Mass., 1972), p. 321.

29. Ruth B. Cowan, "Women's Rights Through Litigation: An Examination of the American Civil Liberties Union Rights Project, 1971–1976," *Columbia Human Rights Law Review* 8 (1976): 381.

30. Irons, *The New Deal Lawyers*, p. 37.

31. Ray Wolters, *The Burden of Brown: Thirty Years of School Desegregation* (Knoxville, Tenn., 1984), p. 222.

32. Vose, *Constitutional Change*, p. 305.

33. Peter H. Irons, *Justice At War: The Story of the Japanese-American Internment Cases* (New York, 1983), p. 313.

34. Epstein and Kobylka, *The Supreme Court & Legal Change*, pp. 343–44 n. 30.

35. Kobylka, *The Politics of Obscenity*, pp. xiii-xiv.

36. Although Koblyka, in his trilogy of responses, does not mention the impact of the Court's rulings on organizations' framing of legal arguments, it is prominent in his discussion. For example, "the legal context narrowed the arguments . . . of libertarian groups." "A Court-Created Contest," p. 1074.

37. Cover, *Justice Accused*, p. 296 n.4.

38. *Louisville, New Orleans and Texas Railway Co. v. Mississippi*, 133 U.S. 587 (1890).

39. Lofgren, *The Plessy Case*, pp. 33–36, 40.

40. Henry C. Lauerman, "The Role of the Judiciary in the Desegregation of the Winston-Salem/Forsyth County Schools, 1968–1975," *Limits of Justice*, p. 505.

41. Tushnet, *The NAACP's Legal Strategy*, p. 135.

42. See ibid., chap. 7.

43. Neal Milner, "Legal Mobilization and the Emergence of Mental Health Rights Litigation: A Comparative Analysis," paper presented to Law & Society Association, 1983, p. 36. See also Milner, "The Right to Refuse Treatment," p. 469.

44. Phillip J. Cooper, *Hard Judicial Choices: Federal District Court Judges and State and Local Officials* (New York, 1988), p. 258.

45. Tinsley E. Yarbrough, "The Alabama Prison Litigation," *Justice System Journal* 9 (1984), 285.

46. Irons, *The New Deal Lawyers*, p. 259.

47. See George R. Osborne, "The NAACP in Alabama," *The Third Branch of Government: Cases in Constitutional Politics*, eds. C. Herman Pritchett and Alan F. Westin (New York), pp. 149–203. See also Walter F. Murphy, "The South Counter-attacks: The Anti-NAACP Laws," *Western Political Quarterly* 12 (1959): 371–90.

48. *Bates v. City of Little Rock*, 361 U.S. 516 (1960); *Shelton v. Tucker*, 364 U.S. 479 (1960); *Louisiana ex rel. Gremillion v. NAACP*, 366 U.S. 293 (1961); *Gibson v. Florida Legislative Investigation*, 372 U.S. 539 (1963).

49. *Adams v. Richardson*, 351 F.Supp. 636 (D.D.C. 1972), 356 F.Supp. 91 (D.D.C. 1973), 480 F.2d 1159 (D.C.Cir. 1973). For history of the early part of the litigation, see Q. Whitfield Ayres, "Racial Desegregation in Higher Education," *Implementation of Civil Rights Policy*, eds. Charles Bullock III and Charles Lamb (Monterey, Calif., 1984), pp. 118–48, particularly p. 133; John Egerton, "*Adams v. Richardson*: Can Separate Be Equal?" *Change* (Winter 1974–1975): 29–36. The most thorough treatment is Rosemary Salomone, "Judicial Oversight of Agency Enforcement," pp. 111–81.

50. Ibid., pp. 128, 135.

51. *Adams v. Bell/Women's Equity Action League v. Bell*, 743 F.2d 42 (D.C.Cir. 1984); *Adams v. Bennett*, 675 F.Supp. 668 (D.D.C. 1987).

52. *WEAL v. Cavazos*, 906 F.2d 742, 744 (D.C.Cir. 1990). See also *WEAL v. Cavazos*, 879 F.2d 880 (D.C.C. 1989).

53. Later the requirement was satisfied by a developer unsuccessful in getting a zoning change, only to have the Supreme Court rule against the civil rights claim on the merits. *Village of Arlington Heights v. Metropolitan Development Corp.* 429 U.S. 252 (1976).

54. *Gulf Oil Co. v. Bernard*, 452 U.S. 89, 99–100, 100 n. 1 (1981).

55. Rosemary C. Salomone, *Equal Education Under Law: Legal Rights and Federal Policy in the Post-Brown Era* (New York, 1986), pp. 116–17.

56. Theodore Eisenberg and Sheri Lynn Johnson, "The Effects of Intent: Do We Know How Legal Standards Work," *Cornell Law Review* 76 (1991): 1151–97. The effect of Supreme Court employment discrimination rulings, particularly individual decisions, on litigation has been questioned. For such an effect to exist, there should have been "a shift in the composition of cases, with cases brought under novel legal doctrines comprising an increasingly important share of all cases filed"—but such changes are not apparent. John J. Donohue and Peter Siegelman, "The Changing Nature of Employment Discrimination Litigation," Working Paper no. 9021 (Chicago: American Bar Foundation, 1990), pp. 10–11.

57. Gabe Kaimowitz, "Response" (to Parker, "The Impact of *City of Mobile v. Bolden . . .*"), *The Right to Vote* (New York, 1981), p. 160. To win *City of Mobile* on remand required the expenditure of "tens of thousands of dollars, at least 6,000 hours of lawyers' time, 800 hours of paralegals' time, 4,400 hours of expert witnesses and research assistants' time, and eleven and a half days of trial." NAACP Legal Defense Fund, Annual Report, 1981/1982, p. 10.

58. Steve Suitts, "Blacks in the Political Arithmetic After Mobile: A Case Study of North Carolina," *The Right to Vote*, p. 47;. Frank R. Parker, "The Impact of *City of Mobile v. Bolden* and Strategies and Legal Arguments for Voting Rights Cases in its Wake," *The Right to Vote*, pp. 111–12.

59. Karen O'Connor and Lee Epstein, "Bridging the Gap Between Congress and the Supreme Court: Interest Groups and the Erosion of the American Rule Governing Awards of Attorneys' Fees," *Western Political Quarterly* 38 (1985): 241.

60. *New York Gaslight Club v. Carey*, 447 U.S. 54 (1980); *Webb v. Board of Education of Dyer County*, 471 U.S. 324 (1985); *North Carolina Department of Transportation v. Crest Street Community Council*, 479 U.S. 6 (1986).

61. *Christiansburg Garment Co. v. E.E.O.C.*, 434 U.S. 412 (1978).

62. *Hensley v. Eckerhart*, 461 U.S. 424, 442 (1983).

3. The Major Litigators and the Proliferation of Groups

1. Jack L. Walker, "The Origins and Maintenance of Interest Groups in America," *American Political Science Review* 77 (1983): 404.

2. Lee Epstein, *Conservatives in Court* (Knoxville, 1985), p. 129. The Women's Law Fund's obtaining Ford Foundation support, for example, caused "a temporary setback to the fund-raising efforts of the newly established WEAL Fund." Salomone, "Judicial Oversight," p. 133.

3. Salomone, *Equal Education Under Law*, p. 116.

4. Gary Orfield, *Must We Bus?: Segregated Schools and National Policy*, (Washington, 1978), p. 361.

5. Jeffrey A. Raffel, *The Politics of School Desegregation: The Metropolitan Remedy in Delaware* (Philadelphia, 1980), pp.3–4.

6. J. Michael Ross and William M. Berg, "*I Respectfully Disagree with the Judge's Order: The Boston School Desegregation Controversy*" (Washington, 1981), pp. 370, 372.

7. Kirp, "Multitudes in the Valley of Indecision," p. 447.

8. O'Connor, *Women's Organizations' Use of the Courts*, p. 145.

9. Karen O'Connor and Lee Epstein, "The Importance of Interest Group Involvement in Employment Discrimination Litigation," *Howard Law Journal* 25 (1982): 714. See also the statement that "the dense litigation field—the large number of other group actors and the diversity of their obscenity interests and goals—worked

against the execution of a coherent litigation strategy." *The Politics of Obscenity,* p. 33. For a portrayal of the range of groups in obscenity litigation, see Kobylka, "The Groups and their Interests," chap. 2 in *The Politics of Obscenity,* pp. 23–66.

10. Salomone, "Judicial Oversight of Agency Enforcement," p. 133.

11. Kobylka, *The Politics of Obscenity,* p. 162.

12. Charles S. Bullock III and Joseph Stewart Jr., "New Programs in 'Old' Agencies: Lessons in Organizational Change from the Office for Civil Rights," *Administration and Society* 15 (1984): 393.

13. Halpern, "Title VI and Racial Discrimination in Educational Institutions," p. 26.

14. Burton A. Weisbrod, "Conceptual Perspective on the Public Interest: An Economic Analysis," *Public Interest Law,* eds. Weisbrod et al., p. 22.

15. " 'Someone Has to Translate Rights Into Realities': Conversation with Civil Rights Lawyer Jack Greenberg," *Civil Liberties Review* 2 (Fall 1975): 123 [Greenberg interview].

16. James L. Gibson and Richard D. Bingham, *Civil Liberties and Nazis: The Skokie Free-Speech Controversy* (New York, 1985), particularly pp. 98–104.

17. Handler, with Edgar and Settle, "Public Interest Law and Employment Discrimination," p. 280.

18. Handler, *Social Movements,* p. 26; Joel F. Handler, Ellen Jane Hollingsworth, and Howard S. Erlanger, *Lawyers and the Pursuit of Legal Rights* (New York, 1978), p. 70.

19. Vine Deloria, Jr., and Clifford M. Lytle, *American Indians, American Justice* (Austin, Texas, 1983), p. 157.

20. Houck, "With Charity for All," *Yale Law Journal* 93 (1984): 1480, 1487, 1495.

21. See Epstein, pp. 45–56, 63–67, 80–88, 89–104.

22. Ibid., pp. 120–29.

23. Handler, *Social Movements,* p. 28. See also Ralph Nader and William B. Schultz, "Public Interest Law With Bread on Table," *ABA Journal* 71 (Feb. 1985): 74–77.

24. Susan Vaughn, "Social Change, and Success, Too," *ABA Journal* 71 (June 1985): 77.

25. At the 1986 annual meeting, when the former director for policy and planning, who had been laid off, demanded both financial accounting and accurate membership figures, his demands were rejected.

26. It may be greater within the NAACP. With racial separation long closing avenues to African-Americans with leadership talent and aspirations, they were left with organizations dealing with African-Americans themselves. With such a very narrow field of play, internal disagreement was likely to be severe, with opposition either suppressed so that the organization can present a common front to the enemy or particularly bitter when it does break out.

27. Lewis Steel, interview by Richard Kluger, March 3, 1971. Brown v. Board of

Education Collection, Manuscript Division, Sterling Library, Yale University, Box 5, Folder 92.

28. Kenneth B. Clark, "The N.A.A.C.P.: Verging on Irrelevance," *New York Times*, July 14, 1983, p. 23. In early 1992, in a fight over whether officers' terms should be limited, the board voted not to reelect the organization's president, and some board members (including a former general counsel) were not returned to office.

29. Gail Diane Cox, "MALDEF Chief Survives Ouster Effort by Board," *National Law Journal*, March 16, 1987, p. 10.

30. Tushnet, *The NAACP's Legal Strategy*, p. 31.

31. NAACP, "The Legal Program and the NAACP Dilemma," *The Crisis* 86 (no. 6, June/July, 1979): 222.

32. Vose, *Constitutional Change*, pp. 317–18.

33. For example, because national NAACP officials in New York did not want to continue the dispute brought about by W.E.B. Du Bois's challenge to the organization's goals, "local NAACP groups were freer for a time to choose targets without fear of censure." Branch, *Parting the Waters*, pp. 52–53.

34. Holden, *The Politics of the Black "Nation,"* p. 61.

35. Branch, *Parting the Waters*, pp. 813–15.

36. NAACP, "The Legal Program and the NAACP Dilemma," p. 221.

37. Tushnet, *The NAACP's Legal Strategy*, p. 100.

38. Ibid., p. 135.

39. Robert B. McKay, *Nine for Equality Under Law: Civil Rights Litigation* (New York, 1977), pp. 11–12.

40. Greenberg interview, pp. 109, 112.

41. O'Neill, *Bakke & The Politics of Equality*, pp. 88–89.

42. McKay, *Nine for Equality Under Law*, p. 12.

43. Ibid., p. 16.

44. Lawyers' Committee, Annual Report 1981–1982, p. 13. For an account of voting rights activity by the project's long-time director, see Frank R. Parker, *Black Votes Count: Political Empowerment in Mississippi after 1965* (Chapel Hill, N.C., 1990).

45. Irons, *Justice at War*, p. 108.

46. Robert L. Rabin, "Lawyers for Social Change: Perspectives on Public Interest Law," *Stanford Law Review* 28 (1976): 212–13; "The ACLU on the Rebound," *National Law Journal*, Sept. 5, 1983, p. 9.

47. Nadine Strossen, "Regulating Racism Speech on Campus: A Modest Proposal?" *Duke Law Journal* 1990: 487 n. 11.

48. William A. Donohue, *The Politics of the American Civil Liberties Union* (New Brunswick, N.J., 1985), p. 20; Irons, *Justice at War*, p. 110.

49. Irons, *Justice at War*, pp. 130, 132, 168, 169.

50. Rabin, "Lawyers for Social Change," p. 212. See generally Samuel Walker, *In Defense of American Liberties: A History of the ACLU* (New York, 1990).

51. The National Prison Project has more autonomy than the others because it "raises its own funds, national 'respects' its work, and the Project has a separate Steering Committee." Karen O'Connor and Lee Epstein, "In Defense of Rights: The National Prison Project of the ACLU," paper presented to Law & Society Association, 1984, p. 5.

52. Danielson, *The Politics of Exclusion*, p. 174.

53. Geoffrey Shields and Sanford Spector, "Opening Up the Suburbs: Notes on a Movement for Social Change," *Yale Review of Law and Social Action* 2 (1972): 311.

54. McKay, *Nine for Equality*, p. 28.

55. Rev. Martin Luther King, Jr., had a "defense consortium" in the tax case Alabama brought against him. "They made an unwieldy team" because not all the lawyers knew each other, and "they came from five different firms in four different cities in three different states." Branch, *Parting the Waters*, p. 287.

56. Cover, *Justice Accused*, p. 161.

57. Stephen B. Goldberg, "Justice Thurgood Marshall: The Long-Distance Runner," *ABA Journal* 78 (1992): 73 (quoting Jack Greenberg).

58. Karen O'Connor, "Litigation as a Form of Political Activity: How Women's Groups Have Used the Courts," paper presented to American Political Science Association, 1977, p. 25.

59. O'Connor, *Women's Organizations' Use of the Courts*, p. 123; Cowan, "Women's Rights Through Litigation," p. 386.

60. John Leubsdorf, "Completing the Desegregation Remedy," *Boston University Law Review* 57 (1977): 94.

61. Olson, *Clients and Lawyers*, pp. 103–104.

62. The seminar was even accredited for mandatory CLE (continuing legal education credit). See *Crisis* (NAACP), May 1988, pp. 19–20.

63. Shields and Spector, "Opening Up the Suburbs," p. 311.

64. Meltsner, *Cruel and Unusual*, p. 114.

65. Vose, *Caucasians Only*, p. 58. See also Genna Rae McNeil, *Groundwork: Charles Hamilton Houston and the Struggle for Civil Rights* (Philadelphia, 1983), pp. 177–78, 180.

66. Meltsner, *Cruel and Unusual*, pp. 144, 238–39.

67. Mark A. Chesler, Joseph Sanders, and Debra S. Kalmuss, *Social Science in Court: Mobilizing Experts in the School Desegregation Cases* (Madison, Wis., 1988), p. 207.

68. E.R. Shipp, "Foes of Abortion Examine Strategies of N.A.A.C.P." *New York Times*, April 2, 1984; Epstein and Kobylka, *The Supreme Court Legal Change*, p. 248.

4. Resources

1. Chesler et al., *Social Science in Court*, p. 4; Neal Milner, "Legal Mobilization," pp. 49, 52.

2. Epstein, *Conservatives in Court*, p. 122.

3. Robert L. Zangrando, *The NAACP Crusade Against Lynching* (Philadelphia, 1980), p. 18.

4. Neier, *Only Judgment*, p. 235.

5. For an instance of the need for further funds to pay lawyers' fees, see Cortner, *A Mob Intent on Death*, pp. 132–33, 160–61.

6. Sorauf, *The Wall of Separation*, p. 42.

7. Orfield, *Must We Bus?* p. 375.

8. Meltsner, *Cruel and Unusual*, p. 35.

9. Allen Redlich, "Who Will Litigate Constitutional Issues for the Poor?" *Hastings Constitutional Law Quarterly* 19 (1992): 775–76.

10. Rabin, "Lawyers for Social Change," 217.

11. Handler, *Social Movements and the Legal System*, p. 31.

12. Governments "tap the local exchequer in order to hire expensive legal talent to prepare their defense" in exclusionary zoning cases. Danielson, *The Politics of Exclusion* (New York, 1976), p. 164.

13. Rabin, "Lawyers for Social Change," 223.

14. Zangrando, *NAACP Crusade Against Lynching*, p. 29.

15. Herbert Hill, "The Equal Employment Opportunity Commission: Twenty Years Later," *Journal of Intergroup Relations* 11 (1983): 47.

16. Danielson, *Politics of Exclusion*, p. 166.

17. Sorauf, *Wall of Separation*, p. 42; O'Connor, "Litigation as a Form of Political Activity," p. 22.

18. Meltsner, *Cruel and Unusual*, p. 109.

19. Orfield, *Must We Bus?* pp. 367–68.

20. Bruce J. Ennis, "A.C.L.U.: 60 Years of Volunteer Lawyering," *American Bar Association Journal* 66 (1980): 1082; Kobylka, *The Politics of Obscenity*, p. 80; Sorauf, *Wall of Separation*, pp. 87–88.

21. Sorauf, *Wall of Separation*, pp. 87–88.

22. Cooper, *Hard Judicial Choices*, pp. 144, 247; Phillip J. Cooper, interview with Louis Jacobs, Columbus, Ohio, April 4, 1985.

23. Bernard Grofman, "An Expert Witness Perspective on Continuing and Emerging Voting Rights Controversies," *Stetson Law Review* 21 (1992): 785 n. 9.

24. Cooper, interview with Louis Jacobs, April 4, 1985.

25. Cortner, *A Mob Intent on Death*, pp. 25, 96.

26. McNeil, *Groundwork*, p. 142.

27. Kluger, *Simple Justice*, p. 256; Meltsner, *Cruel and Unusual*, p. 6.

28. Orfield, *Must We Bus?* p. 366.

29. For the various sources of the LDF's budget in the mid-1970s, see Greenberg interview, p. 115.

30. Lawyers' Committee, Annual Report, 1982–1983, pp. 36ff.

31. Lawyers' Committee, Fifteenth Anniversary Report, p. 12; Lawyers' Committee, Annual Report 1982–1983, p. v; Lawyers' Committee, Annual Report, 1984–1985, p. v. The 1982–1983 report (Appendix A, p. 3) noted that "the market value of these services [donated attorney time] has totaled in the millions of dollars during the past decade and a half."

32. Ennis, "A.C.L.U.," p. 1082.

33. Vose, *Constitutional Change*, p. 337.

34. Norman C. Amaker, "De Facto Leadership and the Civil Rights Movement: Perspective on the Problems and Role of Activists and Lawyers in Legal and Social Change," *Southern University Law Review* 6 (1980): 248 n.76.

35. Karen O'Connor and Lee Epstein, "Beyond Legislative Lobbying: Women's Rights Groups and the Supreme Court," *Judicature* 67 (1983): 139.

36. Tushnet, *The NAACP's Legal Strategy*, p. 110.

37. Randall W. Bland, *Private Pressure on Public Law: The Legal Career of Justice Thurgood Marshall* (Port Washington, N.Y., 1973), p. 23.

38. Orfield, *Must We Bus?* p. 381; Epstein and Kobylka, *The Supreme Court & Legal Change*, p. 95.

39. Casper, *Lawyers Before the Warren Court*, p. 141.

40. Epstein, *Conservatives in Court*, pp. 73–74, 124, 140.

41. Cover, *Justice Accused*, p. 213.

42. Handler et al., *Lawyers and the Pursuit of Legal Rights*, p. 27.

43. Casper, *Lawyers Before the Warren Court*, pp. 72–74.

44. Gregory J. Rathjen, "Lawyers and the Appellate Choice: An Analysis of Factors Affecting the Decision to Appeal," *American Politics Quarterly* 6 (1978): 391.

45. Scheingold, *The Politics of Rights*, p. 170.

46. Ibid., pp. 177–78. See also Robert Lefcourt, ed., *Law Against the People: Essays to Demystify Law Order and the Courts* (New York, 1971).

47. Scheingold, *Politics of Rights*, p. 183.

48. Tushnet, *The NAACP's Legal Strategy*, p. 162.

49. Austin Sarat, comments, panel on cause lawyering, Law & Society Association meetings, May 28, 1993.

50. Gregory J. Rathjen, "Lawyers and the Appeals Process: An Analysis of the Appellate Lawyer's Beliefs, Attitudes and Values," paper presented to Midwest Political Science Association, 1975; Rathjen, "Lawyers and the Appeals Process: A Profile," *Federal Bar Journal* 34 (1975): 21–41.

51. Carrie Menkel-Meadow and Robert G. Meadow, "Resource Allocation in Legal Services," *Law and Policy Quarterly* 5 (1983): 251.

52. Chesler et al., *Social Science in Court*, p. 51 n. 37; Grofman, "An Expert Wit-

ness Perspective," p. 803 n. 103. The case is *Garza v. County of Los Angeles Board of Supervisors*, 756 F.Supp. 1298 (C.D.Cal. 1990).

53. See Chesler et al., *Social Science in Court*, p. 62; see also pp. 69–71, 79–80.

54. Marc Galanter, *Competing Equalities: Law and the Backward Classes in India* (Berkeley, Calif., 1984), pp. 358–59 and 358 n. 6.

55. Armand Derfner, "The Implications of the *City of Mobile* Case for Extension of the Voting Rights Act," *The Right to Vote*, p. 212.

56. Rules like these which the government enforces may result from a bureaucratic mindset, but the ideology of agency officials determines against whom the rule is enforced, making it of little surprise that liberal organizations faced questions from the IRS during Republican administrations. Thanks to Davis Bobrow for the basis for these ideas.

57. Barbara Ann Banoff and Benjamin S. DuVal, Jr., "The Class Action as a Mechanism for Enforcing the Federal Securities Law: An Empirical Study of the Burdens Imposed," *Wayne Law Review* 31 (1984): 65.

58. Handler, with Edgar and Settle, "Public Interest Law and Employment Discrimination," p. 275.

59. Lawyers' Committee, Annual Report, 1984–1985, p. ii.

60. Mark V. Tushnet, "Organizing Civil Rights Litigation: The NAACP's Experience," *Ambivalent Legacy: A Legal History of the South*, eds. David J. Bodenhamer and James W. Ely, Jr. (Jackson, Miss., 1984), p. 178.

61. Irons, *Justice At War*, p. 110.

62. Ibid.

63. Handler, *Social Movements*, pp. 8–9, 144.

64. Rabin, "Lawyers for Social Change," 220 n. 45.

65. Scheingold, *Politics of Rights*, p. 195.

66. Handler, *Social Movements*, p. 110.

67. Greenberg interview, p. 123.

68. See Walker, *Mobilizing Interest Groups in America*, pp. 397–98.

69. Lawyers' Committee, Annual Report, 1980–1981, p. 21.

70. Deloria and Lytle, *American Indians, American Justice*, pp. 157, 159 (concerning Native American Rights Fund, which received almost three-fifths of its 1979 budget from federal government sources).

71. Scheppele and Walker, "The Litigation Strategies of Interest Groups," p. 173. See also p. 177: "the larger the proportion of a group's budget that is supplied by private patrons . . . , the less important litigation is to a group."

72. O'Connor, "Litigation as a Form of Political Activity," p. 22.

73. McKay, *Nine for Equality Under Law*, pp. 8–9; Scheppele and Walker, "The Litigation Strategies of Interest Groups," pp. 165, 169.

74. McKay, *Nine for Equality*, pp. 8–9.

75. Ibid., pp. 9–10.

76. Donohue, *The Politics of the American Civil Liberties Union*, p. 19. Some of those moneys technically went to Columbia University for a seminar on sex discrimination litigation taught by Ruth Bader Ginsburg (later a judge on the District of Columbia Circuit and Supreme Court justice), but its intended use was clear. See Cowan, "Women's Rights Through Litigation," 385.

77. Ford's dominance as a contributor in this area was clear. "Between 1972 and 1974, Ford grants accounted for at least one-half of the $7 billion in foundation grants disbursed for women's programs"; Ford made twice as many grants for such projects in 1976 as any other foundation. Salomone, *Equal Education Under Law*, p. 116.

78. McKay, *Nine for Equality*, pp. 12, 35.

79. See, e.g., Meltsner, *Cruel and Unusual*, pp. 238–39.

80. Zangrando, p. 82; pp. 82, 96–97. It is unclear from historians' accounts how much was actually received; $26,500 had been provided when the $100,000 was voted.

81. Joel Handler, comment at panel on "Litigation as a Strategy for Social Change" Law & Society Association, June 8, 1984.

82. Arthur Kinoy, *Rights on Trial: The Odyssey of a People's Lawyer* (Cambridge, Mass., 1983), p. 264.

83. McKay, *Nine for Equality*, p. 12.

84. Meltsner, *Cruel and Unusual*, pp. 73, 109.

85. O'Connor and Epstein, "Bridging the Gap," p. 241. Because some funds received in one year are attributable to cases from previous years, they do not provide an indication of current legal activity.

86. *Missouri v. Jenkins by Agyei*, 491 U.S. 274, 277, 283 n. 6 (1989). The lawyer had paid over $100,000 in interest on those loans, and had borrowed money to pay the interest. The Supreme Court approved enhancement of the fees for delay in receiving payment.

87. But see *Parker v. Lewis*, 670 F.2d 249 (D.C. Cir. 1981), the District of Columbia Circuit ordered immediate payment of the undisputed portion of an attorney's fee claims in an employment discrimination case and an expedited appeal because lawyers who were not to be paid promptly might not take civil rights cases. Because the government defendant could not be required to pay interest on the award, delay would compound the hurt, they said. And see *Jenkins v. Missouri*, 593 F.Supp. 1485, 1506 (W.D.Mo. 1984).

88. Because of delay in payment, the fees were calculated at the rates current at the time of the claim. The appellate court then remanded this ruling for redetermination. See *Gaines v. Dougherty County Board of Education*, 775 F.2d 1565 (11th Cir. 1985).

89. *Gautreaux v. Chicago Housing Authority*, 690 F.2d 601 (7th Cir. 1982).

90. *City of Burlington v. Dague*, 112 S.Ct. 2638, 2648 (1992) (enhancement of an attorney's fee award to reflect attorneys being retained on a contingent fee basis,

where they assumed the risk of receiving no payment if the client lost). Blackmun dissented, citing amicus briefs by the Lawyers' Committee for Civil Rights Under Law and the Alabama Employment Lawyers Association.

91. See Frances Kahn Zemans, "Fee Shifting and the Implementation of Public Policy," *Law & Contemporary Problems* 47 (1984): 203.

92. Bryant G. Garth, "Privatization and the New Formalism: Making the Courts Safe for Bureaucracy," *Law & Social Inquiry* 13 (1988): 166–68.

93. Theodore Eisenberg and Stewart Schwab, "The Reality of Constitutional Tort Litigation," *Cornell Law Review* 72 (1987): 688–89, based on national data from the Administrative Office of the U.S. Courts and data for 1980–1981 from Central District of California.

5. The Use of Litigation

1. Jack Greenberg, "Litigation for Social Change," p. 20.

2. Kirp, *Just Schools*, p. 50. See also Matthew Holden, Jr., "Litigation and the Political Order," *Western Political Quarterly* 16 (1963): 774–77, where constitutional litigation is seen as an "insurrection without arms" and as "moderate struggle" in which reasonable victory, not punitive victory, is sought, making it different from various bargaining situations.

3. Cover, *Justice Accused*, p. 159.

4. Louis R. Harlan, *Booker T. Washington: The Making of a Black Leader, 1865–1901* (New York, 1982), pp. 297–98.

5. Neier, *Only Judgment*, pp. 227–28.

6. Black, "The Mobilization of Law," 126, 127.

7. Joel B. Grossman and Austin Sarat, "Litigation in the Federal Courts: A Comparative Perspective," *Law & Society Review* 9 (1975): 321.

8. Rathjen, "Lawyers and the Appellate Choice," p. 391.

9. See Scheingold, *The Politics of Rights*, p. 151.

10. *NAACP v. Button*, 371 U.S. 415, 436 (1963).

11. Neier, *Only Judgment*, p. 19.

12. Zangrando, *The NAACP Crusade Against Lynching*, p. 88; Danielson, *The Politics of Exclusion*, p. 161; Ross and Berg, *"I Respectfully Disagree with the Judge's Order,"* p. 4.

13. Richard D. Cortner, "Strategies and Tactics of Litigants in Constitutional Cases," *Journal of Public Law* 17 (1968): 285; Olson, "Interest-Group Litigation in Federal District Court," p. 858.

14. Handler, *Social Movements and the Legal System*, p. 132.

15. Neal Milner, "The Intrigues of Rights, Resistance and Accommodation," *Law & Social Inquiry* 17 (1992): 321.

16. Halpern, "Title VI and Racial Discrimination in Educational Institutions," p. 36.

17. Neier, *Only Judgment*, p. 9; Grossman and Sarat, "Litigation in the Federal Courts," p. 327.

18. Olson, "Interest Group Litigation," pp. 860–61, 863; Koblyka, *The Politics of Obscenity*, pp. 159–60.

19. Koblyka, *The Politics of Obscenity*, p. 160.

20. Epstein, *Conservatives in Court*, p. 68.

21. Marc Galanter, "Why the 'Haves' Comes Out Ahead: Speculations on the Limits of Legal Change," *Law & Society Review* 9 (1974): 98–103.

22. Scheppele and Walker, "The Litigation Strategies of Interest Groups," p. 182.

23. Ibid., p. 164.

24. Jeanne Hahn, "Litigation and the Political Process," unpublished ms. (n.d.), p. 10.

25. Danielson, *The Politics of Exclusion*, p. 162.

26. Cortner, "Strategies and Tactics," 288; see Vose, *Caucasians Only*, p. 251.

27. Lawrence, *The Poor in Court*, p. 118.

28. Patrick J. Bruer, "Studying Interest Group Litigation," paper presented to Midwest Political Science Association, 1986, pp. 21–22.

29. Irons, *The New Deal Lawyers*, pp. 183, 140.

30. Meltsner, *Cruel and Unusual*, p. 36.

31. Shields and Spector, "Opening Up the Suburbs," 325.

32. Epstein, *Conservatives in Court*, p. 144.

33. Cover, *Justice Accused*, p. 160.

34. Casper, *Lawyers Before the Warren Court*, pp. 74–75; Rathjen, "Lawyers and the Appellate Choice," and Susan Ann Kay, "Sex Differences in the Attitudes of a Future Elite," *Women & Politics* 1 (1980): 35–48. See Rathjen, 397. On the weights given by attorneys practicing in federal appeals courts to factors in the equation leading to a decision to appeal or not to appeal.

35. Jeffrey M. Fitzgerald, "The Contract Buyers League and the Courts: A Case Study of Poverty Litigation," *Law & Society Review* 9 (1975): 181.

36. Neier, *Only Judgment*, p. 213.

37. Greenberg, "Litigation for Social Change," p. 10.

38. Scheingold, *The Politics of Rights*, pp. 5, 14.

39. Milner, "The Dilemmas of Legal Mobilization," pp. 114–15.

40. Scheingold, *The Politics of Rights*, pp. 5, 151; Clark, "The Lawyer in the Civil Rights Movement," p. 470.

41. Norman Amaker, comments at panel on presidency and civil rights, American Political Science Association meetings, Sept. 6, 1992.

42. Galanter, *Competing Equalities*, p. 510.

43. Halpern, "Title VI and Racial Discrimination," p. 36; Kirp, "Multitudes in the Valley of Indecision," p. 442; Handler, *Social Movements and the Legal System*, p. 218.

44. O'Connor and Epstein, "In Defense of Rights," p. 9.

45. O'Connor and Epstein, "Beyond Legislative Lobbying," p. 142.

46. O'Connor and Epstein, "The Importance of Interest Group Involvement," pp. 717–18, 720.

47. Paul Burstein and Kathleen Monaghan, "Equal Employment Opportunity and the Mobilization of Law," *Law & Society Review* 20 (1986): 373. See also Paul Burstein and Mark Edwards, "The Impact of Employment Discrimination Litigation on Racial Disparity in Earnings," *Law & Society Review* 28 (1994): 79–111.

48. Lee Epstein and C.K. Rowland, "Debunking the Myth of Interest Group Invincibility in the Court," *American Political Science Review* 85 (1991): 213.

49. Neier, *Only Judgment*, p. 7.

50. Bell, "Serving Two Masters," p. 482; Bell, "Waiting on the Promise of *Brown*," *Law and Contemporary Problems* 39 (1975): 344.

51. Stephen C. Halpern, "Assessing the Litigating Role of ACLU Chapters," *Civil Liberties: Policy and Policy Making*, ed. Stephen L. Wasby (Lexington, Mass., 1976), pp. 159–68.

52. Hill, "The Equal Employment Opportunity Commission," p. 49.

53. Zangrando, *The NAACP Crusade Against Lynching*, p. 108.

54. Neier, *Only Judgment*, p. 140.

55. See Rosenberg, *The Hollow Hope*. As to the limits of this argument, see Michael W. McCann, "Reform Litigation on Trial," *Law & Social Inquiry* 17 (1992): 715–43, and Malcolm M. Feeley, "Hollow Hopes, Flypaper, and Metaphors," ibid., pp. 745–60.

56. See, for example, Louis Ruchames, *Race, Jobs, and Politics: The Story of FEPC* (New York, 1953); Morroe Berger, *Equality by Statute* (New York, 1952; rev. ed., 1967); and Leon H. Mayhew, *Law & Equal Opportunity: A Study of the Massachusetts Commission Against Discrimination* (Cambridge, Mass., 1968).

57. Herbert Hill, "The National Labor Relations Act and the Emergence of Civil Rights/Law: A New Priority in Federal Labor Policy," *Harvard Civil Rights-Civil Liberties Law Review* 11 (1976): 324.

58. See Harrell R. Rodgers, Jr., and Charles S. Bullock, III, *Coercion to Compliance* (Lexington, Mass., 1976), pp. 48–52.

59. A study by the U.S. Civil Rights Commission, cited by Jennifer L. Hochschild, *The New American Dilemma: Liberal Democracy and School Desegregation* (New Haven, Conn., 1984), p. 126.

60. See Orfield, *The Reconstruction of Southern Education*, chap. 4, "Chicago: Failure in the North," pp. 151–207.

61. See B. Dan Wood, "Does Politics Make a Difference at the EEOC?" *American Journal of Political Science* 34 (1990): 503–30.

62. Robert Belton, "Title VII of the Civil Rights Act of 1964: A Decade of Private Enforcement and Judicial Developments," *Saint Louis University Law Review* 20 (1976): 230 n.28.

63. Herbert Hill, "The New Judicial Perception of Employment Discrimination: Litigation Under Title VII of the Civil Rights Act of 1964," *University of Colorado Law Review* 43 (1972): 252.

64. Robert Belton, "A Comparative Review of Public and Private Enforcement of Title VII of the Civil Rights Act of 1964," *Vanderbilt Law Review* 31 (1978): 924, 958.

65. Joseph Stewart, Jr., and James F. Sheffield, Jr., "Correlates of Civil Rights Interest Groups' Litigation Activities," paper presented to Southern Political Science Association, Birmingham, Ala., 1983, pp. 15–16.

66. Danielson, *The Politics of Exclusion*, p. 115.

67. Lawyers Committee for Civil Rights Under Law, Annual Report 1978, pp. 27–28.

68. Zangrando, *The NAACP Crusade Against Lynching*, pp. 17, 139; see also pp. 26–27.

69. Robert Jerome Glennon, "The Role of Law in the Civil Rights Movement: The Montgomery Bus Boycott, 1955–1957," *Law and History Review* 9 (1991): 60.

70. Kirp, *Just Schools*, p. 58.

71. Combs, "The Federal Judiciary and Northern School Desegregation," pp. 14–15.

72. Kirp, "Multitudes in the Valley of Indecision," p. 442.

73. Ibid., p. 491.

74. Kinoy, *Rights on Trial*, p. 193.

75. Bruer, "The Aims of Interest Group Litigation," pp. 6–9.

76. O'Connor, *Women's Organizations' Use of the Courts*, pp. 2–3. See also Sorauf, *The Wall of Separation*, p. 92.

77. Neier, *Only Judgment*, p. 46.

78. Epstein and Kobylka, *The Supreme Court & Legal Change*, p. 29.

79. Drew Days III, comment at panel on litigation and social change, Law and Society Association meetings, June 10, 1984.

6. Litigation Complexity and Choice of Forum

1. In outcomes from 1960–1967 for black litigants in federal district court, "Success ratios in the South were higher than in the North, where cases apparently presented more complex claims." Kenneth M. Dolbeare, "The Federal District Courts and Urban Public Policy: An Exploratory Study (1960–1967)," *Frontiers of Judicial Research*, eds. Joel B. Grossman and Joseph Tanenhaus (New York, 1969), p. 398.

2. See, for Sec. 1983 cases, Eisenberg and Schwab, "The Reality of Constitutional Tort Litigation," pp. 672, 675.

3. Belton, "A Comparative Review," pp. 926, 929.

4. Larry Heuer and Steven Penrod, "Trial Complexity: A Field Investigation of Its Meaning and Its Effects," *Law and Human Behavior* 18 (1994): 30–31.

5. Abram Chayes, "The Role of the Judge in Public Law Litigation," *Harvard Law Review* 89 (1976): 1284.

6. There is an extensive literature on this so-called "public law" litigation, in terms of supposed differences from traditional litigation. In addition to Chayes, "The Role of the Judge in Public Law Litigation," for case studies, see Cooper, *Hard Judicial Choices*, p. 244; and for discussion of whether judges have the "capacity" to handle such cases, see Stephen L. Wasby, "Arrogation of Power or Accountability: 'Judicial Imperialism' Revised," *Judicature* 65 (1981): 209–19, and Ralph Cavanagh and Austin Sarat, "Thinking About Courts: Toward and Beyond a Jurisprudence of Judicial Competence," *Law & Society Review* 14 (1980): 371–420.

7. David L. Kirp and Gary Babcock, "Judge and Company: Court-Appointed Masters, School Desegregation, and Institutional Reform," *Alabama Law Review* 32 (1981): 325, 326.

8. John Leubsdorf, "Foreword," in Ross and Berg, *"I Respectfully Disagree with the Judge's Order,"* p. xx.

9. Salomone, "Judicial Oversight of Agency Enforcement," p. 127.

10. Chesler, Sanders, and Kalmuss, *Social Science in Court*, p. 189.

11. *Hart v. Community School Board*, 383 F. Supp. 699 (E.D.N.Y. 1974), aff'd, 512 F.2d 37 (2nd Cir. 1975). See James J. Fishman, "The Limits of Remedial Power: Hart v. Community School Board 21," *Limits of Justice*, eds. Kalodner and Fishman, pp. 115–66.

12. Geoffrey F. Aronow, "The Special Master in School Desegregation Cases: The Evolution of Roles in the Reformation of Public Institutions Through Litigation," *Hastings Constitutional Law Quarterly* 7 (1980): 754–55.

13. Rabin, "Lawyers for Social Change," p. 223.

14. See *Jenkins by Agyei v. State of Missouri*, 806 F.2d 657 (8th Cir. 1986).

15. They have been made so, William Clune suggests, by the Supreme Court's rulings "particularizing" and "trivializing" the nature of the law involved. Comments at Law and Society Association meetings, Denver, 1983.

16. Halpern, "Title VI and Racial Discrimination," p. 15; Orfield, *Must We Bus?* pp. 375–76.

17. J. Anthony Lukas, *Common Ground: A Turbulent Decade in the Lives of Three American Families* (New York, 1985), p. 236.

18. See Komesar, "Housing, Zoning, and the Public Interest," *Public Interest Law*, ed. Weisbrod, p. 239 n. 78; Danielson, *The Politics of Exclusion*, p. 167.

19. Peyton McCrary, Conference on 25th Anniversary of Voting Rights Act, The Brookings Institution, Washington, Oct. 19, 1990.

20. Robert A. Dentler and Marvin B. Scott, *Schools on Trial: An Inside Account of the Boston Desegregation Case* (Cambridge, Mass., 1981), p. 43; Orfield, *Must We Bus?* p. 367, based on an interview with James N. Nabrit III, Feb. 8, 1974.

21. Tinsley Yarbrough, "The Political World of Federal Judges as Managers," *Public Administration Review* 45 (1985): 662.

22. Belton, "A Comparative Review," p. 928 n. 114; Lawyers Committee, Fifteenth Anniversary Report, July 1978, p. 24.

23. NAACP Legal Defense Fund, 1981–1982 Annual Report, p. 10.

24. Belton, "A Comparative Review," p. 915 n. 51.

25. F. Peter Model, "On the Cutting Edge of the Law," *Perspectives* (Spring 1982): 22–29 (interview with NAACP General Counsel Thomas I. Atkins); Orfield, *Must We Bus?* p. 379. The discrepancy between the attorneys' fee requests and the costs cited by Orfield is accounted for by the fact that much lawyers' time was donated, as indicated, but would still be eligible for attorneys' fee award reimbursement.

26. Jaynes and Williams, *A Common Destiny*, p. 76.

27. Mihelich and Welch, "Omaha, Nebraska," p. 277.

28. See, for example, Elwood Hain, "Sealing Off the City: School Desegregation in Detroit," *Limits of Justice*, eds. Kalodner and Fishman, p. 286.

29. Tony Baez, Richardo R. Fernandez, and Judith T. Guskin, *Desegregation and Hispanic Students: A Community Perspective* (Roslyn, Va., 1980), p. 38.

30. Ricardo R. Fernandez and Judith T. Guskin, "Bilingual Education and Desegregation: A New Dimension in Legal and Educational Decision-Making," *Bilingual Education*, eds. Herman LaFontaine, Barry Persky, and Leonard H. Golubchick (Wayne, N.J., 1978), pp. 59–61.

31. Dentler and Scott, *Schools on Trial* p. 153.

32. Belton, "A Comparative Review," p. 927.

33. Ibid., pp. 928–29.

34. Halpern, "Title VI and Racial Discrimination," p. 15.

35. Interview with William Bradford Reynolds, "A Defense of the Reagan Administration's Civil Rights Policies," *New Perspectives* (1984): 37.

36. Tushnet, *The NAACP's Legal Strategy*, pp. 88, 110.

37. Mark Tushnet, personal communication, March 13, 1989. He observes "that the earlier cases were evidence heavy in relation to resources then available, but not really comparable in absolute size to the later cases."

38. Redlich, "Who Will Litigate Constitutional Issues for the Poor?," p. 776.

39. Fitzgerald, "The Contract Buyers League," p. 186. Because "few lawyers could afford . . . representation without fees which were beyond the buyers' resources," the contribution of lawyers' time was required.

40. Meltsner, *Cruel and Unusual*, p. 15.

41. William L. Taylor, "Mounting a Concerted Federal Attack on Urban Segregation: A Preliminary Exploration," *Racial Segregation: Two Policy Views* (New York, 1979), p. 54; Danielson, *The Politics of Exclusion*, pp. 165, 166.

42. Robert Belton, "Title VII of the Civil Rights Act," p. 229 n. 26; see also pp. 302–303 n. 553.

43. *United States v. Lawrence County School District*, 808 F.2d 1063 (5th Cir. 1987).

44. Lofgren, *The Plessy Case*, pp. 32, 42. A potential complication in the federal route was that it wasn't clear whether "an appeal from the federal Circuit Court

ran to the newly established Circuit Court of Appeals rather than directly to Washington." For the tactic of a state high court petition to succeed, Plessy would have to *lose* there because "Under the existing jurisdictional statute, a case in which a state law was challenged as contrary to the United States Constitution could be carried from the highest state court empowered to decide the issue to the United States Supreme Court only if the state court ruled *against* a claimed federal right." Ibid., p. 37, 60.

45. Grossman and Sarat, "Litigation in the Federal Courts," p. 327.

46. A. James Lee and Burton A. Weisbrod, "Public Interest Law Activities in Education," *Public Interest Law,* ed. Weisbrod, p. 321.

47. Burt Neuborne, "The Myth of Parity," *Harvard Law Review* 90 (1970): 1116, 1119.

48. Paul M. Bator, "The State Courts and Federal Constitutional Litigation," *William & Mary Law Review* 22 (1981): 630–31.

49. Michael E. Solimine and James L. Walker, "Constitutional Litigation in Federal and State Courts: An Empirical Analysis of Judicial Parity," *Hastings Constitutional Law Quarterly* 19 (1983): 241, 246.

50. Sorauf, *The Wall of Separation,* p. 111.

51. "The needle . . . is currently jammed in the 'federal' position." Burt Neuborne, "Toward Procedural Parity in Constitutional Litigation," *William & Mary Law Review* 22 (1981): 733.

52. Sorauf, *Wall of Separation,* p. 111.

53. See Greenberg, "Litigation for Social Change," p. 33.

54. Bator, "The State Courts and Federal Constitutional Litigation," p. 631. He claims this "is no longer of dominating significant in governing the attitudes of state court judges."

55. Tushnet, *The NAACP's Legal Strategy,* p. 51.

56. Sorauf, *Wall of Separation,* p. 112.

57. See, inter alia, Ronald Collins and Peter Galie, "State High Courts, State Constitutions and Individual Rights Litigation Since 1980: A Judicial Survey," *Hastings Constitutional Law Quarterly* 13 (1986): 599–623; and Peter Galie, "The Other Supreme Courts: Judicial Activism Among State Supreme Courts," *Syracuse Law Review* 33 (1982): 731–93; and compare Barry Latzer, "The Hidden Conservatism of the State Court 'Revolution'," *Judicature* 75 (1991): 190–97.

58. William J. Brennan, Jr., "State Constitutions and the Protection of Individual Rights," *Harvard Law Review* 90 (1977): 489.

59. Carl H. Loewensen, Jr., "ACLU Turns to State Courts and Constitutions to Protect Rights," *Civil Liberties,* no. 352 (1985): 7.

60. Shirley S. Abrahamson and Diane S. Gutmann, "The New Federalism: State Constitutions," *Judicature* 71 (1987): 90.

61. See, inter alia, G. Alan Tarr and Mary Cornelia Aldis Porter, "Gender Equality and Judicial Federalism: The Role of State Appellate Courts," *Hastings*

Constitutional Law Quarterly 9 (1982): 919–73; Tarr and Porter, *State Supreme Courts in State and Nation* (New Haven, Conn., 1988); Peter J. Galie, "State Constitutional Guarantees and Protection of Defendants' Rights: The Case of New York, 1960–1978," *Buffalo Law Review* 28 (1979): 154–94, and "The Pennsylvania Constitution and the Protection of Defendants' Rights, 1969–80: A Summary," *University of Pittsburgh Law Review* 42 (1981): 269–311; and Kenneth C. Hass, "The 'New Federalism' and Prisoners' Rights: State Supreme Courts in Comparative Perspective," *Western Political Quarterly* 40 (1981): 552–71.

62. Jack E. Call, "Protecting Defendants' Rights: A Review of Literature on State and Federal Courts," *Courts and Criminal Justice: Emerging Issues,* ed. Susette M. Talarico (Beverly Hills, Calif., 1985), pp. 123–24; Latzer, "The Hidden Conservatism of the State Court 'Revolution'."

63. In the course of one such case, a state judge in Alabama even invalidated a 1956 state constitutional amendment intended to prevent school desegregation.

64. Milner, "The Right to Refuse Treatment," p. 469; *Mills v. Rogers,* 457 U.S. 291 (1982).

65. Milner, "Legal Mobilization and the Emergence of Mental Health Rights Litigation," p. 14.

66. James J. Fishman, Laura Ross, and Steven R. Trost, "With All Deliberate Delay: School Desegregation in Mount Vernon," *Limits of Justice,* eds. Kalodner and Fishman, pp. 370, 394–96, 409.

67. Neuborne, "Toward Procedural Parity," 732.

68. For the effect of public opinion on district judges' sentencing in Vietnam-era draft cases, see Beverly Blair Cook, "Sentencing Behavior of Federal Judges: Draft Cases—1972," *University of Cincinnati Law Review* 42 (1973): 597–633, and "Public Opinion and Federal Judicial Policy," *American Journal of Political Science* 21 (1977): 567–600.

69. Neuborne, "The Myth of Parity," p. 1128.

70. Emmett H. Buell, Jr., *School Desegregation and Defended Neighborhoods* (Lexington, Mass., 1972), p. 70; John Leubsdorf, "Foreword," in Ross and Berg, *"I Respectfully Disagree with the Judge's Order,"* p. xix.

71. Lukas, *Common Ground,* p. 238; Ralph R. Smith, "Two Centuries and Twenty-Four Months: A Chronicle of the Struggle to Desegregate the Boston Public Schools," *Limits of Justice,* p. 57.

72. Fitzgerald, "The Contract Buyers League and the Courts," 171–72. See *Contract Buyers Leader v. F & F Investment,* 300 F.Supp. 210 (N.D.Ill. 1969), aff'd. sub nom. *Baker v. F & F Investment,* 420 F.2d 1191 (7th Cir. 1970); *Clark v. University Builders,* 420 F.2d 1191 (7th Cir. 1970).

73. Steven H. Steinglass, "The Emerging State Court §1983 Action: A Procedural Review," *University of Miami Law Review* 38 (1984): 407, 407 n. 119.

74. Wolters, *The Burden of Brown,* pp. 112–13.

75. Robert F. Williams, "In the Supreme Court's Shadow: Legitimacy of State Rejection of Supreme Court Reasoning and Result," *South Carolina Law Review* 35 (1984): 378.

76. I wish to thank Steven Steinglass for calling this matter to my attention.

77. Charles Wollenberg, *All Deliberate Speed: Segregation and Exclusion in California Schools, 1855–1975* (Berkeley, Calif., 1976), p. 151.

78. *Los Angeles Unified School District v. Los Angeles Branch NAACP,* 714 F.2d 946 (9th Cir. 1983), cert. denied sub nom. *California State Department of Education v. Los Angeles Branch NAACP,* 467 U.S. 1207 (1984).

79. Kinoy, *Rights on Trial,* p. 175.

80. Robert M. Cover, "The Uses of Jurisdictional Redundancy: Interest, Ideology, and Innovation," *William & Mary Law Review* 22 (1981): 646.

81. See Joseph Stewart, Jr., and Edward V. Heck, "The Day-to-Day Activities of Interest Group Lawyers," *Social Science Quarterly* 64 (1983): 177.

82. Edward V. Heck and Joseph Stewart, Jr., "Ensuring Access to Justice: The Role of Interest Group Lawyers in the 60's Campaign for Civil Rights," *Judicature* 66 (1982): 91.

83. Amaker, "De Facto Leadership and the Civil Rights Movement," pp. 245–46.

84. Danielson, *The Politics of Exclusion,* p. 174; Shields and Spector, "Opening Up the Suburbs," p. 309; Kirp, *Just Schools,* p. 136.

85. See Tushnet, *The NAACP's Legal Strategy,* pp. 26–27.

86. Steinglass, "The Emerging State Court §1983 Action," p. 399.

87. Kirp, *Just Schools,* p. 139.

88. Neuborne, "Toward Procedural Parity," pp. 733–34.

89. Steinglass, "The Emerging State Court §1983 Action," p. 416.

90. Victor E. Flango, "Attorneys' Perspectives on Choice of Forum in Diversity Cases," *Akron Law Review* 25 (1991): 68.

91. Meltsner and Schrag, *Public Interest Advocacy,* p. 87; Neuborne, "The Myth of Parity," p. 1120.

92. Meltsner and Schrag, *Public Interest Advocacy,* p. 87; Steinglass, "The Emerging State Court §1983 Action," p. 398.

93. Steinglass, "The Emerging State Court §1983 Action," p. 424.

94. In those surveys, that factor, a preference for the federal rules of procedure, and a concern for judges of high quality, play the largest roles in lawyers' choice of court. Kristin Bumiller, "Choice of Forum in Diversity Cases: Analysis of a Survey and Implications for Reform," *Law & Society Review* 15 (1980–1981): 749–74; Jolanta Perlstein, "Lawyers' Strategies and Diversity Jurisdiction," *Law & Policy Quarterly* 3 (1981): 321–40.

95. Steinglass, "The Emerging State Court §1983 Action," p. 424.

96. Orfield, *Must We Bus?,* pp. 368–69.

97. Steinglass, "The Emerging State Court §1983 Action," p. 413, reporting survey findings.

98. Flango, "Attorneys' Perspectives," p. 66.

7. The "Planned" in Planned Litigation

1. Epstein, *Conservatives in Court*, p. 26; Stephen B. Wood, *Constitutional Politics in the Progressive Era—Child Labor and the Law* (Chicago, 1968).

2. Irons, *New Deal Lawyers*, pp. 240–42.

3. See Epstein, *Conservatives in Court*, p. 110; see also pp. 94–104.

4. Handler, *Social Movements and the Legal System*, p. 117.

5. Greenberg, "Litigation for Social Change," p. 20; Handler, Hollingsworth, and Erlanger, *Lawyers and the Pursuit of Civil Rights*, p. 23.

6. Tushnet, *The NAACP's Legal Strategy*, p. 145.

7. Ibid., pp. 144–46.

8. Jeanne Hahn, "The NAACP Legal Defense and Educational Fund: Its Judicial Strategy and Tactics," in Stephen L. Wasby, *American Government and Politics* (New York, 1973), pp. 393–94.

9. Greenberg, "Litigation for Social Change," p. 12.

10. See Sorauf, *The Wall of Separation*, pp. 121, 129.

11. Hahn, "The NAACP Legal Defense and Educational Fund," p. 393.

12. On use of expert testimony, see Joseph Sanders, Betty Rankin-Widgeon, Debra Kalmuss, and Mark Chesler, "The Relevance of 'Irrelevant' Testimony: Why Lawyers Use Social Science Experts in School Desegregation Cases," *Law & Society Review* 16 (1981–1982): 403–28.

13. Robert L. Rabin, "A Sociolegal History of the Tobacco Tort Litigation," *Stanford Law Review* 44 (1992): 870.

14. O'Connor, *Women's Organizations' Use of the Courts*, p. 17.

15. See Nathan Hakman, "The Supreme Court's Political Environment: The Processing of Non-Commercial Litigation," *Frontiers of Judicial Research*, eds. Joel B. Grossman and Joseph Tanenhaus (New York, 1969), pp. 205–206, for reasons for bringing multiple cases.

16. Belton, "A Comparative Review," p. 929.

17. McNeil, *Groundwork*, p. 135.

18. O'Connor, *Women's Organizations' Use of the Courts*, p. 123; Cowan, "Women's Rights Through Litigation," p. 389.

19. Scheingold, *The Politics of Rights*, pp. 108, 118.

20. Chesler, Sanders, and Kalmuss, *Social Science in Court*, p. 12.

21. Orfield, *Must We Bus?*, p. 374.

22. See *Rothstein v. Wyman*, which was started to protect suburban welfare recipients' welfare benefits, in the event *Rosado v. Wyman*, a major, complex challenge to New York State's plan to reduce welfare benefits, failed. When the carefully

planned *Rosado* case "floundered," a three-judge district court found an equal protection violation in *Rothstein*. See Redlich, "Who Will Litigate Constitutional Issues for the Poor?" pp. 755–56. *Rosado v. Wyman*, 304 F.Supp. 1356 (E.D.N.Y. 1970), rev'd, 414 F.2d 170 (2nd Cir. 1980), rev'd, 397 U.S. 397 (1970); *Rothstein v. Wyman*, 303 F.Supp. 339 (S.D.N.Y. 1969), vacated sub nom. *Wyman v. Rothstein*, 398 U.S. 275 (1970).

23. See Joel B. Grossman, "A Model for Judicial Policy Analysis: The Supreme Court and the Sit-In Cases," *Frontiers of Judicial Research*, eds. Grossman and Tanenhaus, p. 431; Casper, *Lawyers and Civil Liberties*, p. 67.

24. Lawrence, *The Poor in Court*, pp. 49–50; Greenberg, "Litigation for Social Change," pp. 30–31.

25. Greenberg, "Litigation for Social Change," pp. 26, 31.

26. Grofman, "An Expert Witness Perspective," 785 n. 9. "Cases that can best be characterized as mistakes will often be brought by relatively inexperienced private litigators."

27. Greenberg, "Litigation for Social Change," p. 29.

28. O'Connor, "Litigation as a Form of Political Activity," p. 3.

29. Sorauf, *Wall of Separation*, p. 30.

30. Cooper, *Hard Judicial Choices*, p. 168.

31. Casper, *Lawyers Before the Warren Court*, p. 7; see also p. 9.

32. Branch, *Parting the Waters*, p. 189.

33. Anthony Lewis, *Make No Law: The Sullivan Case and the First Amendment* (New York, 1991), p. 161.

34. Kobylka, *The Politics of Obscenity*, p. 33.

35. Sorauf, *Wall of Separation*, pp. 103, 91.

36. Scheingold, *The Politics of Rights*, p. 5.

37. The phrase is Gregory Caldeira's. Conference on 25th Anniversary of the Voting Rights Act, The Brookings Institution, Washington, Oct. 19, 1990.

38. For the former usage, see "*Doe v. Shapiro* was not planned as a test case, that is, using a plaintiff sought out by law reformers." Stephen D. Sugarman, "*Roe v. Norton*: Coerced Maternal Cooperation," *In the Interest of Children: Advocacy, Law Reform, and Public Policy*, ed. Robert H. Mnookin (New York, 1985), p. 377.

39. Zangrando, *The NAACP Crusade Against Lynching*, p. 96.

40. Scheingold, *The Politics of Rights*, p. 109.

41. Orfield, *Must We Bus?*, p. 307; see also p. 361.

42. Lofgren, *The Plessy Case*, p. 29.

43. Tushnet, *The NAACP's Legal Strategy*, p. 35.

44. See Irons, *The New Deal Lawyers*, p. 264, on the NLRB.

45. Irons, *New Deal Lawyers*, pp. 36, 243.

46. Jeremy Rabkin, "Office for Civil Rights," *The Politics of Regulation*, ed. James Q. Wilson (New York, 1980), p. 346.

47. See Lawrence, *The Poor in Court*, p. 45: The Legal Services Program, "to a

large extent, . . . did not have an NAACP LDF-type litigation strategy because the LSP did not begin with a clear notion of the complex interaction between poverty and the legal order. It had not specified its goals."

48. Kluger, *Simple Justice*, pp. 293–94.

49. Comment by Christine Harrington, panel at Law and Society Association meetings, 1983.

50. Greenberg, "Litigation for Social Change," p. 18; emphasis in original.

51. Lawrence, *The Poor in Court*, p. 57; Greenberg, "Litigation for Social Change," pp. 30–31.

52. Cortner, "Strategies and Tactics of Litigants," p. 288.

53. Olson, *Clients and Lawyers*, p. 80.

54. See Belton, "A Comparative Review," p. 934; George Cooper, "Introduction: Equal Employment Law Today," *Columbia Human Rights Law Review* 5 (1973): 266.

55. Greenberg, "Litigation for Social Change," p. 10.

56. Mark A. Chesler, Debra S. Kalmuss, and Joseph Sanders, "Methods of Presenting Scientific Evidence in Court: Panels Versus Party Witnessing in School Desegregation Cases," *Sociological Methods & Research* 11 (1983): 455.

57. Eleanor P. Wolf, *Trial and Error: The Detroit School Segregation Case* (Detroit, 1981), pp. 211–12.

58. 268 F.Supp. 83 (S.D.Ohio 1967) (public officials' awareness of discrimination against minorities by unions, coupled with contractors' acquiescence in that discrimination in public construction projects, is state action subject to remedies under 42 U.S.C. §§ 1981 and 1983).

59. This is based on a point by Tony Freyer, panel at Southern Political Science Association meetings, 1983.

60. Belton, "A Comparative Review," p. 926.

61. Stephanie B. Goldberg, "Justice Thurgood Marshall: The Long-Distance Runner," *ABA Journal* 78 (June, 1992): 71 (quoting Mark Tushnet).

62. Greenberg, "Litigation for Social Change," p. 20.

63. Ibid, p. 32. The same problem can occur in government agency litigation. See Irons, *New Deal Lawyers*, p. 57.

64. Irons, *New Deal Lawyers*, p. 4.

65. Greenberg, "Litigation for Social Change," p. 29.

66. Vose, *Constitutional Change*, p. 307.

67. Epstein, *Conservatives in Court*, pp. 122–23.

68. Casper, *Lawyers and Civil Liberties*, p. 143.

69. Leubsdorf, "Completing the Desegregation Remedy," p. 94.

70. Sorauf, *The Wall of Separation*, pp. 101–102.

71. Orfield, *Must We Bus?*, p. 373.

72. O'Connor, *Women's Organizations' Use of the Courts*, p. 26; see also Greenberg, "Litigation for Social Change," p. 31.

73. O'Connor and Epstein, "The Importance of Interest Group Involvement," p. 718.

74. Irons, *Justice at War*, p. 113.

75. Cowan, "Women's Rights Through Litigation," pp. 390–91; O'Connor, *Women's Organizations' Use of the Courts*, p. 124.

76. O'Connor and Epstein, "The Importance of Interest Group Involvement," p. 714.

77. Vose, *Caucasians Only*, pp. 158–59.

78. Cowan, "Women's Rights Through Litigation," pp. 383, 390.

79. Shields and Spector, "Opening Up the Suburbs," p. 311.

80. Irons, *Justice at War*, p. 105.

81. Ibid., p. 136.

82. Kinoy, *Rights on Trial*, p. 181.

83. Zangrando, *The NAACP Crusade Against Lynching*, p. 72.

84. Epstein, *Conservatives in Court*, p. 76.

85. Lofgren, *The Plessy Case*, p. 33.

86. Interview with Burt Neuborne, "New Appointments Would Strengthen Court's Hostility to Civil Liberties" *Civil Liberties*, no. 352 (Winter 1985), p. 4.

87. Epstein, *Conservatives in Court*, p. 55.

88. Lawyers' Committee, Annual Report, 1984–1985, pp. i-ii.

89. Elizabeth C. Wiggins, Thomas E. Willging, and Donna Steinstra, "The Federal Judicial Center's Study of Rule 11," *FJC Directions*, no. 2 (Nov. 1991), p. 4.

90. Handler, with Edgar and Settle, "Public Interest Law and Employment Discrimination," p. 275.

91. McNeil, *Groundwork*, pp. 219–20.

92. Tushnet, *The NAACP's Legal Strategy*, p. 43.

93. Personal communication, Matthew Holden, Jr., to Stephen L. Wasby.

94. Quoted, from interview, in Connie Pat Mauney, *Evolving Equality: The Courts & Desegregation in Tennessee* (Knoxville, Tenn., 1979), p. 171.

95. Zangrando, *The NAACP Crusade Against Lynching*, p. 110.

96. Bell, "Serving Two Masters," p. 482.

97. Tushnet, *The NAACP's Legal Strategy*, p. 89; Karen O'Connor and Lee Epstein, "Rebalancing the Scales of Justice: Assessment of Public Interest Law," paper presented to Law & Society Association, 1983, p. 6.

98. Clark, "The Lawyer in the Civil Rights Movement," p. 468.

99. Bell, "Serving Two Masters," p. 482.

100. Epstein and Kobylka, *The Supreme Court and Legal Change*, p. 295.

101. Sorauf, *The Wall of Separation*, p. 95.

102. Tushnet, *The NAACP's Legal Strategy*, p. 35.

103. James Q. Wilson, *Political Organizations* (New York, 1973), pp. 33–35, 46–47.

104. Mark V. Tushnet, "Organizational Structure and Legal Strategy: The

NAACP's Campaign Against Segregated Education, 1925–1950," unpublished ms., pp. 1–3—1–4.

105. Armand Derfner, "The Implications of the *City of Mobile* Case for Extension of the Voting Rights Act," *The Right to Vote*, pp. 194–210.

106. J. Harold Flannery, "De Jure Desegregation: The Quest for Adequacy," *Journal of Law & Education* 4 (1975): 142.

107. Sorauf, *The Wall of Separation*, p. 95.

108. Bell, "Serving Two Masters," p. 483.

109. This is the implication of statements by then NAACP General Counsel Nathaniel Jones, quoted by Bell, "Serving Two Masters," pp. 492, 492n.

110. Scheingold, *The Politics of Rights*, pp. 95, 151, 197; Bell, "Serving Two Masters" p. 483.

8. Choosing Areas of Law

1. Dorothy Robyn, *Braking the Special Interests: Trucking Deregulation and the Politics of Policy Reform* (Chicago, 1987), p. 119.

2. Kobylka, *The Politics of Obscenity*, pp. 81, 87–88.

3. See ibid., p. 143.

4. See ibid., pp. 120–21, on lobbying interest groups.

5. Deloria and Lytle, *American Indians, American Justice*, p. 158.

6. See Joel F. Handler, *Social Movements and the Legal System*, p. 144.

7. Handler, with Edgar and Settle, "Public Interest Law and Employment Discrimination," p. 274.

8. Heck and Stewart, "Ensuring Access to Justice," p. 92.

9. Orfield, *Must We Bus?*, p. 367, quoting James M. Nabrit III.

10. *Deal v. Cincinnati Board of Education*, 369 F.2d 55 (6th Cir. 1966); *Bell v. School Board of Gary*, 213 F.Supp. 819 (N.D.Ind. 1963), 324 F.2d 209 (7th Cir. 1963), cert. denied, 377 U.S. 924 (1964).

11. McKay, *Nine for Equality Under Law*, p. 35.

12. Cortner, *A Mob Intent on Death*, p. 3.

13. Tushnet, *The NAACP's Legal Strategy*, p. 145.

14. Ibid., pp. 37, 42.

15. Ibid., p. 104.

16. Ibid., p. 107.

17. Ibid., p. 162.

18. Matthew Holden, Jr., personal communication, Dec. 17, 1992.

19. Holden, *The Politics of the Black "Nation"*, p. 57. See also Gilbert Ware, *William Hastie: Grace Under Pressure* (New York, 1984), p. 35.

20. Greenberg interview, 112–13.

21. McKay, *Nine for Equality*, p. 12.

22. Ibid., p. 11.

23. Greenberg interview, p. 107.

24. NAACP Legal Defense and Education Fund, Annual Report (1981–1982), p. 9. Centrally involved in this work was Lani Guinier, nominated by President Clinton to be Assistant Attorney General for Civil Rights but whose nomination was withdrawn.

25. NAACP Legal Defense Fund, *The 40th Year* [Annual Report] (1980), p. 9.

26. Greenberg interview, p. 122.

27. Jaynes and Williams, *A Common Destiny*, p. 140.

28. Ibid., p. 144.

29. Danielson, *The Politics of Exclusion*, p. 153.

30. NAACP Legal Defense and Educational Fund, *The 40th Year*, p. 4.

31. Greenberg interview, p. 122.

32. Belton, "A Comparative Review," pp. 924, 929.

33. Belton, "Title VII of the Civil Rights Act of 1964," p. 228.

34. Meltsner, *Cruel and Unusual*, p. 109.

35. Ibid., p. 73. Justice Thomas recently called attention to the initial basis of this campaign, in the course of a recent concurring opinion in a death penalty case—in which he agreed with the majority in *not* upholding the claims made by the convicted defendant. *Graham v. Collins*, 113 S.Ct. 892, 904–905 (1993).

36. Meltsner, *Cruel and Unusual*, p. 76.

37. An observer has suggested that LDF appears not to have learned from this earlier failure to persuade judges with statistics, and points to its failure, as part of its overall campaign against the death penalty, to persuade the Supreme Court that race pervaded the capital punishment process, with the Court ruling in *McClesky v. Kemp* (1987) that prejudice had not been shown in individual cases and suggesting that the extremely thorough statistical analysis used by the LDF was flawed.

38. Meltsner *Cruel and Unusual*, p. 106.

39. Ibid., p. 108.

40. Ibid., pp. 36–37. Others, Greenberg in particular, disagree with this account of the genesis of the campaign. Epstein and Kobylka, *The Supreme Court & Legal Change*, p. 44, citing Eric L. Muller, "The Legal Defense Fund's Capital Punishment Campaign: The Distorting Influence of Death," *Yale Law and Policy Review* 4 (1985): 158–87. For another account of the development of the LDF death penalty campaign and early Supreme Court action on the subject, see Epstein and Kobylka, *The Supreme Court & Legal Change*, pp. 43–65, 91–96.

41. Epstein and Kobylka, *The Supreme Court & Legal Change*, p. 95.

42. NAACP Legal Defense and Education Fund, Annual Report (1981–1982), p. 16.

43. Neier, *Only Judgment*, p. 197.

9. Choice of Cases

1. Scheppele and Walker, "The Litigation Strategies of Interest Groups," p. 178.

2. James R. Acker, "Mortal Friends and Enemies: Amici Curiae in Supreme Court Death Penalty Cases," *New England Journal on Criminal and Civil Confinement* 19 (1993): 18–19.

3. Michael Epley, paper for Public Law Field Seminar, State University of New York at Albany, Sept. 30, 1991.

4. Charles R. Epp, "Connecting Litigation Levels and Legal Mobilization: Explaining Interstate Variation in Employment Civil Rights Litigation," *Law & Society Review* 24 (1990): 159.

5. Ralph R. Smith, "Two Centuries and Twenty-Four Months: A Chronicle of the Struggle to Desegregate the Boston Public Schools," *The Limits of Justice*, pp. 110–11.

6. In Legal Services programs, "Both the *size* and *type* of caseload are likely to affect resource allocation decisions." Menkel-Meadow and Meadow, "Resource Allocation in Legal Services," p. 242.

7. See Robert M. Emerson, "Holistic Experts in Social Control Decision Making," *Law and Society Review* 17 (1983): 425, for the argument made in the criminal context.

8. Jessica Pearson and Jeffrey Pearson, "Keyes v. School District No. 1," *Limits of Justice*, p. 187.

9. See Dentler and Scott, *Schools on Trial*, p. 46.

10. Greenberg interview, p. 123.

11. Belton, "A Comparative Review," p. 940.

12. Lawrence, *The Poor in Court*, pp. 46, 52.

13. Tinsley E. Yarbrough, "The Alabama Prison Litigation," *Justice System Journal* 9 (1984): 277–78.

14. Tinsley E. Yarbrough, *A Passion for Justice: J. Waties Waring and Civil Rights* (New York, 1987), p. 199.

15. Sorauf, *The Wall of Separation*, p. 101.

16. Meltsner and Schrag, *Public Interest Advocacy*, p. 77.

17. Rabin, "Lawyers for Social Change," pp. 222–23.

18. Thomas B. Marvell, *Appellate Courts and Lawyers: Information Gathering in the Adversary System* (Westport, Conn., 1978), p. 59.

19. Rathjen, "Lawyers and the Appellate Choice," p. 397.

20. Ibid., p. 399.

21. Lawrence, *The Poor in Court*, pp. 55, 57.

22. Branch, *Parting the Waters*, pp. 332, 410.

23. Irons, *The New Deal Lawyers*, p. 4.

24. Ibid., p. 243.

25. This is based on Matthew Holden, "Litigation and the Political Order," *Western Political Quarterly* 16 (1963): 776–77.

26. Olson, *Clients and Lawyers,* p. 87.

27. Meltsner, *Cruel and Unusual,* pp. 11–12. One civil rights lawyer, who brought up the subject ("You haven't asked about trumped-up cases") provided instances— which he thought crucial in the law's development—in which his organization had developed the case and then sought out a plaintiff.

28. Edward J. Larson, *Trial and Error: The American Controversy Over Creation and Evolution* (New York, 1985), p. 58. A Tennessee ACLU chapter was, years later, to offer assistance, both financial and legal, in a similar case, and the offer was taken by a teacher whose wife said they needed the money; and the leadership of the Arkansas Education Association asked a particular teacher "to stand as its plaintiff in a declaratory judgment action against the statute" in a later test of an antievolution statute, which became *Epperson v. Arkansas,* 393 U.S. 97 (1968).

29. Milner, "The Right to Refuse Treatment," pp. 461–62. Milner notes the absence of case finding when there was a lack of lay participation. Ibid., p. 454.

30. Olson, *Clients and Lawyers,* p. 81.

31. Amaker, "De Facto Leadership and the Civil Rights Movement," p. 234.

32. Lukas, *Common Ground,* p. 218.

33. Amaker, "De Facto Leadership," 228 n. 11.

34. Cooper, *Hard Judicial Choices,* p. 244.

35. NAACP Legal Defense Fund, 1980 Annual Report.

36. Tushnet, *The NAACP's Legal Strategy,* pp. 99–100.

37. Greenberg interview, p. 112.

38. Ibid., p. 117.

39. Handler, with Edgar and Settle, "Public Interest Law and Employment Discrimination," p. 274.

40. Ibid.

41. Sorauf, *The Wall of Separation,* p. 106.

42. Olson, *Clients and Lawyers,* p. 99.

43. Belton, "Comparative Review," p. 934; Handler, with Edgar and Settle, "Public Interest Law and Employment Discrimination," p. 272. However, the number of class actions in the field of employment discrimination, where it had been central to LDF's strategy, has declined, so that "the class action . . . has slipped into a virtual coma." John J. Donohoe III and Peter Siegelman, "The Changing Nature of Employment Discrimination Litigation," American Bar Foundation Working Paper no. 9021, p. 2.

44. Scheppele and Walker, "The Litigation Strategies of Interest Groups," pp. 180–81.

45. Branch, *Parting the Waters,* p. 159.

46. Handler, *Social Movements and the Legal System,* p. 109. At later stages of the

Boston school case, the Harvard Center for Law and Education had difficulty in obtaining plaintiffs. Hochschild, *The New American Dilemma*, p. 171.

47. Irons, *Justice at War*, p. 114.

48. See also Orfield, *Must We Bus?*, pp. 400–402.

49. Ware, *William Hastie*, p. 48.

50. Chesler, Sanders, and Kalmuss, *Social Science in Court*, p. 48.

51. Fairclough, *To Redeem the Soul of America*, pp. 275–76.

52. Chesler et al., *Social Science in Court*, p. 48.

53. Greenberg interview, 116. As an example, he cited *Phillips v. Martin Marietta*, 400 U.S. 542 (1970), an equal pay case involving a white woman.

54. Stephen Engelberg, "Norfolk and Reagan Administration Seek to End Busing in City's Schools," *New York Times*, March 3, 1985, p. 16.

55. Belton, "A Comparative Review," p. 942.

56. Jack Bass, *Unlikely Heroes* (Tuscaloosa, 1981/1990), p. 138, from interview with Jack Greenberg, June 21, 1979.

57. Kaufman, *Broken Alliance: The Turbulent Times Between Blacks and Jews in America* (New York, 1988), p. 115; Greenberg interview, p. 117; Tom Buckley, "25 Years in Battle for Rights, Fund's Lawyer Sees Victory," *New York Times*, May 12, 1974. The lawyer left LDF and did defend Davis.

10. Amicus Participation

1. Emma Coleman Jones, "Litigation Without Representation: The Need for Intervention to Affirm Affirmative Action," *Harvard Civil Rights–Civil Liberties Law Review* 16 (1979): 33.

2. Robert H. Salisbury, "Interest Representation: The Dominance of Institutions," *American Political Science Review* 78 (1984): 71–72. For some discussions of amicus use generally, see Lucius J. Barker, "Third Parties in Litigation: A Systemic View of the Judicial Function," *Journal of Politics* 23 (1967): 52–61, and Robert C. Bradley and Paul Gardner, "Underdogs, Upperdogs, and the Use of the Amicus Brief: Trends and Explanations," *Justice System Journal* 10 (1985): 78–96 (on differences between Warren Court and Burger Court).

3. Susan Behuniak-Long, "Friendly Fire: Amici Curiae and *Webster v. Reproductive Health Services*," *Judicature* 74 (1991): 267.

4. Karen O'Connor and Lee Epstein, "The Importance of Interest Group Involvement," pp. 717–19. Of the eleven cases in which the Lawyers' Committee filed amicus briefs, in two cases, LDF was a direct sponsor of litigation, and in five others, LDF also was an amicus.

5. O'Neill, *Bakke and The Politics of Equality*, p. 61.

6. Jones, "Litigation Without Representation," p. 33.

7. See Wayne V. McIntosh, "Supreme Court Impact on Third Parties: An Ex-

ploration of Amicus Participation in Federal Appeals Courts," paper presented to American Political Science Association, 1984, pp. 7–10.

8. Burstein and Monaghan, "Equal Employment Opportunity and the Mobilization of Law," p. 366.

9. Hakman, "The Supreme Court's Political Environment," p. 210 (table 7.1).

10. Karen O'Connor and Lee Epstein, "Amicus Curiae Participation in U.S. Supreme Court Litigation: An Appraisal of 'Hakman's Folklore'," *Law & Society Review* 16 (1981–1982): 315–16.

11. Lee Epstein, "Interest Group Litigation During the Rehnquist Court Era," *Journal of Law & Politics* 9 (1993): 647.

12. Gregory A. Caldeira and John R. Wright, "Amici Curiae Before the Supreme Court: Who Participates, When and How Much?", *Journal of Politics* 52 (1990): 792–95.

13. See Karen O'Connor and Lee Epstein, "Court Rules and Workload: A Case Study of Rules Governing Amicus Curiae Participation," *Justice System Journal* 8 (1983): 35–45; Edward R. Leahy, "The 10 Commandments of Certiorari," *ABA Journal* 71 (1985): 82.

14. O'Neill, *Bakke and the Politics of Equality*, pp. 47–48.

15. Particularly significant is the fact that respondent had filed a brief in opposition to the Court's granting certiorari in almost all cases (95%) on the Court's "discuss list" (those considered most important and which the justices consider further before granting or denying review). Gregory A. Caldeira and John R. Wright, "Organized Interests and the Discuss List in the Supreme Court," paper presented to American Political Science Association, 1988, pp. 23–24.

16. Gregory A. Caldeira and John R. Wright, "Organized Interests and Agenda Setting in the U.S. Supreme Court," *American Political Science Review* 82 (1988): 1119.

17. An interesting sidelight on the role of accident in litigation is provided by this incident. The lawyer learned of the board's composition because the stationery used for the request to participate as amicus was the type sent to "friends," and the back side of the page contained the board list; usually plain stationery containing no more than addresses was used for such official communications.

18. Epstein and Kobylka, *The Supreme Court & Legal Change*, p. 57.

19. NAACP Legal Defense and Education Fund, Annual Report 1981/1982, p. 2.

20. O'Connor, *Women's Organizations' Use of the Courts*, pp. 4–5; O'Connor and Epstein, "Beyond Legislative Lobbying," p. 139.

21. O'Neill, *Bakke and the Politics of Equality*, p. 215.

22. Epstein, *Conservatives in Court*, p. 60.

23. Ibid., p. 135.

24. O'Connor, *Women's Organizations' Use of the Courts*, p. 3; see also p. 132.

25. Irons, *Justice at War*, p. 305.

26. O'Neill, *Bakke and the Politics of Equality*, pp. 94–95.

27. Ibid., pp. 89–90.

28. O'Neill, *Bakke and the Politics of Equality*, pp. 97, 118.

29. Epstein, *Conservatives in Court*, p. 91.

30. Donald R. Songer and Reginald S. Sheehan, "Interest Group Success in the Courts: Amicus Participation in the Supreme Court," *Political Research Quarterly* 46 (1993): 339–54.

31. Meltsner, *Cruel and Unusual*, p. 229. *McGautha v. California* (and *Crampton v. Ohio*), 402 U.S. 183 (1971), allowing jury unlimited discretion to apply death penalty not constitutional violation, either in single trial procedure (*Crampton*) or bifurcated trial (*McGautha*).

32. O'Neill, *Bakke and the Politics of Equality*, pp. 69, 71.

33. 412 U.S. 507 (1973) (city not subject to jurisdiction for purposes of equitable relief under 42 U.S.C. §1983.

34. Within the government, there is a parallel process by which the decision is made to file an amicus brief, and what its content shall be. For a description of the process within an administration leading to such decisions in the *DeFunis* and *Bakke* cases, see O'Neill, *Bakke and the Politics of Equality*, pp. 179–91.

35. Ibid., p. 57.

36. Ibid., pp. 64, 66, 81, 88 (NAACP Legal Defense Fund), pp. 114–15 (ACLU).

37. See Behuniak-Long, "Friendly Fire," p. 263.

38. Donohue, *The Politics of the American Civil Liberties Union*, p. 18.

39. David O. Stewart, "A Picture Costs Ten Thousand Words," *ABA Journal* 71 (1985): 65–66.

40. O'Neill, *Bakke and the Politics of Equality*, p. 158.

41. Acker, "Mortal Friends and Enemies," pp. 24–25.

42. O'Neill, *Bakke and the Politics of Equality*, pp. 160, 92–93.

43. Vose, *Caucasians Only*, p. 167.

44. O'Connor and Epstein, "Beyond Legislative Lobbying," p. 140; O'Connor and Epstein, "The Importance of Interest Group Involvement," p. 719.

45. O'Neill, *Bakke and the Politics of Equality*, p. 82.

46. Sorauf, *The Wall of Separation*, p. 125.

47. See Epstein, *Conservatives in Court*, particularly p. 66.

48. Behuniak-Long, "Friendly Fire," p. 263.

11. Litigation Dynamics

1. Kirp, "Multitudes in the Valley of Indecision," p. 423.

2. Tushnet, *The NAACP's Legal Strategy*, p. xiii.

3. Kinoy, *Rights on Trial*, p. 180.

4. Leubsdorf, "Completing the Desegregation Remedy," p. 94.

5. Kirp, *Just Schools*, p. 64.

6. Milner, "The Right to Refuse Treatment," pp. 461–62, 467.

7. Belton, "A Comparative Review," pp. 921, 939. *Griggs v. Duke Power Co.*, 292 F.Supp. 243 (M.D.N.C. 1968); 420 F.2d 1255 (4th Cir. 1970).

8. Pearson and Pearson, "Keyes v. School District No. 1," *Limits of Justice*, pp. 220–21.

9. Fishman, Ross, and Trost, "With All Deliberate Delay: School Desegregation in Mount Vernon," *Limits of Justice*, p. 393.

10. See Henry C. Lauerman, "The Role of the Judiciary in the Desegregation of the Winston-Salem/Forsyth County Schools, 1968–1975," *Limits of Justice*, pp. 493–565.

11. Greenberg, "Litigation for Social Change," p. 27.

12. Orfield, *Must We Bus?*, p. 373.

13. Michael A. Rebell, "*Allen v. McDonough:* Special Education Reform in Boston," *Justice and School Systems*, p. 71.

14. Kirp, *Just Schools*, p. 131.

15. Irons, *Justice at War*, pp. 258, 186.

16. In a similar situation, when the *Swann* ruling was announced between the Detroit judge's liability and remedy decisions, he was thus provided with more developed law to apply at the remedy stage. Cooper, *Hard Judicial Choices*, p. 112.

17. See William E. Marsh, "United States v. Board of School Commissioners," *Limits of Justice*, p. 356.

18. Martin E. Sloane, "*Milliken v. Bradley* and Residential Segregation," presentation to Civil Rights Commission conference, Oct. 22, 1974, p. 28.

19. Michael A. Rebell and Arthur R. Block, *Educational Policy Making and the Courts: An Empirical Study of Judicial Activism* (Chicago, 1982), pp. 80–81.

20. See James A. Sartain and Rutledge M. Dennis, "Richmond, Virginia: Massive Resistance Without Violence," *Community Politics and Educational Change*, p. 227.

21. Fishman et al., "With All Deliberate Delay," p. 382.

22. Cooper, *Hard Judicial Choices*, pp. 264–65.

23. Greenberg, "Litigation for Social Change," p. 34.

24. Ibid., p. 14.

25. Irons, *Justice at War*, pp. 104–105, 128, 195.

26. Kirp, "Multitudes in the Valley of Indecision," pp. 447, 465–66.

27. Elwood Hain, "Sealing Off the City: School Desegregation in Detroit," *Limits of Justice*, pp. 248–49.

28. Kirp, "Multitudes in the Valley of Indecision," p. 471.

29. *Adams v. Mathews*, 536 F.2d 417 (D.C.Cir. 1976).

30. See Salomone, "Judicial Oversight of Agency Enforcement," p. 138.

31. Orfield, *Must We Bus?*, p. 355.

32. Gary D. Melton, "Litigation *In the Interest of Children:* Does Anybody Win?" *Law & Human Behavior* 10 (1986): 342.

33. See Milner, "The Right to Refuse Treatment," 461: ("As the scope of the case broadened, its pace slowed.")

34. Rebell and Block, pp. 282–83 n. 22.

35. Richard J. Richardson and Kenneth N. Vines, *The Politics of Federal Courts* (Boston, 1970), pp. 127–29; J. Woodford Howard, Jr., *Courts of Appeals in the Federal Justice System: A Study of the Second, Fifth, and District of Columbia Circuits* (Princeton, 1981), p. 42.

36. S. Sidney Ulmer, "Issue Fluidity in the U.S. Supreme Court: A Conceptual Analysis," *Supreme Court Activism and Restraint*, eds. Stephen C. Halpern and Charles M. Lamb (Lexington, Mass., 1982), p. 322.

37. Lynn Mather and Barbara Yngvesson, "Language, Audience, and the Transformation of Disputes," *Law & Society Review* 15 (1980–1981): 802–805.

38. Wolters, *The Burden of Brown*, pp. 133–34.

39. Tinsley E. Yarbrough, "The Alabama Prison Litigation," *Justice System Journal* 9 (1984): 276–90.

40. Cooper, *Hard Judicial Choices*, pp. 170, 175; Jack Drake, "Judicial Implementation of *Wyatt v. Stickney*," *Alabama Law Review* 32 (1981): 300, 304; *Wyatt v. Stickney*, 325 F.Supp. 582 (M.D. Ala. 1971), 334 F.Supp. 1341 (M.D. Ala. 1971), 344 F.Supp. 373 and 387 (M.D. Ala. 1972), aff'd 503 F.2d 1305 (5th Cir. 1974).

41. Scott Jaschik, "Justice Department Challenges States' Practice of Giving More Money to Black Colleges," *Chronicle of Higher Education* (1991): A1, A22; Goldie Blumenstyk, "Justice Dept. Affirms Federal Backing for Black Colleges," *Chronicle of Higher Education* (1991): A41, A44.

42. See Bullock and Butler, "Voting Rights," *The Reagan Administration and Human Rights*, p. 40.

43. Leadership Conference on Civil Rights, *Without Justice* (Report on the Conduct of the Justice Department in Civil Rights in 1981–1982) (Washington, 1982), p. 3.

44. See Caplan, *The Tenth Justice*, pp. 51–62. See also Philip B. Heymann and Lance Liebman, "Lawyers for Government: The Case of the Segregated Schools," *The Social Responsibilities of Lawyers: Case Studies* (New York, 1988), pp. 136–82.

45. Amaker, *Civil Rights and the Reagan Administration*, p. 96.

46. See also Cooper, *Hard Judicial Choices*, p. 261, on Ohio prison litigation.

47. Note, "Ethical Considerations for the Justice Department When It Switches Sides During Litigation," *University of Puget Sound Law Review* 7 (1984): 406,422.

48. Ibid., p. 421.

49. Ibid., pp. 415, 422.

50. Note, "Professional Ethics in Government Side-Switching," *Harvard Law Review* 96 (1983): 1916.

12. Staff Attorneys and Cooperative Attorneys

1. Meltsner, *Cruel and Unusual*, pp. 8–9.
2. Vose, *Constitutional Change*, p. 321; Casper, *Lawyers Before the Warren Court*, pp. 142–43.
3. Tushnet, *The NAACP's Legal Strategy Against Desegregation*, p. 99.
4. See Vose, *Constitutional Change*, pp. 317–18.
5. Epstein, *Conservatives in Court*, pp. 111–12.
6. Rabin, "Lawyers for Constitutional Change," 219 n.43.
7. Ibid., 217–18.
8. Cowan, "Women's Rights Through Litigation," p. 383.
9. Lawyers Committee, *Committee Report* 2 (no. 1, 1988): 11.
10. Kirp, "Multitudes in the Valley of Indecision," pp. 442–43.
11. Belton, "Employment Discrimination Litigation," p. 234.
12. One government lawyer could serve as a cooperating attorney because his agency allowed lawyers to handle cases of "civic interest"; he felt more free to do pro bono work than many attorneys in private practice.
13. Tushnet, p. 152.
14. Marc Galanter, "Case Congregations and Their Careers," *Law & Society Review* 24 (1990): 389.
15. NAACP Legal Defense Fund, Annual Report, 1981–1982, p. 26.
16. Belton, "A Comparative Review," pp. 930, 951.
17. Wolters, *The Burden of Brown*, p. 209.
18. Kirp, *Just Schools*, pp. 130, 137–40.
19. Mark V. Tushnet, "Organizing Civil Rights Litigation: The NAACP's Experience," *Ambivalent Legacy: A Legal History of the South*, eds. David J. Bodenhamer and James W. Ely, Jr. (Jackson, Miss., 1984), p. 174.
20. Vose, *Constitutional Change*, pp. 314–15.
21. Tushnet, *The NAACP's Legal Strategy*, p. 94.
22. August Meier and Elliott Rudwick, "Attorneys Black and White: A Case Study of Race Relations within the NAACP," *Journal of American History* 62 (1976): 915. For an interesting partial parallel, the use of white lawyers to press Native Americans' interests, where their use was especially problematic because they were "individuals with an untested commitment to the social and political values" of Native Americans, and the legal traditions of client and lawyer also were different, see Jill Norgren, "Lawyers and the Legal Business of the Cherokee Republic in Courts of the United States, 1829–1935," *Law and History Review* 10 (1992): 269, 277.
23. Cortner, *A Mob Intent on Death*, p. 2.
24. Vose, *Constitutional Change*, pp. 915, 920, 930, 933.
25. McNeil, *Groundwork*, pp. 121–22.
26. See Branch, *Parting the Waters*, p. 525, on C.B. King of Albany, Georgia.

27. Amaker, "De Facto Leadership and the Civil Rights Movement," p. 248; Meltsner, *Cruel and Unusual*, p. 8.

28. Amaker, "De Facto Leadership," p. 249.

29. Lofgren, *The Plessy Case*, p. 30.

30. Cortner, *A Mob Intent on Death*, pp. 94, 96–97, 133.

31. Casper, *Lawyers Before the Warren Court*, p. 142.

32. Kinoy, *Rights on Trial*, pp. 187–88, 168, 195.

33. Bell, "Serving Two Masters," p. 476 n. 19.

34. Casper, *Lawyers Before the Warren Court*, p. 142.

35. Quoted in Mauney, *Evolving Equality*, p. 60.

36. Richard A. Pride and J. David Woodard, *The Burden of Busing: The Politics of Desegregation in Nashville, Tennessee* (Knoxville, 1985), p. 265.

37. Irons, *Justice at War*, p. 190.

38. Apropos of Cutler arguing the case in the Supreme Court, one lawyer joked that Cutler's firm "needed some *pro bono*."

39. Rabin, "Lawyers for Constitutional Change," p. 217.

40. Lawyers Committee, Annual Report 1980–1981; Fifteenth Anniversary Report, p. 29.

41. Lena Williams, "N.A.A.C.P. Sues Four of Its Former Lawyers," *New York Times*, Feb. 22, 1987, p. 23; Lynn Byczynski, "NAACP Seeks Fees from Ex-Lawyers," *National Law Journal* March 9, 1987, p. 31.

42. "N.A.A.C.P. Assailed Over Suit on Fees," *New York Times*, April 26, 1987.

43. A federal judge in Cleveland, after enjoining pursuit of the case in Kansas City, dismissed the case against Jones on jurisdictional, venue, and service-of-process grounds, *National Association for the Advancement of Colored People–Special Contribution Fund v. Jones*, 732 F.Supp. 791 (N.D.Ohio 1900), and the remaining parts of the case were dismissed in late 1988 by the judge in Kansas City; Atkins's efforts to have sanctions issued against the NAACP under Rule 11 were denied, and that ruling was upheld. *NAACP-SCF v. Atkins*, 908 F.2d 336 (8th Cir. 1990).

44. *Turner v. Secretary of the Air Force*, 944 F.2d 804 (11th Cir. 1991).

45. Lofgren, *The Plessy Case*, pp. 33, 150–51.

46. Amaker, "De Facto Leadership," p. 274.

47. McKay, *Nine for Equality*, pp. 15–16.

48. The government has done this. At the NLRB, Charles Fahy sent his attorneys on temporary assignments to regional offices for a "brief seasoning in the field" to "familiarize them with the reality of employer–worker conflict, [and] exposed them to combat with company lawyers in hearings." Irons, *New Deal Lawyers*, p. 140.

49. Kirp, "Multitudes in the Valley of Indecision," p. 428.

50. Casper, *Lawyers Before the Warren Court*, pp. 142–43. See also O'Connor, *Women's Organizations' Use of the Courts*, p. 20.

51. Irons, *Justice at War*, p. 110.

52. Ibid., p. 195.

53. Milner, "The Dilemmas of Legal Mobilization," p. 461.

54. Rabin, "Lawyers for Constitutional Change," p. 218.

55. McKay, *Nine for Equality*, p. 14.

56. By contrast, there is "no sense of community at 1790 Broadway"—NAACP headquarters until 1982—said one attorney, expressing the view that "staff attorneys lost their creativity by being on the 10th floor at 1790 Broadway."

57. The five *year* figure has been substantiated in correspondence made available to the author; for some lawyers, the sums involved ran well into five figures. Someone familiar with the situation, on seeing an earlier version of this material, said that saying the NAACP was only five years behind was "generous."

58. Matthew Holden, Jr., personal communication to author.

13. Client and Counsel

1. Amaker, "De Facto Leadership and the Civil Rights Movement, p. 249.

2. Bell, "Serving Two Masters," pp. 476–77, 512.

3. O'Neill, *Bakke and the Politics of Equality*, pp. 78, 115.

4. Douglas E. Rosenthal, *Lawyer and Client: Who's in Charge* (New York 1974), pp. 143, 2.

5. Olson, *Clients and Lawyers*, p. xii; Handler, Hollingsworth, and Erlanger, *Lawyers and the Pursuit of Legal Rights*, p. 82; Scheingold, *The Politics of Rights*, pp. 171, 170 n. 1.

6. Meltsner, *Cruel and Unusual*, p. 36.

7. This is part of what Milner calls "consensual mobilization," in which there are "norms that emphasize shared perspectives and common values." Milner, "The Right to Refuse Treatment," p. 481.

8. Lawrence, *The Poor in Court*, p. 43.

9. Olson, *Clients and Lawyers*, p. 155.

10. Meltsner, *Cruel and Unusual*, p. 107, states, "It was a close question whether a particular [NAACP Legal Defense] Fund client would be helped by tying his fate to a general campaign against the death penalty. Test cases have a way of scaring off judges because their implications are often so enormous." Were this true, death-sentenced individuals might be worse off than if they had not been associated with the larger campaign but had challenged only their own sentences.

11. Meltsner and Schrag, *Public Interest Advocacy*, p. 81.

12. Ibid., pp. 82–83.

13. Rosenthal, *Lawyer and Client*, pp. 57, 133; Olson, *Clients and Lawyers*, p. 137.

14. Olson, *Clients and Lawyers*, p. 151.

15. Amaker, "De Facto Leadership," pp. 248–49.

16. O'Neill, *Bakke and the Politics of Equality*, p. 243.

17. Olson, *Clients and Lawyers*, p. 145.

18. Milner, "The Dilemmas of Legal Mobilization," pp. 115–116.

19. Rosenthal, *Lawyer and Client*, p. 2.

20. Ibid., p. 15.

21. Olson, *Clients and Lawyers*, pp. 141, 150. See also ibid., p. 148.

22. Ibid., p. 132.

23. Ibid., p. 4.

24. Handler, *Social Movements and the Legal System*, pp. 146–47; Vose, *Constitutional Change*, p. 334.

25. *NAACP v. Button*, 371 U.S. 415, 429, 431 (1963).

26. Id., at 421–22.

27. Id., at 420–22.

28. Id., at 422 n. 6, 433.

29. Id., at 443–44.

30. Id., at 460.

31. Id., 449–50, 463.

32. Id., at 450.

33. Id., at 462. That Harlan's concern extended beyond the NAACP context could be seen several years later, when, again in dissent, he raised questions about the lack of personal client-lawyer contact in workmen's compensation cases. *Mine Workers v. Illinois State Bar*, 389 U.S. 217, 231 (1967).

34. This is drawn from Tushnet, *The NAACP's Legal Strategy*, pp. 146–51.

35. "Although there was no evidence in *Button* that any plaintiffs opposed NAACP objectives, more recent desegregation suits suggest that Justice Harlan's concerns were not entirely unfounded." Deborah L. Rhode, "Class Conflicts in Class Actions," *Stanford Law Review* 34 (1982): 1211.

36. Handler, *Social Movements and the Legal System*, pp. 8, 28 (for the structural types), 33. The clientele are "donors who participate by paying for the collective goods but who do not consume them."

37. Amaker, "De Facto Leadership," p. 248. And see the *Chance* litigation, a challenge to discriminatory licensing examinations for New York City principals. Rebell and Block, *Educational Policy Making and the Courts*, p. 114.

38. Olson, *Clients and Lawyers*, pp. 155–57.

39. Fitzgerald, "The Contract Buyers League," pp. 189–90; Baez, Fernandez, and Guskin, *Desegregation and Hispanic Studies*, p. 81 n.42.

40. Olson, *Clients and Lawyers*, pp. 120, 141–42.

41. Neal Milner, "The Symbols and Meanings of Advocacy," *International Journal of Law and Psychiatry* 8 (1986): 12.

42. Clark, "The Lawyer in the Civil Rights Movement," 464–65; Tushnet, p. 82.

43. Lawrence, *The Poor in Court*, p. 76.

44. Neier, *Only Judgment*, p. 201. Amsterdam found a way out of the predicament that solved his immediate dilemma.

45. Ibid., pp. 209–210. Gilmore had told the ACLU to "bug off" (and worse). See Norman Mailer, *The Executioner's Song*.

46. Olson, *Clients and Lawyers*, pp. 29–30. "Civil rights lawyers maintain that the law mandates racial balance remedies whether or not they are effective and whether or not black plaintiffs and the class they represent desire these remedies." Bell, "The Dialectics of School Desegregation," p. 282.

47. Chesler, Kalmuss, and Sanders, "Methods of Presenting Scientific Evidence in Court," p. 455.

48. Rhode, "Class Conflicts in Class Actions," pp. 1206–07.

49. Charles W. Wolfram, "The Second Set of Players: Lawyers, Fee Shifting, and the Limits of Professional Discipline," *Law & Contemporary Problems* 47 (1984): 316. Nonetheless, the Supreme Court said the conflict was not "an 'ethical' one in the sense that [the lawyer] had to choose between conflicting duties under the prevailing norms of professional conduct" as there was "no *ethical* obligation to seek a statutory fee award." *Evans v. Jeff D.*, 475 U.S. 717, 727–28 (1986).

50. Olson, *Clients and Lawyers*, p. 116.

51. Hain, "Sealing Off the City," p. 303 n. 39.

52. Kinoy, *Rights on Trial*, pp. 187–88, describes such a situation in which the NAACP Legal Defense Fund was providing legal expenses in connection with racial disturbances in Danville, Virginia. He quotes one of their lawyers as saying, "'Since the NAACP will be footing the bill, we will want to be able to caution against anything unwise,'" which in this context meant demonstrations.

53. Olson, *Clients and Lawyers*, p. 116.

54. O'Neill, *Bakke and the Politics of Equality*, p. 233.

55. Wolfram, "The Second Set of Players," p. 297; Handler, *Social Movements and the Legal System*, p. 33.

56. Rhode, p. 1223. In one transit case, clients' "lack of experience and assertiveness and the 'crazy hours' the lawyers kept sometimes made it hard for them to keep up with the . . . lawyers." Olson, *Clients and Lawyers*, p. 120.

57. Bell, "Serving Two Masters," p. 483.

58. McNeil, *Groundwork*, p. 189.

59. Rhode, "Class Conflicts in Class Actions, p. 1210. For LSP lawyers, appellate advocacy can be an "important way to give meaning to the drudgery and frustration of their day-to-day practice." Lawrence, *The Poor in Court*, p. 55.

60. Kinoy, *Rights on Trial*, p. 80.

61. Ron Edmonds, "Advocating Inequity: A Critique of the Civil Rights Attorney in Class Action Desegregation Suits," *Black Law Journal* 3 (1983): 175.

62. In one school desegregation case that LDF took over, counsel had not communicated with his clients "for almost two years." Rhode, "Class Conflicts in Class Actions," 1204 n. 84.

63. Rhode, "Class Conflicts in Class Actions," pp. 1185–89, 1191, 1215–16;

Colin S. Diver, "The Judge as Political Powerbroker: Superintending Structural Change in Public Institutions," *Virginia Law Review* 65 (1979): 68–69.

64. Rhode, "Class Conflicts in Class Actions," pp. 1247, 1245.

65. Ibid., pp. 1214, 1212.

66. Ibid., p. 1205.

67. *Mandujano v. Basic Vegetable Products,* 541 F.2d 832, 834–45 (9th Cir. 1976).

68. Rhode, "Class Conflicts in Class Actions," p. 1203.

69. An exception occurred in the Atlanta school desegregation controversy, where dissenting members of the black community pressed for full desegregation rather than a more limited settlement. *Calhoun v. Cook,* 332 F.Supp. 804 (N.D.Ga. 1971). See Leubsdorf, "Completing the Desegregation Remedy," pp. 92–93.

70. Rhode, "Class Conflicts in Class Actions," pp. 1195–96.

14. Interorganizational Relations

1. Walker, *Mobilizing Interest Groups in America,* p. x.

2. McKay, *Nine for Equality,* p. 23.

3. Orfield, *Must We Bus?* p. 373.

4. Ibid., p. 371.

5. Kobylka, *The Politics of Obscenity,* p. 88.

6. Cooper, *Hard Judicial Choices,* p. 244.

7. For instances of the latter in the civil rights context, see Fairclough, *To Redeem the Soul of America,* pp. 80–83, 213–14, 244, 248, 263, 311–12, on relations between the Southern Christian Leadership Conference (SCLC) and the Congress of Racial Equality (CORE), pp. 80–83, and between SCLC and the Student Nonviolent Coordinating Committee (SNCC).

8. Sorauf, *The Wall of Separation,* p. 81.

9. Orfield, *Must We Bus?* p. 189.

10. Gary Orfield, "Congress, the President, and Anti-Busing Legislation, 1966–1974," *Journal of Law & Education* 4 (1975): 116.

11. Dentler and Scott, *Schools on Trial,* p. 92.

12. Orfield, *Must We Bus?* p. 211.

13. Raffel, *The Politics of School Desegregation,* p. 45.

14. Orfield, *Must We Bus?* p. 401.

15. Ibid., p. 373.

16. Cowan, "Women's Rights Through Litigation," p. 401.

17. O'Connor, *Women's Organizations' Use of the Courts,* p. 27.

18. Sorauf, *The Wall of Separation,* p. 59.

19. See, for example, Vose, *Caucasians Only,* pp. 163–67. Such joint participation also occurs among conservative public interest law firms. For example, the Pacific Legal Foundation had several co-plaintiffs in nuclear energy development cases,

including the American Public Power Association, the Atomic Industrial Forum, the Nuclear Energy Liability Insurance Association, "and a number of construction and trade organizations," along with several construction firms. The presence of those firms is said to have raised questions of the "public interest" status of Pacific Legal Foundation. Moreover, consultations about the case "involved parties whose identities overlapped considerably," with a trustee of the Foundation also a partner in the firm representing one of the business firms. Houck, "With Charity for All," pp. 1466–67.

20. *U.S. v. LULAC*, 793 F.2d 636 (5th Cir. 1986).

21. Lawyers' Committee, Annual Report 1980/1981, p. 4; Lawyers' Committee, Annual Report 1982–1983, pp. 5–6, 16.

22. Olson, *Clients and Lawyers*, pp. 105–7.

23. Fairclough, p. 45; Aldon D. Morris, *The Origins of the Civil Rights Movement: Black Communities Organizing for Change* (New York, 1984), p. 120.

24. See David M. Truman, *The Governmental Process* (New York, 1955), pp. 157–67.

25. Morris, *The Origins of the Civil Rights Movement*, pp. 122, 126–27.

26. O'Connor and Epstein, "The Importance of Interest Group Involvement," p. 715 n. 35.

27. Sorauf, *The Wall of Separation*, p. 84.

28. Kluger, *Simple Justice*, pp. 293–94; Vose, *Caucasians Only*, pp. 58, 151; Meltsner, *Cruel and Unusual*, pp. 114, 238–39.

29. See Epstein, *Conservatives in Court*, pp. 55, 61–62, 124, 128.

30. O'Connor and Epstein, "In Defense of Rights," p. 5.

31. Danielson, *The Politics of Exclusion*, p. 174.

32. Walker, "The Origins and Maintenance of Interest Groups in America," p. 401.

33. Heck and Stewart, "Ensuring Access to Justice," p. 91.

34. Cortner, *A Mob Intent on Death*, p. 194.

35. Stewart and Sheffield, "Correlates of Civil Rights Interest Groups' Litigation Activities," p. 6.

36. Casper, *Lawyers Before the Warren Court*, p. 141.

37. O'Connor and Epstein, "Beyond Legislative Lobbying," 139; Epstein, pp. 99, 114.

38. Richard T. Seymour, "Administration Tries to Turn Back Clock on Affirmative Action," *Committee Report* vol. 1 (no. 2, Spring 1987), pp. 17–18.

39. Branch, *Parting the Waters*, p. 186. In oral history interviews, Thurgood Marshall complained that SCLC delegated legal matters to LDF, "dump[ing] all his legal work on us, including the bills." "Marshall's View of Public Figures," *New York Times*, Jan. 31, 1993, p. 32.

40. Lawyers' Committee, Annual Report 1985–1986, p. 5.

41. O'Connor and Epstein, "Rebalancing the Scales of Justice," p. 18.

42. Michael Meltsner, interview by Richard Kluger, Feb. 25, 1971, and March 3, 1971, Sterling Library, Yale University.

43. Branch, *Parting the Waters*, p. 291.

44. See August Meier and Elliott Rudwick, *CORE: A Study in the Civil Rights Movement, 1942–1968* (New York, 1973), for example, pp. 229–32.

45. Stewart and Sheffield, "Correlates of Civil Rights Interest Groups' Litigation Activities," p. 12.

46. Neier, *Only Judgment.* p. 207. See also Epstein and Kobylka, *The Supreme Court & Legal Change*, pp. 46, 48.

47. Houck, "With Charity for All," p. 1477; Epstein, *Conservatives in Court*, p. 155.

48. Shields and Spector, "Opening Up the Suburbs," p. 303; O'Connor and Epstein, "Beyond Legislative Lobbying," pp. 138–39; Salomone, "Judicial Oversight of Agency Enforcement," p. 133.

49. Neier, *Only Judgment*, p. 197; see also Meltsner, *Cruel and Unusual.*

50. Heck and Stewart, "Ensuring Access to Justice," pp. 88, 91, 93.

51. Sorauf, *Wall of Separation*, p. 90.

52. Olson, *Clients and Lawyers*, p. 42.

53. Ibid., pp. 48, 51.

54. Cortner, *A Mob Intent on Death*, p. 106.

55. Sorauf, *Wall of Separation*, p. 59.

56. Buell, *School Desegregation and Defended Neighborhoods*, pp. 93–94; Cooper, *Hard Judicial Choices*, p. 316.

57. See Handler, *Social Movements and the Legal System*, p. 199; Danielson, pp. 190–91.

58. Greenberg interview, pp. 116–17.

59. Robyn, *Braking the Special Interests*, p. 118.

60. Danielson, *The Politics of Exclusion*, p. 122.

61. Clement E. Vose, to author, January 9, 1982. Kunstler's conduct, "penchant for self-advertisement," "exploiting his relationship with [Rev. Martin Luther] King [Jr.]" and "habit of making commitments in SCLC's name on his own initiative," helped alienate people in the Gandhi Society, for which, along with Greenberg, he was acting as principal lawyer. Fairclough, *To Redeem the Soul of America*, p. 178.

62. Kaufman, *Broken Alliance*, p. 106.

63. Kinoy, *Rights on Trial*, p. 264.

64. Zangrando, *The NAACP Crusade Against Lynching*, p. 94.

65. See Dan T. Carter, *Scottsboro: A Tragedy of the American South* (Baton Rouge, 1969/1979). See also McNeil, *Groundwork*, pp. 108–12.

66. The interpretation here would be much more complete if one could hear more of the view of the principal NAACP and LDF actors of the litigation. Matthew Holden, Jr., provided substantial assistance and was particularly generous in

allowing the use of many ideas and words from our discussions and correspondence. However, I bear the sole responsibility for any absence of information, lack of precision, or other defects.

67. Halpern, "Title VI and Racial Discrimination in Educational Institutions," p. 43.

68. Conversation with Davis Bobrow, March 2, 1989. For another instance of the devastating effects of internal conflict on another civil rights litigating group, the Puerto Rican Legal Defense and Education Fund, in which the organization's docket of pending cases was said to have "stagnated," see David Margolick, "Strife Over Aims and Leadership Stalls Puerto Rican Legal Group," *New York Times,* Jan. 2, 1984, pp. 25, 28.

69. Stuart Taylor, Jr., "2 Groups Argue in Court Over N.A.A.C.P. Name," *New York Times,* Jan. 28, 1983, p. B7.

70. *National Association for the Advancement of Colored People v. N.A.A.C.P. Legal Defense and Educational Fund, Inc.,* 559 F.Supp. 1337, 1341 (D.D.C. 1983).

71. Id., at 1342–44.

72. Id., at 1341 n.1, 1343–44, 1345.

73. *NAACP v. NAACP Legal Defense Fund,* 753 F.2d 131 (D.C.Cir. 1985); cert. denied, 472 U.S. 1021 (1985).

74. Robert Carter, interview by Richard Kluger, Feb. 11, 1971. Brown v. Board of Education Collection, Manuscript Division, Sterling Library, Yale University. Box 1, Folder 16; Michael Meltsner, interview by Richard Kluger, Feb. 15 and March 3, 1971. Brown v. Board of Education Collection, Manuscript Division, Sterling Library, Yale University,. Box 4, Folder 66.

75. Kaufman, *Broken Alliance,* pp. 102–103.

76. Lewis Steel, interview by Richard Kluger, March 3, 1971. Brown v. Board of Education Collection, Manuscript Division, Sterling Library, Yale University, Box 5, Folder 92.

77. McNeil, *Groundwork,* p. 135.

78. Lukas, *Common Ground,* p. 234.

79. Such black-white conflict also came to the surface in the mid-1980s in the ACLU when Morton Halperin was chosen to head the organization's Washington, D.C., office. The result was a concerted affirmative action search for the next major staff position, with John A. Powell, a black, selected as legal director.

80. O'Neill, *Bakke and The Politics of Equality,* p. 88; David Margolick, "Ex-Director of NAACP Legal Fund Reflects on State of Civil Rights," *New York Times,* July 5, 1984, p. A9.

81. Meltsner, interview.

82. NAACP, "The Legal Problem and the NAACP Dilemma," p. 222.

83. *New York City Region of New York Conference of Branches v. New York,* 413 U.S. 345 (1973).

84. Steel, interview.

85. NAACP, "The Legal Problem and the NAACP Dilemma," p. 222.

86. Meltsner, interview.

87. Steel, interview.

88. Jack Greenberg, interview by Richard Kluger, February 22, 1971. Brown v. Board of Education Collection, Manuscript Division, Sterling Library, Yale University, Box 2, Folder 37.

89. Meltsner, interview; Steel, interview.

90. NAACP, "The Legal Problem and the NAACP Dilemma," p. 221.

91. Ibid., p. 381. The same tension about the treatment of predominantly and historically black state colleges and universities was evident in the aftermath of the Supreme Court's 1991 *Fordice* ruling on the desegregation of higher education in Mississippi.

92. Robert Carter to Jack Greenberg, May 30, 1974. In file with Carter interview.

15. The Complexity of Civil Rights Litigation: Some Concluding Thoughts

1. Bert Rockman, "What Didn't We Know & Should We Forget It? Political Science & the Reagan Presidency," *Polity* 21 (1989): 792.

2. See William Mishler and Reginald S. Sheehan, "The Supreme Court as a Countermajoritarian Institution? The Impact of Public Opinion on Supreme Court Decisions, *American Political Science Review* 87 (1993): 87–101, particularly p. 95.

TABLE OF CASES

19.01

128370